D1227207

# Television
# "Critical Viewing Skills"
# Education:
## Major Media Literacy Projects in the
## United States and Selected Countries

# COMMUNICATION

A series of volumes edited by
**Dolf Zillmann** and **Jennings Bryant**

# Television
# "Critical Viewing Skills"
# Education:
## Major Media Literacy Projects in the United States and Selected Countries

**James A. Brown**
The University of Alabama

LAWRENCE ERLBAUM ASSOCIATES, PUBLISHERS
1991    Hillsdale, New Jersey            Hove and London

Lawrence Erlbaum Associates, Inc., Publishers
365 Broadway
Hillsdale, New Jersey 07642

**Library of Congress Cataloging-in-Publication Data**
Brown, James A. (James Anthony), 1932–
    Television "critical viewing skills" education: major media
literacy projects in the United States and selected countries /
James A. Brown.
      p.  cm.
    Includes bibliographical references and index.
    ISBN 0-8058-0786-1 (C). — ISBN 0-8058-0974-0 (P)
    1. Television in education.  2. Literacy.  3. Educational surveys.
I. Title.
LB1044.7.B76   1991
371.3'358—dc20                       90-45984
Printed in the United States of America        CIP
10  9  8  7  6  5  4  3  2  1

# Contents

# Preface

RATIONALE

Why another book about education for mass media literacy? Many studies, research reports, and published analyses of specific media projects have appeared during the past two decades. Most of them recounted isolated activities in a single school or district or even by a lone teacher or an educational publishing company. Published studies typically concentrated on individual projects or clusters of similar projects in one region of the world.* None offered a broad perspective of the wide range of projects from far-flung, varying geographic, social, and educational contexts.

The late 1970s saw a surge of systematic efforts to develop integrated curricula and long-term projects in media education, with emphasis on television. By the mid-1980s the heavy tide of federally funded experimental projects had ebbed in the United States. But interest in teaching critical viewing skills for television (sometimes labeled "CVS") remained widespread if less dramatic.† In 1982 in

---

*See Part I for citations of the many reports, monographs, and published books; the References section at the end of this book provides a comprehensive list.

†See chapter 1 for discussion of terminology. This report focuses on mass media study programs with components about television viewing—under various titles (most specifically *critical viewing skills*)—particularly where integrated into formal education and

Grunwald, West Germany, UNESCO sponsored an International Symposium on Education of the Public in the Use of Mass Media; it produced a major document on media education. During that same decade, many projects directed towards television were introduced and continued to develop in other countries, notably in Australia and Scotland. At the close of the decade, a resurgence of interest in media literacy curricula appeared among colleges, private foundations, and national organizations.[1] They explored the status of media literacy activities and sought to lay out anew a national perspective for implementing critical viewing skills. Meanwhile entrepreneurs in other parts of the world were expanding their limited programs, often supported variously by state authority, educational systems, or regional churches.

*Review.* The flurry of organized activity promoting critical viewing skills for television in the late 1970s and early 1980s gradually subsided. Federal government funded several massive projects in the United States only through 1982. Other organizations—usually in education—entered into the effort to prepare systematic instruction in media literacy, notably in Australia and Scotland.

But when major funding dried up in the United States, the largest structured experiments withered. Their principals moved to other sectors such as medical-related projects that were attracting governmental and private funding. In the United States, some directors of projects chronicled in this report were working in disparate fields by the mid- and late-1980s. And former administrators of short-term projects were pursuing goals far different from television "critical viewing skills" which they had promoted in previous years.[2] In Australia, which manifested long-term support for structured curricula in media analysis and appreciation, some key innovators moved on to other responsibilities.[3]

*Compiling the Data.* Successive efforts to gather data in 1981, 1985, and 1988–1989 often yielded limited results. Many respondents to surveys by this author sent massive material, including printed (and in some instances formally published) curricula, outlines, sample workbooks and other texts—even audiovisual support materials. But others replied with only brief letters or anecdotal commentary or, at best, a few representative print-outs of scattered activities. Still oth-

---

offering systematic curricular materials of print and audiovisuals. Despite possible semantic confusion, this report uses a range of terms interchangeably to avoid repeated use of a single term. This seems justified because many programs reported here extend beyond television to other media and so designate themselves; but only their TV components are analyzed here in detail.

ers, especially in some countries of Europe and the Third World, did not respond to inquiries for documentation and commentary about their activities. (This was understandable, with limited funds and staffs, and in some instances with complex, wide-ranging materials from many years in their files.) In some instances, as in areas of South America and parts of Scotland, inchoate projects were maturing only toward the end of the 1980s.

So it was very difficult to obtain relatively complete and reliable information about some media literacy programs involving critical viewing skills for television. Those lacunae show up in this report's descriptions and tabulations of CVS activities around the world. They make data from various countries not always comparable, and evaluating those projects an assumptive exercise. Similarly uneven results from attempts to gather international data were reported by Valerio Fuenzalida (1987) of Chile (for Latin American projects) and by Eddie Dick (1987a) of Scotland (for countries around the world).

Thus, this book is both dated and timely. It is dated because much of the most detailed, concrete material comes from that uniquely active period of 1978–1982, supplemented by further data in the mid- and late-1980s. And yet the book is timely because of renewed initiatives to foster media literacy studies in the context of institutional education and of personal growth in aesthetic, cultural, social understanding of the interaction between society and mass media—especially television.

Precisely because of widespread attention to human communication involving the mass medium of television, coupled with proliferation of educational projects in the field, a need arose for some overview of what has been going on. This survey of the field outlines major patterns of philosophical assumptions as well as of conceptual and operational procedures, and it evaluates major systematic projects that emphasize television.

## WHO MAY FIND THIS REPORT USEFUL

The survey of projects provided in Part II may help others determine which are potentially adaptable to their own situations. In Part III, the conceptual and historical foundations and criteria of Part I are applied to those projects to clarify their aptness according to purposes, assumptions, and principles underlying the respective projects.

Individual educators concerned about the pervasive role of television in the social and intellectual life of their students may find this analytical survey helpful to learn what kinds of television study programs are available and appropriate, often with little adaptation, for their own classrooms. School administrators might refer to this report when assessing inquiries from colleagues or from students' parents about formal courses of "television literacy" in the curriculum. Parents may find guidance to helpful tools for inculcating in their children more discriminating, responsive, and responsible use of the medium of television.

This analysis summarizes the current status of criteria for designing media education programs, and it concludes with major recommendations for designing future programs.

Because they often cut across various levels of age and education, projects are here categorized according to their institutional source or structure: national government-funded projects, regional school districts, local schools and organizations in formal education, individuals, nongovernmental national organizations, and private companies. Administrators and teachers now exploring such projects will find those categories helpful for analyzing contexts similar to their own, because funding or supporting institutional sources are central to the scope and continuity of any media study project, making them feasible. Potential practitioners can draw on sources cited and can assess for their own purposes the relevance and feasibility of discrete projects exhaustively reported in Part II.

Planners can review the range of assumptions underlying different pedagogies, as well as differing purposes and methodologies. They can also learn about the wealth of practical support materials already available, which can be adopted or modified for their own contexts.

Parents, on behalf of their children and also as viewers themselves, can apply what others have tried by perusing the extended excerpts from projects surveyed.

*How This Book Can Be Used.*   Those considering how to introduce serious study of television behavior and reflective judgment about audience responsibilities are faced with many practical questions. Even the antecedent question of *why* critical study of television (for what purpose? to what end? why appropriate for this organization/ institution? is it truly socially, culturally, ethically significant?) carries pragmatic implications. What kinds of study programs are effective with what age groups? What should be the scope of such a program? Should it include all mass media (print, motion pictures, radio, recordings) or only television? Should formal curriculum or study plans with texts and lectures be set off against open-ended inquiry and even entrepreneurial, heuristic exploration? What kinds of written materials might be apt for various levels of participants? What about audiovisual media to exemplify points—when do they distract or dilute content? What about testing? How can results be observed, even measured? Who has prior experience and what resources are available—to provide perceptions, judgments, and recommendations (including cautions)? This report addresses most of those points, often in extensive detail.

Those less familiar with this developing field may find the entire book helpful, including the review of theoretical underpinnings and historical antecedents to media literacy, a brief survey of semiotics, along with ethical and sociopolitical implications of mass media (chapter 1). Those seeking a sense of educational concepts and of research related to media training can peruse chapter 2.

Persons already versed in such topics who wish to review patterns in programs of media literacy training (emphasizing television) will be most interested in the concluding section of chapter 2, which describes criteria for assessing projects, and in chapter 3's sketch of how those projects evolved. Or they might go immediately to Part II (chapter 4) for an overview of purposes and scope of 23 major projects and 10 others worldwide, and for the detailed questionnaire survey of practitioners. They will probably center their attention on details of concrete projects of the 1980s (chapters 5–10), choosing those sections most closely matching their own contexts: elaborate, coordinated projects funded by the U.S. government (chapter 5); American and Australian school districts offering systematic formal instruction in media literacy (chapter 6); projects by individuals—some in collaboration with other persons and organizations (chapter 7); nongovernmental national organizations in the United States (chapter 8); private companies in the United States and United Kingdom (chapter 9); and non-U.S. institution-related projects in formal and informal education (chapter 10)—United Kingdom, Europe, Canada, and Latin America.

Finally, those seeking guidelines for adopting or adapting existing projects and for developing their own curriculum and teaching instruments, might go at once to Part III. Chapter 11 inventories major projects according to criteria established in Part I. Chapter 12 then assesses the projects in detail, noting specific emphases, strengths, and weaknesses. The concluding chapter 13 offers recommendations to those embarking on media education projects specifically involving television and critical viewing skills.

## RATIONALE REVISITED

Valerio Fuenzalida (1987) noted that the very diversity of Latino projects mandates analytical surveys such as his *Education for Critical TV Viewing: Five Experiences in Latin America:*

[I]t would appear that continuity and the accumulation of theoretical and practical experience should be assured. Isolated, short-term projects are of little consequence. Continuity and analysis of results would allow revisions to be made of the nature of instruction in this area. It would thus also be possible to exchange information and experiences between different Latin American projects. (p. 43)

That is precisely the motivation behind this book. So many projects in critical viewing—especially in the United States—seem to have arisen, developed for a short while, then faded from sight. Principal persons have moved to other responsibilities; or they have not received adequate institutional support to ensure longevity. And so the wheel turns, with new persons coming on the scene to initiate similar projects; they can benefit from the record of continuity, and from analyzing previous efforts. This analysis seeks to lay out and measure some of the ground trod by others, to assist newcomers to the scene. It is thus not only timely but important to review major patterns of what has been going on in this significant field of sociocultural interaction with the mass medium of television.

## NOTES

1. Among others worldwide, there were Phoenix College and Community Colleges of Glendale, Paradise Valley, and Scottsdale (Arizona); the University of Windsor (Ontario, Canada); Skaggs Foundation (Chicago) and Benton Foundation (Washington, DC); Media Action Research Center (New York, Los Angeles) and the Center for Media & Values (Los Angeles); Strategies for Media Literacy, Inc. (San Francisco); and Queensland Institute of Technology (Brisbane, Australia). All explored TV media literacy projects; some published newsletters and journals, conducted surveys of media literacy education, and mounted study projects and conferences 1988–1990. Other organizations scheduled for mid-1990 alone four international conferences: in Canada, the Association for Media Literacy and the University of Guelph, Ontario, presented "The New Literacy: Media Education in the 1990's" (May 10–12); in France, the Centre de Liaison de l'Enseignement et des Moyens d'Information joined with the British Film Institute and UNESCO to offer "New Directions in Media Education" (July 2–6); in England, the British Film Institute and University of London's Institute of Education presented IVLA [International Visual Literacy Association] Symposium 1990—"Verbo-Visual Literacy: Mapping the Field" (July 10–13); and in Australia, ATOM Victoria was host to the "1990 ATOM National Media Studies Conference" in Melbourne (September 22–25).
2. For instance, James Anderson, instrumental in media curricula development by school districts in the Far West and Midwest, was engaged heavily in

theoretical communication research; and Donna Lloyd-Kolkin, former director of one of the four major USOE projects, had turned to the field of medicine (but recently returned to activity related to media education).

3. Kelvin Canavan left direct work in media education, which he had pioneered for a number of years, to become a district school administrator.

# Acknowledgments

This book owes much of its inspiration and support to Robert White, S.J., of the Centre for the Study of Communication and Culture in London. He and the Centre initiated the proposal and provided substantial early funding. Other financial support came from the National Association of Broadcasters, plus modest grants from the Research and Grants Committees of both The University of Alabama and its College of Communication. Graduate student assistance was provided at times by the University of Southern California and The University of Alabama. Mary Williams and Tom Waldman assisted in California, Curtis Love in Alabama. Paul Kenney, S.J., of the Centre in London gathered data from Europe.

James Anderson (Utah) and Stewart Hoover (Temple) offered substantial suggestions for restructuring and revising the manuscript draft. Robert White especially guided this project through every stage, offering extensive and valuable observations to strengthen the report. Their counsel is reflected in this work's perspective, organization, presentation, and evaluation of data; shortcomings are the author's own.

Thanks are due to Lawrence Erlbaum Associates, Inc., through Jennings Bryant (Alabama) and Jack Burton, for making this published work available to the many individuals, organizations, and foundations whose anticipation has been long deferred.

Of course, thanks must go to all those worldwide who generously replied to lengthy questionnaires and inquiries, often responding with copious samples of their reports and printed materials. The data they shared—based on their ingenuity, dedication, and practical applications—provide the foundation for this survey and analysis.

In addition to references cited in the text and chapter endnotes and with figures, specifically acknowledged here are formal permissions to cite and/or reproduce samples of copyrighted work by: James Anderson, University of Utah; Charles A Buggé, United States Catholic Conference; Kelvin Canavan, Catholic Education Office, Sydney; Rose Falco, Educational Activities, Inc.; Joel L. LaPray, Idaho Falls School District No. 91; Milton Ploghoft, Ohio University Center for Higher Education; Nelson Price, Media Action Research Center; Marieli Rowe, National Telemedia Council, Inc.; Charles C. Thomas, Publisher, Springfield, Illinois; Diana Zuckerman and Dorothy and Jerome Singer, Yale University Family Television Research and Consultation Center. (Four projects funded by the U.S. Office of Education entered into public domain within 5 to 10 years of publication, as noted in text and endnotes.)

Thanks to these and all others cited throughout the text. We trust that excerpts in this book adequately reflect their important contributions to the field.

*—James A. Brown*

# Introduction

This book analyzes representative media literacy projects focused on television ("critical viewing skills") oriented to typical members of television audiences—in narrow marketing terms, "the consumers." It seeks to identify major patterns, especially strengths, of those widely varying programs, to assist those now designing and implementing similar projects at all levels: grade and high school, college, and adult education, as well as in local, regional, and even national interest groups. After almost two decades of experimenting and implementing in major areas of the world, the time is ripe for assessing what we have learned in media education directed to critical understanding of television.

## WHY STUDY MEDIA—PARTICULARLY TELEVISION?

Mass media are pervasive in contemporary society. In recent decades print and motion pictures have been supplanted by radio and television as dominant forms of communicating entertainment and information to mass publics. Television continually grows in its influence on individuals' and society's use of leisure time, on their awareness of political and social reality, on their forming of personal values in culture and ethics.

Despite an initial appearance of unidirectionality—that is, from the sender through the medium to the individual receiver—the communication process exists by mutual dependence on sender and on receiver. So responsibility for how media are used or abused in society is shared by all parties to the process. Although acknowledging the central role and impact of media organizers and creators—broadcast executives, station managers, researchers and lawyers, as well as artists, writers, production staffs—this study looks to the other half of the communication process, to the users (listeners/viewers) of broadcast media.

## IMPORTANCE OF MEDIA STUDY

Media studies, including CVS projects, make a significant contribution when they analyze not only aesthetic aspects (appreciation of the dominant form of current artistic expression) and technical factors (history, structure, and function) of technology, economics, institutional organization, law and regulation, but also the dynamics between media and individual persons as well as society in terms of human growth and social values—in a word, cultural development, as noted by White (1975, pp. 11–13, 19). That is because media content raise questions about human nature and about the limits of human community, as perceived by those secular media. Issues include human dignity, respect for human beings and life, and the individuals who make up collective society—including minorities, the mentally or physically defective, and the elderly. Media news and entertainment reflect contemporary issues involving human personality, business, government, family, and even spiritual values, thereby at least implicitly interpreting persons' meaning and destiny (see Bamberger, 1975).

Masterman (1985b) has enumerated reasons why media education deserves "the most urgent priority"; typically, his British and somewhat neo-Marxist perspective stresses sociopolitical considerations:

1. The high rate of media consumption and *the saturation of contemporary societies by the media.*
2. The ideological importance of the media, and *their influence as consciousness industries.*
3. The growth in the *manufacture of information,* and its dissemination by the media.
4. The increasing *penetration of media into our central democratic processes.*
5. The increasing *importance of visual communication and information* in all areas.

6. The importance of *educating students to meet the demands of the future.*
7. The fast-growing national and international pressures to *privatise information.* (p. 2)

The medium of television can play a part in the life of audiences either as mere distraction and irrelevance or as a service—as a force for either dehumanizing or liberating a person. That is, the medium can contribute to a sense of alienation and meaninglessness in life, to estrangement from one's own existence; or it can be an instrument for cultural diversity (instead of standardization and uniformity) by contributing to a person's full potential with options of choice. Media can support socialization to the status quo of society or to creative change towards enriching growth in that society. Therefore, a major goal of media education is to help recipients of mass communication become active, free participants in the process rather than static, passive, unresponsive and subservient to the images and values communicated in a one-way flow from media sources.

Alvarado, Gutch, and Wollen (1987, p. 4) look to epistemological aspects of media: "to learn about the ways in which our knowledge is mediated"—that is, about how we come to know about the world, about other people, about ourselves, and about values.

Fiske (1987) noted that television's cultural influence goes beyond its non-stop programming that provides "our most popular leisure activity" to its pervading "so much of the rest of our cultural life—newspapers, magazines, advertisements, conversations, radio, of style of dress, of make-up, of dance steps" (p. 118).

A more immediate purpose is to develop sensitive viewers who seek out and appreciate distinctively qualitative programming and who develop a critical sense of form, format, and content in mass media. Most researchers, critics, and practitioners—those cited earlier but especially Horace Newcomb (1983) and Carey (1988)—emphasize that aesthetic, humanistic role of media curricula.

Fiske (1987), Fiske and Hartley (1978), Worth and Gross (1981), and others advocate developing viewers' competencies in interpreting "codes and modes"—conventions of symbol-systems in various kinds of audiovisual media. They look to both aesthetic and social characteristics of mass media as significant areas for educating viewers.

## HISTORICAL CONTEXT

As described in Part I of this book, media study evolved from analysis of speech and drama, through print, to cinema (especially in the ciné-clubs on the Continent), to radio in the 1940s, and most recently to television. Media study has taken many forms: media topics integrated by teachers in disciplines such as English and social studies, extracurricular groups devoted to film and television appreciation, elective units in secondary schools and colleges, and credit courses integrated into the formal curriculum. Off-campus media study has been offered by organizations such as women's clubs and regional and national associations of parents and teachers, as well as by groups formed precisely to support "better" programming by helping local members of audiences to understand media and how to communicate with media managers about their likes and dislikes. In recent years local churches and national church organizations have mounted educational as well as activist projects to "better" performance by mass media and to train audiences in their responsibilities as media consumers.


## THE SCOPE OF THIS BOOK

This review describes the theoretical foundations and cultural-educational context of recent and continuing media education projects. It proposes criteria to assess the validity and significance of those representative projects as well as of others still being planned. It analyzes in extensive concrete detail, noting commonalities as well as distinctive strengths and weakness, systematic programs of study mounted primarily in the United States, plus selected projects in other countries (mostly English-speaking ones). It can thus guide others entering this challenging field with their students or adult citizens and with their administrators and funders.

Four major designs of media curricula funded by the U.S. government received particular attention because they represent a unique set of pilot projects offering the most developed, comprehensive effort with substantive national support. Other landmark endeavors are selected because they pioneered the field or because they have significant and innovative characteristics, such as detailed supporting materials or valuative testing of project results. Projects from outside the United States were included not so much for comparative purposes as to provide perspective for the American cases. They offer considerable contrast because their contexts and emphases differ from the U.S. experience. Except for several projects in Australia and Scotland, they are less thoroughly treated here—partly because they did not submit extensive material for analysis, but primarily because their widely varying purposes and constituencies made them less susceptible to comparative analysis.

Beyond offering a survey that analyzes purposes, content, and procedures of television literacy projects, this book outlines broad criteria for assessing these and other media study programs. The criteria can thus serve as an evaluation instrument to be applied to projects beyond the representative ones selected for this volume. (Of course, those criteria reflect categories often requiring adaptation when applied to specific contexts so as to reflect localized needs, value systems, and judgments.)

## WHAT THIS BOOK STUDIES

Specifically, this book appraises major projects intended to guide viewers in their media experiences of television. Projects go by various descriptive titles such as *media education, media literacy, television study,* and *critical viewing skills* programs (dubbed "CVS"). Some projects study print and film along with broadcasting; in recent years, most have stressed television. Those projects typically seek to develop more discriminating audiences by clarifying media structures, process, content, and values, and by helping those audiences apply criteria for understanding and evaluating broadcast presentations—the most pervasive popular art in our culture. White (personal communication, November 9, 1988) has noted:

> [W]e have always incorporated cultural and literary education in our curricula and . . . this has always included the popular *print* art (novels, short stories, etc.). Today much of our best 'literature' is in film and television; this is the strongest current of cultural expression today and the major arena of cultural debate (what kind of culture are we creating and do we want to create this kind of culture).

Indirectly, the various projects also hope to influence the quality of media content by developing selective, nonpassive audiences who seek out and support program content of high quality. Some projects also strive to influence directly media decision-makers, structures, and content by activist (or "reactive") involvement.

The report focuses on discrete media-analysis projects emphasizing television rather than on academic degree curricula in media. The latter typically are at the college level, usually surveying all mass media, or else stressing preparation for professional careers.

*Types of Projects Reviewed.* Table 3.1 (in chapter 3) lists major, representative projects in the United States and worldwide that have attempted to guide television viewers toward more discriminating use of broadcast media. In the United States they range from local television station projects (New York and Pittsburgh) to national networks underwriting social research at Yale University (American Broadcasting Company), to entire school districts (Eugene, Oregon; Idaho Falls, Idaho), to research centers whose projects were funded by the U.S. government (Far West Laboratory in San Francisco; Southwest Educational Laboratory in Austin, Texas), to a national coalition of Protestant churches (Media Action Research Center in New York), to the National Congress of Parents and Teachers (National PTA).

Sample projects selected from overseas include the Catholic Education Office in Sydney, Australia; school councils in Wales and in Scotland; the Formation Du Jeune Téléspectateur Actif in Paris; and various applications of a UNESCO-designed media study curriculum applied in nations of Africa, Asia, Europe, Oceania, and Latin America. Other projects from Canada, Latin America, and other parts of the world were described in international studies reported from Chile and Scotland.

*Origins of Projects.*   Projects often sprang into being because of the initiative of a single person or of a small group who enlisted the support of colleagues. Eventually, they attracted clusters of similar-minded educators and administrators in educational systems or in governmental agencies or even in private organizations both local and national. Inspiration for starting media study programs has come in many contexts, from a variety of motivations, and with various priorities for goals and procedures based on educational, religious, social, and other philosophical assumptions.

Thus it seems important to sort out why and how major projects have been mounted and to propose criteria for assessing their validity, their significance, their universality (applicability and feasibility), and their effectiveness.

*Target Constituencies.*   Projects have been directed to a wide range of participants: preschoolers, lower elementary, upper elementary, junior high, high school, college, and postgraduate groups including parents, teachers, and other citizens. They have involved both formal and informal programs, implemented in classrooms or at organizational meetings or in private homes.

*Contexts of Projects.*   Many of the projects are carefully structured, built on deliberately established sets of principles, and elaborately carried out in planning and implementation (with audiovisual materials, and integrated into larger social structures such as school systems). They are well funded and benefit from the collaboration of a small team of persons working exclusively on the activity. Other projects at the opposite end of the spectrum depend on the insight and dedication of a single person, perhaps with the occasional help of cooperative colleagues, but with no allocation of work-load responsibilities or resources to the effort. In some instances—even the multipronged group of projects funded by the U.S. government in 1978–1980—there seemed to be duplicate effort on similar matters, exemplifying the cliché about re-inventing the wheel.

*Formats and Support Material for Projects.* Some projects conduct mock exercises in classroom settings, or view videotaped television programs to analyze their quality, or assign viewing to be done in the home environment. Other projects include assignments to contact local media personnel or to communicate with national media managers to convey personal judgment about program content. Projects variously involve workbooks with fill-in questionnaires and worksheets, flashcards and exercises, filmstrips with accompanying audiocassette narration, extensive reprints of published articles critically evaluating television programs, and supplementary videotaped "lessons" or samples of programming and commercials.

## HOW THIS BOOK REVIEWS THOSE PROJECTS

The projects cited earlier are described in detail in Part II of this book, so that others interested specifically in studying television media can determine which ones might best be suited for local application, based on their own purposes and methodologies and constituencies, as well as available audiovisual materials and budgets. The report offers exhaustive details about most projects so the reader can assess the relevance of the purpose, structure, function, materials, and potential impact of each project. For this reason many and sometimes lengthy quotations are provided from major projects to document their distinctive and significant characteristics. Thus the reader can understand and evaluate specific projects without needing to track down primary source materials.

Beyond offering a composite review or merely an extended annotated bibliography, the present report is intentionally encyclopedic. It can serve somewhat as a manual to assess major "critical viewing skills"-related projects that offer systematic instruction and extensive print and audiovisual support materials.

## BASES FOR SELECTING AND ASSESSING PROJECTS

To assist those designing and implementing television media study, this analysis amply reports those projects that provided significant samples of their printed and audiovisual materials, including statements of educational and media philosophy and goals as well as methodology. The availability of supporting material, coupled with responses to repeated questionnaire surveys and correspondence through the past decade, accounted for the relative space proportioned to respective projects. Some—especially from the United States and Australia—are treated more fully than others that, although sometimes widespread and possessing considerable merit, were unable to provide extended commentary or full samplings of the actual materials used.

Furthermore, because sociopolitical and cultural contexts vary widely around the world, projects differ widely among themselves as to motivation (aesthetic development, social identity, political participation, religious concerns, etc.). So projects within and between categories do not always lend themselves to comparative evaluation, but rather to analysis according to respective contexts of needs and purposes. Projects in the United States and Australia differ in motivation and partly in scope from those of Third World countries such as in Latin America. But so do projects promoted by religious organizations differ in some important ways from ones initiated by school systems or scholarly research institutes.

Therefore the criteria drawn from the initial review of theories and constructs (stated in Part I) cannot be equally derived from or applied uniformly to each of the wide-ranging kinds of projects. But the criteria do help draw a profile of the varying emphases and configurations of media projects, including apparent strengths and limitations. Those disparate experiences offer clues to others about what works, how, and under what circumstances. The intent is not to "rank" projects competitively but rather to explore their strengths and limitations, in order to learn from the range of their experiences, and to identify scope, methodologies, and content for one's own application.

*Sources of Criteria.* Criteria for noting patterns of achievement among domestic and international projects are identified in Part I. Criteria are derived both deductively and inductively. (a) The first part of Part I reviews concepts and historical and other research data as foundations for principles from which can be derived operating standards (drawn from philosophy, sociology, education, etc.) by which to judge soundness (validity), aptness (applicability, feasibility), and value (according to social, cultural, educational, and other norms). Drawn from that review is a list of specific criteria for assessing systematic media projects. The 20 descriptive criteria in seven broad categories are followed by a composite listing of 10 specific criteria for evaluating mass media study programs. (b) Part II describes concrete characteristics of specific projects. Salient aspects common to many—well worked out in concept and application—offer examples of sound factors in stable, consistent, and workable projects. Such patterns, derived inductively, demonstrate and refine the listed criteria.

Despite disparities of context, most projects evince common characteristics whatever their origins or goals. Such patterns turn up in the survey in Part II and are noted in the synthesis in Part III. They include questions of key topic areas to be included in projects, the relation of instructors/leaders to groups engaged in the activity, the underlying educational and cultural premises, and the role of support materials (books, hand-out sheets, quizzes, lecture vs. discussion, sampling media product, pro-active exercises, etc.). Included is the overriding factor of centralized, administrative support vis-à-vis individual initiative in introducing critical study of media. Implied, of course, are the twin concerns of authorization in institutional contexts and of budget feasibility. The historical, analytical survey of projects in Part II provides data related to those kinds of questions.

Part III then assesses the projects in light of the criteria developed, notes patterns, and offers guidelines for applying the criteria to other programs promoting television literacy.

# I

# THEORETICAL AND HISTORICAL BACKGROUND: ESTABLISHING CRITERIA FOR "CRITICAL VIEWING SKILLS" EDUCATION

Part I provides background and foundation for this report. An historical sketch of the development of television media literacy programs follows a review of major aspects of related theory drawn from philosophy, sociology, pedagogy, and other disciplines. Not intended as a theoretical treatise, the chapters in Part I offer a skeletal synthesis of some major theoretical foundations with implications for media education. From them are drawn criteria to be applied (in Part III) to the projects to identify emphases as well as strengths and limitations. The reader is urged to explore further the continually developing body of reception theory as well as communication and education theories generally, including media education and specifically television critical viewing skills.*

## TERMINOLOGY

At the outset some distinctions must be made among terms used in the field and in this report.

---

*Notable and relatively recent are works by Worth and Gross (1981), Fiske (1987), and Carey (1988); plus books fusing theory with application by Ploghoft and Anderson (1981), Worth and Gross (1981), Hefzallah (1987), and Anderson and Meyer (1988) in the United States; and by Masterman (1980, 1985a) and Alvarado, Gutch, and Wollen (1987) in the United Kingdom. Complete citations are in the References at the end of the book.

*Communication education* and the more restrictive *media education* can refer to a wide range of interpersonal as well as technologically mediated transfers of information and meaning. These terms are too broad for what is surveyed in this report. Various proponents of media-training programs, with their respective purposes and procedures (see "Definitions" in Part II), label their work with different phrases.

*Media literacy,* although broader than television or even broadcast study, does emphasize the elements of language and symbol discussed on preceding pages. *Television literacy* would seem to emphasize the medium's content and form as presented visually and aurally, including their codified interrelationships (elements juxtaposed through editing). But literacy is only part of the endeavor. Broader understanding of the structures, processes, and impact of the television phenomenon on society calls for awareness of how media institutions interrelate with that society. Neil Postman was quoted (*Variety,* 1981) as objecting to the term because "television is not a book; you do not learn literacy by watching television" (p. 42). Schwartz (1981) commented on the "post-literate" environment of electronic media, with their vast store of information not requiring the ability to read or write. That, of course, takes the word too narrowly. Proponents of media study programs have used *literacy* analogously. They relate the cognitive and affective processes involved in television viewing to similar processes in reading. And studies have noted not only the affinity between both forms of media experience (TV and print), but concurrent development of reading and thinking skills when TV viewing skills were being developed—reflecting a more holistic phenomenon in human cognitive development. Postman preferred to distinguish television from other communication forms as separate and worthy in its own right because it creates a new "communications context" that eventually will modify "the cognitative [*sic*] habits, social relations, personal styles and political interests" of all viewers, especially children.

The basic constructs in educating to media literacy are perception, reflection, reasoning, evaluation—in short, "critical thinking." Parsley (1981) therefore referred to his detailed program of television study as one of teaching "critical thinking skills" (p. 133). They include understanding the process of valid inferences, abstracting, generalizing, syllogistic reasoning, propaganda analysis, and various forms of problem-solving traditionally exercised in language and mathematics studies.

Electronic media are typically experienced as communication previously packaged and presented to a widespread, anonymous audience that is essentially passive. Thus, Ploghoft and Anderson (1981) labeled as "receivership skills" the learned abilities to respond to media stimuli creatively with sensitivity and discrimination.

Many projects surveyed in this study exclusively concentrate on contemporary television as the medium and the mode for teaching critical thinking and receivership skills, and are called *critical viewing skills* programs.

Called by various names in different parts of the world, these individual and institutional efforts strive not only to guide adults and children to better, more responsible, more responsive and active analysis and reaction to media experience, but also at times to influence the media managers and governmental bodies responsible for overseeing them. Organized projects in North America reflect those purposes in varied terms: *television literacy, critical receivership skills, critical viewing skills,* or more broadly, *critical thinking.* Groups in other countries, notably Australia and in parts of Europe, employ different nomenclature but demonstrate similar purpose and methodologies. All endeavor to guide and train consumers of media to a higher standard of awareness of and critical response to their personal experience of mass media. A brief chronology of how major training programs evolved offers historical context.

Chapter 1 sketches the background of theoretical assumptions about man, society, culture, and communication as bases for identifying criteria by which to assess various media literacy projects. Included is discussion of language and literacy, symbols, ethical and socio-political contexts, research, and educational theories. (Readers familiar with such foundations for teaching media literacy may wish to skim or skip entirely the first chapter.)

Chapter 2 outlines salient characteristics of major projects, noting patterns among their purposes, methodologies, and various definitions of what constitutes critical viewing skills. And it distills 20 criteria reflecting theoretical points drawn from the preceding analysis. Those criteria are applied in Part III to the projects reported in Part II.

Chapter 3 traces the historical development of programs of study in media literacy—their antecedents in film and radio study in the 1930s and 1940s to recent developments worldwide.

# 1

## Foundations of Media Literacy Studies

Because various kinds of media education have proliferated, it is useful to identify their range of objectives and also their differing assumptions about why and how people use mass media and about presumed impact on personal development. Most often media literacy projects occur in a context of formal education, which itself reflects various educational and cognitional theories. And, of course, the sociopolitical and economic environment where specific media study programs exist influence those projects in their assumptions, purposes, structure, and materials. On the following pages these well-springs of communication, media, and education are examined as the foundation for identifying criteria for designing and appraising media education programs.

### HUMAN LANGUAGE, LITERACY, SYMBOL SYSTEMS

The human person possesses a unique characteristic among living beings: the capacity to abstract, reflect, draw relationships, and make judgments. Beyond this power of intelligence is the ability to communicate those thoughts and feelings in arbitrary codification of language, both spoken (linguistic) and written (literary). Grammar, syntax and rhetoric or style are components of this power of language. Competence in these skills—both active (as speaker-writer) and passive (as listener-reader)—is called literacy. These same terms can be extended to the aural and visual media, which include "images" in sound and sight. They are often codified into systematic structures to augment natural (iconic) sights and sounds. The images also demonstrate creative manipulation, just as in spoken and written forms. And they add the essential component of time (length, duration, rhythm) in juxtaposing the aural-visual elements—perhaps making the mass media of film, television and radio as akin to music as they are to literature.

Language is a system of symbols.[1] In a larger sense, symbols can be considered as the form for "organizing ideas by which *people* develop perspectives about their relationship to the world," in Himmelstein's (1981, p. 97) phrasing. This implies the important role played by media creators who select the symbols—and the symbol-structures or codes— that reflect and interpret reality accurately or in a distorted manner. Consumers of media have the task of decoding television sensitively, intelligently, critically in order to give meaning to the medium's content. A body of analysis—developed by Gross (1973, 1974), Worth (1981), Fiske (1987), Carey (1988), Anderson and Meyer (1988), and others—refers to the need for cultural and media-specific "competencies." They involve "modes" of various kinds of media and genres, and "codes" by which signification is imbedded in content and form to be recognized and interpreted by receivers who are the ones ultimately giving "meaning" to their experience of media material. Competence of senders in crafting is related to competence of receivers in interpreting communications distributed through mass media. The process is based on the viewer's "media consciousness" which Altheide and Snow (1979) identify as a "general logic that media professionals and the audience use to 'make sense' out of the phenomenon presented through the media" (p. 200). Widespread media experiences by the mass publics contribute to the collective consciousness of society (Snow, 1983, pp. 10–11).

Underlying all this is semiotics, the science of signs. It studies how signs work and the ways we use them; it analyzes how a sign and its meaning are related, and how signs are combined into codes.[2]

## SOCIAL SYMBOL-SYSTEMS AND TELEVISION

Ironically, the very medium that contemporary society associates with superficial techniques and trivial content is the same medium that respected educators and social researchers seriously look to as an agent for renewed study and growth in cultural experience and understanding. They see this coming about through "total language" of semiotics that lie at the core of communication in any society.

George Gerbner built on the theme that the human person rarely experiences reality directly but rather through symbolic context that gives meaning to perceptions. Echoing Marshall McLuhan, he noted that television is not just a successor to other mechanical-electrical media; it is instead the successor of tribal culture—with its rituals, symbol system, conventions, and continuous involvement and confrontation of the participant-observer. He asserted that analyzing and coming to understand and judge television in our daily living is more than "viewing skills"; it is tantamount to reinstituting liberal education. It attempts to liberate the individual from an unquestioning dependence on the immediate cultural environment, by looking beyond (forward and backward) to science, arts, the classics, and the achievements of mankind, in order to transcend the local, isolated impoverished environment. Thus he asserted that television is truly "the central socializing process of our species in industrialized society" today.[3] Television's conventions, its program schedules of information and entertainment, its pace and patterns of presentation, its omnipresence in homes and on the world scene as an electronic window or mirror all help weave together the fabric of our society that we call contemporary culture—which is broader than "popular culture."

This is so because "stories"—whether creative fiction or selections of factual reality in news, documentaries, interviews, talk programs and so forth—show how things work, what things are, what has value and is worth choosing, and what we are to do about it. These selective perceptions on an institutionalized scale for mass publics form the body of widely recognizable and accepted configurations of how reality is constituted and what is worthwhile in it. In other words, they form our system of "acceptables" and "desirables," our myths and stereotypical patterns of perceiving, comprehending, and evaluating. Society's attention, attitude and behavior are built on such foundations.

This communication process cannot be ignored in our own society. Television today is a major carrier of acculturation and socialization—along with family, school, church, and peer groups, who themselves are all swept into the pervasive phenomenon of television-mediated social agenda and judgments.

Horace Newcomb (1981) looks upon TV as the central symbol field in contemporary western culture. By culture he means a system of shared meaning and value communicated through symbols that are not static and uniform but continually changing. It is a *process* that is constantly redefining symbolic expression of ourselves, our self-understanding, and social settings of other families and businesses and governments.

That experience is shared first-hand at times but more commonly second-hand through communication (conversation, correspondence, print media, film, and broadcasting). Our way of experiencing, understanding, and coming to grips with our world through symbols is mediated continually in our society. More radically, even our thought is shaped by the tradition of linear, causal reasoning that is framed in words—symbols of spoken/written communication. Although "we are accustomed to think of thought as essentially private, an activity that occurs in the head," said James Carey (1975), it is rather "predominantly public and social. . . . Thought is public because it depends on a publicly available stock of symbols" that forms society's system of signs (cited by Newcomb, 1981, p. 12).

That is why critically perceiving and thinking about these mediated experiences is central to being "educated" and to how we live. Critical thinking, in Newcomb's phrase is "a way of living in the world." It has traditionally been exercised in spoken and written forms of analysis and synthesis (speaking and writing clearly, logically, effectively). It lies at the heart of our experience of media as well, if we are prepared to do more than passively let media phenomena wash over us. Television, in its visual and aural form as well as by its very presence in our daily patterns of living, shares in what Milton Ploghoft (1981) called language foundations that involve total language development, not mere skills (as in reading, or phrasing sentences, or constructing syllogistic argument). That total development of mediating symbology is language in the broadest sense. It is not only what is spoken by the tongue or written on a static surface of paper. It also includes perceiving relationships among elements of the message, interpreting the images, evaluating statements and identifying affective appeals as well as logic, drawing conclusions, reacting personally to the message, and recognizing emotional satisfactions from the communication.

In this sense, "critical receivership skills" might be the phrase to describe CVS training as part of a human being's total learning and growing process.* It is medium-specific to television because at this juncture in human history that medium dominates symbol production and myth/reality dissemination in contemporary society. Study of this omnipresent medium can lead by induction to principles about key cognitive processes (perception, reflection) and affective processes (emotion, evaluation).

The phrase "critical viewing skills" (or CVS) is apt because the medium of television—unlike study of cinema, which emphasizes the

---

*For distinctions among labels given to formal study of television media, see "Terminology" listed earlier.

art form and concentrates on analyzing outstanding examples of cinematic art—involves not only content and form in the traditional meaning of "message" but also the pervasive impact on leisure time, on perception and judgment about society, and on the socioeconomic-political environment. This is the far broader meaning of the "medium" that itself is the "message" in McLuhan's felicitously ambiguous phrasing. Television is a sociopsychological phenomenon constituting part of the typical person's conscious awareness and lifestyle, affecting patterns of eating and sleeping, discussion topics among friends, reference points for assessing political and economic life. Viewers often look to television for models of how to dress, speak, and act, and even of how to think. Media images (formulae, symbol-system, codes, cues) become the accepted standard for evaluating and comparing nonmedia reality. The medium's content and format of presentation are even adopted by individuals and institutions in their own sphere of sports, politics, and religion "to interpret and establish meaning in their own lives" (Snow, 1983, p. 166).

This broader scope of television study beyond content and form (grammar, syntax, rhetoric, and time) was noted early on by Lewis in 1948 and UNESCO in 1962.[4]

In many programs of media analysis the social implications have been as important as aesthetics and as students' cognitive development. Unlike film and other public arts, television is not peripheral or intermittent but rather an intimately pervasive phenomenon in contemporary living.

Therefore, one guideline for a comprehensive program in "critical viewing skills" is:

**It should include the study of the broad social context and impact of television as well as the intrinsic aesthetics of the medium.***

*Worldwide Scope of (U.S.) TV Program Distribution.* Concern for how audiences use and are influenced by television is clearly not limited to North America, although the U.S. experience is the main focus of this report. Research chronicles the widespread infatuation with television in most nations, and research has measured the extent to which Anglo-American programming dominates the content on television screens worldwide.

---

*Specific guidelines for appraising television literacy projects are set off from the text from which they are derived. From these guidelines are drawn the criteria listed at the end of chapter 2. Those criteria are used in Part III to assess CVS projects described in Part II.

For example, Murray (1980, pp. 51–57) has outlined the scope of children's television diets in major industrialized nations. In English-speaking countries and industrialized nations where a large amount of television is available, young children's television viewing increases from about 2 hours a day in early years to more than 3 hours a day in pre-teens, until they reach the teen years when viewing decreases. A similar pattern emerges from studies in other European nations, but with amounts of total viewing somewhat less at each stage. Beyond sheer time spent with television, the content of viewing is also identifiable by national source of that programming. American children of course watch programs produced in the United States. But so do children of other countries, including Third World nations. This "media colonization" (on the heels of earlier decades of industrial/cultural infiltration or "imperialism") is reflected in Lee's (1981) analysis.[5] The United States exported to other countries more than three times the total amount of programming exported by the next three nations together. Thus, non-American youth are often exposed to television content similar to American children's TV viewing experience.

Typically, 85% of children's viewing was in evening hours when standard TV fare is on the family screen; only 15% of viewing was during the weekend and early morning periods when programs directed to youth are scheduled. Imported programs are a major fare of evening schedules on the world's TV screens. When Australia imported 65% of its programming, mainly from the United States, France imported 60%; Denmark 52%; Israel and Norway 50% each; Sweden 40%; Finland 35%; and Canada 33% in prime-time plus other imports at other times of day. Ten countries of Central America imported from 60% to 80% of their programs. In the entire Third World of 57 developing nations, 39 imported more than half of their television programming, and two-thirds of those 39 imported more than 60%.[6]

A study of 69 countries in 1983 (Varis, 1984) found the same pattern of one-way exported TV programming as did a UNESCO study a decade earlier (Varis, 1974). Those nations imported one-third or more of their programming, with the United States the dominant supplier.[7]

First World/Western content and format fills not only the Third World's screens, but increasingly those of the Second World (the Soviet sphere in an era of *glasnost* or "openness"). U.S. style of programming, supported by commercial advertising, also sets much of the agenda for mass television structure and styles in non-U.S. countries who look to the United States and United Kingdom as models.

**Any CVS curriculum in whatever country must address the intercultural phenomenon of programming imported from**

**other nations, especially when such programs dominate or constitute a major portion of a country's broadcast service.**

As Sol Worth (1981) observed in quite concrete terms:

> Throughout the world, the air is being filled with reruns of "Bonanza" and ads for toothpaste, mouthwash, and vaginal deodorants. . . . If left unchecked, Bantuy, Dani, and Vietnamese children, as well as our own, will be taught to consume culture and learning through thousands of "Sesame Streets," taught not that learning is a creative process in which they participate, but rather that learning is a consumer product like commercials.
>
> If left unchecked, we, and perhaps other nations like us, will continue to sell the technology which produces visual symbolic forms, while at the same time teaching other peoples our uses only, our conceptions, our codes, our mythic and narrative forms. We will, with technology, enforce our notions of what is, what is important, and what is right. (p. 99)

The role of television in the conduct of business, of education, of cultural activities, and of life itself has relentlessly increased in recent decades. The medium has attracted the attention and touched the senses, emotions, and minds of multi-millions, increasingly with similar form and content of prepackaged presentations of drama, comedy, action, sports, music, talk, and news, plus commercial advertisements.

It is in this context of widespread impact on society that citizens of the world, governmental bodies, and scholarly research teams from the 1950s to the 1990s have become more deeply concerned with how media affect people and, more recently, how people use media.

## PHILOSOPHICAL PREMISES

Among foundations for judging media are premises about the nature of the human person and of society, including implications for the role of government (democratic or authoritarian) and economic structure (such a "big business" in a free-enterprise capitalist society).

One might cite as seminal those thinkers who best reflect one's perspective and value-orientation, such as Aristotle, Aquinas, Hobbes, Kant, Freud, Skinner, and so forth. One may view mankind and human nature by emphasizing a largely deterministic approach that stresses behavioral response to stimuli, of heredity and environmental factors including mass media. In this framework, a person is to a large extent at the mercy of media's current status and must strive to protect oneself with "interventionist" forms of media study. Or one may view

humankind as essentially free, seeking reasons and motives for justifying actions that support personal identity and contribute to social
interaction, and so can learn to react to or modify effects of media, and
even to participate in media.

In the present analytic survey we look to the human person as a
rational, social, symbol-making animal. We assume that the human
being is intrinsically free to learn, to judge, to act. Therefore, media
education should address itself to this fundamental autonomy in the
human condition, as urged by Masterman (1980) and by Minkkinen
(1978).

**A keynote to effective educational process in CVS programs
is to respect the individuality of the person, including their
distinctive upbringing by family, so that they are not indoctrinated with others' opinions and conclusions, but rather
are trained in the process of selective discrimination, analytical observation, and reasoned assessment based on factual data judged according to meaningful criteria. This approach takes into account the context of family, school,
peers, themselves as unique persons, as well as their own
media experience in the past. Freedom and autonomy of the
individual in CVS studies should be coupled with informed
judgment.**

Anderson and Meyer (1988) develop their synthesis of an interactive
model of sender/receiver who respectively imply/infer signification in
media content (or "texts"). They stress the receiver's pivotal role of
interpreting and thus determining the text's meaning for him or her.
They posit their "accommodation theory" by acknowledging that "the
primary characteristic of human life is its performance in social action" (p. 301). Because of the polysemic text—possessing multiple levels of possible meaning for interpretation—individual receivers each
make personalized meaning of media texts in the context of their own
lived experiences and associations. The researcher-theorists assert
that "meaning is in the situated individual, not content" (p. 192) and
"it is, therefore, possible for us both to participate in the 'same [media]
experience' and to achieve radically different interpretations of it" (p.
301). They conclude that *"meaning is a local production and effects
cannot be predicted from content properties"* in the media text, and that
*"meaning is a cultural production"* (pp. 313–314). Therefore they posit
that questions of "meaning"—and, ultimately, of social effects—involve the receivers' personal social context and activity more than
media content.

> Mediated texts are accommodated within these social action routines [of
> a person's daily living] that are, in the main, both prior to and extant
> after the appearance of given [media] texts. . . . Accommodation Theory
> moves the causal agent of any effect from the characteristics of content
> to the local performance of interpretation in which meaning is achieved.
> Further, it holds that the effect, itself, is a product of the social action in
> which the mediated text is accommodated. (pp. 322, 326)

To summarize: Extending previous analyses of Worth, Fiske, and others, Anderson and Meyer look to various receivers' interpreting media
material as based not on the "delivery of meaning" by textual content
but instead by their own "performance" of making sense out of it—
that is, by "accommodating" the media texts into preexisting routines
of personal social involvement. In their theory, "it is the social action
performances that provide for and explain media effects" (p. 49).
Fiske's (1987) analysis puts it this way:

> [V]iewing television is typically a process of negotiation between the text
> and the variously socially situated readers. The value of the theory lies
> in its freeing the text from complete ideological closure, and in its shift
> away from the text and towards the reader as the site of meaning. . . .
> [T]he [media] text [is] a structured polysemy . . . which can only be acti-
> vated by socially situated viewers in a process of negotiation between the
> text and their social situation. (pp. 64, 65)

Such a theoretical stance has direct implications for a media training
program:

**It deemphasizes the role of cultural ideology (including neo-
Marxist and other hegemonic perspectives), of media
creators (in somewhat cynical conspiracy theories), and of
media content (stimulus-response behaviorism) as direct
and primary causes of effects on audiences. It relocates serious responsibility for media's impact to individual media
users, and also to parents and teachers of young viewers.**

The latter point is treated after the following section.

## ETHICAL IMPLICATIONS

The "ethic" as well as the "aesthetic" of a medium is derived from the
nature of the medium that itself reflects the society that spawned and
supports it. A "mass medium" by its nature is intended to reach mas-

sive numbers of people; this implies at the outset a leveling characteristic of the intended audiences and thus of the content presented to
attract them. A mass medium, unlike an esoteric or elitist medium of
expression, is oriented to the general public (large, undifferentiated,
anonymous audiences with little feedback), publicly supported
(through advertising, individual or corporate subscription, or government funding), privately or publicly owned and operated (by corporations, investors, or governmental agencies), and publicly "controlled"
or influenced (by audience patterns of use and at times by governmental authority). Mass media distribute a wide variety of program types
to masses of people; but the media are not masters of a single artistic
standard. This nature of the mass medium nudges it into areas of
content distinguished by Eric Voegelin as sometimes substantive (contributing to the growth of the human personality and of his or her role
in society), often pragmatic (purposeful, in order to indoctrinate—
propaganda, advertising or information), and usually intoxicant (in-
substantial, mesmerizing "escape"—possibly related to a manifesta-
tion of narcotizing dysfunction).

To make judgments about media is to exercise the act of criticism.
That act is constituted by a statement of comparison between what *is*
and what *ought to be*. The critic, and the critical viewer, must be
grounded in two essential areas of this act of critical judgment: the
area of facts (what *is*—informational data) and the area of norms or
standards (what *ought to be*—criteria). It is the act of comparing and
contrasting these factual statements with the normative statements
that results in critical judgment. Thus:

**CVS projects should always be accurate with factual data
based on valid sources and research, eschewing merely
conventional assumptions, commonly accepted but misinformed assertions. Secondly, the contexts of norms being
addressed must be identified, noting the various levels or
categories of criteria such as economic, aesthetic, technical,
social, ethical, legal.**

For example, *economic* norms about what "should" constitute effective mass media communication include reasonable budgets, cost-
effective production and promotion, widespread acceptance, low unit
cost per consumer, and similar factors that result in efficiency and rate
of profitable return or at least a balance between expenses and reve-
nues. They are quite different from *aesthetic* norms about what artistic
quality "ought to be" in communications generally and in mass media
content and form, even for widespread heterogeneous audiences. Both

kinds of normative statements differ from *technical* norms constituting "good" effective electronic signals. And they all differ in kind from *ethical* or moral "oughts" about media content and audience consumption of media products. *Legal* "shoulds" are yet again different from the normative statements or criteria noted earlier. One cannot simply label television as "bad" or "good"except when addressing specific normative categories. Therefore:

> **Critical viewing skills programs must acquaint participants with the constitutive parts of media, including the bi-directional communication process (with both sender and receiver as necessary complements for the phenomenon of communication to occur).**

Some precision of analysis must take into account these varying levels of norms or standards when appraising complex mass media in society.

Many commentators, especially some in Britain and others conducting studies for agencies of the United Nations, stress that

> **ethical and moral values are inherent in any serious study of media; but identification of values ought be elicited from individual reflection and judgment based on values already embraced; educators ought not proselytize on behalf of a given value system.**

Minkkinen (1978) emphasized that these values relate to the family of nations, involving "the formation of man's social relations and his becoming a member of society and a citizen of the world" (p. 38). They include respect for human rights and fundamental freedoms, promoting tolerance and friendship among all nations and racial groups. Because media systems in many nations are oriented primarily to profit-making rather than serving citizens' informational and cultural needs, "an important issue in the field of ethics is whether one takes a stand in respect of the kinds of interests, and whose interests, the outputs of the media and those who provide them should serve" (p. 39). The fact that media product is interchanged so vigorously among nations (as described earlier) suggests international implications for exercising responsibility not only by media suppliers but by media consumers as well. Minkkinen sketched the context of values for mass media:

> Mass communication embodying ethical standards of this nature serves
> to reaffirm and to promote the realization of human dignity and human
> rights while condemning all attempts to infringe them. It does this in a

variety of ways; by standing up for equality between people and nations
and against the inequalities of racism, fascism, chauvinism, apartheid,
colonialism and neo-colonialism; by speaking up for international peace
and friendship and against wars waged for territorial expansion, inva-
sion, domination and war propaganda and the violent repression of
human beings; by reaffirming an optimistic faith in the future of mankind and in science and human intelligence and countering fantasies
about the future which nourish pessimism, and by denouncing fatalism
and unintelligent and unscientific modes of thought. It can take a stand
for tolerance, freedom and thought, opinion and religion and can denounce restraints on speech, ideas and discussion. Mass communication
of high quality can also sustain our sense of beauty and the right to enjoy
art, and can denounce contempt for art and beauty and constraints on
the human need for expression. Love of truth and the search for it are
inherent in this kind of mass communication, enhancing our ability to
think rationally and to perceive clearly the problems arising in our own
society and environment and in the world at large on the basis of fact
and valid generalization. Mass media thus conceived foster interests in
things of the mind and the desire to explore reality and to identify the
contradictions underlying the conclusions arrived at by ourselves and by
other people. (p. 42)

Because critical analysis of media means evaluation based on some
standard of judgment, some of its most trenchant forms occur in Marxist or neo-Marxist and in feminist inquiry. Anderson and Meyer (1988,
pp. 183–186) enumerate class, patriarchy, and hegemony (maintaining the status of any given hierarchical structure such as gender or
race) among ideological theories reflected, supported, and participated
in by mass media.[8] But Gregory Porter (1989, p. 4) reminds that—
despite their differing interpretations and conclusions—Marxists,
capitalists, sociologists, cultural anthropologists, and religious funda-
mentalists all ask similar questions about the role of mass media in
society.


## MEDIA RESPONSIBILITY

Because the mass media process is bi-polar, there is mutual responsibility for what happens when media are used by the masses. This
thesis is stressed by Altheide and Snow (1979, pp. 10, 16, 47) who
underscore the interactive process in media experience—as discussed
earlier. Media are not to be judged, they claim, by deterministic stim-
ulus/response conditioning nor by allegations of conspiracy against
the masses. Because television reflects behavior in society and thereby

helps establish meanings, people develop a consciousness or "media logic" affecting how they relate to and understand their environment. Media experience becomes the framework by which people perceive their world and make interpretations, by which they attain a perspective for judgment. By this symbolic interaction an individual acts voluntarily, creating meaning in concert with others, according to Snow's review (1983, pp. 19, 25, 228, 237, 271). Thus, media influence exists to the extent that media creators (senders) and audience (receivers) uncritically assimilate and accept these symbol systems as standards for evaluating and making comparisons, for interpreting themselves and their world.

Is this latent, self-induced assimilation necessarily intended by media managers? If media's influence and effects cannot be ascribed merely to big business or to bureaucracy but also to people's voluntary interaction involving their own free responsiveness to media, then media managers cannot be seen simply as conspiratorial manipulators. To the extent that audiences freely use media in this way, they must be alerted to their role in the mass communication process and to their shared responsibility for media impact in their lives.

Television attracts and holds an audience through information and entertainment, often relying on stereotypes and idealized norms—which in turn shape the definitions, interpretations, and solutions that are applied to the subjects and issues dealt with by the medium.

In explaining media's influence by focusing exclusively on ideological factors (big business) and sociological ones (organizations, bureaucratic routine) affecting content selection, the "agenda-setting" critique overlooks the more fundamental factors of mass communication linguistics and the perspectives used within each medium to interpret information, including the paramount factor of individual viewers' accommodating the medium "texts" to their own daily social experiences (Snow, 1983, pp. 147, 213).

*Systemic Aspects of Mass Media.* Quite distinct from viewers' making meaning from media programs, the structure of mass media in a given country affects the media process and the relation of senders to recipients of media messages. A "vertical" construct assumes that the source/sender dominates a one-way communication process that induces effects in the passive recipients of messages. Only the introduction of feedback helps soften this stiffly one-way, linear model (unless feedback becomes merely a confirming instrument about the circulation of the senders' program among receivers, as with audience ratings). Alternately, in a "horizontal" model of mutual interaction, a mass medium's leaders can attempt to become involved with the conscious and even unconscious needs and aspirations of the human beings who constitute the public audience, by responding to their cultural state and, in effect, collaborating with them as a dialogue rather than a monologue.

Media study groups have precisely this characteristic:

**They sensitize the receivers to their options of exercising more active roles in the communication process; this is accomplished by internalized reflection and judgment about their own use of media, by interchange with other persons and groups, and even by positive, concrete interaction with media themselves.**

This approach emphasizes the individuality and responsibility of the person for his or her use of and deliberate reaction to the media. It enhances rather than erodes conscious initiative in the very process of participating in media experience. They see it as contributing to a person's human growth, rather than abdicating to one-sided domination of their leisure hours by a medium that allegedly dictates to their cognitive, affective, and behavioral life. In the view of some media analysts, active participation in the creative production of media material is essential. Snow (1983) underscored that:

Media's influence is that it serves as a repository of information and situations for voluntary action by audience members. Therefore, media influence should be understood not as a cause beyond an individual's cont: ol but as something consciously used by people to varying degrees. The media world can become an environment for total immersion, a world tempered by critical evaluation, or an aspect of culture almost totally rejected by an individual. Using a theoretical approach that focuses on establishing and maintaining identity through an interactive process places the ultimate responsibility for behavior squarely on the individual. Yet as most people know, choices often appear limited and often are difficult. (p. 219)

Of course, different sociopolitical milieux prompt differing critical approaches to mass media, as is discussed in the next section. For example, media training curricula in northern European countries (e.g., Sweden, Finland, Denmark, Federal Republic of Germany) stress manipulative tendencies of the media in matters of social concepts; but in Western industrialized countries where media are highly commercialized (e.g., Britain, United States, Australia) media studies emphasize personal ethical values, emotions and tastes (Minkkinen, 1978, p. 28).

## SOCIAL FOUNDATIONS OF COMMUNICATION

To review basic considerations briefly, it is worth recalling that civilization and communication are almost conterminous concepts. A human individual lives isolated until he or she communicates with another human person. Their interrelationship grows and, as more persons join in the give and take of communicating, a bond begins to grow. The individual becomes a sharer in a common environment and together these juxtaposed persons gradually agree on ways to keep in touch and to assist each other while at the same time respecting each other's individuality. When they have advanced to a sophisticated level of interaction they share increasingly complex aspects of living—not only food and shelter, but forms of recreating and of learning to harness the vast world around them. Their formation into a society (*socii*—companions) breeds structures and processes of interchange of goods and means of safety and mutual support. Each is becoming a citizen (*civis*) of an emerging political-economic entity. This has come about through action, reaction, and mutual interaction. It has all been mediated by various forms of communication: first verbal sounds and gesture, then codified signs and symbols, and eventually technical means (*media*) of communicating—person to scattered person through papyrus and then person to multiple persons by copied manuscripts, moveable type, and eventually high-speed printing presses. In this evolving scene in the late 1800s came the electric media of telegraph and telephone, followed by the recording machine, the motion picture camera and projector, and—at the turn of the century—the wireless. Radio fast grew into the electronic communications giant of the 1930s and 1940s, to be supplanted in dominance by pictures-and-sound via electromagnetic energy hurtling with the speed of light. Television continues to dominate the attention of contemporary society in the decades leading into the 21st century.

## SOCIOPOLITICAL CONTEXTS OF MASS MEDIA

Harold Adams Innes (interpreted by McLuhan, among others) looked to the major steps in communication as catalysts for major developments in civilization itself. Sprawling populations coalesced into societies that, in turn, formed into nations of peoples. In parallel stages, if not in time-locked steps, "communication" grew into mass communication and then into competitive mass media systems. Structures and processes of those mass media reflected the culture of society and the social-political matrix of the nations in which they emerged. From this mix evolved mass society with a mass or popular culture.[9]

Social and Cultural Contexts

**Any study of television must take into account the different environments in which various mass media systems developed and now operate.**

The North American experience differs somewhat from other English-speaking countries such as Australia and the United Kingdom. And those differ still more from societies with other heritages: Scandinavian, eastern European, Latin American, African, or Asian. Out of regional cultures and national contexts emerge media systems. Media not only reflect but also play a role in the processes of governing and of establishing cultural priorities and interchange of those respective peoples. Media's role touches upon matters of power and control, in Sol Worth's (1981) view:

> Whereas in earlier times, power and control were seen as being involved with natural and technological resources and with the control of labor and man's production from that labor, political power now seems to be tied more and more to the control of information. . . . If we are to study culture, we are inevitably involved in the study of the power relationships and control over mechanisms, messages, message-makers, and message-receivers. (pp. 103, 106)

But Stewart Hoover (1988) countered "power may be what television is all about (as Gerbner has said), but the power resides in the construction of meaning by the viewer in dialogue with the text, not in an instrumental 'message' of power, or 'exercise' of power by the medium itself" (p. 175).

The development of sophisticated technology for mass communication also reflects an industrialized society's values, often emphasizing economic and political consumerism.[10] Authoritarian or totalitarian systems are reflected in the Soviet bloc and in areas of South and Central America. Various forms of social government are found in Scandinavian and other European nations, and somewhat in the United Kingdom with its nationalized industries. In many countries, including the United States, the private sector is dominant not only in industry but in the relation of government to the people, with concomitant diversity and almost anarchy of the marketplace. In developing countries are found inchoate systems with varying degrees of governmental organization and control.

## MEDIA STUDIES: PROBLEMS POSED BY MEDIA SYSTEMS

Developed countries in the West generally enjoy stable, traditional governmental and economic systems; their standard of living is relatively high. Their media education tends to acknowledge the essential media structure as a "given." So they strive to bring students/viewers to a better understanding of forces that determine content and form and scheduling of the "product" on television screens to which they are exposed. They seek to develop informed, discriminating media audiences. Their media study typically analyzes programming genres (entertainment and news/information), advertising supporting the system, structure of networks/stations licensed by a regulatory agency in the context of whatever constitutional rights are afforded to press and free speech, and audiences (through ratings, measuring program choices and exposure to advertising messages).

In parts of Europe and especially in developing countries of the Third World, media educators often focus on the larger social issue of mass communication as a key agent in society. Some countries have wide class distinctions between the affluent and the indigent; authoritarian forms of government co-exist with international business and foreign banking conglomerates that strongly influence their nation's affairs. Therefore,

**media educators go beyond training in aesthetic sensitivity and beyond insulating from kitsch culture, to teaching informed and competent role-taking in the country's media processes.**

They train participants to interact with existing media systems, to become active in the very process of mass media, and even to develop their own "micro-mass media" such as small-circulation newspapers and local cable channels and other forms of interchange not beholden to or limited by established "macro-mass media" systems. The goal is to develop more pluralistic, democratized media along with personal liberation from established social forces, leading to more "authentic integrity" of the society itself. This perspective considers communication—especially through mass media—to be the foundation and fabric of society. Participatory mass communication becomes a function of an open humanistic society responsive to individuals and subgroups as well as to the power-wielding elite.[11]

Theoretical Perspectives

**Depending on various world views and the theories on which they are grounded, media education designers will assess the role of communications in society and accordingly set objectives and priorities for studying media.**

Grossberg's (1979) analysis suggests an approach to categorizing these constructs of men, media, and society. *Liberalism* stresses the primacy and value of the individual with natural rights; it is coupled with epistemological scientism, which looks to the efficacy of knowledge to promote human progress. Communication is seen in relation to individuals rather than to institutions or social forces, and "effects" research offers significant information for assessing impact of communication on individuals. *Cultural* or *social humanism* looks to a more structural view of communication as a filter that organizes and interprets our social existence, including giving meaning to our experience. (Innis and McLuhan reflect much of this.) *Pragmatism* emphasizes communication as creating community, with the life of that community defining democracy and the source of hope for society. John Dewey and the Chicago school look to mass media as destroying personal and social communication of "face-to-face" contexts, while at the same time contributing to empathic understanding by providing needed information for that very society. This reflects the paradox of the socializing function of communication—"Speech is civilization itself; it is silence that isolates" (Thomas Mann, 1927)—set off against the phenomenon of privatization—"excessive mass communication tends to isolate people from one another and from real experience" (Blake & Haroldsen, 1975, p. 117). Variations on these themes are refined by James Carey who looks beyond mere language of communication to the symbolic content or code systems. Raymond Williams denied a common culture because of multiple strata in society that occasion revolution, so that communication becomes a vehicle for changes in community life (but not a loss of community); he saw contemporary culture in terms of domination and communication.

These world views or theoretical constructs are among the philosophical assumptions that often can be discerned in various projects to train people to more discriminating use of mass media. The projects' goals, objectives, procedures, database, and even materials reflect such assumptions. They are related to both initiators and participants in media study programs.

Porter (1989) noted the successive schools of media criticism, drawing from literature's New Criticism, from semiology, structuralism, and post-structuralism. He nicely charted the progression from "emphasis on media context, to the creative work, to the message imbedded in that work, to a focus upon the *concept* of audience and, finally, to the *real* audience" (p. 4). Horace Newcomb (1986) and others have exhorted colleagues not to focus too narrowly on one or other path of analysis but to bring all to bear on the complex challenge of studying media.

**Media educators ought heed their recommendation to look to the collective findings of researchers with variant theories and methodologies, to develop an increasingly comprehensive and authentic analysis of media.**

This chapter's survey of the foundations of media literacy studies leads to more specific exploration of media systems and education in chapter 2. Guidelines for media education programs (set apart from the previous text) are merged with further guidelines developed in the next chapter; they constitute a list of criteria at the end of that chapter. Those criteria are applied (in Part III) to CVS projects worldwide that are described in Part II.

## NOTES

1. For a readable analysis applied to media see McAnany and Williams (1965, pp. 42–65), "II: The Language of Film."

2. See Fiske and Hartley, (1978, p. 37); cf. Worth (1981, chapters 1 and 2).

3. From notes taken during lecture by George Gerbner at a national conference on topic of "Children and Television: Implications for Education," Philadelphia, Pennsylvania, November 4–7, 1979. See Gerbner (1981, pp. 173–178).

4. For a brief chronological description see Anderson (1983). The International Meeting on Film and Television Teaching, organized in 1962 by UNESCO in Norway, was reported in Hodgkinson (1964), including reprints of major papers presented.

5. During the first two decades of syndicating television programs overseas, American distributors' earnings leaped from $15 million (1958) to more than $230 million (1977). In the late 1970s the United States exported 150,000 hours of programs annually, while the United Kingdom and France each sold 20,000 hours abroad each year; West Germany sold 6,000 hours a year.

6. See Lee (1981, pp. 58–59) and Murray (1980, pp. 58–66). U.S. television program distributors earned two-thirds of their overseas profits from four industrialized nations—from Canada 19%, Australia 18%, Japan 17%, and England 12%. The final third of profits came from all other countries, with Brazil, France, and West Germany the major sources of remaining profitability for U.S. TV exports.

7.  Half of TV transmission time in Latin America (including South and Central America and the Caribbean) was imported programming, three-quarters of it from the United States. One third of Western European nations' television was imported, 44% from the United States. In Asia and the Pacific, TV imports were 36% of all programs, provided mostly by the United States and the United Kingdom. Arab countries imported 42% of their program schedules, one third from other Arabic countries and another third from the United States. (Egypt programmed 54.5% of its schedule with American television.) In urban areas of Africa where television is developed, 40% to 60% of television was from outside countries, about half coming from the United States.

8.  This perspective is found in Masterman (1980, 1983, 1985a, 1985b). For other studies of television's ideological substructures, see also Williams (1975), Fiske and Hartley (1978), and Gitlin (1983).

9.  Cf. Blake and Haroldsen (1975) and Altheide and Snow (1979).

10.  Cf. Ewen and Ewen (1982). Almost all of the world's 179 sovereign nations and 37 dependent territories have broadcast systems; three quarters of them provide television service. Patterns of ownership of television systems in 151 countries: 86 (57%) are entirely government controlled, 29 (19%) are owned by nonprofit public corporations, 16 (11%) are privately owned and fully dependent on commercial advertising, while 29 (13%) are combinations of those three forms. Many government and public systems also include advertising for part of their income. See Head and Sterling (1990, p. 492), citing as source UNESCO's *Statistical Yearbook, 1988*.

11.  Cf. White and Kenney (1982, pp. 2–6) review works by Masterman, Reyes Matta, de Almeida Cunha, and Bauer. Cf. also Minkkinen (1978) and Perez (1971).

# 2

## Media Systems
## and Education

There are many kinds of media education. They work out of differing cultural and educational contexts. They have various objectives. They differ in assumptions about how and why people use mass media. And they vary in interpreting the presumed impact of media on personal development and on society.

Most major projects occur in a context of formal education, which embodies various educational and cognitional theories.

### NEEDS AND PROBLEMS OF EDUCATIONAL SYSTEMS

The process of education itself reflects the socio-cultural melieux and political contexts described in the preceding chapter. Different contexts of educational orientation and emphasis engender varying kinds of media education. For example, public education in the United States (funded by government taxes) differs in clientele and structure as well as some objectives from private U.S. schools and from their "public" counterparts in the United Kingdom. Schooling in villages and towns of developing nations emphasize instruction in hygiene, food preparation, crops, trade skills, and basic communication skills (interpersonal and print literacy). Yet other regions stress social compliance and duty to social structures, including political party and state.

Within those larger forms of education, differing applications of educational philosophy variously feature deduction by lecture and analysis, or induction from experience and discussion, or a combination of both forms of instruction.

And resources of trained personnel, physical facilities, and supporting equipment differ widely according to budget priorities from country to country, as well as between various districts within the same country.

Even where regional circumstances are similar, media study differs according to various perceptions of its value by school boards, commissions, local administrators and individual teachers, as well as by parents.

All these factors affect the purposefulness and feasibility of any effort to introduce sustained study of mass media into formal education.

## POPULAR MEDIA USE AFFECTS MEDIA EDUCATION

How people normally have access to mass media and use them in daily living partly shapes the kind of media study program needed and able to be presented effectively. In some places a single television receiver is available to villagers. Elsewhere, one or more common TV sets serve apartments and houses. In affluent societies, most individuals have personal sets. There are also different stages of media reception: as a child at home with parents, as a teenager visiting friends' homes and places of entertainment, as an advanced student in dormitories with receivers in common viewing rooms, as employed single persons or working adults with families, as elderly relying on mass media to keep in touch with people and events all day long.

Mass media, especially television, may variously be a means of leisure relaxation and even escape, a chronicle of trends in clothing and language, a reservoir of culture (music, drama, poetry), a "babysitter" to occupy children's attention, an interpreter of values about social and ethical dilemmas ("safe sex," birth control, business practices), a reporter of local and national news, a supplier of religious inspiration, a cornucopia of sports, or a purveyor of hedonism. Mass media may also serve the state as a conduit to each citizen's residence. Whatever the mix of purposes, people in all major nations devote large proportions of their waking hours to watching television (from 2–3 hours per person in developing countries, to 4–5 hours in Western nations; the average household in the United States has at least one television set turned on for approximately 7 hours a day). The amount of viewing differs, of course, according to the availability of receivers and program service.

In North America, a TV receiving set is available for every 1.46 persons, compared with one for 2.82 persons in Western Europe, for 3.33 in Australasia and other ocean territories, for 8.08 persons in Latin America, and only one set for every 23 persons in Asia and the Far East.[1]

The way people use media determines partly how media affect or "use people." This is elaborated on later in this chapter. It suggests another in the series of guidelines for implementing media literacy programs in education:*

**To be relevant and effective as well as valid, media study must address the dual relationship between media and users by speaking to viewers' lived media experience in their respective personal contexts.**

## MASS MEDIA AND SOCIAL PROBLEMS

The heavy viewing of television by people worldwide, whatever their status or language or culture, exposes them to enormous doses of programming. Media's content and treatment of social issues can have various kinds of impact on their perceptions of the world around and on their expectations, values, and even behavior.[2]

In fictional drama and comedy, as well as in news and information programming, television treats many major social questions, reflecting the cultural context. Beyond relations of persons in families, views of authority figures, acceptability of dress and language, styles of entertainment (dance, music, sports, etc.), there are also depictions of abusive relations between members of families, violence and sex, terrorism and torture, lying, and so on.[3] How governments operate or corporations manipulate, how thugs extort, how churchmen are altruistic or hypocritical, flicker across the screens of most nations. But those screens are typically opaque or silent about weaknesses or excesses of a nation's political-economic structure itself.

Alvarado, Gutch, and Wollen (1987), reflecting neo-Marxist perspectives common in Britain, stress the pervasive influence of hegemony, and the need to teach

> detailed empirical work about the structure and ownership of the media. . . . for whom maintenance of the status quo is a top priority, but

---

*Guidelines derived from research and experience in media training are set off from the text, as in chapter 1. They are incorporated into the list of criteria drawn up at the end of this chapter.

that very maintenance will also depend, in our view, on the relations of dominance being accepted as apparently natural by those socially and economically subordinated. By teaching about media institutions it is these complex and contradictory relationships that are at stake. (pp. 5–6)

Similarly, Masterman (1980, 1985b), who initially stressed applied training in video skills to understand experientially how media are crafted and communicate images, later expanded his view to include study of how institutional forces determine and control mass media in society.

In increasing numbers of nations, commercial advertising pays for the unending supply of programs—even where media systems are operated by governments and public corporations, as noted in chapter 1. The result is a non-stop barrage of images and associations and implied or expressed values to which viewers are incessantly exposed. Audiences absorb or evaluate or ignore these images and symbols, depending on their awareness of how media are structured and work, and how fiction and nonfiction are created for the sight-and-sound mass medium.

This is precisely where media study can contribute to better understanding and selective, responsive use of mass media.


## RESEARCH: MEDIA AND SOCIETY

Major sources that synthesize decades of research findings in the study of television and its interaction with society include a one-volume distillation of their original four-volume analysis of over 2,500 books, articles, and reports from half a century by Comstock, Chaffee, Katzman, McCombs, and Roberts (1978). A similar but more focused work by Murray (1980) reviewed studies of television and youth, citing 2,886 sources (almost two-thirds of them published between 1976 and 1980), 85% of them English-language publications from North America, Europe, the United Kingdom, Australia, and Scandinavia. Further updating of continuing research has been provided since 1978 by the quarterly *Communication Abstracts,* which draws from published reports in over 200 journals of major disciplines; each issue (of the four to six per year) abstracts 250 published studies. The data in those compilations and in other journals, as well as from governmental and research agencies, together chronicle the sustained efforts to determine the relationship between the medium of television and attention, attitude, and behavior of viewers. Such studies are the touchstone for determining validity of assumptions, assertions, and directives of programs of television media education.

**To the extent that media education programs acknowledge research findings, incorporating valid conclusions and implications into their CVS training, to that extent are the programs founded on stable bases and offer substantive content.**

The reader is directed to those encyclopedic summaries as well as to the broader body of scientific scholarly literature to confirm applicability of hypotheses, methodologies, tabulations of data and findings, interpretative procedures, conclusions, and implications drawn by the researchers. Where CVS projects surveyed in the present report seem to ignore or depart from such research findings, attention is noted in Parts II and III.

## SELECTED PATTERNS OF RESEARCH RELEVANT TO MEDIA TRAINING

Review of research up into the late 1980s note salient patterns, clustering sometimes conflicting findings under such categories as: Children's TV viewing as related to attention span and growth in cognition; purposes in using television ("uses and gratifications") according to typologies such as age, gender, education; televised violence; advertising; "pro-social" programming; TV characters as role models; TV content as real or fantasy window/mirror on the world (social, sexual, ethnic depictions by TV). Most of those relationships studied in formal research have been correlational rather than causal. That is, phenomena may be associated with one another but not necessarily because one causes another (for example, the amount of time spent viewing TV and academic performance). Anderson and Ploghoft (1977) summarized television's effects on cognitive, social, moral, and behavioral development of children under the categories of "TV violence and aggression," "instigation, catharsis, and differential hypotheses about effects," "consumer socialization," and "television as value agent."[4]

Through the 1980s, researchers have increasingly directed attention to the "surround" of people's personal media experience, through naturalistic field study away from laboratory settings, where they observe viewers' patterns of attention, activity, and interaction under actual living conditions. Chapter 1 noted this shift away from media content as determiner of effects to the pivotal role of the individual viewer in integrating their TV activity within their real-life routines.[5] Alvarado, Gutch, and Wollen (1987) stated the case for this approach (without lessening their concern about institutional hegemony shaping and determining mass media structure and content). Their commentary includes what may be highlighted as yet another guideline for media programmers:

> The media and an education system may be massive, but they are *not* massively determining. People clearly read their classroom experiences and the TV programmes they watch very differently. **Thus it is necessary to have a concept not of *a* reading or readings [of media "text" or programs], but of *differential readings*—and these readings are going to be informed by the social positioning and ideological formation of each reader [viewer] within a particular culture.** (p. 254)

Research trends in the last decade reflect increasing attention to the viewers of television rather than to the creators of programming and broadcast schedules. Appearing less significant in social implications is the content itself as a predictor of what effects will occur. More significant is what audiences bring to their viewing experience, the context in which they watch TV ("accommodation"), and how and why they use the medium ("uses and gratifications"). People bring expectations to the medium and choose to use it accordingly (not only time spent, but kinds of programs tuned in, level of attentiveness, and susceptibility to content). Beyond that, viewers shape and interpret meaning rather than having meaning merely thrust on them. Messages are constructed from content by viewers rather than merely delivered by content. The media message is individually personalized and interpreted by each receiver. Each person's own "meaning"—drawn from media's content and form, as well as from life experience itself—is complex, volatile, and subjective.

Therefore, a logical positivist approach that tries to delineate impact of the medium by cataloging types and specific actions (violence, sex) and dialogue is less revealing about TV's actual effects than an interactionist approach. More apposite to identifying the medium's impact is study of the interaction between the audience members and the medium. Despite possibly interpreting Piaget's analysis of stages in children's growth as discrete and distinct steps following a set sequential order, one should note that Piaget's approach is phenomenological: "What a child says he is thinking or doing is what he is thinking or doing."[6] So researchers have increasingly explored the context of the viewing experience itself to better observe the child's (or any viewer's) involvement with the medium as well as with peers and surrounding viewing context. This includes routines of daily living of which television watching is a part.

## CONCEPTS OF EDUCATION AND MEDIA STUDY

Any form of teaching media will reflect broader theories of education. If education is considered to be "any process, either formal or informal, that shapes the potentialities of the maturing organism" including values and habits, then media training is appropriate. This becomes more obvious when one considers that formal education is a systematic effort "to impart the skills and modes of thought considered essential for social functioning" (Harris & Levey, p. 834). Such education reflects that society's attitudes, values, objectives, including "dominant psychologies of learning and systems of ethics." This suggests another guideline:

**CVS projects will reflect currently acceptable theories of education, whether classical, scientific, progressive, or even vocational.**

A society's sources of "truth" and authority affect the content and process of education. Such a legacy might include not only Socrates, Renaissance thinkers, and Rousseau, but also Montessori, John Dewey, B. F. Skinner, and their disciples. That legacy influences how a given nation or region supports advances in education. Within those varied contexts of purpose, process, and expectation any media literacy curriculum must find its place.

**Therefore, a given curriculum will have greater value as it is adaptable to a wider range of educational emphases.**

In the United States, whether it is self-directed Montessori-style education or highly programmatic instruction in the Skinner mode with back-to-basics emphasis, a media educational program must be designed to fit that educational mode if it is to be endorsed by school administrators and also implemented with extensive support materials (print and audiovisual). Otherwise, the entire enterprise is relegated to an extracurricular status, or more probably is reduced to mere segments of a traditional course, subject to the inspiration (or whim) of a given instructor.

For systematic, long-term impact on a society the more formalized means of instruction in the classroom and school are the mechanism for thorough training in media literacy intended to last a lifetime and to interact with the total population.

Beyond the classroom, efforts at media education will depend on para-educational organizations such as associations of parents and teachers, or on church-related groups not in the formal educational system. For citizens generally, especially adults, such groups are effective instruments for reaching an important portion of the media audience, both as viewers themselves and as parents of younger viewers whom they can guide in media use. All of the preceding commentary suggests that:

**A media training program is more significant to the extent that it is organized and sustained (not a brief experiment but used over time and by a number of people and institutions, possibly in more than one region), is based on known research that is valid and relevant, is tested and evaluated for its results with subjects through time, is able to be replicated elsewhere because of its breadth and "open stance" to values and pluralistic forms, and provides detailed audiovisual and print materials supporting the conceptual development.**

*Open stance* refers to values that are not narrowly instructional nor exclusively moralistic in a single tradition, yet not valueless because related to the broad humanistic heritage and to the Judeo-Christian ethic. *Open stance* also refers to pluralistic forms of media: information, persuasion, entertainment; quality programming as well as popular kitsch content; current structures of media and also possibly alternate systems.

Minkkinen (1978, pp. 20, 33) suggested that media training should include three major characteristics, which (paraphrased) provide further guidelines:

**(a) It should involve cognitive and intellectual elements which stress "scientific thinking" that seeks out truth by confirming validity of facts about media institutions, processes, and social connections.**
**(b) It should be aesthetic and creative—inventively applying artistic standards; participants ought not only evaluate media products based on theory and criteria but also search out for themselves quality programs to experience finer media product, so as to enrich the whole human per-**

son (including consciousness, imagination, and emotions as well as cognition and judgment). And it should also involve learning mass media production so as to be able to express opinions through active participation in the media.
(c) It should be ethical—drawn from traditional humanistic values and applied to the context of human social relations; it ought to enhance membership in human society and contribute to citizens' informational and cultural needs in a democracy (rather than merely seeking profitability).

Masterman (1985a, p. 24) insisted that learning practical skills and applying them to concrete video projects is essential for heuristic investigation of how media operate. He stressed that

> *evaluation* of specific, current media presentations should not be the primary goal of media education, but rather *investigation* so that individuals can come to learn for themselves, the way media presentations are formed.

The purpose is to be able to critically scrutinize professional media rather than merely to emulate them. In the process, they also grow in related cognitional skills, including "critical consciousness" able to address media material they will encounter in future years. Students more broadly learn "how knowledge is come by" (epistemology). They observe how we come to know by mediated information—and to some extent how media presentations can reflect, modify, or distort aspects of reality.[7] Students see for themselves how symbol-systems (conventions, codes) mediate our knowledge of the world. This distinctive, pragmatic kind of inquiry is intended to develop what Masterman (1985a) called "critical *autonomy*"; it avoids forming students "who are likely to carry with them for the rest of their lives either a quite unwarranted faith in the integrity of media images and representations, or an equally dangerous, undifferentiated skepticism which sees the media as sources of all evil" (p. 14). He admonished educators:

It is very important, then, that media education
(i) does not degenerate into the stultifying and laborious accumulation of facts, ideas and information about the media
(ii) Should not consist of dehumanising exercises or 'busy work' on the media, designed primarily to keep students occupied
(iii) Should not involve the dutiful reproduction by students of the teachers' ideas. (p. 25)

Minkkinen noted how objectives of education in general have developed in recent decades. European nations have emphasized developing the whole personality of the student. This means training one's thinking abilities, emotions and affective perception, capacity to live with others and to voice one's rights as citizen in an open society in order to contribute to sociopolitical goals (including supporting more equitable distribution of material goods and opportunities). The latter characteristics particularly reflect objectives of education (including media education) in developing countries of the Third World.

**Therefore media training programs should at least address some of these characteristics: Development of cognitive and affective as well as behavioral skills and values—in a holistic experience—linked with the social milieu of one's own culture and nation and even with the peoples of other nations.**

Furthermore, media studies will reflect major theoretical "givens" in the general educational process. For example, attribution theory looks to age, parents' educational level, presence of older children, and child's level of integration with parents and peers as keys to growth. Piaget's cognitive developmental theory posits stages of logical operations. The earlier stage (ages up to 7) involves *pre-operational* thought where children comprehend their world by processing physical stimuli but are limited by "perceptual boundedness" and "centration"; attention and response are primarily to present stimuli, with focus on a limited part of available data such as a single salient feature of an object or experience. This develops into the stage of concrete *operational* thought (ages 7–10+) when a child begins to think logically by seeing connections and relationships and parts of continuing processes. Further steps include social learning theory that involves role-taking and social skills that develop with experience and social cognition. This leads to moral development involving estimates of value and judgments about right and wrong, according to predetermined standards.[8]

A practical application to education, including media study, is Anderson's caution that

**hypotheses should not be constructed nor research conducted as if child subjects were "little adults" with the goal of leading them efficiently to adult reactions to experience such as viewing television.**

For example, a child's playing is often make-believe and experiential for its own sake, not for some larger, maturing goal beyond itself, unlike most activity by adults.[9] This is a corollary to the already noted conclusion that one can more adequately identify the effect of television to the extent that one observes and appraises the child's involvement with and responsiveness to specific television exposure. This is a significant perspective for both teachers and parents to achieve effective CVS training.

*Holistic Interaction of Cognitional Skills.*   Central to legitimizing the arguably narrow study of television "critical viewing skills" is consideration that a person's growth in one form of knowledge acquisition tends to advance that person's capacity and even practical ability in other forms of knowledge acquisition. This holistic approach to human cognitive development involves ratiocinative, enactive, and iconic elements—Bruner's (1962) terms—or symbolic-abstract, kinesthetic, and visual elements—Samples' (1979) terminology. Together, these various forms of perceiving and understanding and judging contribute to a person's growth in "wisdom" in the broad sense. Samples (1979) observed the auditory mode's ability to communicate content in metaphor and the capacity of "sound [to] stand as a representation of a complex idea as surely as it can communicate the phonetic utterance of a spelled word" (p. 80). He likened that to visual and verbal literacy's relation to the radical function of reflective sensitivity and analysis by the total person.

Many authors have emphasized that to understand not just communication through language or other mediating instruments, but even how human thinking itself is processed, demands understanding "a variety of symbolic modes through which we relate to our environment, become human, and become members of our culture"—in Worth's (1981, p. 122) phrasing. Analyzing modes and codes of mass media contributes to that broader cognitional awareness, thereby promoting principal goals of education beyond media-specific learning. Improvement in basic skills of learning—reading, writing, and mathematics—have been found among students in programs of visual thinking or visual knowing.[10] The abstract and logical, linear symbol functions are enhanced along with visual, auditory, kinesthetic symbol formation and study. Because these synthesized growths in skills support a person's interests and inchoate abilities, it has been found that self-esteem and self-confidence also grow. Again, this manifests the holistic nature of a human person's addressing the world of experienced symbols, codes and cues of society which we call culture and civilization.

Newcomb maintained that "the best definitions of culture are those which see it as a system of shared meanings and values expressed through symbols," and he enlists Carey in supporting this holistic role of media education, specifically in teaching critical viewing skills for television. To Carey's (1975, p. 15) words (quoted earlier) "thought is public because it depends on a publicly available stock of symbols," Newcomb (1980) explicitly added "television in all its forms . . . is our most publicly available stock of symbols" (p. 22).

Mass media producers usually knowingly (because competent in harnessing codes of media expression) and perhaps just as often unconsciously (as inheritors of their own culture and milieu) embed in their television programs clusters of symbols that reflect values. The audience is exposed to those clusters and, through selective perception and interpretation, "make sense" out of them in the context of their own experiences and judgments. Newcomb (1980) concluded:

> Thus critical viewing is a dynamic process of criticism: Criticism involves clear thinking that begins in analysis and ends in synthesis . . . not . . . merely the analysis and synthesis of television content . . . (W)e must be involved with the analysis of television in our lived experience, our values, our attitudes, our actions. And we must be equally involved in the synthesis of television into that lived experience in more alert, trained ways. (p. 25)

*"Being and Knowing": Ontological/Epistemological Bases for Methodology.*   Just as there are several kinds of research methodologies, there are varying perspectives or approaches to critical analysis of media. But Gordon (1975) reminded that all theories must "be grounded in a reasonable ontology and construction of nature and a generally accepted epistemology or knowledge system" (p. 49). As stated earlier, any knowledge-system consists of prior value judgments that shape epistemological assumptions. Those judgments include "world-views" and involve scientific, aesthetic, and ethical assessments. That can be the bane of media education featuring teacher-directed, enforced interpretation and evaluation of media content, context, and social implications. Authors and researchers during the 1980s regularly caution against a determinist style of pedagogy:

**Teachers should not advocate or instill absolutes by imposing their own views or "acceptable" or "right" conclusions on trainees engaged in developing truly "critical" viewing skills.**

## CATEGORIES OF ANALYSIS

From theoretical principles, a priori analysis is deductive. Assertions based on intellectual and judgmental premises about the nature of the human person and of reality and society and art are applied to the given media content or process or effects. On the other hand, a posteriori procedure is inductive, drawing from concrete data to discern patterns and then inferences about predictability of associations or causal relationships, to conclusions processed by methodology that processes data from reality. (Of course, those methodologies themselves involve assumptions about levels of reliability and validity which again have an epistemological base.)

Another manner of categorizing research and critical analysis follows Lazarsfeld (cf. Phelan, 1980, pp. 176–182). "Administrative" or functional analysis has utilitarian purposes (such as efficiency in marketing goods or services); it involves experimental and quantitative measurements, including behavioral phenomena. "Critical" analysis typically reflects sociopolitical perspectives and is ideological (implying values), with stress on qualitative aspects of phenomena studied. Or "critical" analysis may instead be cultural, with orientation towards art and the humanities; it is both interpretative (based on values) and holistic rather than atomistic.

All of this suggests further guidelines for appraising media study programs.

> **Media education—just as education in general—ought not limit itself to one form of critical assessment of mass media. In fact, criteria themselves—including ethical concepts— are to be questioned and analyzed.**

Minkkinen (1978) asserted that true criticism exists only when "a critical attitude involves taking a stand for or against certain values" (p. 20).

Beyond contributing to conceptual understanding, media education should have practical applications as well.

> **Education should also be concerned about practical impact on media processes and content as well as on attitudes and behavior of student–viewers, using sound data as the basis for analysis. It should stretch those students to further understanding of sociopolitical perspectives as well as of aesthetic and ethical perspectives. Nor should critical viewing skills programs limit themselves merely to *a priori* lecturing**

**and mandating guidelines, but should be open to heuristic exploration of media experiences by the students themselves who can draw out principles inductively.**

Worth and Masterman repeatedly emphasize the latter approach, as described earlier.

## COMPREHENSIVE MEDIA STUDY

**Media education should address all major elements in the bi-relational process involving media and audience members.**

There is, of course, the very *content and form* of media's programming. This calls for study of the amount, kinds, and frequency of specific content; the prominence or priority of elements of that content; values implied or expressed in those elements selected for presentation; and relationships among elements in the message with their structural meanings.[11] The greater a person's competency in understanding the coding process of the medium, the more that person can be an active (or "interactive") viewer rather than passively assimilating TV without reflective judgment. When an active viewer brings cognitive processing—from other life experiences as well as from formal media study—to watching television, that will influence interaction and whatever effects take place.

## RESEARCH THEORIES AND METHODOLOGIES: IMPLICATIONS FOR PEDAGOGY

**Although it is helpful to acquaint viewers with some study of media *effects* on audiences, including implications for attitude and behavior, media educators should note the tentativeness of many of those findings.**

As noted earlier, they should advert to the shift of research focus from the senders to the receivers in analyzing television's effects. Echoing previous discussion of this point, Fiske and Hartley affirm that, because television is decoded by each viewer drawing on personal social experience and in varying social and personal cognitive environments, the effects of television viewing depend more on the decoder than on the intrinsic nature of the content.[12] Anderson and Ploghoft (1977, p.

11) found that "content is a poor predictor of subsequent behavior in the audience," so concluded that "control of content is not a very useful means for achieving that goal" of increasing pro-social, beneficial effects of the medium.

> **Therefore emphasis should be less on "activist" reforming the medium (structures, senders' input) than on preparing the audience by developing cognitive skills and value perceptions appropriate to translate media content toward pro-social behavior.**

When this is accomplished by introducing curricula to modify the effects of source, message, and medium in the direction of socially desirable effects, it is a form of "interventionist" TV criticism, or "impact mediation."

An area to be integrated into media study and analysis concerns viewers' *uses and gratifications* that prompt them to seek out various media presentations.

> **Media analysis examines why individuals choose to spend time with specific kinds of television.**

Those needs and purposes differ from individual to individual. They are cognitive (acquiring information), affective (desire for emotional and aesthetically pleasurable experience), integrative (personal need for reassurance, self-confidence—and also social need for union with family and friends); and "escapist" (tension-release and diversion).[13]

Various other approaches are observable in different television literacy projects, depending on their content and goals. Anderson's analysis of major projects in the United States in the early 1980s clusters them according to *intervention* (or *impact mediation*—"therapeutic inoculation" against negative effects by media), *uses and gratifications* (or goal attainment), *popular culture* (symbol-systems reflecting society), and *visual literacy* (semiotic study, including techniques of media expression).[14] Those categories have been discussed earlier, based on representative literature in the field.

## GENERAL EDUCATIONAL OBJECTIVE: SELECTIVE, DISCRIMINATING AUDIENCES

Television media education seeks to guide viewers away from unresponsive passivity to becoming "active participants" in the process.

The goal of "active participant" can be taken somewhat *metaphorically,* with the focus primarily on the artistic, aesthetic, and cultural aspects of media experienced by the mass audience. Formal education's traditional role involves transmitting culture, including literature and art. In addition to the classics and recent publications (novels, poetry, short stories), more contemporary communication has included motion pictures, radio, and television. The dominant form of cultural expression—most reaching mass publics, including students and family members—is television. It is important to understand and appreciate the popular art of mass TV in our personal lives as well as in our regional and global culture. Such media analysis grows out of criticism of the traditional arts. It is found in most kinds of projects reported in Part II; it is central to those in the United States.

The assertion about creating "active participants" in media is taken *literally* by many proponents of mass media education. They seek to aid economically deprived citizens—particularly in developing countries of the Third World—to struggle toward broader social justice by directly participating in mass communication, either through direct interaction with media institutions and leaders or by establishing alternate and counter-media.

Typically, media education in the United States tends to reflect and accommodate to the "given" status of mass media structures, stressing the need for sensitive, informed, reflective viewing. It is in less affluent countries where overt class struggle is common that the social-activist model of media education is emphasized.[15]

## CRITERIA FOR ASSESSING "CRITICAL VIEWING SKILLS" PROGRAMS

From the discursive analysis in this chapter, plus parts of chapter 1, can be drawn 20 descriptive criteria by which to assess concrete programs of television literacy or "critical viewing skills."

### Breadth

A.  A project should study the broad social context and impact of television as well as intrinsic aesthetics of the medium.

B.  It should include social, political, aesthetic, and ethical perspectives, including "administrative" analysis (functional, utilitarian, experimental, behavioral—atomistic) and "critical" analysis (judgmental, value-oriented, sociopolitical, cultural, interpretative—holistic).

Scope

C. A media literacy curriculum has greater value to the extent that it is (a) adaptable to a wider range of educational emphases, orientations

D. (b) well organized and sustained over time, by numbers of people and institutions, in more than one place or region.

Individuality and Values

E. It must respect the individuality of the person, including their distinctive upbringing by family, so they are not merely indoctrinated with others' opinions and conclusions.

F. Values presented should not be narrowly instructional nor exclusively moralistic in a single tradition. But the project ought not be valueless; it should relate to broad humanistic heritage and Judeo-Christian ethic.

G. It should not limit itself to one form of critical assessment; even the criteria should be questioned and analyzed.

H. Contexts of norms addressed are to be clearly identified, noting various levels of such categories (e.g., economic, legal, ethical, aesthetic, social, technical—normative statements as criteria).

I. Programs should acquaint participants with constitutive parts of media, including the larger communication process (not labeling the entire television phenomenon as "good" or "bad"): Sensitize viewers to their role in the bi-polar communication process of mutual responsibility of sender/receiver.

Validity and Reliability: Accuracy

J. Projects should present factual data based on valid sources and research, eschewing merely conventional assumptions (commonly accepted but misinformed assertions).

K. They must acknowledge (at least implicitly) research findings and incorporate those conclusions and implications into the content and manner of presenting CVS projects. (Those studies are touchstones for determining validity of assumptions, assertions, and directives for training programs.)

L. Ideally, projects should be tested and evaluated for results with subjects through time.

## Cognition: Developmental

M.  Projects should properly address stages of students' growth in thinking ability—pre-operational (up to 7 years), operational (7–10+)—as well as social cognitional experience and moral development.

N.  They should observe, appraise, and train children *as* children in their responses to specific TV exposure, in accord with children's true state of personal experiencing and cognition (not as "little adults").

## Cognition: Reasoning Skills

O.  Projects should train participants in the process of selective discrimination, analytical observation, and reasoned assessment based on factual data judged according to meaningful criteria.

P.  The process should begin with analysis and end with synthesis, merging learned factual data with receivers' experience of TV and own value-system; it should stress inductive (heuristic, a posteriori) exploration from which principles are drawn out, along with the deductive (a priori) process.

## Pragmatics of Media Education

Q.  Projects should include "a systematic approach to a set of objectives supported by instructional routine and devices"—usually involving a curriculum publicly available.

R.  Major areas in projects might include:

  • media effects on audiences (impact mediation)
  • uses and gratifications (goal attainment; interaction with media)
  • cultural understanding (symbol-systems reflecting society)
  • visual literacy (media techniques, grammar, syntax).

S.  Projects should reflect the diversity of the total TV medium: Information, persuasion, education, entertainment, quality programming as well as popular kitsch content. But selective perception, in context of uses and gratifications, emphasizes the role of the receiver/viewer rather than the content itself;

> interactionist approach is more revealing about TV's effects than logical positivist (content analysis).
>
> T. The project should provide detailed audiovisual/print materials supporting the conceptual development in the program.

These criteria are applied (in Part III) to the major television critical viewing skills projects inventoried in Part II.

## NOTES

1. See Head (1985, p. 327) citing as source BBC External Services, "World Radio and Television Receivers" (London: BBC, 1983). In his unpublished "Update Notes, December, 1987" for that text, Sydney Head reported Tydeman and Kelm's data in their 1986 book on European media: Highest daily viewing was in the United Kingdom at 3 hours 10 minutes per person, the French watched 2 hours 9 minutes a day, whereas lowest viewing was in Norway, 1 hour 18 minutes.

2. George Gerbner's "cultural indicators" research team at The Annenberg School of Communications, University of Pennsylvania, annually reported content analysis of violence depicted in U.S. television programs; the studies over a decade, conducted under grants from the National Institute of Mental Health and the American Medical Association, were regularly summarized in articles in *Journal of Communication*. Cf. also "cultivation analysis."

3. Moralistic critics of mass media include several major groups studied in Part II, such as the Media Action Research Center's "Television Awareness Training" workshops and textbooks for adults, and the National Congress of Parents and Teachers' media projects.

4. See Murray's (1980) analysis of international research in similar categories, with bibliographies under similar headings.

5. Anderson and Meyer's (1988) recent synthesis in their "accommodation theory" expanded themes developed by Williams (1975), Gross (1973), Hall et al. (1980), Fiske (1987), Carey (1988), and others.

6. See Harris and Levey (1975, p. 2142). Jean Piaget's theory of children's cognitive and intellectual development was expounded over decades, such as in *The Child's Conception of the World* (1929), *The Moral Judgment of the Child* (trans. 1932), *The Language and Thought of the Child* (trans. of 3rd ed. 1962), *The Psychology of the Child* (with Bärbel Inhelder, trans. 1969), among other titles. Cf. the symposium on children and television—seven major articles in *Journal of Broadcasting* (Vol. 25, No. 4, 1981), pp. 327–402; the authors review advances in research on children's cognitive development, including affective/emotional and imaginative.

7. Among more recent commentaries, cf. Alvarado, Gutch, and Wollen (1987, pp. 4, 118). Worth (1981, p. 125) cited Piaget (1970): "The problem of intelligence, and with it the central problem of the pedagogy of teaching, has

thus emerged as the link with the fundamental epistemological problem of the nature of knowledge: does the latter constitute a copy of reality or, on the contrary, an assimilation of reality into a structure of transformations?" (p. 28).

8. For a representative research application in this context, see Faber et al. (1982).

9. See Snow (1983, pp. 154–155). Anderson stressed this caveat in several of his writings cited earlier.

10. Samples (1979, pp. 82–83) cited specific instances.

11. See the summary of George Gerbner's "cultural indicators" research, by Fiske and Hartley (1978, pp. 30–36).

12. See Heller (1982, p. 850) in context of citing Fiske and Hartley.

13. These categories are derived from the analysis by Katz et al. (1973); quoted by Fiske and Hartley (1978, pp. 72–73).

14. Anderson variously labeled these four patterns as intervention, uses and gratifications, cultural understanding, and visual literacy (1980), and as impact mediation, goal attainment, cultural understanding, and visual literacy (1983).

15. For reviews and commentary about social oriented publications on media by Len Masterman, Fernando Reyes Matta, Rogerio de Almeida Cunna, and Thomas A. Bauer, see White and Kenney (1982, pp. 2–5).

In addition to those whose work is detailed later in this book, Maddison (1971) surveyed for UNESCO how radio and television were combating adult illiteracy, while Arnheim (1971) analyzed "visual thinking"; Foster (1979) explored the "new literacy" of film and television. McCain (1981) devoted an entire special issue of *Journal of Broadcasting* to children's use of TV. Research methodology for children's television viewing was reported by Wolf, Abelman, and Hexamer (1982), and by Bryant and Anderson (1983). Through the years, workbooks and practical guides for parents, teachers, and individuals have been developed by practitioners such as Kuhns (1971), Heintz and Reuter (1972), and Lelley (1983), and more recently by Tyner and Lloyd-Kolkin (1990).

# 3

## Historical Development of Television Media Education

Noted earlier was international concern that mass media, especially television, contribute to society as positively as possible, and that the media's negative effects be neutralized. Out of this widespread concern have grown various systematic efforts to alert the massive audiences of media to what is happening in this inadvertent love/hate relationship with the television box, particularly among children. Also noted was the shift in emphasis through recent decades from alleged effects of media's content on passive audiences, to the interactive perspective of how and why viewers use a mass medium—including how they create individualized "meaning" of media content within their respective viewing and living environments. More central to the *internal* characteristics of mass media is study of how media are crafted, including aesthetics and art, as well as how they operate and are formed by social, economic, and political factors.

This chapter recounts how analysis of media grew into TV literacy curricula. It chronicles how television study emerged in the educational curriculum. It identifies 23 major critical viewing skills (CVS) projects—most of them in the United States, plus representative ones from other selected countries. The projects are analyzed in detail in Part II (chapters 4–10).

## EVOLUTION OF SPECIFIC TELEVISION LITERACY (OR CVS) PROGRAMS

Succinct reviews of organized activities in the United Kingdom from the mid-1920s can be found in recent books by Masterman (1985a, pp. 38–70) who reviewed conceptual patterns of theory, and by Alvarado, Gutch, and Wollen (1987, pp. 9–38), who tracked organizational developments. Perhaps the most detailed analysis and practical application of critical viewing skills programs in the United States has been provided by James Anderson (1977 to 1988), often with Milton Ploghoft, drawing on research studies in the field. Particularly in two scholarly papers (West Berlin, 1977; Acapulco, 1980a), a published report (*Journal of Communication,* 1980), and a book chapter (Academic Press, 1983), Anderson outlined the origins and development of projects related to critical viewing of television (including his own work with Ploghoft as applied in Idaho Falls, Idaho). We follow his historical outline.

### Mass Media Study: Antecedents to Television Study Programs

Critical thinking was the goal of the Greek peripatetics. Critical reading was an extension of that skill in reflective analysis applied to print communication of the past several centuries. Critical reading of mass media forms of print (newspapers, magazines) developed through the past half century. Some of that kind of analysis was applied in recent decades to motion pictures in the form of discriminating viewing and appreciation. Anderson notes the need for common skills of analysis, for medium-specific skills of receiving and interpreting, and for content-specific skills of understanding—all of which are involved in "receivership" skills of critical thinking/reading/viewing.*

Major institutions only gradually came to recognize the value of systematically aiding audiences in their mass media experiences. In the 1920s and 1930s, teaching film appreciation spread in the United States and England—partly in reaction to the perceived excesses of contemporary movies. Some schools introduced extracurricular clubs and even classes on film appreciation. As early as 1929, a British board of education urged teachers to elevate children's standards of taste and

---

*More recent analysis, including Anderson's own development of "accommodation theory" (1988), avoids delimiting the dynamic process by the term *receivership;* instead, they look to the interactive nature of human cognition amid personal social environment—even when using mass media.

evaluation about motion pictures, by "some specific training . . . either in or out of school, but certainly as part of the general educational process."[1] Out of the London Film Society (1925 and there-after) and the British documentary movement also grew study of "film grammar" in addition to film appreciation and film-making. In the United States, film was taught at secondary level and in colleges since the 1930s, but was not really integrated fully into the curriculum until the 1960s.[2] Film societies in the 1940s and 1950s, like ciné-clubs in France, antedated organizations devoted to promoting support for and critical response to radio programming in those same decades. In 1950 a Society of Film Teachers was formed in England. In the late 1960s film education was still taught in British higher education only in art colleges, contrasted with the wide availability of such courses in col-leges of the United States. By 1972 Britain's Associated Examining Board recognized film study as an integral part of the school curricu-lum, establishing a GCE 'O' Level Mode 3 in Film Studies.

The pattern had originally focused on audience *discrimination* in using film media. That term, commonly used until about 1959, implied negative aspects of mass culture listed by Masterman (1985b, pp. 59–60): essentially negative exercises, absence of commonly accepted cri-teria established from theoretical analysis, ambiguity about validity of applying aesthetic criteria to mass media, moralistic and universal concept of "value," slim relevance to media as "consciousness indus-tries," and practical obstacles for media study in classrooms. Stuart Hall and Raymond Williams promoted a more positive approach to media study, on the broader plane of *appreciation* (the term that came into favor after 1959). In the 1960s, some urged that the somewhat passive term *appreciation* be replaced by *intelligent viewing* to reflect better what was being taught in classrooms.[3] Through the years of developing media study in the United Kingdom, concepts of mass culture spawned the notion of popular culture and then of the popular arts, promoted by the Newsom Report (1963) and by the work of Stuart Hall and Paddy Whannel (1964), among others.[4] The Newsom Report urged that study programs be broadened to include not just the elite or advanced students but also "common" students, especially disadvan-taged ones. And cinema courses in theory and criticism eventually expanded into teaching film skills; by the late 1970s they incorporated vocational elements related to potential careers.

## Formal Study of Television

In the meantime, the new medium of television began to draw serious attention as its presence became ever more widespread—stretching

beyond occasional evening and weekend leisure time to most waking
hours, and pervasively infiltrating the public's consciousness.

A prescient British teacher wrote at the dawn of post-war television
in 1948:

> Television will ultimately develop into an art form in its own right capa-
> ble of being judged by its own standards of criticism, as the cinema and
> the theatre are. And, when it is more widespread, it will become in the
> dramatic field as much a rival, but no more, of the cinema and the
> theatre as they are of one another. But as a medium for the expression of
> ideas and as a social force it will have no rival.[5]

At first, education made direct use of television as an instrument
for teaching. Instructional use of TV was much developed and studied
in the United States and United Kingdom in the 1950s and 1960s.
"Educational television" was also broadly funded in the United States,
particularly by substantial grants from the Ford Foundation and later
by the U.S. Office of Education.

In those same decades, some curricular designs for teaching better
understanding and use of television were developed but not widely
used. Concurrently, regional organizations attempted to promote audience selectivity when they listened to radio, including choosing "better quality" programs from circulated lists, and communicating with
radio managers of stations and networks about programs.

In 1958 a London conference on "Film, Television and the Child"
discussed methods of teaching screen education. Recommendations
from that meeting were repeated and much expanded at an international meeting held in Norway under the auspices of UNESCO in
1962. The report of those sessions (published in 1964) set the perspective for "critical viewing skills" education:

> Because television is already a major channel of communication, and
> will increase in scope and power, we believe it is the responsibility of
> educators to teach our young people to use this medium in a constructive
> way. . . . The aims . . . may be stated as follows:
>
> I.   To help viewers to increase their understanding of what they see on
>      the screen.
> II.  To encourage viewers to become more selective in their choice of
>      program.
> III. To help viewers to become more aware and discriminating in their
>      responses and to develop their power of judgment so that they may
>      benefit from those programs, both imaginative and factual, which
>      have the capacity to enrich their lives.

The aims of screen education thus consort with those of a truly democratic education, namely, to help the individual to respect and uphold
truth and, on the basis of the richest possible personal development, to
share and enjoy with his fellow men the treasures which our civilization offers to the human mind and heart.[6]

Eleven years later the Ford Foundation in the United States af-
firmed "an important need for widened and improved instruction
about mass media in the public schools. . . . [L]iteracy of young persons in regard to the mass media is the proper concern for educational
institutions analogous to their concern about language literacy."[7] The
report of a Television and Children Conference underwritten in 1976
by the Ford, Markle, and National Science foundations recommended
as important for a curriculum:

> such subjects as production conventions, analysis of media appeals, the
> character and role of non-verbal cues, overview of the history and struc-
> ture of the broadcasting industry, the economic basis for television, anal-
> ysis of typical formats for entertainment programming, analysis of the
> values portrayed in television content, standards for criticism of televi-
> sion content, and if possible, some direct experience with television
> equipment.[8]

In 1978 the U.S. Library of Congress and U.S. Office of Education
(USOE) held a national conference on "Television, the Book and the
Classroom" out of which came USOE's request for proposals and its
subsequent funding of four major projects. That agency's definition of
critical television viewing skills was limited to characteristics directly
related to the medium itself (unlike broader social purposes of many
non-U.S. programs):

> to understand the psychological implications of commercials;
>
> to distinguish fact from fiction;
>
> to recognize and appreciate differing and/or opposing points of view;
>
> to develop an understanding of the style and content of dramatic presenta-
> tions, documentaries, public affairs, news and other television program-
> ming; and
>
> to understand the relation between television programming and the printed
> word.[9]

Anderson (1983) noted that—although sporadic efforts to introduce
film and radio education into classrooms paralleled national development of both those media, and provided educational paradigms for

television—there was to that date no systematic curriculum developed, implemented, and made publicly available. By this he meant an "organized, systematic approach to a set of objectives supported by instructional routine and devices" (p. 299).

In Britain, previous application of media study in classrooms did not keep apace with organized adoption in other countries. Masterman (1985a) asserted that since the early 1970s:

> Media education practice is now less developed throughout the educational system of England and Wales than it is in those countries (e.g., Australia, Scotland and most European countries) where teachers have had the confidence to organize themselves, publish their own periodicals, run conferences, develop their own regional networks and confront academics with the challenge of working collaboratively with them in producing 'really useful knowledge,' rather than immersing themselves in what many teachers see as elitist, formalist, and large unintelligible debates amongst themselves. (pp. 43–44)

In 1982 delegates from 19 nations unanimously supported a declaration by UNESCO's International Symposium on Media Education. It lamented that "regrettably most informal and non-formal educational systems do little to promote media education or education for communication."[10] That body addressed recommendations to educators, parents, and students and also "media personnel and decision-makers" as all sharing a role in responsible use of mass media. It called for "competent authorities" to:

> Initiate and support comprehensive media education programs—from pre-school to university level, and in adult education—the purpose of which is to develop the knowledge, skills and attitudes which will encourage the growth of critical awareness and, consequently, of greater competence among the users of electronic and print media.[11]

Almost from the beginning of media study, cultural and aesthetic aspects of media "appreciation" were linked with mass media's social and even ethical implications for society, especially media's impact on younger people. In recent years, emphasis has evolved in many countries to stressing political and economic aspects of media hegemony and the need to counter imbedded ideologies with activist participation in media. Participants were to be well informed and also skillful in applying media techniques. Masterman has been one of the forceful proponents of media study that teaches populist reaction to oligopolistic or state-controlled mass media.

Through the past two decades a number of individuals and schools introduced into curricula structured forms of media study, including television. Two projects in the late 1960s and early 1970s were the first to be organized and distributed for wider use in school districts (in Oregon and New York, building on another conducted in Ohio).[12] Subsequently came other structured programs of television study, particularly four major projects in the United States funded by the Federal government. Selected from more than three dozen proposals to the Department of Health, Education, and Welfare, those projects offered the most comprehensive, interrelated efforts in the United States to systematize training for understanding and responding to television experience.

Concurrently in countries elsewhere around the world, media projects were also being developed, especially in Australia and later in Scotland. American and non-U.S. major television literacy projects analyzed and evaluated in Parts II and III of this report are listed in Table 3.1.

TABLE 3.1
Chronology: Selected Major CVS Projects in United States and Worldwide

| Year Begun | Year Terminated | Project | Targeted Users |
|---|---|---|---|
| | | *U. S. A.* | |
| 1970 | . . . . | WNET/Channel 13, New York | Upper Primary, Junior High |
| 1974 | . . . . | Eugene, Oregon School District | Upper Primary, Junior High, Secondary |
| 1974 | . . . . | Aimee Dorr (Harvard/U.S.C.) | Primary |
| 1976 | . . . . | *Rosemary Lee Potter (Pinella County, Fla.) | Primary, Secondary |
| 1976 | . . . . | National Congress of Parents & Teachers | Primary, Parents |
| 1976 | . . . . | *The Learning Seed Company | Primary, Secondary |
| 1977 | . . . . | Media Action Research Center "Television-Awareness-Training" "Growing with Television" | All levels: children, adults |
| 1978 | . . . . | Idaho Falls School District | Grades 3–6 |
| 1978 | 1980 | Far West Laboratory for Educational Research/Development | Secondary: students, teachers |
| 1978 | 1980? | Southwest Educational Development Laboratory | Grades K–5: teachers, parents |
| 1978 | . . . . | Dorothy & Jerome Singer (Yale/ABC) | Grades 3–5 + Others |
| 1978 | 1981 | Boston University | Post-Secondary, Adult |
| 1978 | × | New York City Board of Education | Primary |
| 1982 | . . . . | U.S. Catholic Conference: "The Media Mirror" | Primary, Junior High, Secondary |

*(continued)*

TABLE 3.1 (Continued)

| Year Begun | Year Terminated | Project | Targeted Users |
|---|---|---|---|
| | | *NON-U.S.* | |
| 1960/ 68+ | . . . . | #Plan DENI—Catholic Cinema Office (Uruguay) | Primary, Teachers, Parents |
| 1970+ | . . . . | #Brazilian Social Communications Union (Brazil) | Leaders; poor rural groups |
| 1970 | . . . . | Catholic Education Office (Sydney) | All levels except college |
| 1975 | . . . . | Southern Arts Assoc. (U.K.) | Upper Primary, Secondary, Adults |
| 1977 | 1979 | Mayfield School/BFI (London) | Secondary |
| 1978 | 1980 | Stichting Audiovisuele Vorming (Amsterdam) | Secondary |
| 1979 | . . . . | Scottish Film Council (Scotland) | Primary, Junior High, Secondary, Adults & Teachers |
| 1979 | 1980 | Powys Education Committee, Visual Literacy (Wales) | Primary, Secondary |
| 1979 | 1985+? | Formation Du Jeune Téléspectateur Actif (France) | Pre-School, Primary, Secondary |
| 1979 | 1980 | UNDA/UNESCO worldwide experimental applications of Minkkinen's model: AFRICA: Gabon, Nigeria; Ile Maurice, Rwanda. LATIN AMERICA: Mexico. ASIA: Korea, India. EUROPE: Italy, Malta. OCEANIA: New Zealand. | (Various) |
| 1980? | . . . . | #Ministry of Education, Western Australia | Primary, Secondary |
| 1980? | . . . . | #Powys (County) Education Committee, Wales | Primary, Secondary |
| 1980? | . . . . | #Clwyd (County) Media Studies Unit, Wales | Primary, Secondary, Teachers |
| 1981 | . . . . | #Centre Cultural & Artistic Enquiry and Expression (Chile) | Secondary, Leaders, Social Groups |
| 1982 | . . . . | #Univérsidad de Playa Ancha de Ciencias dela Educacion (Chile) | Teachers |
| 1983 | 1987 | #Media Education Development Program (Scotland) | (Various), Teachers |
| 1985 | . . . . | #Robert Bellarmino Educational Foundation (Chile) | Primary, Secondary, Teachers |
| 1986/ 89 | . . . . | #Ontario: Media Literacy Resource Guide (Canada) | Upper Primary, Secondary |
| [?] | . . . . | #Latin Amer. Communications Pedagogy Institute (Costa Rica) | Parents, Children (in home) |

* = Series of activities, materials rather than a defined project
+ = Project evolved out of preceding similar activities from prior years
# = Projects not in questionnaire surveys; data received in 1988–89

## SURVEY OF REPRESENTATIVE PROJECTS

Beyond the United States, most detailed data—including supporting audiovisual materials—were available from the continuing program in Sydney, Australia. The plans and curricula for media/television study in formal education were also obtained from the United Kingdom (especially Scotland), France, and various countries where groups cooperated with UNDA and UNESCO in applying Minkkinen's model in Africa, Latin America, Asia, Europe, and Oceania.

It should be noted that many other isolated or collaborative short- and long-term projects have been under way throughout the world. UNESCO reported on many of the early ones (#42 Screen Education; #62 Radio and Television in Literacy; #80 Media Studies in Education—published respectively in 1964, 1971, and 1977). Other sources to be cited later include project directors and representatives from agencies and organizations conducting those works; they include researchers Aimee Dorr and Dorothy and Jerome Singer and also teacher-writer Rosemary Potter. In the United States, data are alluded to from ABC, CBS, NBC, Capital Cities Communications, WQED (Pittsburgh), and such specific enterprises as Prime Time School TV, Teachers' Guides to TV, Parents Participation TV Workshops, The Learning Seed Company, the Television Information Office (of the NAB), and the New York City Board of Education. Also noted are activities in Britain by independent television companies.

Other CVS-related projects are briefly reviewed in a special section because, although not part of the questionnaire surveys in 1981 and 1985, data were submitted in 1988 and 1989. They include activities in Western Australia, Canada, the United Kingdom (England, Wales, and Scotland), and Latin America (Costa Rica, Chile, Uruguay, and Brazil), plus summarized data from various countries around the world made available in 1988 from surveys by the Scottish Film Council and by John Pungente.

*Organizational Sources.* Patterns and excerpted highlights of the most salient projects are recounted in Part II. Projects are clustered according to organizational source and chronology: (1) four projects funded by the U.S. government; (b) six school systems (including one in Sydney); (c) three individuals in U.S. school contexts; (d) five national organizations in the United States; (e) nine private corporations including broadcast companies in the United States and United Kingdom; and (f) four institution-related programs in formal and informal education in the United Kingdom, one each in France and the Netherlands, and ten worldwide with UNESCO. Projects cited earlier as not part of the questionnaire surveys are also reported among the group appropriate to them: one is added to (b) from Western Australia; and included with (f) are two more from Scotland, one each from Wales and Canada, and six from Latin American countries.

*Categories of Theories for Classifying Projects Surveyed.* Major categories include four theoretical foundations for television literacy training: Impact mediation or intervention ("inoculation"), goal attainment (uses and gratifications), cultural understanding (including "literary"), and visual skills (crafts, production, as well as aesthetics). Secondary categories include factors reported in questionnaire surveys and gleaned from supporting materials from the projects: *Motivation* (educational, public relations, religious, ethical/moral, cultural, research); *goals* (media reform, moral, cultural/aesthetic, instructional); *process* (deductive, inductive); *techniques* (discussion, workshop, curriculum); *context* (school, church, home, organization); *participants* (teachers, parents, students at various school levels, citizens generally); and *materials* (readings, lectures, TV programs, scripts, workbooks, tests, activities, etc.).

In Part III patterns and trends in teaching "critical viewing skills" in those specific projects are evaluated according to seven clusters of 20 criteria developed earlier in chapter 2, plus 10 related composite criteria drawn from analyzing projects in Part II.

## NOTES

1. Alvarado, Gutch, and Wollen (1987, p. 17) cited Reed (1950) quoting from the London Board of Education's 1929 *Handbook of Suggestions for Teachers*.

2. See Worth (1981, p. 110).

3. See Masterman (1985b, p. 19), citing Wills (1959).

4. See Masterman (1985b, pp. 51–53, 59–61). He lauded *The Popular Arts* by Hall and Whannel (1964) as *"the* classic text on media education in the 1960's" (p. 299), despite their somewhat negative perspective on television—not unlike the Newsom Report itself that he claimed retarded development of serious study of TV in Britain. Whannel headed the British Film Institute's Education Department.

5. See Andrew Miller Jones (1948), quoted by Alvarado, Gutch, and Wollen (1987, p. 20).

6. See Hodgkinson (1964, p. 78). This was part of the summary of recommendations by an international meeting on film and television teaching at Leangkollen, Oslo, Norway, October 7–13, 1962.

7. See Ford Foundation (1975, p. 31), quoted by Anderson (1983, p. 298).

8. See Ford Foundation (1975), quoted by Lloyd-Kolkin, Wheeler, and Strand (1980, p. 120).

9. Quoted by Lloyd-Kolkin, Wheeler, and Strand (1980, p. 121).

10. See UNESCO, 1982 International Symposium on Media Education at Grunwald, Federal Republic of Germany, January 22, 1982; quoted in full by Masterman (1985a, pp. 340–341).

11. Quoted by Masterman (1985a, p. 341).

12. In the 1970s a consortium of researchers at the Broadcast Research Center and Cooperative Center for Social Studies at Ohio University, in Athens, Ohio, collaborated with school districts in Eugene (Oregon), Syracuse (New York), Las Vegas (Nevada), and Jacksonville (Florida) in developing and pretesting curricular elements for media literacy. See papers presented in West Berlin and in Acapulco, Mexico by Anderson and Ploghoft (1977, 1980a); cf. related articles by them jointly (1980b) and by Anderson (1983).

# II

# ANALYSIS OF REPRESENTATIVE STRUCTURED PROGRAMS OF "CRITICAL VIEWING SKILLS" EDUCATION

$P$art II reports dominant patterns as well as specific details of selected structured programs of media literacy that include training in television "critical viewing skills."

Chapter 4 outlines general characteristics of major projects, drawing on worldwide questionnaire surveys made in the early and middle 1980s.

Specific projects of scope and significance are selected for detailed analysis in the next six chapters. Chapter 5 studies four coordinated national projects funded by the United States government. Chapter 6 explores systematic, formal instruction in school districts—one in Australia and the rest in the United States. Chapter 7 analyzes projects by individuals who worked along or in collaboration with other agencies or organizations—all of them in the United States. Chapter 8 recounts activities by nongovernmental national organizations in the United States. Chapter 9 reviews projects mounted by private companies in the United States and United Kingdom, including broadcasting companies in both countries. And chapter 10 offers material from institution-related programs in formal education from the United Kingdom (including Wales and Scotland), France, the Netherlands, Canada, four Latin American countries, and worldwide under the auspices of UNDA/UNESCO.

# 4

# General Characteristics of Major CVS Projects

As described in Part I, interaction between media audiences and their television experiences has implications for their cognitive and affective growth as well as for their personal and social integrative needs.[1] This widespread and pervasive phenomenon in today's society has prompted serious efforts among researchers and educators to develop systematic programs of study to help viewers, especially youth, to grow in their discriminating use of television and in their critical faculties generally.

## DESCRIPTIVE DEFINITIONS: MEANINGS, GOALS, AND METHODS

Among earliest systematic projects that integrated teaching critical TV viewing skills with formal curricular instruction, and which published detailed accounts, was the work directed by Milton E. Ploghoft and James A. Anderson (1981, 1982) in the early 1970s in Eugene, Oregon, and in East Syracuse, New York. Collaborating with school districts in those and several other cities, Ploghoft and Anderson (1982) identified what they called "receivership skills" that were central to:

> identify and understand our own motives and purposes for attending to TV programs. They include our ability to interpret the influence of our

personal motives and purposes on the way we make sense of the messages we receive—that we may at the outset be more receptive to some
content and less open to other ideas and images. (p. 5)

In a word, viewers were to become selective and discriminating consumers of television programming. Receivership skills, for them, involve comprehending overt and hidden meanings of messages by analyzing language and visual and aural images, to understand the
intended audiences and the intent of the message. These skills include
observing closely the details of program and advertising content and
form, their sequence and relationship—including themes, values, motivating elements, plot-lines, characters and portrayals. To these observations is added reflective evaluation that distinguishes fact from
opinion, and logical from affective appeals. Training in these skills
includes study of the limitations inherent in media and in their messages ("distortions . . . which are contained in the methods selected to
produce this message"). Finally, these CVS projects equip viewers with
criteria pertaining to their own personal reaction to media messages,
in order to help evaluate their own intended responses, motives, and
personal value set on the media experience. All this helps viewers
draw conclusions and make inferences. This leads to comprehending
the medium's impact at both ends of the communication process—the
influence of TV's institutional structure on the message, and the role
of TV in the viewer's own life and thus that role's impact on the message as received. Anderson (1981) summarized the meaning and scope
of this activity:

> Receivership skills refers to those skills related to the assimilation and
> utilization of communication messages for some purposeful action. They
> involve the skillful collection, interpretation, testing and application of
> information regardless of medium of presentation. Skills of this nature
> have had an extensive educational history. Current educational thought
> treats them under the rubric of critical reading and critical thinking.
>     Receivership skills enlarge both of these notions by conceptualizing
> the individual as a consumer of information. As a knowledgeable con-
> sumer the individual has need of common skills of analysis (as in critical
> thinking), medium-specific skills of reception and interpretation (as in
> critical reading for print materials) and content-specific skills of under-
> standing. (pp. 22–23)

Various projects have differing emphases in their definitions of objectives and procedures. Perhaps the clearest statement is by the Far
West Laboratory for Education Research and Development:

Ability to evaluate and manage one's own television viewing behavior
ability to question the reality of television programs
ability to recognize the arguments employed on television and to counter-argue
ability to recognize the effects of television on one's own life.[2]

Both projects cited earlier involved students at the high school level (Grades 9–12); the first one, in Eugene and East Syracuse, also added students in Grades 6 through 8.

A U.S. government-funded project by station WNET in New York City prepared materials for workshops initially held in six states in the United States; participants were students in upper elementary and junior high school (Grades 6–10). Bilowit (1981) outlined what project directors meant by "critical television viewing":

It includes pre-planned viewing schedules, an alertness to television's assets and drawbacks, an ability to evaluate quality, and most of all, an ability to make unique, well-informed judgments about television. Our task is not to persuade people to watch only TV programs that are 'good' for them, but to help them develop the inner resources for setting their own personal criteria about what to watch and how to watch it. More specifically, critical television viewing skills are:

- The ability to analyze what you see and hear on television;
- The ability to evaluate what you have analyzed—for what is good about it, what is bad about it and how it relates to your life;
- The ability to express that evaluation—through something you talk about, through something you may write, through something you may choose to read, or through the television programs you select to watch.

Projects oriented toward younger school children in lower elementary school offer the following descriptions of their efforts. Anderson and Ploghoft (1980a) listed the Idaho State Department of Education's goals for students in Grades 3–6:

To provide young persons with the opportunity to learn about their own personal uses of television; what they like and dislike, how much they watch, when they watch, why they watch.

To provide young persons with analytical tools that will be useful in evaluating the content of entertainment programming.

To prepare young persons to identify the value conflicts that are embedded in entertainment programming content and to provide experiences in value clarification and the consideration of reasonable alternatives to the problem solutions presented in television programs.

To provide young persons with concepts and skills that enable them to analyze the persuasive messages of commercials, to discriminate between product appeals and effective appeals and to become sensitive to the persuasion techniques used.

To provide young persons with concepts that will enable them to use television news with understanding of its limitations and capabilities in comparison with news in other media.

To provide young persons with an understanding of the institutions of the media, their corporate structure, economics and management practices in the context of the effect these elements have on the content of the medium. (pp. 3–4)

The Department of Education's project director (Ashton, 1981) stated their rationale for involving public education in this type of media training:

The development of critical thinking can be enhanced through the study of television.

Basic comprehension skills can be extended and reinforced through analysis of television.

The use of the medium provides a high interest motivational approach with a common instructional base.

Receivership training allows students and parents to become more critical viewers. Hence, program selection is determined on the [basis] of intelligent decision making, rather than passive acceptance and manipulation. (p. 57)

A detailed breakdown of curriculum content areas is offered for children in Grades 3 to 5 by the Singers research team (funded by American Broadcasting Company). They developed a series of lesson plans to help elementary students in lower grades understand the medium of television and use their interest in the medium to advance reading, writing, and discussion skills. Concrete topics for learning about television include the following, slightly rephrased from the Singers' text (1981b, pp. 73–74):

Understand different types of programs.

Learn how programs are created by cooperative effort of different personnel, plus scenery and props.

Learn how TV works in terms of simple electronics.

Learn what aspects of programs are real—how fantasy elements are created for programs and commercials by camera techniques and special effects.

Learn about purpose and types of commercials, including public service or political announcements.

Understand how television influences feelings, ideas, self-concept, identification.

Become aware of TV as a source of information about other people, countries, occupations; learn how stereotypes are presented.

Become more critically aware of violence on television, lack of depiction of its effects on victims or of aggressors' being punished, to understand difference between physical and verbal aggression.

Become aware of their viewing habits, and how they can influence networks, producers, local stations.

Gain experience in using correct grammar and spelling, writing letters, abstracting ideas, critical thinking, expressive language, oral discussion and reading.

Also directed toward children in lower elementary grades (K–5), the Southwest Educational Development Laboratory (Starr, 1979) adopted elements of the CVS definition used by the U.S. Office of Education. It sought to teach what it called "eight primary television viewing receivership skills" that were central to:

Distinguishing program elements, such as music, special effects, setting, color, etc.;

Making judicial use of viewing time;

Understanding psychological implications of advertising;

Distinguishing fact from fiction;

Recognizing and appreciating differing views;

Understanding content of dramatic presentations, public affairs, news, and other programming;

Understanding style of dramatic presentations, public affairs, news, and other programming;

Understanding the relation between television programming and the printed word. (p. 5)

At the other end of the spectrum of formal education, post-secondary and adult viewers were the targeted participants in a CVS project by Boston University's School of Public Communication. Project director Donis Dondis (ca. 1980) broadly purposed:

To teach students how to develop critical television skills.

To create more responsive, responsible, and literate viewers.

To develop a more educationally sound use of television in and out of the classroom. (p. 3)

More value-laden and even moralistic in intent were continuing CVS projects by the Media Action Research Center in New York. Its

*Television Awareness Training* workbooks were used by adults and families as well as college groups. Its "Growing with Television" study program (Griffith, 1980) sought to help participants:

> Look at cultural values in contrast to biblical values;
> learn to use television as a value clarification resource;
> be interested about the content values and the presence of TV;
> develop critical viewing skills;
> to move to new decisions for their lives. (p. 2)

Outside the United States, the long-running, well-structured activity of the Catholic Education Office in Sydney, Australia, had impact not only on the parochial school system but also on state and independent schools—especially at the primary level. The specifically Christian orientation echoes the values of the Media Action Research Center in the United States (Canavan, 1978):

> The AIM of media education in the middle and upper grades is to have the students respond and react to what they view on television and film, to what they read in the press, and to what they listen to on the radio.
> In doing so they will begin to come to some understanding of the nature, techniques and purposes of the media of social communication and thereby be predisposed to develop critical Christian attitudes to television, film, press and radio. The final goal of such media education is to develop persons who will be discriminating truth seekers in their use of the media.
> The fundamental purpose of mass media education is to produce youth who will be appreciative, critical and discriminating listeners, readers and viewers. Ideally, the youth of tomorrow will be equipped to seek the truth in the mass media they and others use.[3]

Objectives are described in terms of growth in knowledge, skills, and attitudes. They include understanding media structure and processes, media's role in society, the Church's views about media, and "the basic elements" of the media. Training in skills augment one's ability to enjoy, appreciate, and judge critically the products of media and also to appraise one's media experience in the context of non-media environment—including formation of public opinion and society's role of responsibility in the mass communication process. The latter includes secular concerns of human needs and social problems as well as religious concerns involving conscience, faith, and Christian morality.

A relatively narrowly focused project in Powys Schools in Wales (United Kingdom) emphasizes "visual literacy" by stressing the "how" of television production rather than the social and cultural "why?" By keeping tabulated logs to observe their TV viewing behavior and by preparing programs with portable videotaping equipment, students "objectify" as well as "demystify" the television experience. Elster (1980) emphasized that "surely the only way that children can be taught to think critically about the medium is to show them through their own experience what *alternatives* might exit to the [professional] broadcast product. . . . The whole principle of community Video work has been to enable ordinary people to create their own alternatives to broadcast T.V., thereby attacking the stereotyped images of their own lives and problems invariably purveyed by the broadcast medium" (pp. 5–6). Even viewing videotaped programs from professional broadcast channels is premised on an *a posteriori* inductive approach "to offering our children analogous critical tools with which to face the T.V. screen"—analogous, that is, to traditional print-oriented study of grammar, syntax, creative writing, and so forth. Contrary to many other systematic CVS projects reported here, this project's premise is based on a caution:

> If our intention is to provide children with critical tools in the hope that they will proceed to discriminate amongst T.V. programmes we shall be frustrated because such discrimination arises in individuals in far more complex ways than the bases of media studies thus far allow. . . . The only viable *alternative* we would suggest is to accept that discriminative ability based on evaluative criteria comes to the individual as a result of life experiences and cross cultural references outside the scope of school-ing. What we can achieve in schools is an awareness on the part of our pupils that there are alternative gratifications available to them while watching T.V. based on new ways of looking at the T.V. product. The aim should be to develop the 'informed eye and mind' and this should be achieved by teaching how the medium produces its effects and by ena-bling children to make use of the medium, ie. [*sic*] make their own T.V. If we limit ourselves to the explication of hidden codes, we may produce an examinable subject but we blind our pupils to the areas of freedom exist-ing in the ground between constraints and to the accidents and freedoms of creativity. (pp. 14–15)

This approach, of course, questions the pedagogical efficacy of media study that looks to structuralism and semiotics—much less ideology analysis—as an avenue to understanding overt and latent "meanings" (codes, symbol-systems, etc.) in media content and form.

But CVS efforts in other parts of the world chose to incorporate both the pragmatic and the theoretical, joining practical experience in pro-ducing amateur programming with analytical observation and judg-ment about sociopolitical as well as cultural factors in the total media experience.

For example, in France the Ministers of Communication, Education, Youth, Sport, Leisure and Agriculture requested the *Fond d'Intervention Culturel (F.I.C.)* to develop a program of formation for young televiewers. The experimental program, called *Formation du Jeune Téléspectateur Actif*, sought to make youth relate actively to television and to give them critical distance from their TV experience so they could better judge the medium and their use of it. Goals include learning about television *comme 'médiateur' entre le monde et le téléspectateur* (by learning how a program is produced with the medium's instruments), *comme moyen d'expression artistique* (crafted by producers' creative perspective, and possessing various genres and styles of image), and *comme phénomène social* (at both the sending and receiving ends of the communication process—including economic and cultural factors in selecting material for broadcast (Gagnier, 1980, p. 10).

More explicit in its social orientation, coupled with emphasis on practical production of media products, was a multinational project conducted by *UNDA—Association Catholique Internationale pour le Radio et la Télévision* under a contract from UNESCO (Dessaucy, 1980). Its scope included modest experimental or pilot projects in ten countries on five continents. Its intent was to put into practice Sirkka Minkkinen's UNESCO-funded report, *A General Curricular Model for Mass Media Education.*[4] Television was one component of that paradigm for a broad-based training in media literacy and activism. This process of what they termed *l'éducommunication* reflected the broad sweep of Minkkinen's proposal for analyzing social, political and cultural as well as aesthetic and ethical aspects of media in society:

> *L'objectif de l'éducommunication: Rendre conscient l'usager des médias, de leur impact sur la vie sociale, culturelle et politique. C'est-à-dire, expliquer comment fonctionnent les médias, exposer leurs objectifs, leurs contraintes et leurs limitations, decrire comment ils exercent leurs éffets, pour le meilleur et pour le pire.*[5]

A means to achieve this was practical use of media tools as well as discussions with media practitioners. In fact, the ten lessons used by experimenters were almost exclusively devoted to learning basic skills of the various media.

A brief summary of the kinds of purposes and meanings given to various programs are provided by responses to a questionnaire survey from those for whose projects little supplementary material was available. In the United States, a public school coordinator for Eugene, Oregon, stated:

Critical viewing is the application of receiver skills in television observation: selection, observation, analysis, conceptualization of intended messages and those which are received through frame of reference and incidentally. Assessment and evaluation are natural conclusions.[6]

The response from the Parent-Teachers Association's Commission on Television emphasized the medium's negative attributes and effects:

The PTA is educating about television, as an art form and as an industry—providing viewers with skills to read television on the intellectual, the affective, and the subliminal level. In addition to developing an appreciation of the media, the trained viewer will recognize and avoid harmful effects of it: unrealistic and stereotyped portrayals of individuals, groups and lifestyles; false, unreal and misleading ideas about the world and influence to consume unneeded goods and services; lack of stimulation of academic, social, and physical skills.[7]

Mpre explicitly concerned with theoretical and sociopolitical implications was the Southern Arts Association in Winchester, Hampshire (England):

Awareness of the social, cultural, ideological and technical determinants of (primarily) film and television products. Recognition of the influences exerted over an audience/viewer by the programme-makers' choices (of subject, style, editing, relation of sound image, etc.).[8]

And in Amsterdam, "critical viewing skills" means simply "awareness how media producers use language of images and sounds and how they, the trainees, respond to the media."[9]

It is in this mix of perspectives and emphases that contemporary training in "media awareness," "media literacy," "receivership skills," and "critical viewing skills" was taking place around the world in the decade of the 1980s.

## QUESTIONNAIRE SURVEYS

The first step in this review was to identify those actively engaged in CVS-related projects and to obtain samples of their written and audiovisual materials. Then a three-page questionnaire was sent to those individuals and organizations to get comparable factual data about their projects. That survey early in 1981 was supplemented by a follow-up questionnaire in 1985 to determine the later status of those projects. (Both questionnaires are reproduced in the Appendix.) Supplementary data were solicited in 1988 and 1989, with responses from Australia, Chile, France, Canada, and the United Kingdom (Wales, Scotland, and England).

In most instances, questionnaire responses correlated with prior analysis of printed and other materials from those projects. But in some cases respondents indicated slightly different categories of content, format, purpose, or intended participants than were able to be determined from the materials themselves. Representatives of 17 projects returned completed questionnaires in 1981; seven responses were supplemented by follow-up questionnaires returned in 1985. Additional commentary and reports obtained from other countries in 1988–1989 offered contemporary descriptive information (not quantified for tabular comparison of data drawn from questionnaires). The list of projects surveyed in this investigation appears in Table 4.1. The U.S. projects are clustered according to three major categories reported in detail in this report, plus a fourth category of projects only summarized briefly. Projects from beyond the United States are listed separately. (For a chronological listing, see Table 3.1 in Part I.)

Of 11 projects in the United States, Number 13 (American Council for Better Broadcasts) only completed one-half the original (1981) questionnaire, and Number 15 (Television Information Office) only one-sixth; both indicated that remaining questions did not relate to their activities. Those 11 questionnaires and the 6 returned from other countries provided a profile of the kinds of "critical viewing skills" projects developed by the early 1980s. (See Table 4.2; respondents are identified by alpha-numeric listing in Table 4.1.)

All projects cited the purpose or motivation of the organizing source as "education." Three respondents added "research," and each of four others added "religious," "ethical/moral," "public relations," or "other: cultural."

The specific goal to be achieved with participants in their activity was identified as "educational" by all but one of the respondents. Six added a second goal as "cultural/aesthetic" results. Three also included "media reform" as part of their goal. And one included "ethical/moral" in its multiple response.

Although one project had been initiated in the early 1970s, and another in the mid-1970s, most began at the end of the decade. (Question #4; see chronological list in Table 3.1 in Part I.)

All but two of the projects were conducted under some form of institutional auspices; the exceptions were in Tel Aviv and in Florida where individuals oversaw media projects.

Three groups directed their efforts to preschool children, as well as

TABLE 4.1
CVS-Related Activities Surveyed 1981, 1985

---

*United States*

---

Projects Funded by U.S. Government
+  1. Southwest Educational Laboratory (Austin, Texas)
*  2. WNET/Thirteen (New York)
*+  3. Far West Laboratory (San Francisco)
*+  4. Boston University
School Districts
*  5. Idaho Falls
*  6. Eugene, Oregon
   7. East Syracuse, New York
   8. New York City Board of Education
Organizations
*+  9. Singers/Yale University/ABC (New Haven, Connecticut)
*+ 10. Media Action Research Center: "T-A-T"/"Growing w. TV" (N.Y.)
   10a U.S. Catholic Conference: "Media Mirror" (Washington, D.C.)
* 11. National Parent-Teachers Association (Chicago)
   12. Learning Seed Company (Illinois)
* 13. American Council for Better Broadcasts (Los Angeles)
   14. Action for Children's Television (Boston)
   14a Rosemary Potter (Florida)
Broadcast-Related Companies, Agencies
* 15. Television Information Office (New York)
   16. National Broadcasting Company (New York)
   17. CBS Inc. (New York)
   18. Capital Cities Communications (New York)
   19. American Broadcasting Companies, Inc. (New York)
   20. Time-Life, Inc. (New York)
* 21. Metropolitan Pittsburgh Public Broadcasting, Inc./WQED

---

*Other Selected Countries*

---

*  A. Catholic Education Office (Sydney, Australia)
*+ B. University of Stirling (Scotland)
*+ C. Southern Arts Association (Winchester, Hampshire, U.K.)
*  D. Stichting Audiovisuele Vorming (Amsterdam, The Netherlands)
*  E. Tel-Aviv University (Israel)
   F. Schools Council/Powys (Wales, U.K.)
*  G. Formation Du Jeune Téléspectateur Actif (Paris)
   H. UNDA/UNESCO (Africa: Gabon; Nigeria; Ile Maurice; Rwanda)
                  (Latin America: Mexico)
                  (Asia: Korea; India)
                  (Europe: Italy; Malta)
                  (Oceania: New Zealand)

---

* = Questionnaire returned, 1981 (with usable data)
+ = Updated questionnaire returned, 1985 (not all original respondents were included in updated survey)

TABLE 4.2

Questionnaire Responses, Selected Questions, 1981 Survey

|  | 2 | 3 | 4 | 5 | 6 | 9 | 10 | 11 | 13 | 15 | 21 | A | B | C | D | E | G |
|---|---|---|---|---|---|---|---|---|---|---|---|---|---|---|---|---|---|
| **# 2: *Purpose or "Motivation" of Organizing Source*** | | | | | | | | | | | | | | | | | |
| Education [=all] | 2 | 3 | 4 | 5 | 6 | 9 | 10 | 11 | 13 | 15 | 21 | A | B | C | D | E | G |
| Public relations | | | | | | | | | | 15 | | | | | | | G |
| Religious (church-related) | | | | | | | 10 | | | | | | | | | | |
| Ethical/moral | | | | | | 9 | | | | | | | | | | | |
| Research | | | | | 6 | | | | | | 21 | | B | | | | |
| Other: [cultural] | | | | | | | | | | | | | | C | | | |
| **# 3: *Project's Specific Goals to be Achieved With Program Participants*** | | | | | | | | | | | | | | | | | |
| Education | 2 | 3 | | 5 | 6 | 9 | 10 | 11 | 13 | | 21 | A | B | C | D | E | G |
| Cultural/aesthetic | 2 | | | | 6 | 9 | | | 13 | | | | | C | | | G |
| Ethical/moral | | | | | | | 10 | | | | | | | | | | |
| Media reform | | | | 5 | | | 10 | 11 | | | | | | | | | |
| **# 9: *Levels of Participation by Participants*** | | | | | | | | | | | | | | | | | |
| Pre-school | 2 | | | | | | | | | | | A | | | | | G |
| Elementary (1–8) | 2 | | | 5 | 6 | 9 | | 11 | 13 | | 21 | A | | C | | E | G |
| High school (9–12) | 2 | 3 | (4?) | 5 | 6 | 9 | | 11 | 13 | | 21 | A | | C | D | E | G |
| College | | | 4 | | | | 10 | 11 | | | 21 | | B | C | | | |
| Postgrad/extension | | | 4 | | | | 10 | 11 | 13 | | 21 | A | B | C | | | (G) |

#10: *Approach Emphasized*

#11: *Techniques Used*

#14: *If School-Related Project, This Activity is: (? = not specified)*

#16: *Form of Involvement With Television Media*

#19: *Testing/Measuring to Evaluate Project Materials, Methodology, Effects*

#20: *Findings Compiled: Results and Measured/Reported Effects*

| | 2 | 3 | 4 | 5 | 6 | 9 | (10) | 11 | 13 | 21 | A | B | C | D | E | G |
|---|---|---|---|---|---|---|---|---|---|---|---|---|---|---|---|---|
| **Deductive** | | | | 5 | 6 | 9 | (10) | | 13 | | | B | C | D | E | G |
| **Inductive** | | 3 | 4 | 5 | 6 | 9 | 10 | | 13 | 21 | A | B | C | D | E | G |
| **Lecture** | 2 | | | 5 | 6 | 9 | | 11 | | 21 | A | B | C | D | | |
| **Discussion** | 2 | 3 | | 5 | 6 | 9 | 10 | 11 | | 21 | A | B | C | D | | |
| **Workshop** | 2 | 3 | 4 | 5 | 6 | 9 | 10 | | | 21 | A | B | C | D | | |
| **Curriculum (formal)** | 2 | 3 | 4 | 5 | 6 | | 11 | 13 | | | A | B | C | D | | |
| **Readings** | | 3 | | 5 | | 9 | 10 | 11 | 13 | 21 | A | B | C | D | | G |
| **Other: [miscellaneous]** | | | | | | | | 11 | 13 | | | B | | | | |
| **Curriculum Integrated** | 2 | 3 | | 5 | 6 | | 11 | | | 21 | A | | C | D | E | |
| **(a) Required** | ? | | | | | | | | | | × | | | ? | | |
| **(b) Elective** | ? | × | | × | × | | × | | | | | | × | ? | × | |
| **Extracurricular** | | | | | | 9 | | | | 21 | A | | C | D | | |
| **"Active"** | 2 | | 4 | 5 | 6 | 9 | 10 | 11 | | 21 | A | B | C | D | | G |
| **"Passive"** | 2 | 3 | 4 | 5 | 6 | 9 | 10 | 11 | | 21 | A | B | C | D | | G |
| **#19** | | 3 | | 5 | (6) | 9 | | 11 | | 21 | | B | C | | E | |
| **#20** | | 3 | | 5 | | 9 | | 11 | | 21 | A | | C | D | E | |

(Numbers/letters refer to CVS projects listed in previous table) to students through the next 12 years of schooling. Seven U.S. projects and four non-U.S. ones worked with students in elementary grades (1 through 8). Seven and five groups, respectively, worked with high school children. Five U.S. projects and two non-U.S. projects were directed to college students; those same groups plus one more non-U.S. group worked with adults.

All respondents to Question #10 except one (Sydney, Australia) stated the "inductive" approach was emphasized; but three U.S. and four non-U.S. respondents also added "deductive" as well.

As Table 4.2 indicates, most groups employed a diversity of techniques in training people to be more discriminating users of television. Workshops were employed by most groups, with formal curricular courses, readings, and discussions used almost as widely. Least utilized was lecture; only three U.S. and four non-U.S. projects included that form of presentation among their several other techniques.

Where media literacy training was conducted as a school-related project, it was an integral part of the curriculum in six U.S. and four non-U.S. projects (all elective, except one non-U.S. where it was required). It was an extracurricular activity in two U.S. and two non-U.S. projects.

Fourteen respondents (9 U.S., 5 non-U.S.) described their participants'/students' form of involvement with television training as "passive" (by selective viewing and by evaluating media content). Nine of those also indicated "active" training (writing letters, contacting media organizations, and/or presenting media programs).

Eight groups claimed to have some kinds of testing or measuring to evaluate their activities. Some sent what reports were available, but most did not have succinct summaries, only materials in files not easily accessible for this survey. But five U.S. and four non-U.S. groups did state that they had compiled data about measured effects of their work and some made portions of those data available. Several other groups outside the United States sent descriptive reports in 1988–1989.

## GENERAL PATTERNS

Some clear patterns emerged from responses to the questionnaire survey by directors of "critical viewing skills" projects. The great majority were educational ventures with no stated intent to make moral or ethical value judgments about television, either as part of their purpose in mounting programs or as a goal to be achieved with program participants. (The only exceptions were the research-related activities by the Doctors Singer at Yale University and, more predictably, the church-related Media Action Research Center in New York.) A few organizations noted "research" as part of their purpose: the schools in Eugene (Oregon), the educational television group in Pittsburgh, and the University of Stirling in England. Presumably, the Singers looked to CVS activities as the fruit or application of their scholarly research in the field, rather than as the matrix for research itself. And one would expect the National Association of Broadcasters' Television Information Office to include "public relations" among its purposes in carrying on "critical viewing" efforts. Only the Southern Arts Association in Winchester (United Kingdom) added "cultural" to its reasons for involvement in this work. None of the respondents reflected Minkkinen's UNESCO mandate for social and even political orientation to media study. Some in Central and South America as well as Europe, including the United Kingdom, might find this a shortcoming in a statement of purpose or motivation. Their perspective reflects social oriented—even Marxist oriented, if not doctrinaire—purposeful harnessing of media so common persons can understand forces at work in society and can eventually participate in controlling them—reflecting "ideology in action."

Further analysis (in following chapters) of specific project materials determine to what extent "education" motivation and goals do in fact include educating about sociopolitico-economic aspects of society at large as well as in media.

Only three organizations stated "media reform" among their goals for participants: the Idaho Falls school district, the Media Action Research Center, and the National Congress of Parents and Teachers (National PTA). So "media activism" by participants as audience-consumers was not a major focus of the projects reviewed in this study.

Most respondents to the questionnaire survey indicated multiple levels of school/age engaged in their projects. Only the Far West Laboratory in San Francisco and Stichting Audiovisuele Vorming in Amsterdam limited their work exclusively to a single sector, high school students; and the Singers at Yale in Connecticut focused solely on elementary school students. All other projects engaged at least two tiers of school, and many of them three or more (including preschoolers and adults). Because many projects were exploratory or experimental, some with "seed" funding by governmental agencies, they prepared a range of introductory materials with broad potential applications. But the diffuse focus could affect the relevance and effectiveness of materials assembled for the projects, precisely because participants ranged across a wide spectrum of developmental stages and personal experience—including media exposure.

Clearly respondents did not favor an exhortatory, analytical approach more often associated with apodictic lecturing—whether disseminating informational material or offering standards for appraising the performance of mass media. Only the Catholic Education Office in Sydney listed its activity as exclusively deductive in analyzing media. All others responded that inductive exploration, including heuristic experience of media, was a major portion of their approach; half of those also employed deductive pedagogy. (The following analysis of specific project materials notes the kinds of materials and procedures employed by specific projects.)

This emphasis is confirmed by responses to the next question about techniques used. Lecture—the traditional vehicle for analytical study based on enunciated principles and criteria—was cited as the form least used in educating participants. That question was ambiguous because it listed "Curriculum (formal courses)" as a technique distinguished from "lecture"; but many curricular courses rely on positive teaching in lectures as well as on other processes that more actively engage students. (Again, later detailed analysis of specific project materials clarifies this point.) But almost all respondents (14 of the 17) cited "workshops" as the mode for studying media. Workshops are typically "hands-on," interactive, exploratory forms that involve active participation. The category of "readings" is ambiguous. It depends on whether readings are primarily sources of data and a wide variety of judgmental statements—to be discussed and debated to form one's personal perspective—or rather presentations of absolute principles, norms, and final assessments of media—similar to lectures that outline, define, and judge for the recipient.

A number of project workbooks and instructors' manuals explicitly caution against attempting to inculcate the teacher's own views and values. They urge that participants be free to experience media, to react to them, to reflect on their reactions, and to voice those reflections without being preconditioned artificially or "indoctrinated" and without having their observations and opinions evaluated as "right" or "wrong" or "good" or "bad." Exercises are intended to sensitize participants to their personal experience of media and to encourage them to reflectively appraise that experience from their personal framework of likes/dislikes and values.

Where CVS activity is related to schools, in all instances except one (the Catholic Education Office in Sydney) it is optional study when integrated into the curriculum or it is an extracurricular activity. Motives may well be mixed for participants who choose media studies in school, but they are free to select or avoid it everywhere except in Sydney. On the other hand, does this diminish the stature of media study in the minds of students as well as of administrators and faculty? And are curricular resources, including flexible scheduling and audiovisual support, adequately provided for what are scheduled as electives and extracurriculars?

Finally, 14 respondents to Question #16 described their programs of study as "passive" in orientation, with 9 of the same respondents describing them also as "active." Whereas both forms were mingled in many programs, the dominant approach confirmed the original purpose or motivation and goals of the projects: Education and enlightenment based on personal experience and reflection. Far less attention was given to activist involvement in media such as producing media materials or attempting to influence media managers by writing letters or contacting media organizations. This reflected slight social and political orientation in most programs. Does that make them objective and free of ideological bias? Or does it imply acceptance of the status quo of media systems and content and their influence on society (which is itself a bias)? Is it better for media study programs not to impose values? Or should they present ranges of values and prompt participants to reflect and select value-systems consonant with their own? Can media study be "valueless"? And what kinds of values, structures, principles are apt for what age-groups? (Once again, analysis of specific project materials throws light on how each goes about this challenging task.)

## MAJOR CHARACTERISTICS OF CVS PROGRAMS

Based on information provided by the 1981 questionnaires, other patterns and some exceptions to those patterns emerged. Throughout the decade of the 1970s, various individuals and organizations mounted CVS-related projects both in the United States and abroad. Only in 1972 and 1973 were no new projects mounted (at least by respondents to the survey). In every other year at least one new project was started, with two initiated in 1970 and again in 1979 and six in 1978. Among those six were the four major projects funded by the U.S. Office of Education, although one (WNET/Thirteen) had already been under way in the New York area since 1970 and only then was receiving 2-year federal support. Nine reported no terminal date for their projects; the rest were to conclude in the early 1980s (three in 1980, two in 1981, one in 1982). Those terminations were related to funding from national governmental sources, both in the United States and elsewhere. The continuing projects were typically in school districts or associated with national or regional (private) organizations.

*Administrators* of programs (including clerical and research staff, and teachers or "trainers" in workshops) numbered from 2.5 to 8 in structured projects, and a wide range of staff and assistants in far-flung workshops—variously reported as "9 + 30," "17 + 433," "4-to-40 + 7000 volunteers and 6000 'monitors'" (PTA). Totals reported in 1985 roughly corresponded to the earlier data submitted in 1981. Differences could be attributed to the fact that many projects had been concluded 4 years earlier, so respondents in 1985 did not have precise information about previous activities.

*Project participants* in 1981 were often reported as in the thousands, either because many schools were part of CVS activities or because workshops or other short-term formats were offered regionally or nationwide. For instance, the Southwest Lab reported 2,200 participating at 17 schools, Idaho Falls involved 9 schools, the Singers at Yale worked with 14 schools. The Sydney project included over 5,000 classes and 500 homes; the Winchester activity involved 450 persons, 20 schools, and 12 organizations; MARC/T-A-T noted "thousands" over 4 years of their project. (In 1985 MARC answered that same question with "hundreds of thousands" whereas other responses were closer to their previous estimates.) In short, endeavors to advance "telemedia literacy" were far-reaching; they were not merely relegated to small clusters of persons in research laboratories or isolated classrooms.

The *sizes of groups* were related to the context of CVS activity as well as to forms and foci of analysis. Those are noted when individual projects are analyzed in detail in subsequent chapters. Some projects offered discrete workshops confined to a total of 6 hours (Boston University), whereas others offered two hour-long meetings each week over an entire year (the Singers' research-oriented study). Other workshops extended through 2½ days (MARC/T-A-T) to 4 days of 8 hours each (WQED). The University of Stirling's sessions were presented three to four times a week for between 1 and 2.5 hours (averaging 6 hours a week). Winchester had longer periods of 2 to 3 hours for 8 to 12 weeks, similar to Amsterdam's 2 hours a week for 7 weeks. In Tel Aviv the sessions were 2 hours long, four times a month. Length and frequency depended on the purpose and structure of the project.

*Funding* depended on the initiating or supporting agency. Projects supported by the U.S. government were funded at levels of $400,000 over 3 years (Boston University), $410,000 over 2 years (Far West Lab). American Broadcasting Companies, Inc. provided $160,000 over 2 years (Singers/Yale). Idaho Falls School District invested $111,080 over 3 years. Three national church organizations underwrote MARC's project of Television Awareness Training with $12,700 a year. The National Parent–Teachers Association's funding joined national membership contributions in providing between $36,000 and $84,000 a year. WQED worked with $10,000 a year. And the American Council for Better Broadcasting used $4,000 annually. The only non-U.S. specific figure quoted was £75,000 provided in Winchester (United Kingdom). Other funding was nonspecific in the general budget for education (Sydney), in University funds (Stirling), or by ministries of education (Tel Aviv) or culture (France).

With the exception of WNET/Thirteen in New York, U.S. Office of Education (USOE) projects were somewhat experimental efforts granted "seed" money by federal government to establish prototypical projects within 2- or 3-year periods. The intent was to provide not only direction but also materials and research evaluations to others wishing to emulate them. USOE projects were large, staffs ample, and results swiftly orchestrated into extensive printed materials (workbooks, manuals, etc.) put in the public domain with copies able to be purchased from project offices.

## OTHER FEATURES

The initial questionnaire survey in 1981 reflected other characteristics of CVS activities. Only one project (Tel Aviv) did not treat television but rather film and advertising. Five projects included study of print (WNET, Eugene, Singers, Sydney, and Stirling). Four added film to TV (all outside the United States—Sydney, Stirling, Winchester, Amsterdam). Sydney also included material on sound recordings. Three projects added radio to their activity (Eugene, Sydney, and Stirling). (American Council for Better Broadcasting had grown out of a many-decades tradition of monitoring and critiquing radio broadcasting; but it responded only to the first questions, so no detailed data were provided.)

Two aspects of content were also surveyed in 1981: CVS topic areas and sources for establishing norms for evaluating media content and practices.

*Topic areas* were listed in the questionnaire in the following order:

A. Time spent with TV.
B. Program viewing patterns.
C. Impact of TV on reading, speaking, other cognitive skills.
D. TV's form and format: Schedules, techniques of camera, sound; plot, character, dialogue.
E. TV's structure and processes: Advertising supported, government regulated; industry/art of stations/networks/producers-suppliers.

F.  How people use TV: Uses and gratifications—needs, desires, preferences, choices in context of other media/leisure activities.

G.  What TV does to people: Effects of viewing on attitudes, behavior.

H.  Kinds of TV: ( ) entertainment; ( ) news, public affairs.

I.  Advertising: Commercials (appeals, "values," weaknesses).

J.  Consumer roles: ( ) writing; ( ) joining organizations to affect media decision-makers; ( ) other.

K.  Other.

Five responded by checking *all* items in the list as topics covered in their CVS projects (one added "program evaluation" but that was intended to be included under *D*, *G*, and *H*). Another two in the United States checked all except *C* (TV's impact on personal communication experiences) and *J* (consumer roles). MARC checked all except *C* and *D* (production and aesthetics)—typically concerned more with social and ethical impact of TV than creative and artistic aspects. That differed widely from non-U.S. emphasis. The University of Stirling excluded topics *A*, *B*, *C*, and *J* (viewer/consumer inventory and activities). Winchester indicated they covered only *D*, *E*, *G*, and *H* (program content and genres, media's internal structure, plus audience effects). Amsterdam marked only *D* and *H*—eschewing all statistical, structural, social, economic, moral/ethical, and activist aspects of critical viewing skills training.

What about *sources* used to determine standards for evaluating the media? The questionnaire checklist included:

A.  Originators/leaders of project.

B.  Professional educators.

C.  Professional media persons.

D.  Research reports.

E.  Published books, articles.

F.  National office of organization.

G.  Other.

Only the respondent from France marked all choices as sources utilized for their project. Three in the United States marked all items except *F* (a national office or organization). Most tended to rely on sources relatively close to themselves. The National PTA relied on its 6,000 members who participated in a survey. Idaho Falls, Eugene, and Tel Aviv looked to *A* and *B*—the principals in the project or professional educators (admittedly the latter were often researchers and scholars with access to data in *D* and *E* as they developed criteria for assessing media). Amsterdam reported only *B* (professional educators) as sources for norms, whereas MARC noted *A* plus *D* and *E* (research reports and published books and articles). Far West Laboratory depended more on outside sources, *C, D,* and *E*. Stirling leaned on sources other than *A* and *F* (project originators and organization). Winchester cited A and B and to a "limited extent" *E* plus *G* ("Other: films, broadcast TV, non-Broadcast video") from which to draw norms for analyzing and evaluating television.

There is considerable diversity in how different CVS groups analyze broadcast media. Each has strengths and weaknesses. One who looks to these previous major projects for guidance and materials in implementing a local CVS activity must take into account the varied approaches and criteria to determine which best serve one's own purpose and need.

## QUESTIONNAIRE UPDATE, 1985

Brief questionnaires to update information were sent to 17 major respondents to the earlier questionnaire (1981); 7 responded again. All USOE funding for projects had terminated in 1980 (in accordance with terms of the contracts), as had ABC's grant for research by the Singers at Yale University. But some activities continued there as well as at MARC, the University of Sterling, and in Winchester. All three were receiving some support from department funds or from multiple other sources.

*Staffing* reflected the extent of those seven programs. The largest staff was 33 at Yale; 17 were at Boston University when the project was terminated in 1981, whereas 13 continued at MARC, 6 at Far West Laboratory, 5 at Winchester, 4⅔ (including part-time) at University of Stirling, and 3 at the Southwest Educational Development Laboratory. The numbers of participants "to date" (1985) were 300 at Stirling; 1,500 plus 30 organizations in Winchester; 2,500 at Far West Laboratory; 14 schools during the project, and more than 100 since then, with the Singers' work; and "hundreds of thousands" in far-flung workshops and classes participating in MARC's national activities ("T-A-T").

*Evaluation.* CVS groups often attempted to evaluate materials, methodology, and effects of their projects. The Far West Lab worked with Educational Testing Service and 25 teachers in the United States to help assess the project during formative stages. Boston University pretested workbook materials. The Singers conducted extensive research and testing (and reported results in formal papers). Other groups employed examinations, essays, and activities to discern effects or results of CVS projects. Only the Singers systematically reported findings on results of their media-study activities. They and MARC also had documented reactions from parents, leaders, and participants—usually in the form of letters. (Respondents to the initial survey also noted that correspondence constituted the bulk of their evidence about reactions and appraisals by those in the CVS programs.)

## RELATED STUDY OF CVS PROJECTS

Question #3 in the 1981 survey asked about specific goals of the projects. Fifteen responded "education," five listed the broader category "cultural/aesthetic," three noted activist "media reform," and only one the value-oriented "ethical/moral." Anderson (1983) identified 11 major categories of instructional objectives in eight major television literacy curricula.[10] In all eight projects he found management of viewing (both amount of time spent and program selection); grammar and syntax of television (aural-visual elements, semiotics, form and formats); and technical knowledge of TV (production, distribution). Objectives in seven projects involved advertising techniques and consequences; comparative strengths and weaknesses of different media (in presenting news and drama); and the television industry and society (sociological and economic, including legal, but not anthropological or cultural aspects). Six projects focused on value analysis (commercial messages, news, dramatic themes). Five studied consequences of TV viewing (social and individual effects, both positive and negative); and evaluation, criticism, and analysis (through content analysis and assessment traditional in literary contexts). Five projects also were specifically directed to news programming (to understand processes and to evaluate potential biases); and to fantasy/reality (TV's depictions vs. "what is"—according to the project creators' perspective, at least). A few other objectives were sought by one or other project, including integrating television literacy into existing curricular programs such as English and social studies. He did not identify as a specifically stated objective growth in analogous cognitive skills (speaking, reading, logical reasoning).

Anderson interpreted those 11 objectives as reflecting four kinds of activities constitutive of television literacy. More than two-thirds of instructional texts were devoted to two of them: exposition/description (of data, categories) and identification (applying those data to TV experience). Less than one-third of project materials was directed to the other two activities: analysis (of personal purposes in viewing, value formation, news and its sources, and distinguishing fantasy from reality) and attribution or decision-making (regarding choices and consequences of televiewing). Anderson asserted that those eight projects generally incorporated in their objectives and activities most elements developed a priori in early concepts about "receivership skills" in the early 1970s (and paraphrased at the beginning of this chapter):

> [Television literacy] skills begin with those skills needed to identify and understand our own motives and purposes for attendance. They include the ability to interpret the influence of those motives and purposes [i]n the way we make sense of the messages we receive. That those motives, for example, may facilitate the acceptance of certain statements and the rejection of others.
>
> They provide the ability to grasp the meaning of the message; to comprehend language and visual and aural images discriminately; to interpret 'hidden' meanings; to specify the working elements of the message; to identify to whom the message is directed and its intent.
>
> They foster the observation of details, their sequence and relationships; the understanding of themes, values, motivating elements, plotlines, characters and characterization.
>
> They direct the evaluation of fact, opinion, logical and affective appeals. They identify fanciful writing and images.
>
> Receivership skills include an understanding of the sources of bias inherent in the medium of presentation, and a comprehension of the grammar, syntax and meanings contained in the methods chosen to produce the message.
>
> Finally, the individual trained in receivership skills can recognize intended affective reactions and motives; can relegate personal value to the message; identify emotional satisfaction and their sources in the messages; relate the message to other experiences and information; can make inferences, draw conclusions and establish predictions or other criteria for evaluation.[11]

In the following chapters each project's stated purposes, content, procedures, constituencies, and support materials are analyzed in detail. Data about several non-U.S. projects that submitted reports in 1988–1989 (without previous questionnaire responses) are incorporated into the text with appropriate groupings—in chapters 6 and 10—along with projects profiled by 1981/1985 tabulated information.

## ANALYSIS OF CVS PROJECTS

All projects but one (Television Information Office) represented in the 1981 questionnaire survey listed "education" as their sole or major

TABLE 4.3
CVS Projects Clustered by Institutional/Individual Source

### A. *Projects Funded by U.S. Government*

Southwest Educational Development Laboratory (Grades K–5)
WNET/Thirteen, New York City (Grades 6–8)
Far West Laboratory for Educational Research and Development (Grades 9–12)
Boston University (Post-secondary and Adults)

### B. *School Districts (Systematic, Formal Instruction)*

Idaho Falls School District No. 91 (Grades 3–6)
Eugene (Oregon) Public School District 91 (Grades 4–8, 9–12)
East Syracuse, New York (Grades 6–12)
New York City Board of Education (Grades K through 9)
Catholic Education Office, Sydney, N.S.W. (Grades K–6, 7–12)
#Ministry of Education, Western Australia (Grades 8–12)

### C. *Projects by Individuals—Collaborative and Individual*

Aimee Dorr *et al.* (Harvard/Univ. of Southern California)
Dorothy and Jerome Singer (Yale/ABC)
Rosemary Potter *et al.* (Pinella County Schools, Florida)

### D. *National Organizations (Nongovernmental): U.S.*

National Association for Better Radio and Television
American Council for Better Broadcasts
Congress of Parents and Teachers (National PTA)
Media Action Research Center (MARC)
(a) "Television Awareness Training" ("T-A-T")
(b) "Growing with Television"
U.S. Catholic Conference ("The Media Mirror")

### E. *Private Companies: U.S., U.K.*

The Learning Seed Company
Television Learning, Ltd.
Prime-Time School Television
Television Information Office/Teachers Guide to Television
Capital Cities Communications
National Television Networks (U.S.): CBS, NBC, ABC
Independent Broadcasting Authority & Independent Television Companies (U.K.)

### F. *Institution-Related CVS Programs in Formal Education*

Powys (Wales)
#Clwyd (Wales)
Mayfield School, Southwest London (England)
Southern Arts Association, Winchester, Hampshire (England)
Scottish Film Council (Scotland)
#Media Education Development Project (Scotland)

(*continued*)

TABLE 4.3 (*Continued*)

---

#Media Education Research Project (Scotland)
  Formation Du Jeune Téléspectateur Actif (France)
  Stichting Audiovisuele Vorming, Amsterdam (Netherlands)
#Media Literacy Guide, Ontario (Canada)
#Latin American Communciations Pedagogy Institute (Costa Rica)
#DENI Plan—Catholic Cinema Office (Uruguay)
#Robert Bellarmino Educational Foundation (Chile)
#Centre of Cultural & Artistic Enquiry & Expression (Chile)
#Univérsidad de Playa Ancha de Ciencias de la Educacion (Chile)
#Brazilian Social Communciations Union (Brazil)
  UNDA/UNESCO—Worldwide: various countries

---

(# = Project not included in questionnaire surveys)

goal of CVS activity. The majority of projects reviewed in this report were directed to elementary school children, with overlapping age-ranges. Some CVS programs were for students from kindergarten through the fifth grade (K–5), others were for Grades 3–5 or 3–6 or 5–8 or 6–8 or even 1 through 8. A number of those also were directed to secondary school students, Grades 9–12 (or only 9–10). And several were also directed to college-level students. Projects developed for adults were intended to reach younger people through teachers and parents in those CVS training programs. Therefore, projects could not be categorized usefully according to intended participants. Instead, they have been grouped according to sponsoring or controlling agency (as listed in Table 4.3). A chapter is devoted to each: (chapter 5) four projects at successive levels, funded by the U.S. government; (chapter 6) school districts in four U.S. cities, and in two Australian regions; (chapter 7) three projects by individuals (associated with schools); (chapter 8) six projects by five national nongovernment organizations in the United States; (chapter 9) nine projects by private corporations, including broadcast companies, in the United States and United Kingdom; and (chapter 10) institution-related programs in formal and informal education—seven in the United Kingdom (Wales, England, and Scotland); one each in France, the Netherlands, Canada, Costa Rica, Uruguay, and Brazil; three in Chile; and ten worldwide with UNESCO. As noted earlier, the several projects for which data were obtained in 1988–1989 are described in appropriate parts of the text; but data were not included in the tabulated comparative analysis because they did not participate in the 1981/1985 questionnaire surveys.

## NOTES

1. Cf. Fiske and Hartley (1978, pp. 72–73).

2. Cited by Lloyd-Kolkin (1981, p. 93). See this organization's project *Workbook (Vol. 2),* in U.S. Office of Education's funded series discussed later in text.

3. See Canavan (1978, p. 2). The same statement is printed by Canavan (1975, p. 23) in the curriculum guide for secondary schools.

4. See Part I of this book for comments about Minkkinen's analysis and proposed plan of media study.

5. See Dessaucy (1980, pp. 9–10). Thus, to them, the objective of "éducommunication" is to develop reflective use of media, their impact on social, cultural, and political life. That is to say, to explain how media function, to expose their objectives, their constraints and limitations, and to describe how they exercise their effects, for better or worse.

6. Melva Ellingsen, curriculum specialist, School District No. 41, Eugene, Oregon. Questionnaire response.

7. Marion R. Young, consultant to PTA Action Center in Chicago, Illinois. Questionnaire response.

8. David Altshul, film officer, Southern Arts Association; Winchester, Hampshire. Questionnaire response.

9. Unsigned questionnaire response, Stichting Audiovisuele Vorming, Amsterdam.

10. In addition to three USOE projects (Southwest Educational Development Laboratory, Far West Laboratory, WNET/13), Idaho Falls School District (ESEA IV-C Project), and ABC-Singers/Yale, were: the Milford, Ohio, project (Fransecky & Ferguson, 1973; Shorr, 1978); East-Syracuse/Minoa Receivership Skills Project (Anderson was consultant to project 1975–1980); and the Anderson-Ploghoft curriculum (see citations in Part I).

11. Adapted by Anderson (1981, p. 23) from the 1973 statement.

# 5

## Projects Funded by U.S. Government

This chapter offers a national perspective of American major CVS programs: The four "seed" projects underwritten by the U.S. government. They represent collaborative effort by teams of specialists in education and media throughout the country.

### SOUTHWEST EDUCATIONAL DEVELOPMENT LABORATORY (GRADES K–5)

The SEDL project was one of four founded in 1978 by the U.S. Office of Education. The intended constituency included elementary school teachers of grades K through 5 and also those students' parents, plus youth leaders. The context for CVS activity was both classroom and home, plus community organizations. SEDL acknowledged the difficulty of introducing new components to school schedules, therefore proposed incorporating the program into existing courses. Although their stated "motivation" was educational, goals also included cultural/aesthetic and social aspects.

*Purposes.* SEDL sought to train teachers, parents, and youth leaders to communicate principles to youths. Those principles are stated succinctly; appendices in the training manual substantiate major assertions and conclusions, most from aptly selected research literature.

Stated premises include children's heavy television viewing, young-sters' various levels of maturation and cognitive development, and the general availability of parents in the home setting where most television is viewed. Children's interpreting their TV experiences is to be supported by parents' "co-viewing" with direct or indirect intervention through questions and discussion about programs being watched. Beyond merely limiting children's amount of viewing, the intent is to guide purposeful selection of program content.

SEDL sought to prepare adults to work with children over a long period of time to help them benefit from television by matching TV viewing habits with maturation in cognitive skills. The training manual and workshops outline strategies for developing more critical awareness of television and better habits of using and responding reflectively to the medium. This includes ability to evaluate whether TV content is "real" or reflects reality, to what extent it is relevant to one's life, and to understand motivations and psychological implications of characters, dialogue, and action. Manual (Starr, 1979) stated that "the goal of teaching children these skills is to reduce the undesirable consequences of television viewing on students and to maximize the potentially positive learning opportunities" (p. 6).

SEDL's content reflects the basic components of USOE's outline of what constitutes "critical television viewing skills." They include the ability to:

1. distinguish program elements [music, special effects, costumes, settings, color, etc.]
2. make judicious use of viewing time
3. understand the psychological implications of advertising
4. distinguish fact from fiction
5. recognize and appreciate differing views
6. understand content of dramatic presentations, public affairs, news and other television programming
7. understand style of dramatic presentations, public affairs, news and other television programming
8. understand relation between television and the printed word. (pp. 42–43)

*Support Materials for Teachers and Parents.* SEDL prepared a "Training Manual for Teaching Critical Viewing Skills" and a set of 56, 5×8-inch "Teacher Cue Cards" with specific activities outlined for various subjects in the regular curriculum (e.g., art, mathematics, language, social studies). Those and a series of four-page, 8½×11-inch printed pamphlets serve in place of a structured CVS curriculum or

FIG. 5.1. Handout sheets, lesson cards, booklets, and board game developed under grant from U.S. Office of Education by Southwest Educational Laboratory, 1979, Austin, Texas.

study plan (see Fig. 5.1). The keynote was flexibility and adaptability to the local context.

SEDL's orientation, according to the project director, was to provide materials capitalizing on students' habitual use of television as well as on teachers' desire to teach academic and social concepts, by integrating TV usage with basic subject areas. Thus television was to be considered "as still another learning resource to teach reading, language arts, social studies and math."

Teacher Cue Cards serve that purpose directly, to enhance various subject areas by harnessing TV viewing (see Fig. 5.2). Seven subjects (art, language arts, math, music, physical education, science, and social studies) are represented on color-coded cards, each noting appropriate age ranges for the activity involving TV. Every set of activities suggested on the cards is accompanied by topics for discussion. The cards reflect an inductive approach to exploring television critically; no judgments or conclusions are suggested. The tactic is to draw out students' own reactions to TV experiences, helping children reflect about them.

For other than teachers, the series of six-page booklets titled "Television: A Family Focus" presents themes about TV's content, structure,

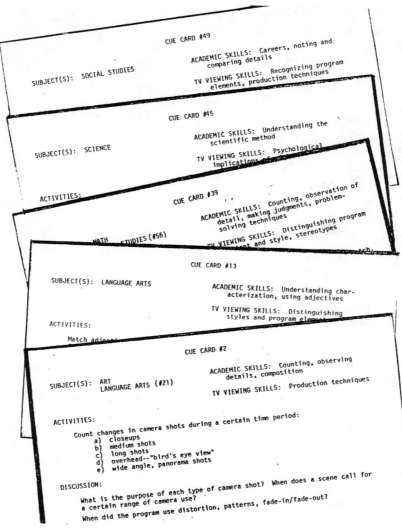

CUE CARD #49

SUBJECT(S): SOCIAL STUDIES

ACADEMIC SKILLS: Careers, noting and comparing details

TV VIEWING SKILLS: Recognizing program elements, production techniques

CUE CARD #45

SUBJECT(S): SCIENCE

ACADEMIC SKILLS: Understanding the scientific method

TV VIEWING SKILLS: Psychological implications

ACTIVITIES:

CUE CARD #39

ACADEMIC SKILLS: Counting, observation of detail, making judgments, problem-solving techniques

TV VIEWING SKILLS: Distinguishing program and style, stereotypes

MATH STUDIES (#56)

CUE CARD #13

SUBJECT(S): LANGUAGE ARTS

ACADEMIC SKILLS: Understanding characterization, using adjectives

TV VIEWING SKILLS: Distinguishing styles and program elements

ACTIVITIES:

Match adjecti

CUE CARD #2

SUBJECT(S): ART
LANGUAGE ARTS (#21)

ACADEMIC SKILLS: Counting, observing details, composition

TV VIEWING SKILLS: Production techniques

ACTIVITIES:

Count changes in camera shots during a certain time period:
a) closeups
b) medium shots
c) long shots
d) overhead--"bird's eye view"
e) wide angle, panorama shots

DISCUSSION:

What is the purpose of each type of camera shot? When does a scene call for a certain range of camera use?
When did the program use distortion, patterns, fade-in/fade-out?

FIG. 5.2.   "Teacher Cue Cards" for student assignments. From CVS materials developed by C. Corder-Bolz (Dir.), 1979, Austin, Texas, Southwest Educational Development Laboratory. (No copyright noted, but organization's related material copyright 1979 by Southwest Educational Development Laboratory and U.S. Office of Education; subsequently in public domain.)

and impact. Each booklet offers positive information, plus several activities and stories and games. Parents can use them with their children to help sharpen critical awareness about TV stereotyping, distortions, plots, motivations of characters, commercial advertising, and selective viewing. The booklets succinctly cite research data. They emphasize information and especially analyzing one's TV use and one's own thinking about topics noted earlier. Materials are generally not judgmental (yet not valueless because implying them) but leave it to parents and individual viewers to form their own conclusions after being prompted to think about their TV experiences. Printed materials parallel the outlines and suggestions for teacher-training workshops: Interaction among groups should be free-form, with only limited positive data and no recommendations or conclusions to direct discussions. Resource and reference material is provided in the appendices but is not keyed into the workshop guidelines for discussion; that limits its efficient practical use.

*Printed Material for Children.*   Booklets and a board game involve children in media-related activities. Seven booklets of a "frog fable" featured episodes about that animal and a young girl. Both characters are depicted observing the workings of a television station; through them young readers learn about technical production of programs and the editing involved in entertainment, news, and commercials. A teacher's manual describes the "research basis" and the "rationale" for each of the seven storybooks. These fanciful stories developed for youngsters' level of comprehension cover topics such as judicious use of viewing time, distinguishing program elements in TV and also fact from fantasy, psychological implications of advertising, and each of the other eight elements in the USOE definition.

Similarly, the TV Discovery Game is based on research about youth's perceptions of TV's structure, purposes, and manner of presenting fiction along with ads and news. The board game is played while watching television. Cards with questions about their concurrent viewing are intended to prompt children's awareness of specific elements in programs and commercials, particularly when parents participate to judge answers as right or wrong. Undercut, however, is the child's experience of TV as TV; it becomes a vehicle for the board game that leads to a "winner" rather than to a fuller experience of the senses and emotions with their own coherence and for their own sake. (Recall Anderson's cautions about judging children as if they were adults with similarly mature reactions.)

*Testing and Evaluation.*   Materials developed in this USOE-underwritten project were evaluated in 26 states by over 100 teachers who used the materials with their students, and by more than 70 families in 24 states. Some minor modifications resulted, mostly slight changes in wording. According to project director Charles Colder-Bolz (1980a), "the evaluation results indicate that the materials significantly and substantially increase elementary school-age children's critical TV skills" (p. 38).

*Assessment.*   The entire project was grounded on research findings that the major predictor of children's perception and use of TV is how their parents use it. SEDL's intent was to help children see TV as only a representation of life, not life itself, and to interpret those depictions as filtered through a medium. Further, television as an art form was to be evaluated as an aesthetic, artistic, and "artificial" presentation. All was to be accomplished without intrusive curricular additions but by linking present TV usage with traditional classroom studies, utilizing parents in the home as crucial to the developmental process.

While emphasizing the medium of television for its own sake, the materials often employ television to enhance study of language arts, social studies, and similar subject areas. The project uses television as a resource for learning other skills; it harnesses TV to serve teachers' needs in teaching specific academic and social concepts. As with a number of other CVS projects, the effort here is to teach both with television and about it.

But larger themes of ethical/moral value-judgments are not part of the SEDL approach to CVS.

The role of parents and teachers is emphasized in activities suggested on cards and in other materials. Clearly dominant in the SEDL's project is mediation, which—to use Anderson's (1983, p. 302) phrasing—is "essentially protectionistic in its approach and therapeutic in its outcomes." The project director noted that parental interaction directed toward programs viewed—not mere presence while children watch TV—is "critical," based on research studies conducted by SEDL (Colder-Bolz, 1980b, pp. 106–118). Parents are to serve as "primary social agents" to complement, clarify, and inoculate against television as a "secondary" but significant agency of social information affecting children's understanding.

## WNET/THIRTEEN, NEW YORK CITY (GRADES 6–8)

Noncommercial television station WNET's Education Division had been serving educators in the New York area since 1972, by visiting schools to conduct workshops in critical television viewing skills. With funding from USOE in 1978 it began to develop and test formalized curriculum materials and to conduct training sessions across the country for both educators and community leaders. Ten such sessions were planned for school administrators and teacher trainers in the United States to assist them in conducting their own CVS workshops for teachers. A similar number of sessions was planned for community leaders and public librarians in the country to help them present workshops to parents and children, focusing on home-viewing.

*Purposes and Procedures.*   As with other grade-school CVS programs, this was intended to be an integral part of language arts or social studies curricula as well as to be used at home. Teachers who field-tested the original material recommended as options: (a) an intensive mini-course of three to five class periods per week through 5 weeks; or (b) one activity as a small part of each regular class period throughout a semester or school year; or (c) as a series of mini-courses, clustering two or three consecutive chapters at a time; or (d) simply selecting material from throughout the workbook as it related to current class work in a given subject.

Creators of the WNET/Thirteen material emphasize (Kane, 1980) that this CVS curriculum is also a "critical *thinking* course" because skills can be applied to reading, math, social studies, and other disciplines: "A major objective of the curriculum is, in fact, to show students the relationship between television and the printed word" (p. 13). They also noted that the curriculum did not seek to increase or decrease a person's use of television, or even to change their viewing to different programs, but only to prompt them to reflect on their TV experience and assess it for themselves. (This is, of course, both a strength and a weakness.) They acknowledged that, because the materials can be used in sixth through eighth grade (or, variously, Grades 5 to 9—in some of their literature), the text might be too sophisticated for younger students or too obvious in parts for older students. Teachers on the scene were asked to adapt the assignments to the appropriate cognitive levels.

*Pretesting and Evaluation.*   In 1978 the staff formulated its curriculum goals and objectives with the aid of an advisory committee of dozens of educators, curriculum designers, media specialists (including prominent broadcasters and TV critics), teachers, and parents.[1] They then conferred with teachers and students to assess viability of the proposed objectives. Next, they drafted the text while consulting professionals in television and education (including language arts specialists, school administrators, and classroom teachers). In 1979 a com-

**Purpose:** To identify news sources.

**1. Start-up**

a) **Say:** Do you remember when you received your homeroom assignment for this school year? How did you find out? Who told you? (Probably a letter from the school, the teacher or a friend. Accept any reasonable response.) You got your information from a **source**. The person who informed you was your source. Reporters also have sources of information. Do you think you would prefer some sources over others? For example, would you prefer to learn your new homeroom from your friend, your teacher, or your neighbor? (Accept reasonable responses. Students might prefer receiving the information from a teacher rather than a friend who may have limited information or a neighbor who may not be connected with the school at all.)

b) **Say:** I will give you another example. Let's say there has just been a major marathon race. From what source would you prefer to learn about (sample answers are given in italics):
- the rules of the race? *(a marathon judge, the runners)*
- the history of marathon races? *(a professional runner, a marathon coach, a historian)*
- the crowd's reactions? *(a member of the crowd)*
- the runners' attitudes about marathon training? *(people close to the runners, such as relatives or coaches)*
- the winner's reaction? *(the winning runner)*

c) If time allows, you may want to discuss preferred sources for learning about a world event. Point out that it is not probable that students will ever speak directly to those involved in the event. Encourage students to discuss how this might affect their choice of news media.

**2. To Do Activity A**
Read the top half of the page with students.

**3. Follow-up**
To reinforce the content of the page. Read the following statements out loud. Ask students to complete each sentence.
- Sources give a reporter *(information about an event)*.
- Sources can be *(people who were involved in the event or who saw it happen)*.
- Sources can be *(experts on topics involved)*.
- Sources can be *(reports in other media)*.

**4. To Do Activity B**
Read the definitions of the five types of sources with students.

---

## V. Looking For The Source

"When I watch a TV news report I try to figure out where the reporter got the information for the story."

**A. What is a source?**

One way reporters find out about events is that they are at the event when it happens. But usually they need more information to do a complete story. Sources give a reporter information about an event.

Sources can be people who were involved in the event or who saw it happen. Sources can be experts on the topic involved. Sources can even be reports in other media.

Knowing who the source is helps you decide:
- whether or not the statements are complete,
- whether you are hearing fact or opinion,
- if the story affects you,
- if you need to find out more information,
- where to find more information.

**B. What are the different kinds of sources?**

**1. The main source**
These are the people who are involved in the event. If possible the reporter interviews these people directly. We may see and hear the interview. If the story is about a disagreement, the reporter may interview two main sources — one from each side.

**2. People close to the main source**
These are people who know about the event. They may be friends or relatives of the main source. They may be official representatives of the main source. They may be people who just happened to be watching as bystanders. If a TV reporter talks to one of these sources, we may see and hear the interview as part of the television report.

**3. Reporters**
Sometimes reporters themselves were at the event when it happened. They may be the only people you see and hear during the report on TV. They may give the report from the scene of the event or from the TV news set in a studio.

**4. Other Media**
Reporters sometimes get information from other media, such as newspapers, magazines, radio, books or journals.

**5. Experts on the topic**
These are people who are not involved in the event being reported on, but they do know a great deal about the topic.

74

---

FIG. 5.3. Sample pages of teacher's manual with integrated pages reproduced from student workbook. From Kane (1980) *Critical Television Viewing: A Language Skills Work-A-Text: Teacher's Annotated Edition.* (Copyright © 1980 by Educational Broadcasting Corporation, Inc. until entered public domain after 1987.)

C. Which sources do you trust most?

When you watch the news on TV, you will be hearing from many sources. It is important for you to decide if you are hearing the story from the source you trust the most. If not, you might want to see if you can find the source you trust the most in another news media.

1. Here are four reports about two teen-agers who were lost in the woods. On the line above each report, identify the type of source. Use a number from the Source Key.

**Source Key**
1 — The main source
2 — People close to the main source
3 — A reporter
4 — Other media
5 — Experts on the topic

a) Source _____ 3 and/or 4

"This is HLK reporter, Getty Scoop. I was at the scene when the rescue team found the teenagers. They were in a forest at the foot of the mountain and looked tired but relieved."

b) Source _____ 3

"This is Paul Anchor for 'Eye Saw It News.' The New York Times reported today that two teen-agers, who spent a freezing night lost in the woods, survived what could have been a fatal tragedy by keeping awake throughout the night."

c) Source _____ 2

"We are happy that our children are alive and well. We knew they'd have the good sense to share the food in their backpacks and to stay awake."

d) Source _____ 1

"We knew it would be best to stay in the general area and to keep walking. Luckily, we had some candy, but we had no matches. We were glad when we saw the rescue team in the forest."

2. Look back at the sources and the reports. Circle the source you would trust the most. On a separate piece of paper, write a paragraph giving three reasons why you trust that source most. Consider these questions:
   a) Are you hearing fact or opinion?          Answers will vary.
   b) How does the story affect you?
   c) If you need more information, where would you be most likely to find it?

75

**5. To Do Activity C**

a) Read the paragraph at the top of the page and the directions to #1 with students. If necessary, students can refer to the previous page to review the different kinds of sources.

You might point out to students that the news report is based on the same true event as the script in Chapter 3.

b) Have students write in answers to #1.

*Here are some sample advantages and disadvantages of each source:*

■ Getty Scoop has the perspective of an on-the-scene witness, but to only part of the drama. Certainly the rescue team could provide details as to the state the teens were in when rescued.

■ The parents of the teens can't add any factual information about the ordeal or rescue, but the human interest aspect could be useful as a feature.

■ The teens' account is potentially the most accurate and factual, yet people just out of a perilous situation may not be able to recount what has happened to them with great accuracy after having been in such a stressful situation.

■ For b, students may answer 3 (a reporter) and/or 4 (other media). In the example, the reporter clearly identifies his source as The New York Times. The viewer's source however, is Paul Anchor, the reporter on "Eye Saw It News."

c) Students will need additional paper to complete #2. Answers should be supported with reasons.

**6. Follow-up**

a) Conduct a class discussion in which students share their answers and reasoning for their responses to #2.

b) Ask students to become reporters for their school. Suggest that in addition to current events, students could investigate and write about the history of the school and community or research and prepare biographies of some teachers.

Fig. 5.3 (*Continued*)

mercial research firm evaluated the material, based on field tests among 45 teachers and over 1,300 students in six school districts: Newark, New Jersey; Nashville, Tennessee; Lafayette Parish, Louisiana; Stamford, Connecticut; Palo Alto, California; and Salt Lake City/Sandy, Utah. Finally, the text was revised and reviewed to confirm compatibility with curriculum goals currently in U.S. schools.

*Support Materials for Teachers.*    The workbook text is complemented by a 160-page *Teacher's Annotated Edition*. That manual reproduces each page of the student workbook reduced to half a page (see Fig. 5.3). Surrounding each boxed half-size student page are detailed explanatory notes; they include "overall purpose," "rationale," and guidelines for leading discussion on specific topics and for directing student activities from the workbook.

The information is well suited to student exercises; it is clearly and briefly stated, yet complete. Cross-references to other parts of the "Work-A-Text" curriculum as well as recommendations for further related activity are provided throughout the teacher's guide.

*Printed Materials for Students.*    WNET's original "Criti-Kit" grew into *Critical Television Viewing: A Language Skills Work-A-Text* (complemented by the *Teacher's Annotated Edition*). Writing and thinking skills included in the exercises are listed for each of the ten chapters. Skills relate to reading and observation, criticism and judgment, composition, listening and speaking, and media interpretation. Although television is the direct subject of the students' activities, related cognitional learning specifically includes: recognizing main ideas, classifying details, recognizing and interpreting literary elements (characterization, plot, conflict, setting, mood, tone, theme, point of view), sequencing, symbolism; making inferences, drawing conclusions, interpreting graphs and charts, distinguishing fact/opinion, reasoning and examples, developing criteria for evaluating, persuasive language, stereotyping; descriptive writing, writing summaries, business letters, essays, reviews, short stories; conducting interviews, role-playing, using sound effects, recognizing dialects; analyzing presentations, techniques, and effects of a variety of media, relating media to one's own life, developing standards for evaluating media.

The text offers "non-judgmental" data for study, emphasizing the structure and process of developing television entertainment, news, and commercials. Interpretative areas include reflection on one's use of TV: the amount of time, the selection, and the reasons (chapter 1); persuasive advertising and programs (chapter 5); criticism of television content (chapters 8–9); and assessment of one's own television diet (chapter 10).

Daily exercises are combined into composite reviews at the end of each unit. Additional activities are suggested.

No other support materials or special film or television equipment are needed to implement the project. The workbook includes many reproductions of photographs and TV scenes to clarify concepts and provide examples; numerous line-drawings add interest (although some are rather jejune).

*Assessment.* Work-pages for students are well designed and well organized. Most offer basic information, then provide blanks for students to answer the nondirective questions. Apt examples illustrate explanations about media. Graphs, charts, and checklists illuminate the subject. Layouts are clean and attractive, with clear headings and subheads to clarify relationships in developing the topic. Occasionally, instructions for students seem extremely explicit and obvious, overly simplified. At those points the text is less mature or sophisticated than that developed for the K–5 age group by the Southwest Laboratory; for example, on p. 33, examples of 1-shot and 2-shot camera views are described, followed by the question: "Guess what a shot of three people or objects is called? Write in your answer on this line" (for eighth graders?).

But the content is appropriate for WNET's objectives and intended participants. In fact, the complex project in chapter 7 asks students to schedule a network's programming based on program strategies (p. 114). Again, mature research is needed for suggested "follow-up" activity: "Ask students if a TV program they like has ever been canceled (or if one that they dislike has been kept on the air). Have them investigate why by studying old ratings, reviews, contacting executives at local TV stations or writing to network executives" (p. 115). Later, students are told that program ideas should be submitted by registered mail to protect their creative rights in a property (p. 117)!

This projects eschews explaining much about economic bases of the business of broadcasting. The first reference to financial considerations, including advertising as it relates to audience size, is in a half-sentence almost "thrown away" on p. 43 of the students' workbook. Even the following chapter on advertising focuses on commercials as a form of persuasion, with "target audience" the only concept related to economic considerations. (But paradoxically, students are told about writing to major ratings companies to obtain tabulated statistics about program audiences.) This CVS project clearly stresses the creative and artistic or literary aspect of the medium, not the socioeconomic-political structure and its causal impact on programs and audiences.

Not until the last 10 pages of the students' 120-page workbook are good analytical materials presented, such as the recommendation to write letters to broadcasters (too late to incorporate TV managers' responses into course discussions). Another weakness is the absence of exercises to stretch the students' experience of different and some-times "quality" material available through television—which tends to be overlooked or unknown among youngsters. Only the final para-graphs of the workbook's last page mention that students might watch something else on TV they haven't seen before. But in these final pages an exercise does nicely guide students to apply newly learned perceptions and skills towards planning their own diet of future televiewing.

The teacher's edition of the workbook provides very detailed guide-lines, including step-by-step directives for student activities. This is perhaps the clearest, best organized, and easy-to-use teacher's guide available among CVS projects, because the format of combined texts keys all commentary directly to the student workbook sheets re-produced on the same pages. This eliminates shuffling back and forth between teacher's guide and student workbook or hand-out materials; everything is bound in a single series of successive pages.

## FAR WEST LABORATORY FOR EDUCATIONAL RESEARCH AND DEVELOPMENT (GRADES 9–12)

A third project funded by the United States Office of Education in 1978 (for 2 years, as with other CVS projects) was directed to second-ary schoolers. The Far West Laboratory for Educational Research and Development (FWL) was principal contractor with a grant of $410,000.

*Purposes and Procedures.*  FWL's mission was described as fourfold: to identify TV skills apt for teenagers; to develop and field-test curric-ulum materials for student, teachers, and families; to prepare training material and to conduct workshops for educators, parents, and leaders of organizations; and to publish and distribute those materials.[2]

The FWL first outlined an initial curriculum based on research literature.[3] Those data were complemented by experiences and obser-vations of the two panels, plus the staffs of FWL and the two sub-contractors. They determined that their CVS classroom-oriented cur-riculum should involve four areas of critical viewing abilities:

> To be able to evaluate and manage one's own television viewing behavior,
>
> to question the reality of television programs,
>
> to recognize the persuasive arguments and messages on TV and to be able to counterargue, and
>
> to recognize the effects of television on one's own life. (p. 122)

They later added a fifth skill: "the ability to use television as a mechanism to enhance family communications." For this they developed a special booklet, "A Family Guide to Television," to complement the classroom materials.

To develop those skills, the curriculum sought to help students understand television's economics and regulation and how TV programs are produced. The curriculum stressed "an experiential activity-oriented approach to learning." It sought progressive growth in knowledge and skills, and use of primary materials where possible (such as scripts, industry and government documents). It stressed critical thinking skills relative to television: prompting students to form questions about TV, to find how to get information for answers, and then to evaluate and draw conclusions from those answers. The curriculum also sought to reinforce skills in reading, writing, speaking, and listening.

The basic premise of Far West Laboratories states (Lieberman, 1980a, p. 3): "As viewers, students can develop standards of judgment to determine for themselves their own best use of television." Those standards are gradually formed from practical everyday experience of TV, coupled with learning what this curriculum text provides, and then reflecting about it all. "Students do require training to develop the ability to analyze and evaluate those messages, know the capabilities and limitation of this medium, and make conscious decisions about when and what to watch."

FWL decided to use print as the medium for presenting their curriculum lest it depend on availability of video equipment in classrooms, and also so it could be either presented as an independent course or integrated into language arts, social studies, or communication courses. They developed seven units for the curriculum, presented in a textbook, a teachers' guide, and a thick set of worksheets for local copying and distribution (see Fig. 5.4).

*Pretesting and Evaluation.* FWL was assisted by the Office of Radio and Television for Learning at public station WGBH-TV in Boston, which wrote curriculum materials, and by Educational Testing Service, which reviewed and helped revise draft materials based on evaluations by 35 educators in 14 states. FWL also formed two panels—one of parents–teachers, the other of students—to help work out details of the project's mission.

Three dozen reviewers enlisted by ETS across the country rated the draft material highly. They favorably noted its effort to address teenagers as adults able to comprehend a broad view of the medium, its stress on creative thinking and writing, the concepts reflecting many disciplines, and the range of activities suggested. But many ques-

FIG. 5.4. Worksheets, book, poster, teacher's guide, and workshop handout pages developed under grant from U.S. Office of Education, 1980, by Far West Laboratory for Educational Research and Development, San Francisco, and WGBH Educational Foundation, Boston.

tioned whether students with poor reading ability would benefit adequately from the material.

Project staff members, panelists, and consultants revised the original draft to reduce the level of reading difficulty, and they shortened or eliminated some readings.

During 1979–1980, the second year of the grant, 17 schools conducted "demonstration classrooms" and more than 2,200 teachers and parents attended training sessions held at national conventions across the country. Five regional "leadership workshops" were conducted in the spring of 1980 for members of school districts and state departments of education in an effort to enlist administrators in the effort to bring CVS into systematic instructional programs. Late in 1980 they distributed a list of names, business affiliations and titles, addresses, and telephone numbers of 81 persons in 31 states as "State Trainers/Critical Television Viewing."

*Support Materials for Teachers.* The well-planned and well-printed 57-page *Teacher's Guide to Inside Television* (White, 1980b) closely parallels the structure, layout, and typeface of the student textbook. It cautions that students are not to be instructed to change their viewing habits for the exercises; rather they should grow in skills "to make their own determination about how best to use television wisely" (p. xi). Teachers are urged to select and adapt exercises to the levels and needs or interests of their respective pupils. (If all "synchronized" lesson plans are followed in order, the entire course of seven units is structured for 78 days.) This is particularly important because some activities have sophisticated content and complicated procedures. Throughout, the *Teacher's Guide* offers very detailed and concrete projects as options. The manual raises valid points for reflection.

A separate set of 72 worksheets (fill-in completions, multiple choice, charts, excerpts of material for analysis, and guidelines for role-playing simulations) are carefully typed, ready for photocopying and immediate use in classrooms; they are keyed to specific sections of the printed text (see Fig. 5.5). The entire package provides a teacher with all the tools immediately necessary to present CVS study to high schoolers.

*Printed Materials for Students.* The basic document produced by FWL is a well organized, detailed, nicely laid out 161-page hardcover text for students, *Inside Television: A Guide to Critical Viewing,* by Ned White (1980a).

The author of the curriculum texts employs nondirective, inductive procedures by enlisting students in gathering personal data about viewing patterns in their own homes to compare against national statistics and other research. Classroom discussion about their findings is supplemented by excerpted readings representing diverse views about TV's role and impact in society. The kinds of questions and some of the homework assignments, of course, imply interpretations or even directives.

The textbook *Inside Television . . .* provides a variety of data, graphics (charts, graphs, photographs), and lengthy excerpts from interviews and major articles and books (see Fig. 5.6). The seven units analyze TV's pervasiveness and impact in society; the structure and processes of the American television industry, including the roles of government and advertising; programming and production; commercials and political and public-service persuasive announcements; television news, including governmental factors (First Amendment, "fairness doctrine," cross-ownership); the social environment of the medium, including stereotyping and effects; and TV's potential in the context of alternate technologies and of audiences' providing critical feedback. The author provides good succinct explanations or definitions of each new term as it occurs in the text.

Worksheet 7.4        Why I Watch TV, Now

While you are logging your viewing activities this week, keep track of the reasons why you watched those programs. Every time you turn the set on, every time you sit down to watch a set that's already on, every time a new program comes on, place a hatch mark (/) in the appropriate column below. Sometimes you may have more than one reason for starting to watch a particular program. In that case, draw hatch marks in the two or more columns that apply.

If you are watching TV for a reason not listed below, write the reason(s) in the spaces provided at the bottom.

I am watching this             Number of Times    Total    Rank
particular program because:

1.   I want to be informed or learn someth

2.   I want to relax and be entertained.

3.   I just want to kill time.

4.   I want to see something stimulating
     and exciting.

5.   I don't want to have to talk to p

6.   I want to join people (family, fr
     who are already watching.

7.   I want to forget about my proble

8.   I want to see a particular TV p
     star, sports figure, etc.

9.   I want to learn about human re

10.   I want to avoid loneliness; p
      characters on TV are good com

11.   I want to avoid certain obli
      (homework, etc.)

12.

13.

At the end of the week, total
write the number in the "Total
each program you watched durin
to 11 (or 1 to whatever number
you have in your log. (The re
one with the next most should

---

Worksheet 6.2

Who's on TV

Choose a single half-hour or hour-long dramatic program that is aired time, one you normally watch. For this exercise, make a log of all the who have speaking parts on the program and write down the information below.

| Character Number | Sex Male/Female | Approximate Age | Ethnic (White, Other-- |
|---|---|---|---|
| 1 | | | |
| 2 | | | |
| 3 | | | |
| 4 | | | |
| 5 | | | |
| 6 | | | |
| 7 | | | |
| 8 | | | |

When you've completed this part, fill in the table below from the information just gathered.

I.   Elderly Characters (approximately 65 and older)
     Total Males _____   Total Females _____   Total Elderly Characters _____
       White _____        White _____        White _____
       Black _____        Black _____        Black _____
       Other _____        Other _____        Other _____

II.   Adult Characters (approximately 20-65 years old)
     Total Males _____   Total Females _____   Total Adult Characters _____
       White _____        White _____        White _____
       Black _____        Black _____        Black _____
       Other _____        Other _____        Other _____

III.   Young People (from small children through age 20)
     Total Males _____   Total Females _____   Total Young People _____
       White _____        White _____        White _____
       Black _____        Black _____        Black _____
       Other _____        Other _____        Other _____

     Total Males, all ages _____    Total Females, all ages _____

FIG. 5.5. Sample hand-out sheets for student exercises. From White (1980a) *Inside Television: A Guide to Critical Viewing—Worksheets.* (Copyright © 1980 by Far West Laboratory for Educational Research and Development until entered public domain after August 1985.)

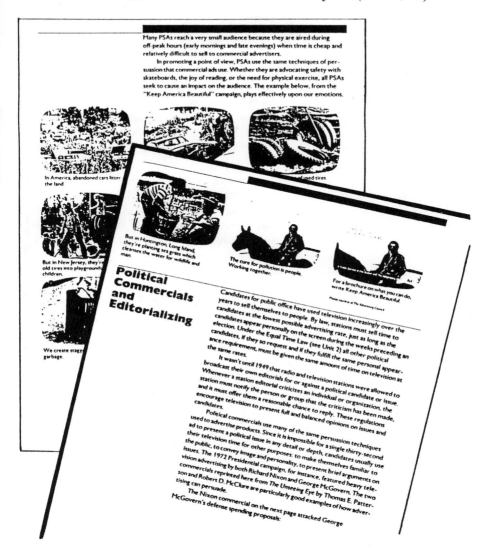

Many PSAs reach a very small audience because they are aired during off-peak hours (early mornings and late evenings) when time is cheap and relatively difficult to sell to commercial advertisers.

In promoting a point of view, PSAs use the same techniques of persuasion that commercial ads use. Whether they are advocating safety with skateboards, the joy of reading, or the need for physical exercise, all PSAs seek to cause an impact on the audience. The example below, from the "Keep America Beautiful" campaign, plays effectively upon our emotions.

In America, abandoned cars litter the land

But in Huntington, Long Island, they're planting sea grass which cleanses the water for wildlife and man.

But in New Jersey, they're old tires into playgrounds children.

We create stagg garbage.

The cure for pollution is people. Working together.

For a brochure on what you can do, write Keep America Beautiful.

## Political Commercials and Editorializing

Candidates for public office have used television increasingly over the years to sell themselves to people. By law, stations must sell time to candidates at the lowest possible advertising rate, just as long as the candidates appear personally on the screen during the weeks preceding an election. Under the Equal Time Law (see Unit 2) all other political candidates, if they so request and if they fulfill the same personal appearance requirement, must be given the same amount of time on television at the same rates.

It wasn't until 1949 that radio and television stations were allowed to broadcast their own editorials for or against a political candidate or issue. Whenever a station editorial criticizes an individual or organization, the station must notify the person or group that the criticism has been made, and it must offer them a reasonable chance to reply. These regulations encourage television to present full and balanced opinions on issues and candidates.

Political commercials use many of the same persuasion techniques used to advertise products. Since it is impossible for a single thirty-second ad to present a political issue in any detail or depth, candidates usually use their television time for other purposes: to make themselves familiar to the public, to convey image and personality, to present brief arguments on issues. The 1972 Presidential campaign, for instance, featured heavy television advertising by both Richard Nixon and George McGovern. The two commercials reprinted here from *The Unseeing Eye* by Thomas E. Patterson and Robert D. McClure are particularly good examples of how advertising can persuade.

The Nixon commercial on the next page attacked George McGovern's defense spending proposals:

FIG. 5.6. Pages from hardcover textbook on CVS. From White (1980a) *Inside Television: A Guide to Critical Viewing.* (Copyright © 1980 by Far West Laboratory for Educational Research and Development until entered public domain after August 1985.)

The teacher, of course, plays a central role in facilitating this critical viewing training. Although the students' text and worksheets are to a large extent self-contained, and despite the intent to have the teenagers discover for themselves and come to a heuristic assessment of TV in their lives, the classroom teacher will select and assign and guide the many optional activities suggested in the text. Those involve tasks for individuals and for groups; others are writing assignments; still others pose specific questions for class discussion and response. Many are to be carried out in class; others are meant to be homework assignments. For example, optional activities in Unit 2 include gathering research data on the audience ratings history of any recently canceled program; or to "buy" stock in each of the three networks and then monitor their daily price fluctuations; or again, to write to networks for their annual reports. In Unit 3, one activity is to investigate the role of unions in the economics of producing a TV program, including wage levels and restrictions on working conditions. Explaining and interpreting these activities falls to the teacher.

*Assessment.*    This is one of the most carefully orchestrated and instantly usable sets of material for CVS training found among the projects studied for this report.

The author of *Inside Television* . . . sustains the premise that this project does not impose value-judgments but rather sources of data and varying interpretations so that students may arrive at personal conclusions about television and their use of the medium. Generally the commentary is brief and balanced, and it progressively covers key points, aided by thought-provoking interviews and reprints of readings integrated into the text. However, on a few points the text presents a broad negative statement or overstated or misleading comments not fully supported by research findings but rather by assertions of critics or practitioners quoted in the excerpts. The accompanying worksheets do lead students to reflect on their own specific patterns of viewing, and to assign personal reasons for viewing.

The contents cover a wide range of topic areas. But some sections seem very heavily detailed with factual data that may be confusing, even frustrating, to high school students. (At times, the text seems almost more appropriate to junior college and beyond.) Beginning the text with arcane demographics and detailed analysis of complicated ratings seems daunting, although germane to the opening of topic of TV's place in today's society. Similarly in later sections, and in some worksheets, technical points from research and the professional industry seem unnecessarily complicated (e.g., agency's buying of TV spots in a "scatter plan" and the networks' "step deal" with program producers, too much about quarter-hour average shares, and excessive use of business' argot or "in-terms"). Worksheet exercises are well worked out but sometimes ask for too complex detail (such as logging specific characters with speaking parts in programs, by age, gender, and ethnic status—while viewing the programs at home.)

Although the layout design of *Inside Television* . . . is organized and consistent, it is sometimes difficult to coordinate various books and worksheets by using the subsection numbers; and the text at times seems cluttered, with little white-space to help show relationships between material and to highlight sectional divisions.

Discussion questions suggested in the *Teacher's Guide* contribute to the broader CVS purposes. Although nondirective, the questions guide students to evaluate their patterns of TV experience. In that manual, succinct, clear, and usually accurate summaries of many complex and significant topics are provided for the teacher (such as the "fairness doctrine" and implications of cross-ownership). Regrettably, only the final pages recommend specific procedures for audience feedback, including where to write to networks, stations, and government to pose questions or lodge complaints. It would be enlightening as well as useful for students to engage in this activity during the course, so that responses could be shared with the class.

*Related Activities.* The Far West Laboratory also conducted training workshops, for which they prepared a *Trainer's Manual* of 25 pages plus appendices, and a 17-page booklet of *Workshop Handouts* (Lieberman, 1980a, 1980b). The workshops were designed to guide teachers, parents, and community leaders wanting to help young people learn how to become more knowledgeable and discriminating users of television, specifically by using the textbook *Inside Television* in their classrooms, homes, and organizations. The two booklets were designed to help "trainers" set up and run the workshops (names and addresses of 80 such trainers in 31 states were listed in Appendix C of Volume I, *Trainer's Manual*).

The *Manual* briefly states the rationale for workshops about critical viewing training, and offers concrete agenda for structuring and running them (including hour-by-hour schedule and audio-visual materials). As with the basic curriculum, FWL's approach is to prompt reflection and to elicit discussion about participants' own observations and judgments about TV. The manual suggests sample activities similar to those in the curriculum, including viewing TV and writing critiques about programs, filling in selected worksheets, and visiting TV stations for information. It includes a three-page grid that cross-references 46 worksheets (by name and page number) and 35 activities

Workshop Activity Ideas
from INSIDE TELEVISION's
Student Activities and Worksheets

| Worksheet Subject | Worksheet Number | Warm-Up | Economics | English | Home Economics | Humanities | Journalism | Mass Media | Psychology | Social Studies | Video Production |
|---|---|---|---|---|---|---|---|---|---|---|---|
| TV Viewing Questionnaire | 1/1 | x | x |  | x |  | x | x | x | x |  |
| Favorite Programs | 1/2 | x |  | x |  | x |  | x | x |  | x |
| Viewing Log | 1/3 |  |  |  | x | x | x | x | x | x |  |
| Evening Viewing Log | 1/4 |  |  |  | x | x | x | x | x | x |  |
| Why I Watch TV | 1/5 | x |  | x | x | x | x | x | x | x | x |
| Class Evening Viewing | 1/6 |  | x | x | x | x | x | x | x | x |  |
| Class Percentage | 1/7 |  | x | x | x | x | x | x | x | x |  |
| Class Totals | 1/8 | x |  | x | x | x | x | x | x | x | x |
| The Ratings Game | 2/1 |  | x | x | x | x | x | x | x | x |  |
| The Prime Time Game | 2/2 |  | x |  |  | x |  | x | x | x | x |
| Complete the Schedule | 2/3 | x | x | x |  |  |  | x | x | x |  |
| Plotting "Gifts" | 3/1 |  |  | x |  |  |  |  |  |  | x |
| Lassie: "The Challenge" | 3/2 |  |  | x |  |  |  |  |  |  | x |
| 30 Minutes | 3/3 |  |  | x | x | x |  | x |  |  | x |
| The Soaps | 3/4 |  |  | x |  |  |  |  |  |  | x |
| Good Times | 3/5 |  |  | x |  |  |  |  |  |  | x |
| Life Script vs. TV Script | 3/6 |  |  | x |  |  |  |  |  |  | x |
| **419 Calif. St.** |  |  |  |  |  |  |  |  |  |  |  |
| Intro. to Characters | 1 |  |  | x |  | x |  |  |  |  | x |
| Developing Characters | 2 |  |  | x |  | x |  |  |  |  | x |
| Plot Development | 3 |  |  | x |  | x |  |  |  |  | x |
| Script Development | 4 |  |  | x |  | x |  |  |  |  | x |
| TV Drama | 5 |  |  | x |  | x |  |  |  |  | x |
| Count the Shots | 4/1 |  |  | x |  |  |  | x |  |  | x |
| The Pitch | 4/2 |  |  | x | x |  |  | x | x | x | x |
| Fill in the Video | 4/3 |  |  | x |  | x |  | x | x |  | x |
| Write a Commercial | 4/4 |  |  | x | x |  |  | x | x | x | x |
| Choose Your News | 5/1 |  |  | x | x | x | x | x | x | x |  |
| Compare Newscasts | 5/2 |  |  | x | x | x | x | x |  | x | x |
| Local News Log | 5/3 |  |  | x | x | x | x | x |  | x | x |

FIG. 5.7.   Grid of subject areas apt for CVS topics, drawn from White's (1980a) *Inside Television* book and worksheets. From Lieberman (1980a) *Volume I: Trainer's Manual—Critical T.V. Viewing Workshops for High School Teachers, Parents, and Community Leaders*. (No copyright noted, but organization's other material copyright 1980 until entered public domain after August 1985.)

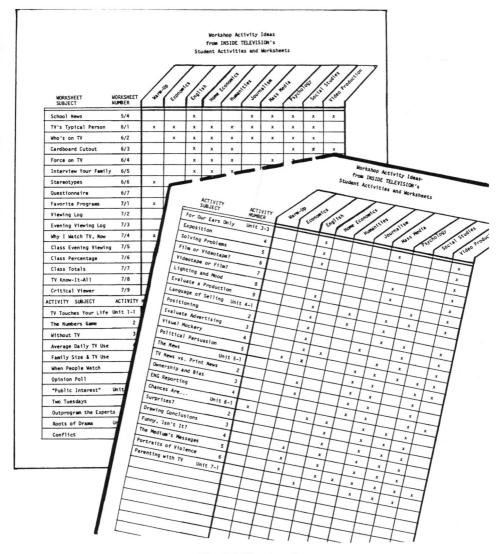

Fig. 5.7 *(Continued)*

(by unit and number) to related or cognate academic areas: economics, English, home economics, humanities, journalism, mass media, psychology, social studies, and video production (see Fig. 5.7). It also includes samples of posters and flyer announcements as well as of pithy outlines for overhead projection during workshop presentations.

Volume II, *Workshop Handouts,* provides printed materials that can be reproduced for distribution to participants. They include restatements of the purpose, structure, and components of FWL's total curriculum package of materials; a "TV Fact Sheet" with 16 statistical information items, a five-page bibliography, a two-page "Resource List of Organizations"; and a reprint of their eight-page folder, "A Family Guide to Television." The latter offers a sampler of data from the curriculum text—in checklists and multiple-choice questions plus brief quotations—offering families one-time exposure to data about social implications of television.

Some form of compiled findings about the results of this project was said to exist in the early 1980s, as were valuative comments by workshop participants; but they were not readily available. Later information acknowledged no such report.[4]

## BOSTON UNIVERSITY (POST-SECONDARY AND ADULTS)

The final project in the USOE series was conducted by the School of Public Communication at Boston University. Funded for approximately $400,000, it began in September 1978, and ended on July 31, 1981.

*Purposes.*    This project was directed to college students and especially to teachers and parents, with the purpose of having some impact on the medium itself, according to project director Donis Dondis (1980):

> The effort must be begun with adults: the parents, teachers—the present and future gatekeepers [*sic*]—and the producers of television programming if we are to have any influence on the young minds growing up in front of the television screen. (p. 51)

This intent was stated more specifically in a pamphlet that emphasized the role of critical viewing skills for adults in continuing education programs, non-profit organizations, and community groups. According to a pamphlet (Dondis, ca. 1980), such training "enables these audiences, in their present or future roles as parents, educators, business people, and community leaders, to comprehend and influence programming decisions" (p. 3).

*Pretesting.*    Preliminary curriculum materials were tested at nine locations in the United States, then revised. They consisted of four sets of interrelated but self-contained textbooks, workbooks, and instructors' guides. The respective topic areas were: Television literacy (technical, aesthetic, and social aspects), persuasive programming (commercials and public/political announcements), entertainment programming (forms, formats, and production characteristics), and informational programming (news, documentaries, and public affairs—including visual, economic, governmental, and ethical factors influencing content and coverage).

A series of day-long (6-hour) workshops was held throughout the country beginning in the spring of 1980. Conducted by project staff members from Boston University, they sought to provide teachers and parents with practical experience in using the curriculum materials. These activities involved "several hundred [persons] in all categories" of families, schools, churches, and organizations.[5]

In both 1981 and 1985 questionnaire surveys, project principals responded that they had compiled no formal evaluations, other findings or measured effects, or documented reactions and appraisals by leaders or participants.

*Printed Materials for Students and Teachers.*   Initially, the first module in the series of four was labeled "Television Literacy." The four sets of spiral-bound typewritten texts and workbooks for the modules were subsequently combined into a single staple-bound book of 158 pages (the textbook portion was compactly typeset), under an umbrella title *Television Literacy.*[6] The first portion was retitled "Behind the Scenes," whereas the three others retained their original titles relating to forms of programming: persuasive, entertainment, and informational. The text in both versions remained essentially the same, almost verbatim. Space and cost were conserved by eliminating the excellent large photographs, the lengthy readings (20 to 29 pages of several major excerpts in each module) and bibliographies, some charts or multiple samples of scripts, and much white space.

Each of the four curriculum components (or modules) contains six sections. Each section presents introductory information followed by various exercises, both from the workbook and also based on outside activities. Instructors' guides supplement the texts with itemized learning objectives, background material, questions for discussion and quizzes, and other class exercises. Teachers are urged to select freely and flexibly to suit the needs of their students.

Module #1 covers the organizational structure of the American television industry, production techniques, the creative process in programming, the economics of TV as a business, federal regulation of broadcasting, and some aspects of TV's effects. Module #2 focuses on persuasive program announcements, including kinds of appeals, impact and effects, methods to affect attention and interest and credibility, claims, the form and structure of commercials, and kinds of

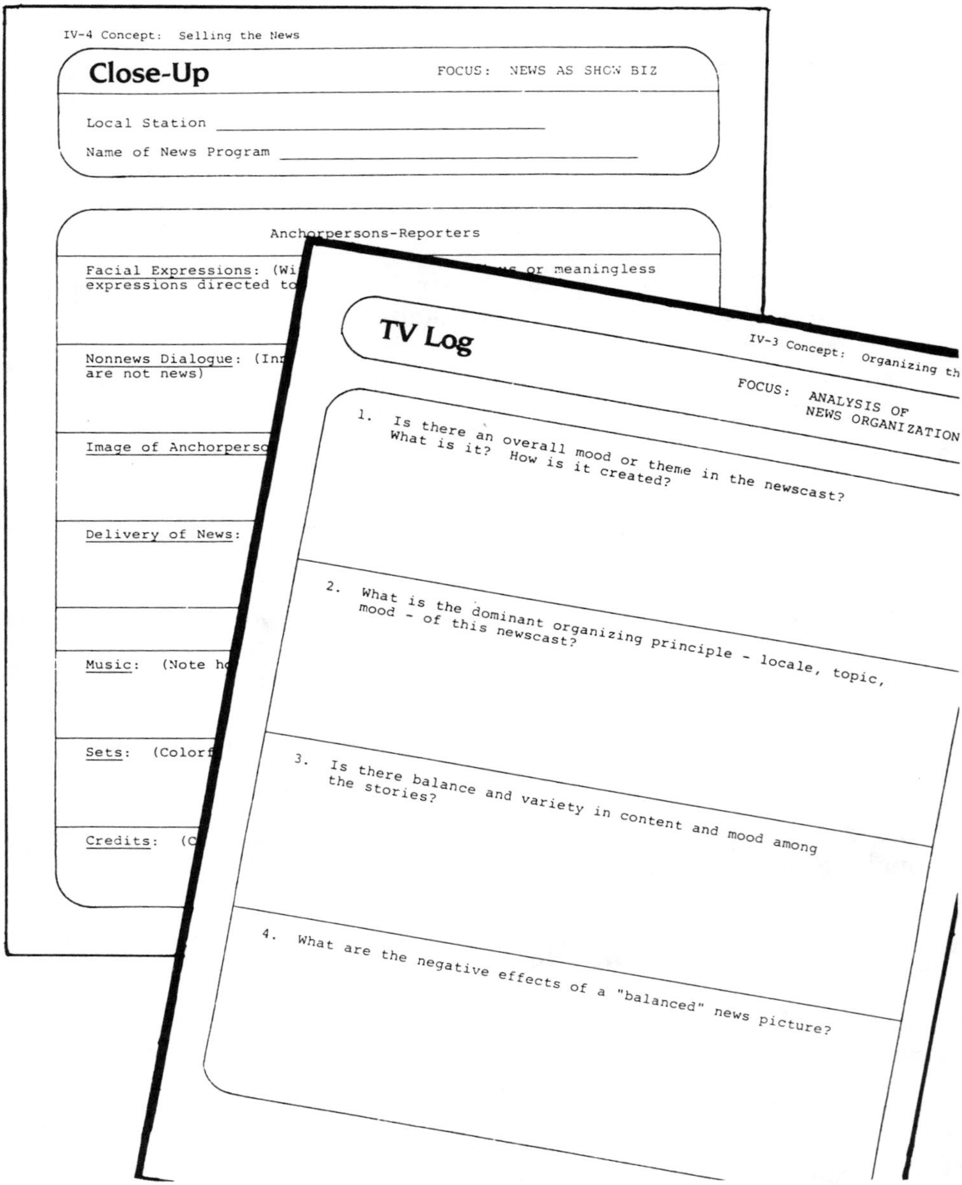

IV-4 Concept:  Selling the News

## Close-Up

FOCUS:  NEWS AS SHOW BIZ

Local Station _____

Name of News Program _____

Anchorpersons-Reporters

Facial Expressions: (Wi_____ or meaningless
expressions directed to_____

Nonnews Dialogue: (In_____
are not news)

Image of Anchorperso_____

Delivery of News:_____

Music:   (Note h_____

Sets:   (Color_____

Credits:   (C_____

## TV Log

IV-3 Concept:  Organizing th

FOCUS:  ANALYSIS OF
NEWS ORGANIZATION

1.  Is there an overall mood or theme in the newscast?
    What is it?  How is it created?

2.  What is the dominant organizing principle - locale, topic,
    mood - of this newscast?

3.  Is there balance and variety in content and mood among
    the stories?

4.  What are the negative effects of a "balanced" news picture?

FIG. 5.8.   Student exercise sheets for CVS assignments. From Barnett
(1981) *Television Literacy: Critical Television Viewing Skills—Workbook.*
(Copyright © 1981 by the Trustees of Boston University until entered
public domain after 1990.)

advertising research and testing. Module #3 analyzes the structure and ingredients of prime-time shows, entertainment themes, social behavior as reflected in popular programming, genres of talk-game-variety programs, and TV as popular culture. Module #4 explores origins and social-governmental constraints on television news, gathering and selecting as well as organizing news, influence of commercial sponsorship, mutual impact of government and news media, and documentaries and special news coverage (see Fig. 5.8).

The text and workbook as well as instructor's guides are nondirective. They offer a range of information and viewpoints, with a minimum of interpretation, so that CVS trainees can arrive at their own observations and judgments.

*Assessment.* In general, the authors of these CVS materials provide a useful range of background information, factual data, and apt quotations about most of the topics so that teachers and students gain essential knowledge about the complexity and interacting factors involved in television. They offer jejune treatment of topics, usually factually correct (except for some technical legal aspects of news, politics, and controversy as well as several other points regarding advertising, and audience research). The tightly written information is augmented by fuller details developed in workbook exercises—not merely redundant applications but developing the text's information Despite occasional overload of technical jargon ("inside stuff" from the broadcast industry) the language is appropriate for adults in its vocabulary and succinct style. The body of the text includes clear rather than ponderous citations of sources. Some workbook exercises are excessively detailed ("busy-work") for the intended benefits. But most prompt one to systematically gather factual data by first-hand experience of media and then to reflect on implications of those findings.

The text's neutral posture in explaining how and why things happen in television might make the entire project seem supportive of the status quo in American broadcasting. But this does not necessarily imply that "to know it is to accept it." The whole point of CVS is to increase knowledge and sensitivity to what happens in the total television experience, in order to develop perception and discrimination—precisely not accepting it as an absolute, immutable "given." Often the data presented are themselves neutral or favorable to the current system of commercial broadcasting. But readings (regrettably omitted in the revised version), discussion questions, and even some exercises guide participants to more thoughtful analysis of what goes into television, what comes out of it, and to what effect. These characteristics of factual foundation and balance, plus discussion points and exercises are reflected in the treatment of controverted topics. Topics include the economic-legal structure of the television industry, commercial advertising, consumer activist versus corporation/advertiser, research into behavioral effects, program stereotyping of male/females and minorities, treatment of sex, family trends in programming, sources of non-objectivity in news, and factors affecting presentation of news in an entertainment medium. Sample items: "lack of seriousness and sensitivity that surrounds sex on television"; "the difficulty TV creators have in portraying reality in a dramatic form"; viewers "are encouraged to sift through all the chatter of typical talk shows and search for interesting and often valuable information." The books in the bibliography reflect this balanced appraisal of television's multifaceted role in contemporary society. Although optimistic, the authors' stance is not naive; nor is it cynical, despite quotations from highly critical books by Jerry Mander, Ben Stein, and Frank Mankiewicz and Joel Swerdlow.

The revised format of the text offers a readable, comprehensive, and coherent outline, to provide a source-book for individuals selecting only portions of the total curriculum. Similarly, workbook sheets are arranged in a format easy to select and reproduce for class use.

*          *          *

Because these four pilot projects were funded by the U.S. Office of Education, their handsome publications are all in the public domain. Curriculum designers and classroom teachers will find in the pretested (but not formally evaluated) projects—developed by competent collaborators nationwide—paradigms for their own TV literacy curricula. They can also literally reproduce the well-structured and detailed texts, readings, exercises, and worksheets for use in their CVS courses.

Following this national perspective, the next chapter reviews systematic CVS instruction in local school districts.

## NOTES

1. One consultant to the project was David R. Sirota, PhD, of the Institute of Film and Television at New York University's School of the Arts. He cautioned against the unfeasible challenge of attempting serious television criticism, especially because the "medium's social and cultural force [is] often seen at odds with education at all levels." He feared that introducing commercial television and discussion thereof into the classroom would corrupt formal education. He warned that TV's entering the schoolroom "bestows upon it a cred-

ibility and legitimization [and] a sanctioned place within the context of public education." He cited social thinkers to whom "the introduction of commercial broadcasting into the school system would be seen at best as socially and culturally deteriorating and at worst cataclysmic." He himself seemed to denigrate any positive value in television viewing by grudgingly admitting that formal study might inoculate viewers against the medium's destructive impact: "Granted, developing a critical viewer, a more prudent and vigilant viewer is a noble ambition, for by better understanding television and its structure, its influence might be mitigated. . . . From the vantage point of those who are most concerned with television as corruptor of culture, i.e., the arts, its introduction into main stream school life would be a disaster. . . . The content which it presents is at best non-art and at worst aesthetically destructive and corruptive." But most disappointing in this consultant's stance of despair was his lament that one cannot and possibly should not even try to reflect seriously about any closely and intimately experienced phenomenon. "The task in making the shift from passively and easily absorbed entertainment television to television as data for analysis is extraordinary. It will become necessary for students of television to view the medium differently than they would as casual observers. This would seem to present a major difficulty. . . . Now the student will be prompted to become detached and critical. In a sense it is like asking a child to become objective about a parent, sibling, or close friend. In general, the student will be asked to understand a way of life. . . . To primary, middle and secondary school age students television is simply a fact of life. The task of making clear that television should be a subject to probe when automobiles, garbage cans, bookshelves and family are all exempt is monumental. . . . Teachers not trained in media criticism but like most of us, over adept at media absorption, will have to struggle to separate fantasy from truth. . . . [T]elevision will need to be viewed in a new and discriminating fashion, taking into serious account important social and political implications. This will be no less a reenculturation process for the teacher than it will be for the student." But he concludes that criticism is essential for all aspects of American life, including television, yet "the entire process of implementing critical television viewing skills into the public schools should be approached with the utmost caution." See Sirota (n.d.), 10-page report on WNET's response to the U.S. Department of Health, Education and Welfare's (subsequently U.S.O.E.) request for proposals to teach CVS curricula. [Syntax and punctuation corrected in excerpts quoted here.]

2. A clear chronological account of the genesis and development of the projects and its materials is provided by the project director (Lloyd-Kolkin, Wheeler, & Strand, 1980). It confirmed data from other sources and offered complementary information for these pages of this book. (In the 1981 questionnaire they reported the staff as two administrators, two clerical/research persons, one teacher/"trainer," one writer, and two evaluators; in 1985 they listed their previous staff as one administrator, one clerical/research person, one teacher/"trainer," plus three staffers at subcontracted WGBH—an administrator, writer, and research assistant.)

3. Lloyd-Kolkin, Wheeler, and Strand (1980, p. 122) reported that at the

time they found only one study explicitly analyzing critical TV viewing skills: A paper presented by Graves (1979) to the American Psychological Association.

4.  Response to #20 in the 1981 questionnaire, about any findings compiled: "report is about 5″ thick and available for review in office only"; response to #21 about documented appraisals by leaders or participants: "reactions/reviews by workshop participants—too bulky to append" (Donna Lloyd-Kolkin, project director). Responses to #20 and #21 in the updated 1985 questionnaire were "No" checked for both questions. The director of the Far West Laboratory had moved to a successor project called Friends Can be Good Medicine, sponsored by the California Department of Mental Health. (By the late 1980s she was associated with Strategies for Media Literacy based in San Francisco.)

5.  Questionnaire response in 1981 by Donis Dondis (project director). The staff consisted of two administrators and one clerical/research person (1981 reply), or three administrators, five clerical/research persons, and nine teacher/"trainers," according to reply to follow-up inquiry in 1985. (Respondent was Phyllis Robbins, assistant to the Dean of the college and familiar with the project at that time; Dean Dondis had left her deanship the year after the project ended, and died 2 years later in 1984.)

6.  The original edition of four sets of books was copyrighted 1979 and 1980; the revised edition in one set of books was copyrighted 1981; see Barnett (1981). All publications were produced by Boston University's School of Public Communication under contract with the U.S. Department of Education (originally, U.S. Office of Education in the Dept. of Health, Education, and Welfare). The final composite edition was distributed by Dendron Press, Boston.

# 6

## School Districts (Systematic, Formal Instruction)

IDAHO FALLS SCHOOL DISTRICT NO. 91 (GRADES 3–6)

The Idaho Falls project, begun in 1978 and continuing in the next decade, grew out of James Anderson and Milton Ploghoft's collaboration with public school administrators and teachers. James F. Parsley, Jr. (1980), district school superintendent, introduced critical television viewing as an integral part of the language arts and social studies curriculum. He considered this "essential . . . for practical application and soundness of curricular approach" (p. 30). That reflected Ploghoft and Anderson's (1982, pp. 6–7, 24–26) recommendation based on their experience with schools in Eugene, Oregon, and Easy Syracuse, New York and elsewhere.

First, the major objectives of critical viewing skills instruction share a common psychological base with the major objectives of the language arts and with selected objectives of social studies. This condition is a requirement for the integration process. In other words, integration of a new element into a curriculum area can be done only where there is extensive compatibility between the objectives of the new curricular element and the existing curriculum area into which the new element will be integrated.

Comprehending the message is an objective that is pursued in the most traditional language arts programs and it is a major objective of critical viewing skills instruction. . . .

Integration, then, is feasible where the objectives of the existing program will not be replaced by the objectives of a new curriculum element, but where the existing objectives will provide a support base for the pursuit of the new program objectives. (p. 25)

Because of limited public funds, "feasible" integration included restricting technical equipment for CVS study to what was already available in schools.

A second major element of this project extended beyond the classroom, involving parents in their children's media exercises while watching television at home.

*Purposes and Procedures.*   The curriculum's overall goal in school is to develop analytical thinking, and at home to foster leadership and interaction among family members (with television as the catalyst). The purpose includes developing viewers able to identify value-laden statements and images in media presentations—not judging them from material provided in the curriculum but rather through discussion with teachers and parents in schools and homes (Ashton, 1981):

The project does not address the issue of right or wrong values or acceptable and non-acceptable role models. However, instruction within the project does teach that values *are* present in programming and that most characters hold specific value systems which can be transmitted to students, either through social learning or a lack of perceived reality. It is the intent of the project to encourage parents to communicate with their children concerning the values that are expressed on television in relation to their own family value system. (p. 60)

Intelligent choice and reflective reception are to replace passive acceptance. And discussing media experiences would improve communication between parents and children. Focus was not so much on what received over TV, but on how it was received by the viewer.

The curriculum's 4 years are vertically integrated, so each succeeding grade builds on the prior year's media study. Each extends over the entire academic year, with two sessions totaling 1½ hours weekly. (The project director noted that an alternate plan, using the same materials, could be a consolidated 54-hour unit of instruction.)

*Support Materials for Teachers.*   A "Teacher's Guide" for each of the four elementary grades (3–6) outlines the curriculum, provides background data and explanations, and supplies master copies of material to be reprinted and distributed to students and to parents (see Fig. 6.1). The spiral-bound 8½×11-inch sheets, printed on one side, total 80, 86,

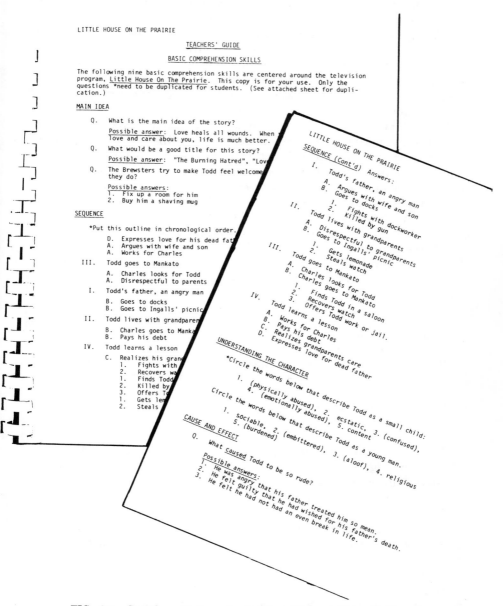

FIG. 6.1. Sample guidelines for teachers. From Ashton, Moll, and Rinaldi (1981) *The Way We See It: A Project to Develop Analytical Tele-viewing Skills—Teacher's Guide.* (Copyright © 1981 by Idaho Falls School District No. 91. Reprinted by permission.)

and 143 pages for each of the first three grades (a copy of the fourth booklet was not available for this report).

The guides provide master sheets for making copies to hand out to students in class, sometimes in conjunction with overhead projections of transparencies, and at other times to be taken home to parents—informing them about project activities for family participation. The project generally relies on Socratic method of question-and-answer to elicit responses from students. Many series of specific questions constitute the bulk of the teachers' guides. The intent is to draw out the students by challenging them to reflect and think and make judgments with little a priori direction from the instructor. After each question multiple "possible answers" are listed as a guide to the teacher. Succinct information sheets prior to each set of questions provide minimal, essential facts. Some are to be distributed; usually hand-out sheets list open-ended questions to be filled in by students.

Even when treating the concept of values, the procedure is nondirective through questions, often providing multiple choices for discussion. For example, values are stressed as one of the seven sections in Grade 5. The *Teacher's Guide* (Ashton, Moll, & Rinaldi, 1981) outlines objectives:

Students will be able to:
A. Identify a value.
B. Understand that not all people have the same value system.
C. Understand that television deals with a vast number of viewers who have differing interests and values.
D. Understand that they need not change their value system to that shown on television. (p. 27)

The source of values—the judgment placed on doing something as right or wrong—is described as varying among people, drawn from parents, family, church or synagogue, school, friends, and also media presentations.

The teacher's guides provide sets of questions about the videotapes that the teacher can present verbally to students for open discussion or as hand-out sheets for them to fill in. Each sequence of questions reflects content and procedures related to cognitive skills, using television as the referent.

Evening meetings are to be held for parents at each school to acquaint them with the CVS project. And six discussion guides are provided to parents to help when they are appraising television with their children. For example, one "home component" for parents of sixth graders studying TV news describes various kinds of bias found in television information programs: direct and indirect bias, selective reporting, and manipulative persuasion. Parent and child are asked to observe a TV news program to identify such characteristics. The teacher's guide directs teachers to instruct parents: "it is important that you emphasize to him/her [their child] that drawing conclusions on any news story or event should be made on a variety of informational sources and not just one news report."

*Printed and Audio-Visual Materials for Students.*    For both classroom and home, many typewritten materials were reproduced for distribution. The general theme was positive: to understand television by analyzing and evaluating programs while viewing them, and by planning and producing amateur programs. Curriculum materials were first developed by Anderson and Ploghoft, based on objectives formulated by district teachers. The materials were later refined as those teachers developed specific learning activities to be included in the "Teacher's Guide" for the project, labeled *The Way We See It* (Ashton, Moll, & Rinaldi, 1981).

The curriculum for third grade emphasizes commercials, teaching the basic skill of persuasive language. A "personal use component" for that grade is consumerism.

Instruction in fourth and fifth grades stresses entertainment programming; skills for both are literary elements and basic comprehension, plus value identification for fifth graders. Under the rubric of "personal uses" children learn about alternatives, motivations, and stereotyping in fourth grade, and about social learning, modeling, and value identification in fifth grade.

The sixth-grade level studies news broadcasts; skills pertain to the communication process itself. The "personal uses" section covers drawing conclusions and forming judgments.

The "personal uses" component in each year is intended to help students track and appraise their own use of television: What they like, how they watch, when they watch, and why they watch TV. They keep a detailed log or diary of their own viewing to gather personal data for later analysis.

Tape recordings to be played in class provide positive background information to aid both teacher and students. For third grade, an audiocassette presents Barry Manilow with commercial songs. Six videocassettes (two of 35 minutes duration, three 15 minutes long, and one 5 minutes) treat major types of commercials; advertising appeals such as puffery, claims, unstated qualifiers; major selling tactics; skills in making decisions; and analyzing and evaluating commercials.

For Grades 4 and 5, entertainment programming curricula include eight special videotapes and large portions of 14 commercial TV programs, including two to be taped off the air locally to represent students' currently favorite programs. Titles (and lengths in minutes) for fourth grade are: "Production Techniques" (30 min.), "Special Effects in Star Wars" (50), "Trade-Offs" (15), "Puff the Magic Dragon" (20), "The New Fat Albert Show" (20), "Eight is Enough" (50), "Mork and Mindy" (20), "The White Shadow" (50), and "Little House on the Prairie" (50). For fifth grade the videocassettes are: "Production Techniques" (50 min.), "Scheduling and Sequencing" (15), "Values Presented on T.V." (60), "Classifying Information" (15), "Furious Flycycle" (10); plus "The Brady Bunch" (20), "The Lion, the Witch and the Wardrobe" (110), "The Return of the King" (110), "Little House on the Prairie" (40), "The White Shadow" (40), "Weep No More, My Lady" (20), and "Little Women" (180).

In each grade a basic vocabulary is introduced (via the teacher's guides) to familiarize students with conceptual and technical terms in TV advertising and programming.

For Grade 3, words include such terms as: persuade, assume, analyze, compare, evaluate, exaggerate, puffery, symbol, slogan, needs versus wants, association, identification, advertiser, commercial, competitor, target audience, promotional or "promo" ad, public service announcement, camera angle, and sound effects. The teacher's guide also outlines steps in making a decision that children should understand: define the problem, list alternatives, state criteria, evaluate alternatives, make decision, check results of the decision. Students learn the meaning of these concepts by applying them to specific television activities in school and at home. Thus growth in critical televiewing is at the same time growth in critical thinking—perceiving and reasoning.

In Grades 4 and 5, words and concepts presented as part of the lessons include: Advertising versus entertainment versus news, plot, major/minor characters, setting, plot resolution, values, sequence, cause and effect, predicting outcomes, inference, context, fact versus opinion, and summarizing. Technical terms (used both in analyzing programs and in preparing amateur productions) include: Audio and video elements, special effects, script, storyboard, wide/tight/ establishing/insert shot, zoom in/out, pan/tilt, dolly/truck, graphics, editing, fade-in/out, dissolve, cut, superimposition, dubbing, credits.

In the fifth grade, students also learn to analyze and outline constitutive parts of programs, and to classify information. Sixth graders study the structure and content of television news. They learn limitations and capabilities of TV news (time constraints, story selection, editing, visual impact, concise news summaries, many items clustered in a short time), and they practice verifying TV news in relation to other information sources.

In each grade, CVS training culminates in students' planning and producing on film or videotape their own commercials, entertainment and news programs.

What the project calls "home components" are activities for students when at home, usually with their parents (see Fig. 6.2). The child initiates the activity to involve parents in media-related skills and reflection coinciding with in-school CVS study. From three to five such components are structured into the media curriculum of each of the four grades. On each occasion an explanatory letter, sometimes accompanied by reprints of informational or explanatory material, is forwarded to parents through the students.

*Testing and Evaluation.* Three of the six schools (all relatively similar) in Idaho Falls District 91 participated in the CVS project: six third-grade classes, five fourth-grade, six fifth-grade, and five sixth-grade classes. Testing and evaluation was conducted by consultants Anderson and Ploghoft (1980a), and by Idaho State University's Bureau of Educational Research and Services. The former developed a test of "television literacy" called the "Television Information Game," in which students demonstrate progressively more advanced cognitive skills in analyzing short segments of television material—including identification, analysis of syntax, and perceiving implications and consequences.

Anderson (1983) reported that testing before and after participation in the CVS study program

> found that third grade students showed rapid gains in cognitive skills vis à vis television and performed nearly at sixth-grade levels. Fourth-, fifth-, and sixth-grade students also showed significant posttest increases, but those increases were better explained by maturation than by the instructional intervention. Subsequent evaluation . . . on fourth, fifth, and sixth grades showed fifth- and sixth-grade students who received instruction posting greater gains than control students at the same grade levels not receiving instruction. Fourth-grade findings remained equivocal. (pp. 314–315)

But he noted that trained fifth graders achieved no higher scores than untrained sixth graders. He interpreted this as showing that "neither the provision of information nor the demonstration of mastery of that information is enough to promote critical viewing skills." He concluded that instruction must be keyed to children's respective levels of developmental needs if it is to be effective, sometimes with even "spec-

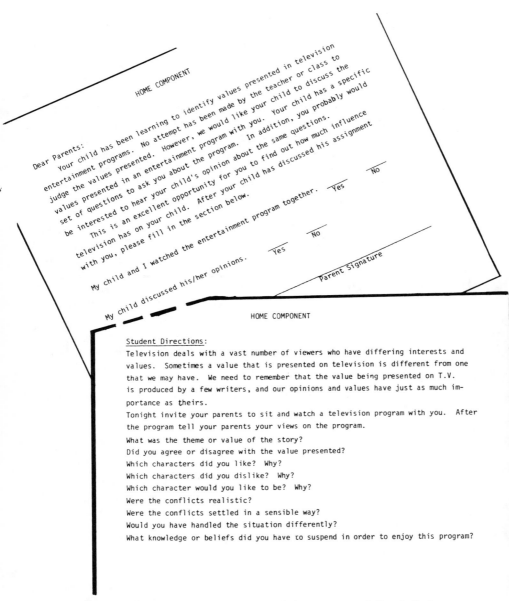

FIG. 6.2. Sample "home components" for parents and for students.
From Ashton et al. (1981) *The Way We See It: A Project to Develop
Analytical Televiewing Skills—Teacher's Guide.* (Copyright © 1981 by
Idaho Falls School District No. 91. Reprinted by permission.)

tacular results"; otherwise it is wasted. Further, he noted that students more successfully learned content than critical analysis skills. Reflecting on developmental research, he saw two contradictory inferences possible. Such training might be too late because traditional linguistic-oriented education may have already suppressed instinctive ability with visual and aural images (symbolic memory superseding eidetic or visual-image memory). Or else it might be too early because, according to Piaget's theories, formal cognitive operations central to critical viewing skills only emerge at about the fifth- or sixth-grade level. But the success with third-grade students suggests implementing the project earlier rather than later in a child's education.

Idaho State University's third "audit" or progress report was conducted in 1980 at three schools where eight classes of sixth-grade students studied the unit on television news. Interviews found teachers enthusiastic about the project: content of materials, organization, and format. Most faculty judged the 9-week period (the fourth quarter of the academic year) too limiting for fully integrating the project into regular subject areas; some recommended a full year for covering the material. Most found the quizzes and worksheets useful, but some did not use them widely because of time constraints. Teachers estimated that their students were fairly successful in achieving the six objectives of the news unit (most ranked their charges at about 4 on a 5-point scale, 5 being "excellent"). Fewer than two dozen students were tested; they demonstrated fairly good knowledge of most material covered, especially the section on interviewing (conducted at home, for the most part). They enjoyed the project, although they liked some of the pre-printed written activities the least. Parents responded to a questionnaire that children demonstrated increased interest in media news despite continuing to view about the same amount of news. More formalized analysis of testing indicated that all experimental schools did significantly better than the control school, and all grade levels demonstrated significant gains in mean scores.

*Assessment.*     This well-structured project reflected reasoned development based on research, and was integrated into "real-world" administrative contexts. The coalition of scholars and educational practitioners engaged schoolroom teachers and parents at home, attempting to address almost the total context of children's TV viewing experience. Antedating Anderson's later formulated "accommodation theory" (described earlier in Part I), the project enlisted all the agents involved in the typical youngster's "TV discourse" world—teachers, parents, peers—and partly focused on the domestic site of most TV viewing by youngsters. This holistic approach avoids theoretical compartmentalizing the child's viewing and "making meaning" of TV images into an abstract exercise. It also avoids the narrow approach to studying only alleged "effects" of TV content, or "uses and gratifications" attributed to viewers' patterns of TV use.

Although nonjudgmental in its content, the project leans heavily on the already established values—explicit and implied—of individual teachers in classrooms of youngsters and of those children's parents. It promotes reflective analysis of broadcast media without outlining expected specific outcomes. It relies on the interactive context between viewers and the medium and among viewers, including classmates and those in the family circle.

Extensive printed material for students and teachers is complemented by audio-visual items. Curricular support data continually relate training in critical viewing skill to fundamental cognitive abilities (not merely to course subjects).

This was one of the rare projects to conduct major systematic testing after being conducted in a broad, "real-life," yet controlled setting. Project directors-researchers drew restrained conclusions from the data. They offered partly optimistic but also partly cautious interpretations of sometimes ambiguous data about complex relationships between human beings and mass media, and about the measurable results of this project.

## EUGENE (OREGON) PUBLIC SCHOOL DISTRICT
## (GRADES 4–8, 9–12)

This systematic program, initiated as a pilot project in 1970, was supported by district funding throughout the decade. It was one of Ploghoft and Anderson's early collaborations with public institutional programs. The school district's representative chose to use the term "receivership skills" coined early on by that research team. The project involved grades 4 to 8, plus high school.

*Purposes and Procedures.* The district incorporated CVS course-work as an optional elective for students in language arts and social studies curricula. Program components were distributed to related academic areas. Developing observational skills and studying news and persuasion techniques came in social studies; analyzing dramatic forms in entertainment and information programs and commercials fell within performing arts; speech and script writing were part of language arts. Additional "in-service training" during the school year an summer workshops was judged by the district's media specialist (Ellingsen,

1981) "essential to the success of the viewer skills instructional program" (p. 89). Both teachers and students worked with video equipment, to learn new techniques and to engage in a shared media experience, as well as to further develop the CVS program and align it with community and school needs.

*Printed Materials for Students.* Although no printed materials were available for the present report, their returned questionnaire indicated that the educational and cultural/aesthetic goals were met by most methods and materials therein listed: inductive and deductive approaches together with lecture, discussion, workshop, and formal course material as elective portions of the curriculum. Materials included workbooks, scripts, audio-visuals, tests and quizzes, viewing programs, study sheets, guides for parents and teachers, and checklists for monitoring TV. In addition to selective viewing and evaluating media content, participants prepared their own programs and contacted media organizations. (But according to another response in the same questionnaire, students were exposed to all topic areas for TV activity except consumer roles—writing, joining activist media organizations—and TV's impact on reading, speaking, and other cognitive skills.)

The Eugene school district project reflected *Television and You,* the first of six curricular modules developed by Anderson and Ploghoft (1977, pp. 15–17). Seven chapters offer topic areas about how television and cable operate and produce commercials and programs including news, TV's effects on viewers, and how viewers can respond to their television exposure. The second module, "You and Your Television Set," directs students to complete a 9-day diary of their viewing patterns and then to write a case-study analysis. Modules #3–#5 respectively analyze values in dramatic programs, commercials, and news. The sixth module offers simplified creative experience in preparing first imitative and then innovative productions.

*Testing and Evaluation.* Sources for establishing norms were project originators and professional educators, but not published books or research reports, professional media persons, or other organizations. Despite the decade of activity, they did not compile findings or measure project effects, nor did they document appraisals by leaders or participants. But the district's curriculum specialist provided anecdotal appraisal, recounting teachers' reports about students' success and enthusiasm for the commercial portion in particular. Further positive effects of the CVS curriculum included increased interaction among local schools, college, parents, and local media because CVS materials including keeping logs of personal TV habits were shared with the community (Ellinsen, 1981, p. 90).

*Assessment.*   This project had many positive characteristics similar to the previous one (Idaho Falls, cited earlier) by the same scholar-researchers, except it lacked formal evaluation of effects.

## EAST SYRACUSE-MINOA (NEW YORK) CENTRAL SCHOOL SYSTEM (GRADES 6–12)

Yet another school district involved in Anderson and Ploghoft's early field work, the East Syracuse-Minoa system emphasized training teachers in CVS who could then pass this along to their students.

*Purposes and Procedures.*   Conducted in four phases over four summers (1976–1979), the voluntary training sessions consisted of 5 half-days of curriculum study and planning. Under the CVS mentors' guidance, teachers from social studies and language arts as well as communication skills learned basic concepts and explored ways to integrate CVS into their various subject areas. They developed objectives to fit into current curricular areas such as "The Language of Symbols" (Grade 6), "Semantics" (Grade 10), social studies and sociology (two sets: for junior high and for high school levels). They next wrote exercises to match those objectives. And they visited local television stations to observe production techniques and procedures.

*Assessment.*   This experimental effort helped teachers develop goals and materials to implement CVS in local school curricula. Content reflected previous Anderson–Ploghoft models. But it depended on the initiative and commitment of self-selected teachers, with little of the systematic integration enjoyed by school districts described earlier. (No questionnaire was returned in the 1981 survey.)

## NEW YORK CITY BOARD OF EDUCATION (GRADES K–9)

Little information was available except for the 68-page draft of a booklet for teachers, *TV and Growing Up.*[1] Despite its inchoate stage, it is included here as the fourth CVS project in formal school jurisdictions. Like many others, this project began in 1978.

*Purposes and Procedures.* Drafters of the document stated their assumption that American television, despite government regulators and activist groups, will probably remain pretty much as it is. But the medium can still be a potent ally for learning critical thinking. They quote Harrison (1977) approvingly:

> Critical thinking is not just the habit of criticizing; it involves the ability to suspend judgement, to examine before accepting, to consider alternatives before making a choice. In developing this art, children need all the help they can get—and they should get it early.[2]

That help is seen as coming from teachers' harnessing omni-present TV as a vehicle for teaching critical viewing skills. The authors claim to present a balanced assessment of the medium, and look to TV as "a motivational resource to stimulate learning."

*Support Materials.* The booklet *TV and Growing Up* provides teachers with background information about television as well as exercises for their students. Five chapters include introductory material about TV, clarifying values, information about the medium's structure and program production, how to improve TV experience by changing the medium itself as well as one's use of it, and an analysis of mass communication and the future of television.

Each chapter offers several pages of suggested learning activities for students, questions for discussion, and other materials for class use. These options are aptly divided into clusters of suggestions for different age groups: Grades K–2, 3–4, 5–6, and 7–9. They seem suited to respective levels of cognitive development and TV experience. They tend to be nondirective, assigning tasks to which the children respond from their own experience and viewpoints; subsequent discussion may then be directed by the teacher. Obviously some topics are themselves value-related, such as fantasy versus reality (stereotypes—racism, sexism), material possessions as indicator of personal worth, violence, and persuasion in commercials. Value orientation is generally "middle-class" sociocultural, but not economic or political regarding the U.S. system of business or government vis-à-vis alternative structures in the world.

A number of film or videotapes are suggested as aids, but the children's normal use of TV at home is the basis for most discussion. No other materials were prepared for those using *TV and Growing Up* in New York City schools.

*Assessment.* The material offers a good introduction to effectively using and evaluating television, condensing to utter succinctness information covering much ground about mass media's interaction with society. Although this pithy overview of major concepts is generally balanced, many of the short quotations tend to be negative (with repeated citations of highly negative criticisms by Jerzy Kosinski and especially Mankiewicz and Swerdlow—the latter's *Remote Control* cited in 22 of the 66 footnotes). Brevity of treatment makes for a sketchy outline, generally offering only a brief quotation or two as source material and rationale for generalizations and evaluations abut complex and widely controverted topics. (Among sources cited *passim* are articles published in *TV Guide, New York Times, McCall's,* and *Women's Day,* in addition to more scholarly publications.) Teachers are directed to further information in useful references tersely cited in the notes. But they are left much to their own devices in interpreting and applying assertions made in the text.

## CATHOLIC EDUCATION OFFICE, SYDNEY, AUSTRALIA (GRADES K–6, 7–12)

A CVS project for a comprehensive school jurisdiction was developed under Roman Catholic auspices in Sydney, Australia. Its constituency ranged from preschoolers to the end of high school, plus adults. It was also intended for use in churches and homes. The project is well developed in both its widespread application and duration as well as the quality of printed and audio-visual support materials (see Fig. 6.3).

*Historical Development.* During the 1970s Kelvin B. Canavan (1980) prepared a series of curriculum-related outlines and other publications for the Catholic Education Office in Sydney.

In 1971 the Catholic school system had requested an interim media curriculum that was prepared for upper primary schools in 1972. A series of workshops helped teachers implement the curriculum. That same year the Australian Episcopal Conference introduced mass media education into all Catholic schools. Subsequently Canavan and co-authors (1974/1978, 1975/1978, 1974/1979) prepared a set of four workbooks for students, *Mass Media Activities* (published by Longman in 1974, with 60,000 copies sold within 5 years). In 1973 the bishops' Committee for Mass Media had requested a full curriculum be prepared for Grades K through 12. Nineteen Catholic Education Offices in Australia were enlisted to determine behavioral objectives and strategies. In 1975 the Catholic Education Office in Sydney published

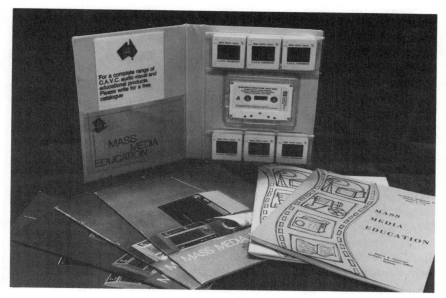

FIG. 6.3. Kit of 35mm slides and audiocassette (top), plus booklets of student assignments and curriculum guidelines for teachers. Developed as *Mass Media Education* by Kelvin Canavan et al., n.d., Homebush, NSW, Australia: Catholic Audio Visual Centre.

Canavan's *Mass Media Education: Curriculum Guidelines for Primary Schools, Years 1–6,* and *Mass Media Education: Curriculum Guidelines for Secondary Schools, Years 7–12* (in half a decade 8,000 copies were sold). In 1978 they prepared for groups of teachers and parents a presentation of 80, 35mm slides and an audiocassette soundtrack, *Mass Media Education, Why? How?* (60 sets were distributed). Those curricular materials are detailed after the next section.

*Purposes and Procedures.* According to the questionnaire returned in 1981 and confirmed by published materials, the overall purpose of the media-study projects was educational, not religious, although the text occasional refers to specific Christian and Catholic values. They favor a deductive rather than inductive approach—emphasizing philosophy, theories, and application of principles. Procedures include lecture, discussion, workshop, and readings. The material is part of schools' formal curricula, either integrated into existing course material or else presented as separate class content. In either case, the subject area is not an optional elective; all students are required to study mass media—which included print, film, and radio as well as television.

Canavan published in final form in 1975 two books: *Mass Media Education: Curriculum Guidelines for Primary Schools / Years 1–6,* and *Mass Media Education: Curriculum Guidelines for Secondary Schools / Years 7–12.* They spell out in great detail the rationale and range of procedures to accomplish objectives of media study. (They reflect the philosophy and guidelines presented in the 1978 publication *Life in the Media Age,* described later.) The two similar books—52 pages for primary schools and 54 pages for secondary schools—each devote the first 17 pages to identical presentations of factual data about media and audiences, including summaries of major research trends in stimulus-response effects and in systems or process transaction among media, messages, audiences, and cultural/viewing environment. The last two pages add a specifically moral and theological perspective, with lengthy excerpts from the Catholic church's formal documents addressing Christian values and media in society.

Nine major assumptions underlying the curriculum are drawn from that first section of the books (Canavan, 1975/1976). They include the socio-cultural influence of mass media on students and society at large, implications for formal schooling and for family life, and specifically "that children are capable of reacting critically to what they hear, read and view" (p. 17). The final three assumptions, although general, paraphrased positive concepts drawn from the Decree on Social Communication by the Second Vatican Council in 1963:

7.   That all people have a basic right to be fully and accurately informed.
8.   That all people should be able to receive information, education and entertainment from the mass media.
9.   That, due to economic considerations, publishers and producers are to some extent governed by the prevailing tastes in society, and therefore it is the reader, listener and viewer who is [*sic*] primarily responsible for the content presented by the mass media. (p. 17)

This expands a bit the abstraction in the curriculum guide at the outset of "Preamble to the Course" on p. 19: "Ideally, the youth of tomorrow will be equipped to seek the truth in the mass media they use" (similar to abstract wording in *Life in the Media Age*). Clarifying that statement is the accompanying assertion that:

All people have a right to be fully and accurately informed, and, in these days of mass communication, people will only be well informed, and hence free from potential coercion, if they possess the knowledge, skills and attitudes necessary to understand the nature, techniques and purpose of radio, press, television and film. (p. 19)

The 26-page booklet *Life in the Media Age* (Canavan, 1978, pp. 11–13) summarizes main lines of media education developed through curriculum-oriented publications. The general purpose of media education in the four lowest grades is to help youngsters "begin to respond and react to what they see on television in order to predispose them to the subsequent development of appreciative and critical attitudes to television." That later development was to come in subsequent grades when they learned to "respond and react to what they view on television" and in other media. Objectives of media study include knowledge, skills, and attitudes. Students are to gain *knowledge* of how television operates as well as its role in their country, plus the Church's assessment of the medium. Their *skills*—in addition to being able to enjoy and appreciate media and to have "effective viewing skills"—include ability to compare and contrast programs, to rate programs according to personal enjoyment and enrichment, to analyze elements in TV commercials, to appreciate TV's role in developing public opinion, to exercise critical judgment of content viewed in context of previously acquired knowledge, to form opinions about various viewpoints on issues presented in TV, and "to form judgments as to the responsibility of society for conserving truth in television." Media education is to develop the *attitude* of a "continuing desire" to develop critical viewing ability, to synthesize information learned from media, to grow in sensitivity to human needs and social problems presented by media, and "to relate his or her judgment of film and television to the demands of conscience, of faith and Christian morality."

The keynote in classroom activities is a high level of student involvement, stressing skills to help students use media confidently and intelligently. (This suggests inductive experience, in addition to the exclusively a priori emphasis noted in the questionnaire response.)

*Support Materials for Teachers and Parents.*   Material in the two books *Mass Media Education: Curriculum Guidelines . . .* (1975) was intended to be incorporated into existing academic studies such as English, social science, and religious education. While allowing maximum flexibility for adapting the material to given school years and specific classrooms of students, the curriculum guidelines suggest that Grades 1–3 study television and Grades 4–6 study television and film, the press, and radio—in that order. But for secondary school students (in Australia, Grades 7–12), the curriculum suggests introductory study of mass media in Grade 7, followed by press in Grade 8, radio in Grade 9, television and film in Grade 10, and cross-media study in the two final years.

Some 253 goals, "goal components," or objectives of the curriculum were sent to 19 Diocesan Directors of Catholic Education, responsible for education of 95% of students in Catholic secondary schools in Australia. The majority of them (15) responded and were "generally supportive" of the initially stated objectives. Revised curricular guidelines incorporated their comments. Objectives are stated in behavioral terms, but did not discount less easily perceived and measured affective results. "Learning experiences" are also itemized, based on those stated objectives.

Two matters discussed in the primary curriculum are not in the booklet for secondary level. Teachers of Grades 1–6 are reminded that, while leading their pupils to be "discriminating truth seekers in their use of the mass media," that responsibility must be tempered (Canavan, 1975/1976):

1.  Preaching against the mass media and generally imposing his own tastes on the pupils will not produce the desired long term effect.
2.  As a Christian educator he cannot stand aside and simply let the pupils decide what is good and bad in the mass media.
3.  With great care and skill the primary school teacher can gradually raise the media tastes of the pupils in his class. This is not achieved overnight. It is a long term objective of every lesson in mass media education. (p. 19)

Second, a brief section called "Communication with Parents" is added to alert them to their child's media study, especially because younger children's media experience is mostly in the home and no teaching about discriminating use of media can succeed without parents' support.

In the lower primary years (Grades 1–3), 10 objectives for TV study include awareness of differences among programs and between them and commercials, verbal recall of highlights viewed, comprehension and interpretation of principal themes in programs, and opinions about them, plus ability to state reasons for watching a program. Although the authors caution teachers to adapt materials to the level of maturity of their charges, they still expect youngsters to learn to differentiate between situations "that are good and those that are bad" as well as those that are true and false, real and unreal—at least in elementary ways. They then provide over three pages of fine-printed questions for class discussion and specific activities involving television.

For upper primary grades (4–6), some 28 "behavioural objectives" list intended results of media study, including film, press, and radio in addition to television. Some are broadly stated: "The pupil will be able to *enjoy and appreciate* the film and television he or she views" (emphasis in original). Others are more advanced levels of the same skills for lower grades. Yet others are somewhat more sophisticated, including ability to "rate" programs according to enjoyment and information, and to analyze and evaluate program elements such as fact, opinion, fantasy, and bias or emotional factors and persuasion in presentations. Each specific section on television and film, on the press, and on radio is divided into two pages of questions and activities about "using" the medium and three pages of questions and activities for "studying" it. Each integrates study of the respective medium with traditional educational areas: critical thinking, English, social studies, catechetics, and mathematics (for press) and music (for radio). Students are to make inventories of their media diet to analyze patterns. Written and oral exercises based on media experiences lead students to reflect on media habits, program content and format, characterizations, and implied values in entertainment forms, drama, cartoons, news and documentaries, and commercials. The authors cite Bruner and Piaget for recommending concrete projects from which children can learn concepts—such as making photographs, slides, and home movies, including planning theme, plot, and characters.

Distinctive in the primary-level curriculum (Canavan, 1975/1976) is the intermittent inclusion of religious orientation. The section on "Using Television and Film" comments on catechetics and media:

> Conscience is formed by our environment, by the behaviour of the people about us. Moral education has become more difficult in the television age. The children see their heroes, pop stars on television, admitting to what we would regard as real moral deviations. Because they are their heroes, they are affected by this. We have to let them see that a conscience is a personal and an individual thing. The heroes of the Church must be presented to these children in such a way that they will not appear 'inferior' to the television heroes, and so the child will grow to see his own dignity and responsibility as a Baptized member of the Church. (p. 30)

Similarly, teachers are urged to select programs that can lead "children in deprived areas . . . to experience something of the grandeur of God's world" and to compare in programming "how man has despoiled the world" contrasted with "how man works to obey God's command given in the Book of Genesis 'to cultivate the earth and care for it'."

For secondary schools (Grades 7–12), no fewer than 79 "objectives of the course" are itemized for television and film alone. Including those for print and also for radio, the list totals 252 objectives from which teachers can select. Most repeat on a somewhat higher level what was presented for primary students. Additional or more developed objectives include: the structure of the Australian television industry, ethical questions including political bias and role of values and unstated assumptions in editing and news reporting, impact of TV and film on attitudes and values, role of mass media as agents of change and "creators of taste," some production elements of TV and film, critical assessment of one's own viewing by comparing "attitudes" presented by media against one's own attitudes and by attempting to "resolve discrepancies between" them, appreciation of artistic qualities of music in media, examination of a variety of viewpoints on significant issues and ability to revise judgments, and general awareness of human values and judgments about society and Australian life as presented by mass media. A final objective was that pupils exercise personal responsibility for television by using it selectively and by contacting "producers and [governmental] authorities" when productions are either above average quality or are offensive.

Only a single paragraph mentions the religious dimension of study in television and film for secondary school students: "The pupil will *know the Church's attitude* toward television as expressed in the Decree of the Media of Social Communication (1963) and the Pastoral Instruction on the Means of Social Communication (1971)" (Canavan, 1975/1979, p. 28).

"Suggested Learning Experiences" for secondary students list 90 concrete activities involving television and film, many with subsections, in ascending order of difficulty. Again, teachers are urged to pick and choose apt clusters of assignments most suited to their students, to best achieve objectives selected from the previous section. They include monitoring media, making lists, hearing guest speakers, producing their own TV program or film, class discussion topics, and research topics such as TV audience ratings and regulations and movie ratings system. None of the activities relate explicitly to religious values. The inductive emphasis (again, despite the questionnaire response) using Socratic method is apparent even in the value-oriented topics, such as "90. Have the class debate the following question: Do the popular television shows reflect what most of us value? Or do they actually educate us in what we should value?" This section admonishes that "the teacher's role is seen primarily as that of stimulator, questioner, and facilitator and not that of a lecturer" although "this is not to imply that there is no place in the curriculum for teacher input" (p. 33).

A final section in booklets for both elementary and secondary levels offers a grid listing "Guidelines for Evaluation of Television, Film, Press and Radio"; it is based on material from the National Council of Teachers of English. Categories comprising "standards" include aptness for audience's age level, meeting "needs for entertainment and action," stimulating worthwhile activities, possessing artistic qualities, using suitable language, and having an overall desirable effect. Two other standards in that grid address values, indirectly relating to religious ones:

> STANDARD: 3. Does it add to one's understanding and appreciation of himself, others, the world?
>
> DESIRABLE—IF . . . It is sincere, constructive, informative; gives a balanced picture of life; encourages decent human relations; is fair to races, nations, religions, labour, and management.
>
> UNDESIRABLE—IF . . . It is one-sided, or propagandist; arouses or intensifies prejudice; takes advantage of immaturity and lack of knowledge.
>
> STANDARD: 4. Does it encourage worthwhile ideals, values, and beliefs (concerning such matters as family life)?
>
> DESIRABLE—IF . . . It upholds acceptable standards of behaviour; promotes democratic and spiritual values, respect for law, decency, service.
>
> UNDESIRABLE—IF . . . It glamorizes crime, indecency, intolerance, greed, cruelty, encourages bad taste, false standards of material success, personal vanity, intemperance, immorality.[3]

The summary booklet *Life in the Media Age* by Canavan (1978) suggests specific questions and exercises to prompt students to comment on their own experiences with media and to discuss among themselves media patterns and implications. Almost all activities are based on home viewing, about which students are to reflect and respond—as in ranking favorite programs, describing ethnic stereotypes viewed, listing and timing items in news programs. Through class discussion students eventually develop a set of criteria for evaluating television.

For media study in homes, the booklet cautions parents to adapt television exposure and analysis to the developmental level of their children. It recommends to parents activities similar to those for classrooms (cited earlier), with parental questions and guidance the matrix for their children's growth in critical viewing. Most questions suggested are nondirective, seeking children's responses about how a program began and then developed, about alternative endings possible, and about characters they liked and why. Other activities include limiting the amount of time spent viewing, preparing a diary of programs viewed for subsequent analysis and ranking, and writing letters of inquiry or complaint to broadcast companies.

For adults, *Life in the Media* emphasized activism: letters and other forms of communication and social action to broadcasters, advertisers, and governmental agencies; and harnessing opportunities for positive use of media, such as through phone-in programs and access time in schedules by appearing in or even producing programs. Strategies for adult groups repeat some classroom exercises and add communal viewing of programs as a basis for discussion, followed by writing to stations about the group's favorable and unfavorable reactions. Also suggested are gathering of data about media ownership, holding seminars to assess how media serve the public, discussing program patterns and media standards, and analyzing values portrayed in programming vis-à-vis Christian values.

*Printed Materials for Students.*   The earliest set of publications, *Mass Media Activities 1, 2, 3,* and *4,* was printed in 1974 and reprinted without revision through the 1980s.[4] The first two booklets are 30 pages long, the last two 46 pages, all with glossy photo covers. Less than one-third of each booklet is devoted to television (respectively, 9 of 30 pages, 9 of 30, 14 of 46, and 13 of 46); other sections treat newspapers and radio. They present brief, simple, and practical exercises. Usually by fill-in questions and multiple checklists, students are asked to record their media experiences, their impressions and understanding of them, and sometimes their judgments and projections (e.g., create an ending for a program, analyze "weak" programs and write a sample letter to a station manager). Some questions require gathering of data or assistance from a teacher or book, such as determining when the first television station was established in the area. Other reflective and judgmental questions require considerable analysis and reasoning. Questions are ordered to provide students with progressive steps for reflecting and reasoning (or critical thinking).

*Audiovisual Support Materials.*   Because of widespread favorable response to the Catholic Education Office's curricular materials, coupled with requests for audiovisual support material, Canavan designed a custom-bound package of 35mm slides and audiotape for teachers and groups of parents.[5] Color photographs and accompanying 23-minute narration with occasional music and on-site sound were produced with professional quality. The first 40 slides summarize the rationale for implementing mass media education at home and in school. Based on a balanced assessment of research, this even-handed explanation concludes with a brief exhortation to mount media studies in curricula. The second group of 40 slides offers very practical suggestions and demonstrates samples for parents and teachers "who are concerned with preparing children to enjoy and use discriminately the mass media."[6] This phrasing reflects the positive perspective throughout all the Catholic Education Office's materials. The recorded narration concludes with the statement:

> The press, radio, film, and television have emerged as powerful agents of education alongside the traditional agents—home, school, peer group, and church. All educators need to recognize the role of the media in the growth and development of young people and to coordinate their efforts to help them use the mass media intelligently. Although the modern communication media must certainly be accepted as influencing young people, they should never be deemed too powerful to be corrected or mitigated or utilized. The media are intrinsically good. They are a constant reminder of the creative talents of modern man.

Although many slides and narrative comments pertain generally to mass media, most statements and examples relate directly to television. Among the final 40 slides, 7 specifically refer to newspapers and magazines, and 4 to radio.

*Testing and Evaluation.*   Although formal evaluation of results was not conducted, one indication of success was widespread use of the curricula without subsequent revision. In 1978, as a result of these and related efforts, 56% of all Catholic Primary Schools in Sydney presented lessons in mass media education at least once a week, 17% offered lessons every 2 weeks, 16% presented one to three lessons per term, and 11% offered no lessons. A survey of those same primary schools in 1981 revealed somewhat reduced attention to media education, with fewer weekly lessons but more bi-weekly and occasional lessons per term (see Table 6.1).

On the other hand, although such education was becoming an integral part of the curriculum in many schools at the primary level, Canavan (1980, p. 11) observed that "the introduction of media study

TABLE 6.1
Media Education in Classrooms, Sydney, Australia
Catholic Primary Schools: 1978, 1981[7]

| Frequency | 1978 Classes | | 1981 Classes | |
|---|---|---|---|---|
| At least once a week | 56% | 874 | 43% | 709 |
| Every 2 weeks | 17% | 258 | 21% | 341 |
| 1–3 lessons per term | 16% | 243 | 26% | 426 |
| No lessons | 11% | 172 | 10% | 156 |
| TOTALS | 100% | 1,547 | 100% | 1,632 |
| (Total Students) | (36,600) | | (37,500) | |

programmes appears to have been severely hampered by the subject-based administrative structure" which cannot fit media neatly into a single subject area. In the latter 1980s primary schools moved away from subject compartmentalizing to a more integrated curriculum—making it difficult to monitor mass media education as a specific study area.[8] But many secondary schools offered various media courses.

The curriculum guidelines published in 1975 were never revised and late in 1988 continued to be used by many teachers. The Catholic Education Office/Sydney project was not formally evaluated. Many of the concepts of Canavan's outlines and reports can be found in subsequent work by Departments of Education overseeing public schools in Australia. Samples of their curricular materials follow.

*Assessment.* Canavan's 1975 publications nicely synthesize the state of research findings relating to media education. His review of the field is balanced, lucid, and appropriate. The books, addressed to curriculum planners and teachers, are neither condescending nor simplistic. They provide reasoned, reasonable analysis of the communications process, drawing implications for media education based on a broad range of sound research.

The 1978 booklet is similarly broad in scope. It leans heavily on the home environment and parents for effective media exercises. Its value-orientation remains objective, while promoting social activist roles for parents.

The handsome publications offer exhaustively detailed lists of suggestions for guiding youth's media use. They are supported by professionally crafted printed and audio-visual materials.

## MINISTRY OF EDUCATION, WESTERN AUSTRALIA (GRADES 8–12)*

Early in the 1980s, teachers of media study formed an association of Australian Teachers of Media (ATOM); they held their first national conference in Sydney in May 1984 and a second in Brisbane in September 1988. Key figures in promoting media studies while providing theoretical perspectives and pragmatic resource materials (outlines, curricula, bibliographical material) were Barrie McMahon and Robyn

---

*Although not included in either questionnaire survey (1981, 1985), this project is listed in comparative tabulations in Part III. Material received in 1989 offers some comparison between this secular CVS program and the previous one by a religious group in Australia.

Quin. McMahon was senior curriculum officer and assistant for media to the Ministry of Education (East Perth, Western Australia), including policy related to media; and Quin was president of ATOM while serving as department head of Media Studies at Western Australian College of Advanced Education (Mount Lawley Campus). Both published and spoke widely about media education theory and practice, including training teachers.

*Purposes.*   McMahon and Quin (1986) explain that syllabi from various educational systems in different Australian states "exhibit different philosophies, rationales, and emphases. . . . Course content is determined by a separate state curriculum authority" (p. 3). Television gradually dominated media studies curricula in Australia; and study of television constitutes the major component for senior years in Western Australian schools.

A key objective of the Ministry is to foster literacy in the broad sense: the ability to control language in both comprehending and composing—understanding others as well as in expressing oneself. A tightly composed "Rationale" defined the broad scope and purposes of the curriculum for lower secondary level (Grades 8–10):

> Media studies is the study of the modern mass media, namely television, radio, film, mass print and photography as it occurs in the mass print.
>
> These communication systems are seen as being most significant forms of communication in modern society. In order to understand their impact it is necessary to understand the languages of the mass media. This involves understanding the links between the languages and the cultures which generate them, the economic factors which affect the production or reception of mass media messages and the ways that audiences develop understandings from the media messages. The latter involves audience perception of both surface and deeper (cultural) meaning associated with the mass media messages.
>
> The organizing pedagogy for the study focuses upon the nature of communication, the codes and conventions associated with the language systems, the narrative patterns that are developed and the social implications of the messages. (p. 3)

The curriculum stresses that media audiences are not merely passive recipients of messages but instead are active in "making meaning" from the messages. The material avoids the "inoculation" approach of attempting, in McMahon and Quin's (1986, p. 4) wording, "to build within students a protective shell which will guard them against the evil influences of the media." Included are the literary or "discriminatory" and the "cultural" approaches. The curriculum recommends applied, practical exercises but cautions about making skills activities an end in themselves; and it suggests that quite modest audiovisual equipment is adequate for most of the projects. (This differs widely from some British projects where hands-on application of media devices and techniques is stressed as central to learning principles and forming evaluations of media content and procedure.)

In Western Australia's primary grades (Grades 1 to 7), prior to 1981, pilot programs in media studies were integrated into existing courses. At the secondary level (Grades 8 to 12), although study of mass media has been integrated into present courses—usually English—by several hundred teachers, it has also been widely developed as a separate subject. Institutional support is provided by the Ministry of Education's various committees, especially the Media Studies Syllabus Committee (chaired by Mr. McMahon).

*Curricular Materials.*  In March 1987 the Education Department of Western Australia (1987) published its revised edition of *The Unit Curriculum: Media Studies* for lower secondary schools. The unit is structured to promote both analytical and practical skills, through 40 hours of instruction in six stages devoted to these themes:

Introduction to media education
Development of understandings about media language
Understanding of narrative and genre
Study of representation
Understanding of the Australian social context
Investigation of media issues. (p. 1)

The six stages, each developing threefold topics, very closely match a media education paradigm developed in Scotland (see chapter 7). Television is treated explicitly in only 4 of the 16 "cells" of topics. TV is implied in 3 others ("stars and stereotypes," "advertising," and "media images of Australia"), and is an option in all three developmental cells in Stage 6, which offers a media case study and two media projects.

Curriculum materials are organized according to five objectives for each teaching unit: the nature of communication, codes and conventions, narrative, social context, and skills.

Each 2- to 3-page single-spaced sheet in the syllabus includes "Notes for Teachers" with tips and strategies for adapting material to classroom circumstances.

Course structure for both Grades 11 and 12 offers the same thematic development:

(a) The problematical nature of the mass media
(b) Media products as constructions
(c) Methods of construction
(d) Control of the constructions
(e) Value systems of the constructions.[9]

Those somewhat arcane titles include most major topics. (a) In addition to analyzing implications of the terms *mass* and *media* and specific characteristics of film, radio, and television, the Year 12 curriculum adds theories of media analysis. (b) This includes study of genres in film and TV, radio formats, and realism. (c) *Methods* includes media selection processes (of words, images, sounds), terminology, narrative and rhetoric forms, codes and conventions, and temporal and spatial parameters of media. (d) *Control* looks to political, economic, and historical factors, plus specific study in Year 12 of "implications of corporate ownership across the Australian media." (e) *Value systems* explores stereotyping, media representations as "normal" or "natural"; and, added in Year 12, representation of authority figures, connotation and myth, dominant cultural factors affecting audiences' receptivity.

*Support Materials for Teachers.*   In 1988 the Ministry of Education published a 71-page printed *Media Studies Resource Catalogue* listing complete references to books, articles, videotapes, films, and audiotapes—all keyed section by section to the curriculum guideline documents. Complete mailing addresses and other information expedite teachers' access to these resources.

Much briefer guidelines were prepared for Years 11 and 12 (eight and nine typewritten pages, respectively, plus two pages of bibliography). They were complemented by teachers' resource guides (36 and 44 typewritten pages) offering very concrete tips on classroom activities, plus detailed references to specific portions of audiovisual and printed resources—each segment keyed to verbatim portions of the curriculum statements. Great flexibility is left to the on-site teacher, including selection of apt exercises and readings as well as the time devoted to each topic. Each "teaching point" is accompanied by citation of a chapter or even just several pages in the many sources, so that teachers can prepare each lesson with explicit information and conceptual understanding.

*Assessment.*   Although including many topics subject to debate and disagreement, curriculum guidelines do not inculcate a preset perspective (although desirable implications are fairly evident). Education administrators espouse open-ended study of media with true freedom for students to develop processes of thinking and judging by exploring and discovering for themselves. They see this as the goal of critical thinking—using media as the matrix—instead of attempting to indoctrinate students with what is considered "good" or "not good" aesthetically, socially, or otherwise. Useful printed support material promotes flexible adaptation by local teachers. The entire project assumes teachers to be well informed, balanced, creative, and able to stimulate students to look below the surface of media appearances and to question mass media processes, content, and forces—including big business, government, and audiences, as well as creative media practitioners. But nowhere does the curriculum promote an activist stance.

*        *        *

Beyond the context of formal institution-mounted programs reported in this chapter, other forms of teaching critical viewing skills are carried on with little or only indirect administrative support. Chapter 7 reports projects mounted by individual researchers and teachers. (Chapter 10 explores institution-related programs around the world.)

## NOTES

1. The 68-page typewritten manuscript by the New York City Board of Education (1978) was made available to this researcher by the Television Information Office of the National Association of Broadcasters.

2. Quoted by New York City Board of Education (1978, p. 27).

3. Canavan (1975/1979, p. 49) cited as source Boutwell (1962).

4. Canavan, Slattery, Tarrant, and Threlfo (1974/1979 and 1975), and Canavan, McGuiness, Blaney, and Davis (1974/1978 and 1975/1978). Entering 1989, those original curriculum guidelines were still used without revision, according to personal correspondence to this author from Kelvin Canavan, dated September 29, 1988 (but received January 4, 1989).

5. The Curriculum Development Centre at Canberra provided $1,800 funds for the slide-tape package produced in 1978. In 1979 a similar package was produced with the support of $3,000 donated by the Federation of Australian Commercial Television Stations to the Child, Education & Media Sub-Committee of the International Year of the Child; it was distributed by the Catholic Audio Visual Centre.

6. See Canavan (1978/1979), p. 2 of folder accompanying the slide/sound package.

7. Source: Kelvin Canavan, Executive Director of Schools, Catholic Educa-

tion Office, Sydney, in personal communication dated September 29, 1988, with accompanying excerpt from report.

8. Informal updated report to this researcher by Kelvin Canavan, Executive Director of Schools, Catholic Education Office, Sydney; enclosed with personal communication dated September 29, 1988 (but received January 4, 1989). These and accompanying data, including tabulations in Table 6.1, are from his correspondence at the end of 1988.

9. Education Department of Western Australia (ca. 1988, p. 2). Undated, the report was sent to this researcher by the government office, January 27, 1989. Identical material is in *Media Studies: Year 12,* p. 2.

# 7

## Projects by Individuals: Collaborative and Independent

Individual persons have always been in the forefront of most major innovations in society, including education and media. Their professional work has often involved institutions with which they collaborated or to which their media explorations were applied. At other times they have been individual entrepreneurs.

Among such figures important in media literacy training in the United States have been Aimee Dorr, Dorothy and Jerome Singer, Rosemary Potter, and private business persons who have harnessed their awareness of media's significance with ventures in publication. Chapters 7, 8, and 9 report their activities in developing systematic training for critical viewing skills.

### AIMEE DORR ET AL. (HARVARD/UNIV. OF SOUTHERN CALIFORNIA)

Representative of scholars who conducted formal experimental study of teaching media literacy were Dr. Aimee Dorr and her associates at various universities. Her earliest formal study, conducted in Boston from 1974 to 1976 (supported by a grant from the Office of Child Development), was similar in scope, participants, and results to the Singers' projects at Yale University in 1978 and thereafter (Dorr, Graves, & Phelps, 1980).

*Purposes.* In an effort "to modify some of television's effects—to make children more critical evaluators of its content," these researchers developed and tested curricula with more than 200 White, Black, and Hispanic persons—half of them elementary school children and the rest adolescents and adults.

Their investigation drew on available research suggesting that media's effects on audiences could be modified when viewers were able to evaluate the source of program content and motivations for presenting it, as well as to perceive the degree of reality intended. Dr. Dorr and her colleagues developed curricula "to diminish the credibility children ascribed to television" by teaching about production processes and the economic purposes of the industry, to help children assess the reality of TV content, to compare it with information from other sources, and finally to evaluate that content.

*Curricula: Content.* They developed three curricula, two of them new.

1. The "industry curriculum" taught eight facts about how entertainment programs are produced and affected by economic factors (Dorr, Graves, & Phelps, 1980, p. 73). Plots are made up, characters are really actors, incidents are fabricated, and settings are often artificially constructed. Further, programs are broadcast to earn profits, money for programs comes from advertisers purchasing air time, ads are intended to sell products to viewers, and audience size determines broadcast income.

2. The "process curriculum" taught children procedures and sources for evaluating TV content: Entertainment programs are made up, they vary in their degree of realism, viewers can decide for themselves how realistic programs are, and TV content can be evaluated by comparing it to one's own experience, by asking other people, and by consulting other media sources. In both curricula, students were to use that information to understand the reality and fantasy of entertainment programs.

3. Used as a control, the third curriculum was modified from an existing one about "social reasoning," teaching role-playing skills through discussion and other interaction. Its purpose was to help children grow in understanding by observing, asking, and talking with others and then using that information to reason about social dilemmas common to their age.

*Procedures.* Eight experienced teachers taught the curricula to small groups in six 1-hour lessons. They followed detailed curriculum guides and used audiovisual material. They emphasized games and role-playing.

*Testing and Evaluation.*   Pre- and posttesting included written forms and interviews. Results indicated that children did learn material in the curricula, and could use it to discuss the level of reality in television programming; but they did not use that material to mediate attitudinal effects of viewing. Even in just 6 hours of such CVS training, young children were able to learn much about how television works and creates programs, as well as how to seek out alternative sources of information; they were also able to apply that information when asked to assess how real programs are. But the study did not demonstrate clearly whether their knowledge of the medium would actually lead them to be more selective in future viewing.

## DOROTHY AND JEROME SINGER (YALE UNIVERSITY/ABC)

Since 1978 the Doctors Singer, both professors of psychology at Yale University (New Haven, Connecticut), directed successive formal research studies of youths and television. Their work was funded by major organizations, including the National Science Foundation and American Broadcasting Companies, Inc. Although many of their experimental projects related to cognition and developmental growth in young children, several activities directly pertained to teaching critical television viewing skills. They published papers based on their research, with very practical conclusions and guidelines embodied in two published works similar in content and structure.

The Singers' previous years of research laid the foundation for their systematic plans of CVS study. They founded and continued as co-directors of the Family Television Research and Consultation Center at Yale University. Some salient aspects of their reported research follows. Many CVS projects begun in the late 1970s and early 1980s embodied many of their conclusions, implications, and recommendations—which have contributed to the body of literature relating to cognitive and behavioral development of youngsters vis-à-vis television viewing experience.

*Research Basis: Procedures.*   The Singers preferred field research to laboratory settings or surveys for most of their data. Subjects included 3- and 4-year-olds, and classroom experiments were first with students in Grades 3 through 5 (134 in the experimental group, 98 in the control group), later in Grades K through 2. The project typically involved eight 40-minute lessons over a 4-week period. In addition to hand-out materials and work-pages, materials included narrated videotapes for each lesson, with sample clips from current TV shows. The tapes were 7 to 10 minutes long for the older group. For the younger group, video was reduced to only program excerpts interspersed through the local teacher's presentation—usually a total of about 3 minutes for each lesson. Pretests were conducted 2 weeks before the lessons began, post-tests 2 weeks afterward. Students were retested 3 months later.

*Research Findings.* The research team consistently reported that children's attitudes and behaviors, including growth in imagination and in "prosocial orientations," related closely to the presence and behavior of parents when television was turned on. They stressed the transactional context of television viewing instead of linear stimulus/response causal relationships between TV content and children's behavior patterns. The former involves individual predisposition (intellectual ability, imagination, etc.) and the social context of television viewing, in the family context or with peers. They related these findings to aggressiveness (over 10-year spans) but also to positive behavior such as cooperation, creativity, and language development. They also related these data to socioeconomic status, race, and gender. They (Singer, Singer, & Sherrod, 1979) concluded that "these dimensions of individual/environmental variability do not determine the relationships [between TV viewing and behavior] although they do seem to mediate them" (p. 13). Because of the "bidirectionality" and thus shared responsibility of both viewers and producers of programs, they asserted that discovering why certain children prefer some kinds of programs was as important as learning the consequences of viewing those programs.

Although noting that television can provide "a host of archetypes, identification and stereotype figures around which children can organize their imaginative experience," Jerome Singer (1977, pp. 22–32) cautioned that parents play a pivotal role in helping the child interpret and assess the significance of those models and values in their own lives. He provided a foundation for CVS study programs by inferring from social-psychology research data some desirable forms of controlling use of the medium in households. Turning off the set was not a feasible option. Rather, controlling *patterns* of viewing (amount of time and frequency as well as selections) should be joined with more effective TV viewing experience by an adult being present when preschoolers watch together. And children should be engaged in alternate activities involving imaginative play as an antidote to potential aggressive influence of televised violence.

The husband–wife research team noted their own explorations in preparing materials to facilitate teachers' and parents' attempts to guide children's use of television:

> Parents need some guidance in what to look for in programming, what elements to focus on, how to restrain their didactic tendencies from time to time and still play a teaching role. . . . Dorothy Singer and I have worked out cognitive training materials that can be linked to television viewed jointly by parent or teacher and child and are trying them out with parent groups . . . [including] preparation of parent-training manuals in how to use the TV medium for cognitive development. (pp. 28, 29)

Jerome Singer added only a brief reference to the importance of "pressuring the commercial and public TV producers to increase the number of carefully-designed child-oriented programs and to evaluate them systematically" (p. 31). That approach was more fully developed in the Singers' "Parent's Kit for Television" (described later).

In their reports, the Singers offer balanced assessment of behavioral research, noting the positive as well as negative characteristics that correlate (not necessarily causally) with levels of televiewing.

*Curriculum Projects: Purposes and Procedures.*   From their original research base, the Singers embarked on building a paradigm for systematic instruction of CVS in schools. With financial support from the government, foundations, and the broadcast industry, they and their staff consulted with principals and a media specialist and subsequently with teachers. The plan was to present two topics a week during 4 weeks in selected elementary schools. Out-of-class activities were designed for 15 to 30 minutes to correspond to expected amounts of homework. Lesson plans included specific details for concrete implementation, to expedite teachers' use. All centered around discussion and activities, to engage the children, coupled with emphasis on skills in writing and critical thinking. Short videotapes of 7 to 11 minutes each were prepared to accompany the lessons. Those lessons were subsequently modified so they could be presented effectively without the need for audio-visual support equipment.

When they introduced the lessons as a regular part of the school curriculum they conducted observation and questionnaire surveys of teachers about their students to assess any behavioral changes. They established workshops for teachers and then for parents. As with the videotapes, they later "wrote out" those workshops from later versions of the curriculum published in two books cited later.

*Testing and Findings.*   Testing showed that students engaged in CVS lessons progressed in specialized learning more than did control groups; but the former's viewing habits and preferred programs and characters were not significantly influenced by the lessons (Singer, Singer, & Zuckerman, 1979/1980, p. 17). Subsequent testing indicated retention of much of what was learned.

Beyond documenting the initial effectiveness of their curriculum lesson materials for teaching children about television as well as vocabulary, writing and thinking skills, and even mathematics, the study (Singer, Zuckerman, & Singer, 1979) cited as a "second major finding . . . that the parents were very influential role models for their children's television viewing and for their attitudes towards television" (p. 14). The Singers concluded that "television viewing tends to be more strongly related to the examples set by the parents, rather than to expected predictors such as parents' educational levels, mothers' employment status, or child's IQ" (p. 15).

They adapted their original curriculum (Grades 3–5) to youngsters aged 5 to 7 years (Grades K–2). The number, objectives, and content of lessons were simplified. Briefer units of videotape (only 3 minutes each) were interspersed throughout lessons. They emphasized play activities and homework assignments relying on concrete, visual thinking—addressing the children's pre-operational stage of cognitive development (in Piaget's terms).

Pre- and posttesting indicated significant progress in all areas covered by the tests. They concluded from these and other data that "children benefit from the curriculum regardless of the level of their intellectual ability, reading or social skills. . . . Overall, there was clear evidence of improvement in comprehension in practically all the areas covered in the curriculum" (Rapaczynski, Singer, & Singer, 1981, p. 8; 1982). Pupils and teachers alike responded favorably to the experience. The latter regretted, however, that more time was not given to these and similar exercises; they recommended greater elaboration of the concepts and activities throughout the entire school year.

The Singers subsequently formulated their behavioral research and initial development of tested lesson-plans for young students in two books directed respectively to students and to parents.

Both books were published in 1981. *Teaching Television: How to Use TV to Your Child's Advantage* is a somewhat sophisticated explanation for parents and teachers to use while interacting with children. *Getting the Most Out of TV* is a soft-cover workbook for use by the children themselves, which includes much of the other book's background and explanatory material for parents and teachers (see Fig. 7.1). Both refer

72 ____ Action and Violence

The purpose of this lesson is to teach the children that the violence on TV is not real and should not be imitated. The focus should be on teaching children why violence is not fun, and on discussing other ways of solving problems.

**PRESENTATION OF LESSON**

1. "Action shows are shows which portray a lot of activity, such as car chases, fights, and people running to catch someone or to escape from someone. What action shows do you watch?" (Teacher lists these on the board. Cartoons may be considered action shows.)

2. Discuss vocabulary words.

3. Teacher reads a violent passage from a TV script (see below). Teacher asks if reading about vi_____
   of special effects,

**TV Script**

An old blue car pulls shar____
someone jumps into the passe____
corner and speeds away.

A man starts his motorcycle____
traffic. The blue car then pulls____
the same alley from the other____
and skids into some trash ca____

The motorcyclist gets up a____
end of the alley, bends down ____
car. The car is hit and immed____

4. "Many programs s____
   you to think for a ____
   seem real? (Stress t____
   that? (Teacher ack____
   the real world.) W____

5. Teacher explains th____
   as funny? Is it true____
   will never hurt me"____
   sion?" (Teacher ack____
   TV, but not in rea____
   verbal aggression.

6. "Sometimes people____
   TV." (Teacher gives____
   ever noticed yours____
   What can we do t____

7. "We laugh at the m____
   would you feel if y____
   ever thought of th____
   long periods of h____
   people who are vi____

# ACTION AND VIOLENCE 5

**OBJECTIVES**

1. To understand that the violence portrayed on TV is sometimes distorted.

   a. Violence is not as common in the real world as it is in the TV world.
   b. Violence on TV often seems fun or exciting, because the consequences of violence are not usually shown on TV.

2. To understand that there are other ways of solving problems that are preferable to violent confrontations.

3. To understand that television programs can be exciting or suspenseful without showing violent scenes.

4. To develop familiarity with vocabulary words related to physical and verbal aggression.

**MATERIALS**

1. Aggression Chart.

2. Verbal Aggression Chart.

3. Special Words and Ideas List: action-packed, bloodshed, aggressive, aggression, verbal aggression.

4. Vocabulary List: conflict, alternatives, consequences, excitement, exciting, gory, grief, suspense, violence.

**BACKGROUND INFORMATION**

In the last few years, there has been great concern about the amount of violence on television. Psychologists have found that children tend to imitate the violence that they see on television, and this is especially true for children who have a tendency to be aggressive.

Many children watch violent programs, and their favorite TV characters are often violent heroes and superheroes. However, when we asked elementary school children about television violence, many of the children were aware that TV violence influences them in negative ways. They described how they sometimes imitated TV violence by chasing their friends on bicycles, and frequently described angry interactions with family members. Many children said they were angry "right after watching a program that had a lot of violence."

71

FIG. 7.1.  Explanatory material for teachers. From Singer, Singer, and Zuckerman (1981a) *Getting the Most Out of TV* (Copyright © 1981 Goodyear Publishing.)

throughout to a wide range of published and unpublished research over the decades, including their own studies since 1976 involving teaching media literacy.

The two publications embody the authors' conclusions about structuring a systematic program for introducing CVS to youngsters in Grades 3 through 6. They also suggest adaptation for younger or slightly older boys and girls. Key findings lead to their emphatic recommendation that responsibility is shared between media audiences and media producer-suppliers. They emphasize the role of parents and teachers in acquainting children with ways to get more out of their present TV viewing. The authors did not intend to lessen the typically heavy viewing diet but rather to redirect it somewhat, stressing reflective analysis of programs watched.

*Purposes.* Their field research as well as the literature grounded their assumption that children watch television heavily—usually reflecting the patterns of TV viewing by their parents—and cannot be weaned away from it. But children can be helped to watch more selectively, with more perception and understanding, and with judgmental reflection. The Singers offer little moral or ethical assessment. But their pragmatic perspective does seek to mediate youngsters' TV experience, even to inoculate them against it, in order to lessen negative social and cultural effects on their attitudes and behavior.

The authors offer a balanced perspective about the negative and positive impact of television on young people. They favor harnessing TV instead of decrying it without changing children's habits. They begin by describing key characteristics of pre-adolescents' perceptions, attitude, and behavior. They then summarize trends and major examples of significant laboratory and field research (their own is mostly field tested). They note that "parents' viewing habits were the most important predictors of their children's" habits with television (Singer, Singer, & Zuckerman, 1981b, p. 30). Their readable and fairly complete survey of scientific findings to date provides a useful background so teachers and parents may understand how the rest of the practical lesson materials relate to growing children.

*Procedures and Content.* The eight-lesson plan was presented experimentally in differing forms, first to children in the Orange and Wilton, Connecticut school systems, and then in field testing among students in eight cities scattered around the United States.[2] Although the lessons in the two books do not directly match, most are similar in content, structure, and sequence except for news which is treated only in passing in the hard-cover book, *Teaching Television.* . . .

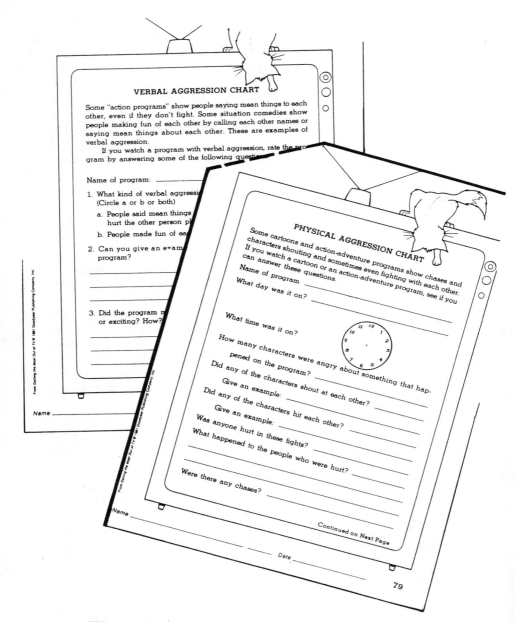

FIG. 7.2.  Sample worksheets for students. From Singer, Singer, and Zuckerman (1981a) *Getting the Most Out of TV*. (Copyright © 1981 Goodyear Publishing.)

The sequence of topics includes: technical aspects of the medium, the creative personnel whose decisions develop different kinds of programs, special effects and fantasy versus reality, stereotyping and role-models in characters, action and violence, commercial advertising and its influence, and the roles of government and audiences in influencing media leaders.

*Assessment.* Both publications are useful for parents and teachers because each offers factual data, summaries of research findings, explicit outlines of purposes and intended outcomes for lessons, supporting readings, guides for eliciting discussion on specific points about the medium and TV viewing, and very concrete activities to engage the youngsters by getting them to look closely at and to think about their television experience (see Fig. 7.2). Except for those applied exercises (accompanied by many tear-out pages of illustrations and fill-in assignments in the soft-cover workbook), the perspective and language of the texts are fairly sophisticated, "talking down" to neither parent– teacher nor child.

In summary, the hardcover *Teaching Television . . .* is intended (in content, layout, and language) for adults who can then apply the principles and reproduce the sample activity sheets. The soft-cover workbook *Getting the Most Out of TV* is suited for children to work with directly (despite the extended explanatory material at the start of each lesson).

The Singers also developed a more judgmental and activist-oriented 13-page report *A Parent's Kit for Television* (Singer & Singer, 1979). In it they primarily warn against youngsters' overuse and misuse of TV; they also urge parents to contact organizations and broadcasters to lodge their complaints. That 13-page kit reflects some of their other guidelines published for parents. It attempts to protect children from negative effects of unsupervised TV viewing, and looks to the medium as a vehicle for enhancing cognitive and social skills useful to growing up. Only a small part offers positive analysis of television. Heavy emphasis is on commercial advertising and its blandishments. Similar emphases are found in materials prepared for parents workshops (Part III, "Helping your child to use television constructively," Sessions 1 to 3).

## ROSEMARY LEE POTTER ET AL. (PINELLAS COUNTY SCHOOLS; CLEARWATER, FLORIDA)

Although well-read in related research, Rosemary Lee Potter, EdD, emphasized heuristic application of TV-related exercises to teach her elementary and middle school students traditional skills in reading, writing, arithmetic, and thinking. The distinctive notes of her many activities were practical application, concrete teaching materials, and employing TV in the service of traditional educational objectives and content. Her major purpose was to enlist children's TV experience and interests in the cause of the standard curriculum. Only part of her broad focus was specifically "critical viewing skills" to enhance personal television experience.

In addition to her daily classroom teaching, Dr. Potter was a prolific writer of articles for popular and professional journals, in which she recounted her discovery and development of TV as a learning tool as well as a valuable medium in its own right.[3] She participated widely in seminars and conferences of educators and others concerned about the role of television in educating children. Her personal involvement in the classroom context led to entrepreneurial projects that provided many kinds of specific teaching aids: books, pamphlets, filmstrips, audiocassettes, reproducible master worksheets (for distribution), and sets of cards outlining concrete exercises for students.

Her initial experience in harnessing TV for the classroom began in 1965 with first-grade students. Subsequent applications evolved in her other elementary grades (1–8), and as a certified reading resource teacher and specialist for those grades and for high school (Grades 9–12).

In 1976 she published *New Season: The Positive Use of Commercial Television with Children,* reprinted (minus the first two words) in 1981 by the National Education Association; it was directed to teachers in primary, intermediate, and secondary grades. In 1979 she produced a kit of resource materials for Grades 5 through 12, titled *Channel: Critical Reading/TV Viewing Skills.* In 1980 she collaborated with the same company to produce *TV Readers Skills Kit* for Grades 1 through 6, with materials updated in 1982 (Potter, 1976, 1981). Those major products are reviewed here because they were developed from Potter's first-hand classroom experience coupled with formal study of research and her own experimental projects, and were made widely available to teachers. They were among the several CVS sources offering the most sophisticated "packages" of media-enhanced materials.

Rosemary Lee Potter's premise remained the same throughout the years: Commercial television programming can be a functional referent in the classroom to "support both the instructional goals set for growing children and encourage steps towards TV literacy" (1979, pp. 19–20). She did not recommend viewing commercial TV fare in school but advocated exercises and discussion among students based on their regular home viewing. In fact, she noted in her first book (Potter, 1981) that "commercial television today has in itself little positive value for children" and the book's exercises "neither approve present TV fare nor encourage more extensive viewing" but rather "are designed to capitalize on the wealth of data and TV viewing experiences students already have, turning it to studies they must address" (pp. iv–v). In a sense, her approach sought to redeem TV or capitalize on it for other educational goals rather than to discover and analyze the medium's own positive assets. She urged "tie-ins" of TV viewing with books on the subject and with reproduced scripts, to foster interest in reading. Yet she lauded early efforts to teach media literacy to help teachers, parents, and students "manage TV in their lives and to learn from it and enjoy it."

The bulk of her 126-page book *New Season: The Positive Use of Commercial Television with Children* (pp. 21–107) consists of 57 out-lines of specific "learning experiences," derived from commercial tele-vision programming and tested in her classroom, each of which relate to a cognitive skill or content area. Teachers are to select and adapt these model exercises to the personal television viewing experiences of their students. Briefly, TV programs and characters are referents cited in exercises such as learning the alphabet, recognizing auditory cues, selecting details to suit an author's purpose, identifying story parts and logical sequencing, recognition of character traits of stereotyped classes, distinguishing reality from fantasy, and recognizing rela-tionships in analogies. The intent is to link new learning skills and concepts with personal TV experience commonly shared among peers. In one exercise, thinking processes are to be developed by relating to specific game show formats the following concepts: comparison, es-timation, auditory recall, visual memory, generalization, and analy-sis/synthesis. In another, values that motivate human beings as well as value-conflicts were to be discussed by analyzing roles and story-lines in popular evening TV programs. In yet another exercise, stu-dents were to use TV schedules printed in newspapers and *TV Guide,* to learn how to find and use such information in making decisions about viewing. Most exercises teach cognitive skills. Others pertaining directly to television provide nondirective questions without implied judgments, to draw out students' personal perceptions about television.

Only on a single page near the end did Dr. Potter list recommenda-tions for parents to guide TV patterns in the home. The 13 points emphasize interaction between parent and child, including shared viewing and discussion about programs and commercials. Parents should support selective, planned viewing of both entertainment and news, and they should encourage non-TV activities such as reading and sports.

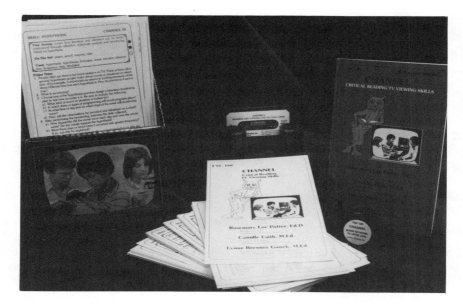

FIG. 7.3.  Kit of lessons cards, filmstrip, audiocassette, and manual in *Channel: Critical Reading/TV Viewing Skills* by Potter, Faith, and Ganek (1979).

*Support Materials.*    That book was followed several years later by the first of two resource kits. *Channel: Critical Reading/TV Viewing Skills* (see Fig. 7.3). The kit provides teachers with concrete instructional aids to help motivate students in upper elementary grades (5–8) and secondary school (9–12), to enhance their reading and viewing skills:

By reading and viewing selectively.

By linking TV viewing to reading, balancing time for both and also for other leisure activities.

By learning to analyze and evaluate what they watch and read.

By encouraging them to communicate with publishers and networks.[4]

This elaborately boxed set includes a 62-frame filmstrip with accompanying audiocassette soundtrack, a 21-page reference manual (including a brief bibliography, list of agencies and sources for TV curricular materials, and alphabetical index of topics on "skill cards"), a brief teachers guide, and 87 "skill cards" (5½×8½-inch sleek stiff cardboard) with specific instructions for assignments and activities relating to critical reading/TV-viewing skills.

*Procedures.* The material is intended to be integrated into traditional courses over a full semester or a school year. In addition to their use by teachers in regular classes, the materials can also be used as supplementary, enrichment material for advanced students to use independently. Potters' underlying premise was "the rich and integral critical links between television and print media." The sound/filmstrip oriented participants to those "links." (Appropriately, a lynx is the cartoon "logo" in the filmstrip, booklets, a poster, and cover of the kit.)

The eight-page *Teacher's Guide* provides a sample form for logging students' daily diet of television, 21 nondirective questions for discussion prior to and after viewing the sound/filmstrip, and a cross-index of categories of skills involved in the 87 cards—relating them to critical thinking, reading, and television viewing.

The cards can be used in any sequence. Each is self-contained and includes five sets of information/instruction. A somewhat forced use of media jargon is intended to capture attention by translating traditional educational terms into the argot of TV. Each card includes: "Fine Tuning" (Objective), "On the Set" (Materials), "Cues" (Vocabulary), "Prime-Time" (Activity), and "Spin-Offs" (Additional Activities). Each card is marked with a stylized code indicating "mature/difficult," "average," or "easy" level of material, and whether the material thereon includes "content reading." In addition to being used in full classrooms or by small subgroups, they can be used for field work and reports by individuals or committees, by parents at home with their children, and for assigned classwork or homework as well as for extra-credit or make-up work. The cards are meant to be a flexible resource to teachers in a range of courses.

Because the activities are open-ended, for learning through discovery in practice, there are no "answers" or key provided. Students' explorations and findings are to be shared and discussed, with the teacher's cooperation and guidance. But no claim is made for progressive, systematic, and measurable growth in critical reading/viewing skills: "CHANNEL provides experience in the skill[s]—field work, rather than entry or exit level testing of such skills."

The "Skill Cards" are carefully worked out by Dr. Potter and her two associates (both experienced classroom teachers and one also involved in the HEW-funded CVS project in New York). They include more specific references to television than to print, but they continually mingle both media. Topics are wide-ranging with sometimes challenging questions and assignments to find more information. Unlike the sometimes simplistic-sounding filmstrip soundtrack, these card exercises in some instances could be demanding for advanced students and even for adults. The thrust is more toward critical *thinking,* with both print and electronic media serving as the sources for references and examples.

"Skills Correlation" in the teacher's guide clusters cards by their numbers according to major categories of "Comprehension" (including topic areas of word meaning, and literal, interpretive, and critical comprehension); "Location/Study Skills" (advertising, following directions, interpreting pictorial representations, library skills, note-taking, outlining, and book parts, skimming/scanning, and organizing); "Literature/Language Development" (figurative language, literary technique, oral language, written language, and listening); and "Reading in Content Areas" (art, career education, consumer education, health, journalism, law, literature, mathematics, music, physical education, science, and social studies). Included within those ares are the otherwise abstract topics of context, analogy, cause and effect, relationships, analyzing characters, criticism/evaluation, inference, reliability/validity, extrapolation, and development and interpretation of oral language.

The following year Potter and one of her colleagues collaborated with a new third partner on a *TV Readers Skills Kit,* produced by the same company in 1980, with updated materials added in subsequent years.[5] The well-packaged materials intended for Grades 4–8 included 8 elaborate booklets with large photographs (averaging 35 pages each), 8 accompanying audiocassettes, 16 "reproducible worksheets," and a brief teacher's guide (see Fig. 7.4). Added in 1981 were three 20-sheet sets of ditto masters to make copies for distribution to children in Grades 1–2, 3–4, and 5–6, respectively, with three teacher's guides.

*Purposes.*    The same rationale lay behind these instructional aids as for the previous *Channel . . .* kit:

> to link students' interests in television with the teaching of basic reading skills both to improve reading and TV literacy. TELEVISION BEHIND THE SCENES [*sic*] promotes more and better reading. It encourages a better understanding of television, but not more viewing.[6]

Students received practice in major reading and thinking skills through reading texts while listening to the audiocassettes, discussing the topics, answering multiple-choice questions at the end of each booklet, and filling in the two worksheets for each. At the same time they learned many details about the structure, processes, personnel, and effects of the television medium. The booklets need not necessarily be read in sequence. Titles, intended skills to be learned and exercised, and content for each booklet are:

FIG. 7.4.  Kit of audiocassettes, booklets, worksheets, and teacher's guides developed as *TV Readers Skills Kit* by Potter, Hanneman, and Faith (1980).

"Ready Three! Take Three!"
  SKILL: *Synthesis*
  Shows the process involved in taking an idea to the TV screen
"How We Got Into TV by Me, Jake Reynolds"
  SKILL: *Analysis*
  Shows development of a VTR news show by middle-schoolers—problems, suggestions, situations
"TV Typewriters, Brushes, and Pens"
  SKILL: *Seeing Relationships*
  Shows relationship of words to TV; print and art careers in the medium.
"What It Takes to Be a TV Star"
  SKILLS: *Classification, Fact/Opinion, Reality/Fantasy*
  Shows honest background on TV "talent" and the nature of performers' work.
"And Now This Message"
  SKILLS: *Cause/Effect, Main Idea*
  Explains how TV advertising works, using a fictional product.
"Television On Trial"
  SKILL: *Analysis*
  Considers problems with TV and children, using family and home as setting.

"TV Tricks with Camera, Machine, Cast, and Props"
   SKILLS: *Problem-solving, Reality/Fantasy*
   Explains how special effects are achieved.
"Television! All Summer Long?"
   SKILL: *Sequence*
   Shares the past, present, and future of television in a storefront museum.
   (p. 2)

*Assessment.* The well-written booklets clearly presented accurate and detailed information about the television industry. The full-page photographs offered graphic examples of technical information in the text. The accompanying audiocassettes were professional in technical quality. They carefully integrated appropriate "upbeat" music during opening and closing paragraphs, and at transitions to "punctuate in sound" the development of the material; and judicious use was made of apt sound effects to augment the listening experience—reinforcing students' appropriate interpretation of the printed words and their context. The written text and the style and pace of the reader are not condescending, interpreting the text dramatically and carefully for interest as well as comprehension.

But the extended detail of precise and often technical information about how television operates may detract from the broader purposes of the materials. The "skills" listed for each booklet may be overly general and optimistic about what students may actually derive from this immersion in the minute details of a professional industry. For example, the effect of reading the first booklet might be to understand the complexity of creating television programs; but the claimed skill of "synthesis" may be a quite indirect learning goal. Accompanying worksheets reinforce the emphasis on mechanics and techniques of TV program planning and production more than on direct analysis of combining and synthesizing elements into a coherent whole. Much seems left to the ability and imagination of the local teacher to support learning of "synthesis."

All but one booklet in the series contributed only indirectly to critical viewing by acquainting readers/listeners with major elements of the medium, its operation, and personnel; such understanding might help demystify programming. But connections to personal viewing habits and reactions would probably have to be made by local teachers for effective impact on children in Grades 4–8. Only the sixth booklet, "Television on Trial," explicitly discusses major elements of critical television viewing. Points are made by realistic dialogue in a fictional dramatic setting, involving youngsters and their parents who attempt to resolve family differences about misuse of television in their home.

Generally, the perspective in the materials is one of "status quo"—neutral description and explanation, with little value judgment implied other than acceptance of television programs and advertising as "givens." Yet the sixth topic does offer judgment about TV programming's positive values as well as about harmful ways of misusing the medium. Focus is on viewer misuse (viewing too much, to the detriment of other leisure activities and duties, and without positive selection). Few questions are raised about excesses or problems arising in the medium itself (such as stereotyping, violence, images and values, or misrepresenting reality in news). However, all the booklets and audiotapes seek to counter stereotypical images in general by emphasizing females in important positions in the stories and photos, alternating female and male voices on the eight audiocassettes, featuring minority children and adults in photos, and alluding occasionally to real-life domestic situations such as children of divorced parents, alcoholism, and handicapped persons.

The related set of material carries the title "Contrast: A TV Study Strategy for Basic Skills Improvement." These three sets of purple ditto masters were intended to "provide a practical way to teach critical TV viewing skills while also . . . teaching basic school skills" to children in lower elementary grades.[7] The authors stated that children perceive the medium as separate from school learning and even from skills in thinking. Because school schedules permit little time to examine TV viewing skills, Potter and Faith offered these exercises for integration into teaching basic subjects, "linking the practice of print and video skills essential to critical thought and making efficient use of time." They noted that children find TV-related activities interesting and motivating, thus making more relevant the traditional subjects linked with television study. They "reexamined" the CVS skills offered by the Office of Education's funded projects, "reinterpreting" them according to their own experience with youngsters' needs and the goals of schools. They selected those skills in the USOE projects that were also found in standard elementary school curricula for language arts, reading, and social studies:

1. Understanding extent, self-control and preplanning of viewing using TV schedules, etc.
2. Discriminating among different kinds of television programming: shows from commercials, children's shows from adult programming, and programming types.
3. Recognizing internal characteristics of TV: purposes, persuasive techniques, and reality from fantasy.
4. Recognizing the tie-ins between television and everyday life: language, music and sports, and feeling.

5. Recognizing some of TV's potential and problems: content, scheduling, access to faraway places, and stereotyping.[8]

Four ditto worksheets are devoted to each of those areas of skills in each set of grade levels (1–2, 3–4, and 5–6). With variations in sequence and in level of sophistication among the three sets, the exercises relate those five TV-specific skills to broader, more basic skills that include: Analyzing, following directions, recalling details, sequencing, classifying, determining main idea, estimating, making inferences, determining fact from fiction, recognizing cause and effect, noticing patterns, extrapolating, classifying themes, comparing, listening, analyzing feelings, and stereotyping. The upper two levels also include these skills: Estimating, developing vocabulary, problem solving, recognizing distortion, judging appropriateness, making decisions, criticizing, writing letters, and improving written expression.

An important feature was that many exercises are to be done at home and even shared with parents for discussion or assistance. At the outset each student is to take to their parents a sheet explaining the purpose of these activities. Included are disclaimers: "We will not be encouraging extra television viewing by your child" (1–2 level) or "We neither encourage nor approve additional television watching with this unit" (3–4 level). Alternate options are made available where home viewing does not fit into family patterns. Parents are encouraged to use these home-based exercises as opportunities to learn more about how their children relate to television and about their growth in general skills in the context of TV experience.

Exercises for each grade level begin with students logging and analyzing their own TV viewing habits, including listing their reasons for watching various programs and comparing how time is spent on other kinds of activities day and night. Unlike previous booklets and audiocassettes, these exercises progressively move toward implied assessments of positive and negative values of various programs and commercials. Although the worksheets do not state judgments, students are guided to reflect on what they view and to compare it with related experiences in their own life, adding their personal evaluation. Further, they are shown how to respond to material they judge poor: by refusing to view such on television, by writing to broadcast companies (New York addresses of major networks are listed), and by joining consumer groups objecting to industry practices. In progressive steps, the exercises thus guide the youngsters through a series of activities involving gathering and learning data, reflecting about the medium and its role in their daily living, and eventually making judgments about programming.

The six-page teacher's guides for each set of materials succinctly note the purpose and scope as well as concrete objectives of each ditto worksheet, together with tips for using them effectively in the classroom. They also caution teachers not to be judgmental about the responses children write on the sheets, but rather to "be prepared to be a learner."

*     *     *

The research and applied projects of individuals recounted in this chapter represent initiatives taken elsewhere around the world by persons working on their own or in collaboration with others—often at academic institutions. The next chapters turn to major organizations and private companies that advanced media literacy including critical viewing skills for television.

## NOTES

1. Cf. Singer and Singer (1980); Singer (1980); and Zuckerman, Singer, and Singer (1982).

2. See Singer, Singer, and Zuckerman (1981b, p. vii). Although the authors note that field testing was conducted "in fourteen different school systems around the country" (p. ix), they cite in their "Acknowledgments" only 10 in addition to the original two in Connecticut: Phoenix, Arizona; Stamford, Connecticut; Cary, North Carolina; Lafayette, Indiana; Brookfield, Wisconsin; Valley Center, California; Santa Rosa, California; Omaha, Nebraska; Deerfield, Wisconsin; and Portland, Oregon.

3. Since 1976 Dr. Potter wrote regularly for *Teacher* magazine ("TV Talk" column); in the late-1970s she also wrote a weekly syndicated column on using television wisely, and contributed articles to various publications since then, including *NCCT Forum* (see Potter, 1979).

4. "Reference Manual," p. 2, in kit by Potter, Faith, and Ganek (1979).

5. See Potter, Hanneman, and Faith (1980–1982). Potter wrote eight of the booklets, Hanneman and Faith each wrote two. The booklets and worksheets were copyrighted in 1980, audiocassettes and teacher's guide in 1981; the additional three sets of purple ditto masters and teacher's guides were copyrighted in 1982.

6. See Potter, Hanneman, and Faith (1981). Title of this 4-page teacher's guide (coded BC 331) differs from the rest of the kit (items coded AKC 331).

7. Identical wording was at the beginning of teacher's guides for each of the three grade levels— "Tony the TV Turtle," "Another Look: Understanding Television," and "More Than Fun: Understanding Television"; each was subtitled "Contrast: A TV Strategy for Basic Skills Improvement." These materials (coded D226, D227, and D228) were included in the kit described earlier and were copyrighted in 1982.

8. Potter, Hanneman, and Faith (1981), p. 2 of teacher's guide for Grades 1–2 (coded D226). Wording differed only slightly on p. 2 of the other two guides.

# 8

# *National Organizations (Nongovernmental), U.S.*

Systematic programs of training in critical viewing skills were also prepared by organizations not associated with government, school districts, or institutions. Unlike most of the other "value-neutral" curricula, these programs were generally oriented to value-systems. They usually included elements of consumer activism, seeking to affect media industries as well as media viewers. Projects described in previous chapters represented specific schools and districts in the United States and in other regions of the world. Typically they were intensive where they originated—in specific classrooms and campus-related testing sites. What might be call their "vertical" structure contrasted with the broad "horizontal" scope of CVS programs mounted by national organizations. This chapter describes four such major entities in the United States: the American Council for Better Broadcasts, the National Parent-Teacher Association, the Media Action Research Center, and the U.S. Catholic Conference. But briefly noted first is an early related organization.

## NATIONAL ASSOCIATION FOR BETTER RADIO AND TELEVISION

A forerunner to organized critical evaluation of broadcast media was the National Association for better Radio and Television. Created in

1949 as the Southern California Association for Better Radio and Television, two years later it expanded in name and activity to national scope. This primarily activist public interest group participated in the public arena by conducting studies and surveys, providing information to viewers and agencies concerned about media content, testifying at governmental hearings about alleged media abuses, and consulting with leaders in media industries for redress of complaints. As an important feature of its work, NAFBRAT developed printed guides for parents and teachers evaluating children's and other programming. Among its 11 "aims and purposes" listed in a four-page booklet was "8. To encourage the development of high individual standards of radio and television appreciation both in the schools and in the homes" (NAFBRAT, ca. 1960, p. 1).

The first issue of the *NAFBRAT Quarterly* (summer 1960, pp. 1, 8–12) reported its 10th annual national survey of children's programs. It described 14 TV programs ranked in their category of "excellent," 13 as "good," 14 "fair," one "poor," 12 "objectionable" (including "Disney Presents," "Lone Ranger," "Rin Tin Tin," "Roy Rogers," and "The Three Stooges"), and one as "most objectionable" ("Superman"). For radio, they judged four programs as "excellent" and one each as "good" and "fair." They listed each program's advertisers. Their evaluations primarily targeted depictions of crime and violence, even in programs of fantasy (including animated cartoons) and ones with traditional "good/bad" values where law, justice, and "right" triumphed.

NAFBRAT alerted parents to program content it judged might adversely affect children. The organization distributed to members and opinion leaders reprints of published criticisms as well as its own evaluations, to help families use broadcast media more selectively.

## AMERICAN COUNCIL FOR BETTER BROADCASTS/NATIONAL TELEMEDIA COUNCIL

An early broad-based activity in systematic critical appraisal of media was the American Council for Better Broadcasts. The ACBB was founded in 1953 by representatives of 18 national and 16 state organizations. It evolved out of the Wisconsin Association for Better Broadcasting, an organization formed in the early 1930s in Madison, Wisconsin, by English teachers of the American Association of University Women's local chapter. Their concern about radio's cultural and social impact led to a monthly listing of "some good radio programs" and "helps" to listening. The organization's director (Rowe, 1989) said their objective was to promote "awareness, critical evaluation, and appreciation of quality programming." Their positive perspective acknowledged and awarded excellence in media programming. ACBB also sought to influence broadcasters and government regulators by enlisting viewers to evaluate programming publicly and to communicate their judgments to media leaders. By actively monitoring TV programs, participants were to become more discriminating and judgmental about their television experience, thereby learning "the critical viewing skills needed to develop television-wise consumers of the medium."

The year it was formed, the ACBB (1980, p. 1) created its "Look-Listen Opinion Poll," soliciting listeners' and viewers' qualitative evaluations of radio and television programming. The poll has been conducted annually since then. Thousands of members nationally reviewed drama, music, news, information, and children's programs. They rated them as excellent, good, mediocre, or poor and then explained briefly their reasons for so rating them. In the 1979–1980 poll, viewers were presented for the first time with specific questions "designed to probe the reasons behind the viewers' ratings and opinions and in order to facilitate criteria for evaluation. But fully two-thirds who participated that year were teenagers or younger. Because assessments were subjective, "the preferences expressed in this poll do not constitute a recommended list or guide for viewing. They are grassroots judgments from all regions of the country based on the desires of individuals."[1] The published report of the 1960 poll totaled 28 pages; the 1980 report filled 60 large pages, including 6 pages of statistical results and analysis, and 51 pages of excerpted qualitative comments; the 1989–1990 report totaled 5 pages, plus 11 pages of appended material. The ACBB (ca. 1960) also published the findings in a national newsletter to members, with the purpose of encouraging "discrimination in choosing broadcasts for enrichment." The organization emphasized positive values; its newsletter listed only programs highly rated by its constituency. It did not promote boycotting material disfavored by poll respondents. In fact, since 1965 it presented Sponsor Recognition Awards in order to recognize and encourage support for programming excellence.

The ACBB also promoted media literacy by conducting summer workshops where teachers each developed their own curriculum, and by providing materials and guidelines for classroom use. The latter appeared in the bi-monthly newsletter *Better Broadcast News* and were also distributed as reprints. One of the ACBB's earliest efforts at organizing curricular materials, ca. 1960, was a 33-page mimeographed compilation subtitled "A tentative outline, especially helpful to teachers of English and Speech." A brief explanation of the rationale and procedures was accompanied by quotations from specialists and by extended reprints of articles. An outline for evaluating drama for two weeks and news and informational programs another two weeks offered assignments and points for discussion. Lessons included reading, viewing kinescopes (filmed recordings of TV programs), and class discussion about elements in drama and news and about the medium's structure and form. The final day was devoted to determining how best to communicate with broadcasters by writing letters. Additional pages of media data, including definitions, were supplemented by material to help students take part in the annual programing poll—labeled the "Look-Listen Project." Similar treatment was offered for news programs, plus some information about commercial advertising. Samples were added about how critical viewing exercises were conducted among elementary school children in several schools in the Midwest, and another described group procedures "to foster discriminating viewing of television" for all ages.

In 1983 the ACBB changed its name to the National Telemedia Council; its national office remained in Madison, Wisconsin. In the mid-1980s the council shifted the focus of its national surveys from individual home viewers' opinions to promoting critical, evaluative viewing by school children. It changed the format and name of the annual project from "Look-Listen Opinion Poll" to "Project Look-Listen-Think-Respond," stressing reflective thought instead of mere reaction. Working exclusively with classroom teachers across the nations, the organization intended its TV viewing/analysis project to serve as an instrument for teaching youngsters to "be reflective about the media they consume and . . . express in writing what they think" (Wyman, 1990, p. 1). Students' written comments about specific programs were used for class discussions to develop their own criteria; extended excerpts were compiled in the council's annual published reports for teachers, "reinforcing a mutually supportive network to promote media literacy" (p. 43).

Late in 1989 the National Telemedia Council's executive director (Rowe, 1989, p. 2) outlined five major obstacles to media educational development in the United States: (a) Established practices in formal education exclude television. (b) Teachers and administrators resist change. (c) Mass media, much less media literacy, are not recognized as significant. (d) The meaning of "media education" is often confused with TV as an audiovisual tool in teaching. And (e) teaching media literacy is difficult, requiring new attitudes and forms of teaching. She added that "media literacy cannot be taught by rote, or by simply following a 'plan,' but requires the creative skills of a truly reflective teacher.

The ACBB/National Telemedia Council's openness to pluralistic values was reflected in a newsletter column (Baime, 1980). (It provides a bridge to the next cluster of CVS organizations that clearly espouse sets of values.) The columnist addressed the delicate issue of standards for evaluating programming, and thus of criteria for critical viewing skills themselves.

> As a shortcut or expedient to complete a task it is reasonable to develop a list or guide to direct one's efforts. This can be effective in the resolution of one's personal affairs. But to impose one's personal list of criteria upon others for accomplishing their tasks is perhaps, a bit naive. . . . I believe this simplistic method for assessing complex problems is similar to the teacher who has developed her/his own standards for critical viewing of television and imposes them upon the students. They might have served the teacher well, but their impact will be lost in translation by students. An inherent danger of printed lists or 'canned' learning units is that they can immobilize the creative energy of the class and define the limits or range of activity. This may not be the intent of the originator, but it is a reality in the classroom.
>     If lists of specific unit materials are to have significance for their students, they should develop their own. In the act of producing such material they are compelled to examine or research the media in depth. Through this process a genuinely critical attitude will take root.
>     Student involvement in developing their own material for 'TV literacy' has the additional value of encompassing the collective value system represented in the class.
> . . . . . . . . . . . . . . . . . . . . . . . . . . . . . . . . . . . . . . . . . . . . . . . . . . . . . . . . . . . . . . . . . . . . .
>     Faced with endless variables in TV taste in the classroom, the teacher might give up in exasperation with, 'No way can such variety be pulled together and become critical TV viewers.'
>     But—it's precisely the variety, which if looked at realistically and creatively, is the single greatest resource to the teacher! The challenge is to direct the synergy from seeming chaos. From it the process for critical viewing can develop.
>     Perhaps it's this, the process, rather than an end product, which should be sought in developing a critical viewing public. Process connotes movement, an adaptability to change. In a fast-moving world, any attempt at developing 'TV literacy' must include techniques as dynamic as the areas to be criticized. (p. 8)

The ACBB acknowledged the dilemma such an approach raises for training media teachers and for conducting classroom instruction. Its newsletter outlines possible approaches:

> At one extreme is the strictly defined set of guidelines which tell the student directly, with authority, and with specific examples, what is a

good program and what is a bad one. Such approaches are easier to carry out but are arbitrary in the imposition of standards and values.

A more subtle, but still advocacy-oriented approach, will guide the student to the desired conclusions by means of well-chosen examples which single out and emphasize the specific positive or negative values to be illustrated and learned.

By far the most difficult approach involves an entirely non-judgmental way, which allows the student freely to come to his own conclusions and to develop his own criteria and values as a result of non-judgmental presentations in which he acquires the *tools* for intelligent, discriminating use but must develop his own answers. The ultimate goal is self-generated rather than outside control. It is primarily a value-building process based on knowledge and awareness. (p. 8)

This premise is similar to that of the next organization described. (Both of them differ considerably from the orientation of the third and fourth organizations described later.)

## NATIONAL CONGRESS OF PARENTS AND TEACHERS (NATIONAL PTA)

Throughout the 1970s the National Congress of Parents and Teachers publicly criticized the quality of national television. It monitored programs, published lists of ratings, held public hearings, conducted symposia, and fostered letter-writing campaigns to broadcast companies and government agencies. By 1978 the organization began to explore ways to promote better television programming on behalf of children and families; that eventually included developing plans for a CVS curriculum.

One effect of eight regional hearings it held in 1976–1977 (resulting in 50,000 pages of transcribed testimony) was an eight-page booklet (National PTA Television Commission, 1977) summarizing their "findings." They predictably indicted television and its programming. But they also noted that responsibility for the medium's impact in society was shared; not only broadcasters and program suppliers but also government and parents and teachers as well as individual viewers had roles to play in proper use of television.

Those hearings also resulted in a Program Review Guide that the National PTA began publishing in 1978. The 21-page booklet responded to requests from parents and teachers for specific aid in supervising their children's viewing. The booklet (National PTA TV Action Center, 1978) reported balloting by PTA members "from thousands of local units in all 50 states and the District of Columbia actively engaged in monitoring television" (p. 2).[2] Prime-time programs were appraised in three general areas, with a 5-point scale for each of 21 subcategories to be ranked from 1 (poor) to 5 (excellent). Data were derived from forms filled in around the country. The report identified the 10 most commended programs and the 10 most objectionable in each category; it evaluated and ranked each network. On 11 pages the booklet described 70 regularly scheduled programs plus "specials" aired by each network, with excerpts from presumably representative comments by PTA reviewers. It added ratings ranging from four stars down to no-stars. The 10 programs rated with four stars received double space, each featured in ruled boxes with accompanying photo. Distribution of these booklets supplemented the considerable national press coverage of the PTA's annual program evaluations.

*CVS Curricula.* Quite different from its 4-year-old monitoring activity that publicly praised and denounced each season's "best" and "worst" prime-time TV programs, a new project was announced in 1982. The PTA's new direction emphasized positive, constructive approaches to limit alleged negative impact of the medium as well as to encourage producers and programmers to improve TV content for an increasingly selective mass audience. The organization planned to develop four CVS curricula for Grades K–2, 3–5, 6–8, and 9–12.

*Purposes and Procedures.* Their rationale was similar to that of the American Council on Better Broadcasts: Help train a sensitive, discriminating, and demanding audience with good taste and judgment in using media, so that programmers would respond by creating content of "quality" for that growing audience. Intended as neither "anti nor pro television in its approach," the project sought advice and assistance from a broad range of educators, specialists in child development, and advertisers and professional broadcasters as well as creators of programming. The project set out to create student study guides, worksheets, and viewing assignments for classroom and home, videotaped material "developed to heighten understanding and critical skills," supplementary viewing activities for home, and TV program libraries available in school.

*Curriculum Content.* Topics included quality of content and form (plot, characterization, production techniques, special effects, etc.), stereotypes, advertising accuracy and persuasion, propaganda, and television as an industry.

Initial planning of that CVS project back in 1979 had produced a sample workbook to be presented to the PTA's national convention.

That experimental workbook for upper elementary/middle grade levels consisted of three lessons (each six pages plus two pages of teacher's notes). They were to field test the total curriculum of 36 lessons about television's "special effects." Each brief lesson included classroom and take-home assignment sheets following each two-page explanation of basic points about some TV production techniques. Exercises tended to be pragmatic "how to" and "hands on" activities such as filling in questionnaires after viewing programs at home, or making a monster mask out of plaster. Teacher's notes explained the reasons for studying "special effects": to diminish fear when watching horror programs, to differentiate between reality and TV illusions, and to understand the process of making TV programs. The notes provided concrete examples for class, discussion questions, and optional follow-up activities, as well as brief bibliographies. Printed lesson booklets were supplemented by audio-visual materials.

In 1980 the National PTA developed another curriculum package on the topic of "family awareness." Its objective was to help students differentiate between television's often stereotypical and distorted portrayals from real-life families, with their variety and complexity of interactions and daily household problem-solving.[3] The PTA developed two different sets of 36 lessons each for Grades K–2 and Grades 3–5 (Dietsch, Young, & Maley, 1982). The first set included a 78-page teacher's manual and 72 sheets of illustrative cartoon-like drawings as exercises to be done in class in conjunction with the teacher's verbal explanations and read-aloud vignettes (both in the manual). Children were to analyze components of real-life families by reflecting on their personal home experiences and then to compare those with families depicted in TV programs. Exercises and class discussions were to help youngsters realize the discrepancies between real and fantasy family contexts, personalities, dialogue, and relationships. This sociopsychological emphasis was unlike most other CVS curricula that included cultural and aesthetic qualities of programs as well as informational and economic aspects of the medium (news, commercials, etc.). Only Lessons 7 and 8 explicitly focused on the structure and characteristics of how the medium is crafted by analyzing how programs are developed by executive, creative, and technical personnel with specialized equipment that selects and edits content.

The second set of curricular materials, for Grades 3–5, included 72 pages of teacher's notes and 72 sheets in a student activity book. Again the emphasis was on substantive issues in interaction and life style of real families, including the students' own. The curriculum continued to use television as a referent against which children could discuss personal experiences of their own families at home. The purpose was still to wean students from TV depictions as the ideal or normative or even as representing real life. Topics for discussion included chores, arguments, feelings and their expression, alcoholism, divorce, foster children, single adults, and other problems affecting adults and children in a family. Every sixth lesson was labeled "The Video Family Review," which reviewed previous topics while presenting information about how television is structured and works—how economics and techniques and personnel determine the TV families seen on the screen. In the final lesson, the teacher's manual noted: "This conceptual leap between watching TV families as if they were slices from life and watching TV families as actors playing roles before a camera crew is fundamental to the child's ability to critically view TV" (p. 74). The students' sheets provided considerable data in textual form and in diagrams or cartoons; they included fill-in questions and charts or other pen-and-pencil tasks to develop the point of each lesson. Each lesson had a two-sided sheet, most of which was devoted to the concepts about family as such; but each had a small portion at the bottom of the back side to note when the lesson's examples were observed in specific TV programs. Every sixth sheet pertained directly to television, but offered only jejune information about broadcast techniques. For example, in Lesson 18, nine short sentences noted the artificial limits of program time blocks, and in Lesson 24, there were 13 even shorter sentences describing program ratings. Only in the final Lesson 36 of the Student Activity Book were three sentences devoted to how a program is produced in a studio:

> Video Facts: While TV actors play their parts, there are many people around them who stand where the camera cannot see them. They are always there, however, for without them, no TV show could be made. They are the technical crews and the director, plus the camera operators and support personnel. (p. 71)

Neither the PTA nor the Center fully carried out similar plans for the upper two sets of grade levels. Some curriculum material for Grades 6–8 was "available" but not distributed; material for Grades 9–12 was developed but not available for this report.[4] The national Phi Delta Kappa organization did not conduct planned regional workshops; nor did it evaluate the use of effectiveness of the distributed curricula for the two sets of lower grades.

*Assessment.* The PTA curriculum stressed teaching understanding of family living against the backdrop of television programs about families. But it offered very limited information and guidance to teachers or students about characteristics of the TV medium. Critical viewing focused almost exclusively on how the medium depicted families in a limited and often inaccurate way. This agenda for study implied a clear set of values: the quality and variety of family life, and acceptance of a wide range of family structures, contexts, and experiences—including non-traditional ones—as not abnormal despite TV's stereotyped portrayals. Any learning about how television operates and affects program content as well as viewers' perceptions of the real world was done indirectly, at best.

## MEDIA ACTION RESEARCH CENTER

One of two major church-related organizations that mounted extensive critical viewing skills projects was the Media Action Research Center (MARC). Organized in 1974 in New York City, it was formed with grants from foundations, government, and religious denominations to research and design educational media programs. Its religious orientation clearly advocated a "values approach" rather than a neutral one.[5] MARC responded to the 1981 questionnaire that, in addition to an educational and religious purpose or motivation, its goals were ethical/moral and media reform.

In 1977 it collaborated with the Church of the Brethren, American Lutheran Church, and the United Methodist Church to develop its first major project, Television Awareness Training (or "T-A-T"). It developed a 280-page *Viewer's Guide* and various kinds of workshops and training sessions for teachers and parents. Its second curriculum project, *Growing with Television,* consisted of 11 large booklets and audio-visual support material. It promoted specifically Christian biblical values in conjunction with television viewing.

The Television Awareness Training project in its early years was run by five administrators, two clerical/research staff members, 10 teachers/"trainers" and another 433 trained "T-A-T leaders" in 44 states. By 1985 there were an administrator and another staff member, with 11 teachers/"trainers." Workshop participants during its first 4 years numbered "thousands" of collegians and adults; by 1985 participants in the T-A-T program's books, seminars, and workshops were estimated at "hundreds of thousands."[6]

*Procedures.*   MARC/T-A-T conducted workshops in two steps: *Regional* workshops offered leadership training to those who then went on to conduct *local* workshops in their respective areas. Typically, MARC sponsored ten or more regional workshops annually in major cities of the United States, and by the mid-1980s also in Canada, Brazil, Norway, Japan, Australia, the Philippines, and Hong Kong. Leaders used nine films/videotapes of sample TV content, a leader's manual, and the basic workbook text. The Media Action Research Center (1980b) conducted workshops during 2½ days of a weekend, with eight 2-hour sessions.

> The workshop process is designed to assist television viewers in understanding how TV programming and advertising affects behavior and attitudes. . . . in a significant skill-and-awareness building experience around television's effect on 'values.' . . . Actual programs and commercials will be examined to see whether they encourage problem-solving through negotiation and cooperation or through violence and conflict, whether the characters perpetuate stereotypes or foster caring relationships. Workshop participants analyze, read, role-play, brainstorm, and enjoy the fun of sharing, questioning and working out solutions together. (p. 1)

In 1978 eight areas of television experience were developed for the workshops: an overview of the medium, violence, human sexuality, stereotyping, advertising, children's programs, news, and strategies for change. By 1981 four more areas were added: sports, minorities, theology, and soaps/game shows. In 1984–1985 the units were condensed into five: children, violence, stereotyping, advertising, and human sexuality—all as portrayed by television.

*Purposes.* Workshops were designed to assist individual parents, teachers, and religious leaders in guiding their young people's use of television as well as their own. The workbook and exercises were intended to be applied in the home by individuals and entire families, although they were also used in high school and college courses and in adult education and continuing education for teachers. Unlike most other formal curricula, these were not primarily intended for systematic classroom instruction and use. Although intermittent rather than sustained, workshops and exercises could nevertheless be more integrated or "organic" with the medium in the viewing context as commonly experienced. This is reflected in the complete title of the major text (cited in the following).

*Television Awareness Training.* Beginning in 1977 MARC published various editions of *Television Awareness Training: The Viewer's Guide / For Family and Community.* Whereas MARC's purpose was to protect values, it sought to help individuals find or form those values for themselves. The co-editor (Logan & Moody, 1979) emphasized in the first paragraph of the first page of text:

The relationship each of us has with television is very personal, and any study of that relationship must be equally personal. Another person can't move into our minds, tell us how we now use TV, and what changes will make television a more creative part of our lives. . . .

Again, it is each of us as an individual who can best find the answers—if we will take some time and energy to study our relationship with TV. (p. 5)

Nevertheless, the project was strongly oriented to standards drawn at least indirectly from the extensive readings in the workbook as well as from the orchestrated "two-step" workshops led initially by leaders closely associated with institutional churches.[7] Co-editor Ben Logan noted that readers "will find in the rest of this book a lot of different kinds of clues, starting points and insights from the minds of a lot of different persons" (p. 11).

The workbook is divided into two parts, one with 12 chapters or lessons (in the revised 1979 edition), the other with reprints of 19 major articles that usually relate directly to television. More than other CVS projects, this one offers a range of lengthy readings that involve not only information but also interpretative perspective and judgments about media and their influence. Supporting its stated attention to "values," the T-A-T text offers assessments and implied or expressed criteria for evaluating television. Therefore, despite worksheets accompanying each of the first 12 readings, the emphasis is on deductive analysis—assimilating others' viewpoints and principles, then noting how they apply to the medium.

A negative tone tends to dominate the readings (some of them commissioned, most reprinted from previous publication). The concluding bibliography lists 46 books, newsletters, teachers' guides, and audiovisual support material. Approximately 12 of them reflect a positive stance toward mass media, 9 neutral analyses, and 25 with somewhat negative perspective. Yet TV's undesirable impact is attributed not only to broadcasters but also to viewer's tolerance and lack of selectivity in using the medium. Hence "Television Awareness Training."

Chapters analyze television in relation to: violence, stereotypes, advertising, children, human sexuality, news, sports, minorities, theology, daytime genres (soap operas and game shows), and strategies for change. Each closely printed page carries the equivalent of two printed book pages. The first 12 chapters devote 80 pages to text (approximately 5 pages per article, including extensive footnote documentation in some). They add 5 pages of selected quotations, 5 pages of resource lists, and 80 pages of worksheets (each set of exercises total about 6 pages per chapter). Exercises relate to preceding articles (see Fig. 8.1). Often they are checklists or grids; usually they are open-end

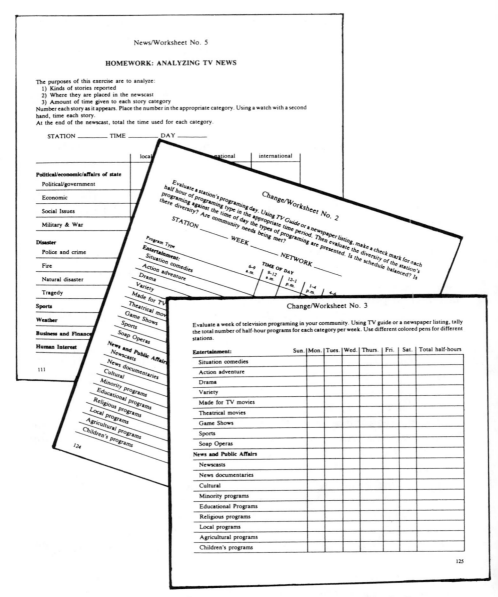

News/Worksheet No. 5

**HOMEWORK: ANALYZING TV NEWS**

The purposes of this exercise are to analyze:
1) Kinds of stories reported
2) Where they are placed in the newscast
3) Amount of time given to each story category
Number each story as it appears. Place the number in the appropriate category. Using a watch with a second hand, time each story.
At the end of the newscast, total the time used for each category.

STATION _____ TIME _____ DAY _____

|  | local | national | international |
|---|---|---|---|
| **Political/economic/affairs of state** | | | |
| Political/government | | | |
| Economic | | | |
| Social Issues | | | |
| Military & War | | | |
| **Disaster** | | | |
| Police and crime | | | |
| Fire | | | |
| Natural disaster | | | |
| Tragedy | | | |
| **Sports** | | | |
| **Weather** | | | |
| **Business and Finance** | | | |
| **Human Interest** | | | |

111

Change/Worksheet No. 2

Evaluate a station's programing day. Using *TV Guide* or a newspaper listing, make a check mark for each half hour of programing type in the appropriate time period. Then evaluate the diversity of the station's programing against the time of day the types of programing are presented. Is the schedule balanced? Is there diversity? Are community needs being met?

STATION _____ WEEK _____ NETWORK _____

|  | TIME OF DAY | | | | |
| Program Type | 6–9 a.m. | 9–12 a.m. | 12-1 p.m. | 1-4 p.m. | 4-6 |
|---|---|---|---|---|---|
| **Entertainment:** | | | | | |
| Situation comedies | | | | | |
| Action adventure | | | | | |
| Drama | | | | | |
| Variety | | | | | |
| Made for TV | | | | | |
| Theatrical movies | | | | | |
| Game Shows | | | | | |
| Sports | | | | | |
| Soap Operas | | | | | |
| **News and Public Affairs** | | | | | |
| Newscasts | | | | | |
| News documentaries | | | | | |
| Cultural | | | | | |
| Minority programs | | | | | |
| Educational programs | | | | | |
| Religious programs | | | | | |
| Local programs | | | | | |
| Agricultural programs | | | | | |
| Children's programs | | | | | |

124

Change/Worksheet No. 3

Evaluate a week of television programing in your community. Using TV guide or a newspaper listing, tally the total number of half-hour programs for each category per week. Use different colored pens for different stations.

| | Sun. | Mon. | Tues. | Wed. | Thurs. | Fri. | Sat. | Total half-hours |
|---|---|---|---|---|---|---|---|---|
| **Entertainment:** | | | | | | | | |
| Situation comedies | | | | | | | | |
| Action adventure | | | | | | | | |
| Drama | | | | | | | | |
| Variety | | | | | | | | |
| Made for TV movies | | | | | | | | |
| Theatrical movies | | | | | | | | |
| Game Shows | | | | | | | | |
| Sports | | | | | | | | |
| Soap Operas | | | | | | | | |
| **News and Public Affairs** | | | | | | | | |
| Newscasts | | | | | | | | |
| News documentaries | | | | | | | | |
| Cultural | | | | | | | | |
| Minority programs | | | | | | | | |
| Educational Programs | | | | | | | | |
| Religious programs | | | | | | | | |
| Local programs | | | | | | | | |
| Agricultural programs | | | | | | | | |
| Children's programs | | | | | | | | |

125

FIG. 8.1. Sample worksheets for students in MARC workbook. From Logan and Moody (1979) *Television Awareness Training: The Viewer's Guide for Family and Community.* (Copyright © 1979 by Media Action Research Center, Inc. Reprinted by permission.)

questions, to be filled in. Many of them require more ample explanation (possibly by leaders trained in the T-A-T workshop system); sometimes they are unclear or unstructured, relying on on-site discussion and interaction by participants.[8] Occasionally they merely elicit random recollection of media experiences; more often they propose gathering detailed factual information about TV content and viewer use.

In some chapters, worksheets suggest various activist responses to television's impact on (or intrusion into) viewers' lives. But other worksheets offer a neutral stance, leaving it to those filling out the exercises to arrive at their own judgment. For example, in chapter 2 on violence, a section of exercises on "coping with the anti-social messages of television" outlines options for individual response, for family reaction, for community and for national and governmental action. In addition to personal selectivity and family discussion of TV patterns, the T-A-T workbook (Logan & Moody, 1979) listed these options: join consumer groups; write letters of protest to broadcasters, advertisers, and government agencies; challenge license renewals of stations; boycott advertisers' products; and discuss the issues of censorship and alternative resolutions possible. The authors concluded

2.  b. It is ludicrous to use our most powerful and pervasive medium to primarily sell goods and to unintentionally teach anti-social and destructive behavior. The basis for program decision-making must move to a higher morality than simply what will secure the largest audience for advertisers.
3.  Alternatives
    a. Create laws defining excessive violence and sex. Allow the jury system to determine what is objectionable.
    b. License stations on a part-time basis so that the community can create programs which are more directly prosocial and useful.
    c. Create a National Television Program Board and Community Television Program Boards to participate in program decision-making.
    d. Develop others. (p. 28)

But even here there are positive suggestions offered, such as: introduce courses in television viewing literacy at all levels of the school system; use TV programs as curriculum in church schools for children and adults; use TV in the church "as a moral/ethical/theological laboratory for preaching and teaching"; and "use television production in church and public schools to demythologize the medium" (p. 27).

Similarly, in the next two exercise sheets for the same chapter, "psychological aggression" is to be monitored. Viewers are to:

tabulate the number of discounts or put-downs. Become aware of the way in which humor often is at the expense of the personhood of another.

> Listen especially for cues from the laugh track or live audience. This is
> an interesting exercise, too, for the game shows and the soaps. (p. 30)

On the next page a checklist with "almost always," "often," and
"rarely" prompts reflection on how one typically turns on TV when
returning home, plans to watch favorite programs, prefers to watch TV
rather than to be with others, and centers conversation on TV programs and personalities. The concluding advice modestly suggests: "If
your answers are weighted to the left ["almost always/usually"], you
may want to consider whether you want television to be that much a
part of your life" (p. 31).

The chapter on stereotypes in TV characters provides rather heavy
reading of statistical data, including 35 footnotes for the four-page
article that summarizes formal studies and experiments.

Some chapters such as "Television and Children: Regulating TV at
Home" recount personalized experiences, with common-sense conclusions; others like "Television and the Young Viewer" are heavy trea-
tises. The latter offers an excellent synthesis of patterns of research
findings through two decades, especially regarding aggression. This
balanced 10-age review is nonjudgmental, urging general and positive
response to TV's role, offering "a bridge between research and policy":

> All too often the social scientist venturing into television policy consid-
> erations makes naively sweeping recommendations with no understand-
> ing of the enormous complexity of responding to all the pressures and
> necessities of production. At the same time, some responsible members
> of the television industry take refuge in a defensive posture about the
> implications of the research findings. . . .
> Perhaps the most compelling reason for more collaboration among all
> sectors—industry, researchers, the viewing public, foundations, and gov-
> ernment agencies—is the common objectives held. Television is now a
> dominant voice in American life. It is a formidable teacher of children.
> Its healthy future should be the interest and responsibility of all of us.
> (Rubinstein, 1979, p. 69)

Exercises for this chapter on TV and children offer good concrete, step-
by-step strategy for modifying family members' use of television,
searching for positive program content as well as dropping negative
programs, viewing specific programs rather than merely "watching
TV."

Some worksheets are broad and even a bit vague, not offering much
definition or direction but leaving it to the adult to apply (presumably
based on previous participation in a workshop). But others are very
specific, providing lists of questions for discussing the topic by drawing
from individual TV experience.

Chapter 6 offers a sensitive analysis of "Television and Human Sexuality" with "There's More to Sexuality Than Sex." The article notes that "seldom are erotic relationships between people seen or discussed in the context of a warm, loving, stable relationship" and "one is struck by the lack of genuine intimacy portrayed" (pp. 83, 84). The authors acknowledge TV's impact by its daily repetition "of a limited range of human relationships, meanings and feelings"; they thoughtfully conclude:

> Given this perspective, there is no one right way for sexuality to be portrayed on television. No one right way to handle a bedroom scene, a dual career family, or a young boy's first love affair. It is true that a list of do's and don'ts might reassure public interest groups and seem to make life easier for the industry executive. However, that kind of specificity would only perpetuate misunderstanding about televised sexuality by suggestion that it can be conveniently compartmentalized, monitored, and regulated.
>
> Responsible television does and must deal with issues of sexuality. These issues are central to our humanity and they are at the core of human comedy and drama. Through discussion and exploration of such issues as masculinity/femininity, intimacy, love, relatedness, vulnerability and affection, perhaps the public and the television industry can come to understand the fullness of human sexuality and television's responsibility to presenting the diversity of this human experience with honesty, compassion and accuracy. (Roberts & Holt, 1979, p. 85)

The companion article in this chapter excoriates television for sniggering treatment of sex-related topics and for misinformation.

A worksheet offers potentially controversial options when it lists 10 situations involving unmarried sexual relationships, homosexual couples, rape, divorce, and prophylactics. Two such situations are: "In a short comedy sketch a mother deals with her 13-year-old about masturbation" and "Create a television commercial for prophylactics" (p. 93). The exercise directs: "Select one or more of these situations . . . and write a brief description of how you would develop the situation(s) for TV in a way that provides helpful accurate information and is in keeping with our own values." (It is not clear whether "our own values" refers to the MARC coalition of churches, or is a misprint intended to read "your own values.") The next two exercise sheets offer a check-list of 30 topics, plus 22 subtopics, related to sexuality; they are to be related as "a common human experience," "people need info about," "could be treated sensitively on TV," "I have seen it treated on TV: Good / Bad," or "Not for TV." Obviously discretion must be used for the latter instruction: "This worksheet is for your own information and for sharing as you desire with the group" (p. 94). Some of the topics are: petting, intercourse, masturbation, wet dreams, involuntary erection, inability to have orgasms, absence of lubrication, premature ejaculation, homosexual lifestyle, abortion, sterilization, contraception, incest, group sex, prostitution, transvestism, transsexualism, and voyeurism.

The most exhortative article is by Stewart M. Hoover, a co-founder of Television Awareness Training. In "Television: Strategies for Change" he emphasized personal responsibility for TV by pragmatic steps toward more discriminating personal viewing and toward working for change by contacting broadcasters and government agencies. Although recommending positive meetings with managers, he also offered accurate information about gathering data and even seeking legal assistance. He added five pages of resources "for decisions and action"—organizations, publications, advertisers, and dates of station license renewals by state.

A good treatment about minorities and stereotyping in television analyzes specific programs and characters. Among the eight exercises are worksheets with nonjudgmental questions to prompt discussion between parent and child based on data tabulated from their own viewing.

Curiously, the two final chapters seem inverted. The penultimate piece on "Television and Theology" is followed by a concluding article "Television's Soap Operas and Game Shows." The former four pages by Conklin and McFadden (1979) consider viewers' "transactions" with television as a reflection of our human condition when turned away from a creating God by sinfulness to a substitute relationship with the created world; "we attempt to find ultimate meaning for our existence in television, but such meaning is not there to be found" (p. 154). A Christian theological perspective can help individuals "see that our stewardship of television is an issue of human community," with responsibility mutually shared by producers, advertisers, and viewers. The authors warn viewers to consider how they substitute the medium's fiction (drama, comedy) and non-fiction (news) as well as commercial advertising—and even TV religion—for deeper realities and transcendent values. One exercise picks up that theme by posing the question "What god or gods are you being asked to worship?" (p. 158). The most explicit moral assessment in the T-A-T program is posed:

> There are unresolved theological tensions between the message of the Christian Gospel and the medium of television. Can a Gospel which assumes dialogue be communicated through a medium whose current technology broadcasts a monologue, inviting no response from the audience except conformity to suggested patterns of behavior? . . . Where,

in the midst of television's beautifully told stories and charming myths, is there room for the message that the ultimate story is the story of God's love affair with humanity? . . . The nature of the Gospel is such that it calls into question the system of values proclaimed by television, and, indeed, ultimately calls into question the structures—technical, social, economic, and political—which shape television as it presently exists.

### Conclusion

Television participates in our turned-awayness from God. It often dehumanizes people; it presents the idols of society in dazzling imagery; its monologue says that ultimate worth is to be found in the things of this world.. . . . A theological reflection on television must begin with ourselves and the uses we make of television, must continue with the uses it makes of us and of all Creation, and must result ultimately in our choice of a new relationship with this aspect of Creation. (pp. 156–157)

Appropriating that general moral judgment to the variety of religious groups in pluralistic society, "Theology/Worksheet No. 4" offers an ecumenical exercise:

Most theologies include an acknowledgment of good and evil in ourselves and our world and provide value standards that help individuals define what is good and what is evil. Watch at least one situation comedy episode and at least one action adventure episode and using your own understanding of good and evil, write down instances where they appear in the programs. (p. 161)

Although moralistic, the T-A-T approach is broadly conceived to embrace various religious/ethical stances founded on Judeo-Christian tradition. Specific moral assessments are left to individuals drawing on their respective value systems.

Part II (pp. 179–267) of the book consists of 19 articles averaging about four pages each. Some pieces analyze the social and educational phenomenon of mass media, providing behavioral concepts for serious study of television, including media impact on cognition and resulting actions. Others offer extended factual details about the structure and economics of broadcasting, about its processes and techniques (including audience measurement and production of commercials). Still others describe ways to respond to and harness the medium in a family setting, offering positive concrete steps for parents to take when dealing with children's use of TV.

Typical of T-A-T's stance for individuating value structures is Aimee Dorr's practical advice to parents about maximizing their children's learning and behavior in accord with their own values. She urged parents to familiarize themselves with TV programming so that, knowing what television routinely presents "and how it matches your own values, you can make wiser choices about your children's television viewing"—including regulating how they use it (p. 217). Again, she encouraged parents to help their youngsters develop skills to evaluate television "in terms of both its accuracy and its congruence with your family's values." She alluded to the great variety of people in society with their range of values: "Each family and each child within that family has its own values and interests, strengths and weaknesses. What is right for you and your children is what you must choose to do" (p. 219).

A number of reprinted articles address television's socializing function, both negative and positive, with both anecdotal and research data.

In the concluding essay, William F. Fore offered a broad analysis of mass media's nature and role in society, emphasizing Christian values and assumptions. His remarks have added importance because of his long service as Assistant General Secretary for Communication in the National Council of Churches, and because of his prominent participation in national media and church conferences. He explored media's function in providing myths, symbols, images, and fantasy that contribute to the "commonality" of society—its stability, cohesion, and common purpose—sometimes for better, sometimes for worse. Among myths central to contemporary society he cites:

The fittest survive
Power, including decision-making, starts at the central core and moves out
Happiness consists of limitless material acquisition
—consumption is inherently good
—property, wealth and power are more important than people
Progress is an inherent good
There exists a free-flow of information. (p. 264)

He then described values in our culture as communicated by mass media: power over others, power over nature; the value of wealth and property; everything can be purchased; consumption is an intrinsic good; and narcissism, immediate gratification, and creature comforts.

Thus the mass media tell us that *we are basically good,* that *happiness is the chief end of life,* and that *happiness consists in obtaining material goods.* The media transform the value of sexuality into *sex appeal;* the value of self-respect into *pride;* the value of well-to-live into *will-to-power.* They exacerbate acquisitiveness into *greed;* they deal with insecurity by generating more *anxiety*. They change the value of recreation into *competition* and the value of rest into *escape*. And perhaps worst of all, the media constrict our experience and substitute media-world for real-world so that we are becoming less and less able to make the fine value judgments that such a complex world requires. (p. 265)

In a broad indictment of the media, he countered those standards by appealing to the broad range of religious beliefs:

What is the Christian response to this value system? The answer is obvious and undeniable. Regardless of your theology, whether you are conservative, liberal, or middle-of-the-road, and regardless of whether you believe the Bible word for word or demythologize it piece by piece— the whole weight of Christian history, thought and teaching stands diametrically opposed to the media world and its values I have just been describing. (p. 265)

As an antidote, the author looked to media education with three aspects. First, it must restore two-fold vision, adding a transcendent perception to the scientific-technocratic view of reality promoted by media; the Bible is the reference point that transcends current culture. Second, face-to-face interaction in small groups, notably in church gatherings, must be the venue for analyzing media—not in mass contexts where propaganda (in the broad sense) numbs perception and judgment.

Media education would have a different focus with different groups. Among the poor it would aim at helping them define what the media says about them, and then to define their real problems and their real role in society—which could very well lead to action to get out of that role. Among the vast middle class workers and consumers it would help them understand the ways in which they are being manipulated to ends not their own, and to evaluate the satisfactions held out to them by the media in terms of their reality, and then to establish values independent of those of the media, and develop lifestyles which can achieve *their* goals instead of media goals. As this is happening, new myths, new symbols and images would develop which would move into competition with the old and which could help transform the society into one better suited to meet human needs. (p. 266)

Third, media education should involve direct social and political action to modify media structures to make them more responsive to viewpoints differing from the norm. This is to be accomplished in the United States by testimony and lobbying before the Federal Communications Commission and Congress, by lawsuits in courts, and by economic leverage of stockholders. He disclaimed media as merely "being manipulated and mishandled by greedy people at the top"; instead, media managers as well as consumers are swept up in the same valueless system. "The solution is much more radical: a change in the beliefs and assumptions and economic base of the entire society" (p. 267). He concluded with the assertion that "our Christian theology is fundamentally at odds with the theology of our society, and the mass media happens to be the arena where the matter is going to be resolved."

*Growing with Television.*    The characteristics of "Television Awareness Training"—emphasizing Christian values as criteria for assessing television's values and impact—were brought forward by the Media Action Research Center to its next media project, *Growing with Television: A Study of Biblical Values and the Television Experience.*

*Purposes.*    Premises similar to the T-A-T project were joined by explicit reflection on individual Christian belief or faith, based on sacred scripture. MARC (1984) promoted this book as stressing criteria for Christian living: "For church educators, television can provide yet another opportunity for self-development through examining and defining cultural values, personal values, and Biblical values" (p. 2). Christian values are discussed as a means of tempering or enhancing TV viewing experience.

The *Program Guidebook* (Griffith, 1980) summarizes the goals of helping participants:

- Look at cultural values in contrast to biblical values.
- Learn to use television as a values clarification resource.
- Be intentional about the content values and the presence of TV.
- Develop critical viewing skills.
- To move to new decisions for their lives. (p. 2)[9]

Throughout the guidebook, MARC acknowledges positive as well as negative aspects of television's content and implied values:

> The thrust of Growing with Television is that television can be a positive influence on us. . . . [T]he focus of the series is not on television, but on values as TV can help us examine them. . . . We are using the 'teachings' of television to compare and contrast with the teachings of the Bible. That's what the course is really about! . . . The fact is that this is not a 'stop-watching-TV course.' (pp. 17–18)

Introductions to each of the five *Leader's Guides* are similar. At the outset each repeats a balanced assessment of television (Price, 1980b):

Some of what is on television affirms those Christian values, bringing us positive models of persons in close relationships, enriching us with new ideas, personal growth experiences, new understanding of widely diverse types of persons, a view of the world we might never get any other way. At the same time, compared to Christian values, some of TV's values are crass, thing-oriented, violent, stereotyping, sensationalized and cheapening of humanity. That duality is a reality of the television experience. (p. 5)

The *Guides* note how CVS studies relate to critical thinking: "Helping children examine their television experiences in a values context can be the beginning of a lifelong habit of making thoughtful and intentional decisions" (p. 6). The intent is to give young people confidence in themselves as persons, in their ability to make judgments and decisions, and to act on them independently of external sources such as television programs, personalities, and commercials.

*Curriculum: Content.* MARC developed this sophisticated, well organized set of printed and audiovisual materials as a curriculum for church schools; it can also be adapted for homes and other kinds of groups (see Fig. 8.2). The package presents similarly structured themes for each of five age levels: younger elementary, older elementary, junior high, senior high, and adults. Each course level offers four units of study; each unit presents three topics for separate sessions (partly in group discussion, partly by private viewing at home). Unit 1 on world views analyzes what is learned—including implicit values and "belief characteristics"—from TV and from the Bible about reality and fantasy in life. Topics for sessions are: "The American Dream," "Simplistic Problems and Solutions," and "Real or Unreal" (fact and fantasy). Unit 2 on lifestyles explores the theme of people's lifestyles as depicted by television, by the Bible, and in real life; it includes the influence of commercials. Sessions are: "Consumerism," "Happiness," and "Uniformity vs. Diversity." Unit 3 on relationships looks at stereotypes in sessions on "Images of Others," "Sex and Sexuality," and "Isolation/Community." Unit 4 on concept of self analyzes human and divine evaluation of persons, compared with television's evaluation— and guidelines for reacting to others. Sessions are: "Images of Self," "Models of Behavior," and "What to Do?"

MARC developed the project over two years. They designed it to be used by relatively untrained leaders (unlike the scheduled workshops required of T-A-T group organizers). But the "Program Guidebook" does offer many concrete suggestions for preparing and effectively implementing the program in churches, schools, and organizations.

FIG. 8.2.  Kit of phonograph disks, filmstrip, folders, and booklets developed as *Starter Kit: Growing with Television* by Media Action Research Center (1980a).

*Support Materials.*    Resources include the *Program Guidebook* (for planners and administrators) for the entire project, *Leader's Guides* for each of the five age levels, leader's packets for each of the lower two levels, and a set of 12 student leaflets for each level (each leaflet with four pages 8½×11-inch format). *Leader's Guides* analyze the scriptural foundation and offer step-by-step outlines of suggested procedures for each weekly session (see Fig. 8.3). Leader's packets augment the guide with posters, a 33.3-rpm recording (seven brief songs and one voiced dialogue to accompany a filmstrip), and two 35mm color filmstrips with eight frames each). Student leaflets for each week's session offer material for reading and discussing at home, class discussion, and viewing assignments.[10]

All materials were field-tested in churches and evaluated by "Christian education specialists" during the 2 years of development.

*Procedures.*    The *Program Guidebook* notes that well-planned lessons are needed for effective sessions (see Fig. 8.4). But it adds that teachers must feel free to innovate. They should be flexible with the material,

---

# UNIT I
# WORLDVIEWS
# SESSION 1 — THE "AMERICAN" DREAM

---

## Session Summary

*Resources*
Student Leaflet 1 – The American Dream
*Materials*
Chalkboard and chalk or newsprint and markers
Paper and pencils
*Session Plan Outline*
Introduce world view focus.
Read scripture and commentary and make lists of characteristics.
Do Hermit Exercise.
Read "What Is the American Dream?"
Use scripture story to look at two sets of characteristics.
Assign homework.

## Main Idea and Objectives

*Main Idea:* TV presents an image of a fulfilled American Dream (which could also be called a North American Dream) with people abundantly blessed with material possessions and position in the world. The implication is that such abundance is available to all and that it is what life is all about. There is a de-emphasis on wide-ranging problems like those of the urban poor, and there is the implication that technology can solve all problems. *In the Christian Faith, the good life does not consist of getting and having, but of serving and taking care of (as in stewardship).*
*Session Objectives:*
   Compare the characteristics of the American Dream shown on mainstream TV and of the "good life" according to the Christian faith.
   Become more aware of the contrast between the two.
   Begin to check your own values against these.

## Background and Preparation

As you prepare for the first session in this series, think about the personal nature of TV viewing.

People will often be eager to talk about TV; they may also be sensitive. Avoid antagonizing anyone unnecessarily. Giving some thought to that possibility in advance can make you more aware of people's unconscious feelings. Probably the most important thing to remember is that this is not a study of TV but of values, *using TV.*

Since TV is the vehicle, some preparation will be helpful, even though you may be an expert on TV already. Here are two ways to become a more self-aware viewer and to get a better sense of how the study will be using TV:

*'Why I Watch TV' Analysis* (assign values of 1 to 5, with 5 being the most weighty)
For entertainment
For information
To learn what to wear
   what to buy
   how people relate
   what issues are important
   how I should act
To occupy time
To escape
To relax
To be with people
To avoid being with people
To be with TV people
To avoid doing something I should do
To avoid figuring out something else to do
Others _____

Give close attention to what the good life is according to television. It would be good to watch one soap, one drama, at least one situation comedy (sit-com), one action-adventure, and to notice the commercials during these shows. Look for current and concrete examples of the good life. During the first session especially, you will be the only person specifically prepared.

   **In preparing for this session and all others,** walk through all exercises, both the homework and those to be done in class, to imagine how the use of them might go. Remember, you often won't be able to do everything and will need to select.

10

FIG. 8.3.   Teacher's guidelines in MARC's "Starter Kit." From West (1980) *Leader's Guide/Adult: Growing with Television—A Study of Biblical Values and the Television Experience.* (Copyright © 1980 by Media Action Research Center, Inc. Reprinted by permission.)

using it as a guide rather than a blueprint, in order to focus on the students and their interaction with TV and with one another while exploring these themes. It provides six pages of detailed options for procedures that promote thought as well as interaction among participants. Suggested group activities always include viewing of television followed by discussion.

The Guidebook stresses six sessions (totaling 3 to 6 hours) of teacher training. Seventeen pages supply structure, outline, materials, and

TRAINING SEGMENT 4
## "Testing the Waters"

### CHECKLIST OF SUPPLIES NEEDED FOR THIS SEGMENT:

_____pencils at each chair
_____books/magazines to serve as lap desks
_____handout entitled "Walk in the Shoes of Your Students" (see page 23)
_____student books for *Growing with Television*
_____"Real and "Unreal" discussion questions *typed*
_____material as outlined in the last exercise of this segment
_____crayons, magic markers (for younger elementary teachers in the last exercise)

### GROUP PREPARATION FOR THE TRAINING EVENT:

• Scripture: "I do not understand my own actions. For I do not do what I want, but I do the very thing I hate" (Romans 7:15).
• Prayer:
*Loving God, so often we are uncertain about the "whys" of our life. We wonder who we are and why we do some of the things we do. And it becomes clearer all the while that if we neglect or forget to apply the teachings of your Word to our lives, we will continue to ask the "why" questions without receiving any satisfaction whatsoever. Lord, be with us as we struggle. Amen.*

### DIRECTOR:

In this session, some of the activities we do are from **Growing with Television**.

This is experiential education. Experience is a personal thing, even if it turns out to be like the experience of someone else. As we experience things, we do so at our own level of ability and readiness. In the classroom a specific event will be experienced by the participants in a variety of ways, with a range of different possible meanings—just as you will experience the following exercises in a different way than the students.

To begin this segment find one person with whom you have had no conversations or only few conversations during these teacher training sessions.

Each person has **4 MINUTES** to interview the other. Discuss the responses after both interviews have been done. I will notify you when **4 MINUTES** have passed. Okay. Please begin now.

(**At the end of 4 MINUTES** alert the pairs. They continue for **4 MORE MINUTES.**)

Thank you. Please stop. It will add a tremendous wealth to your teaching preparation to interview several children before and during the teaching of this course. Face-to-face interviews will be considerably more meaningful than telephone interviews. Consider interviewing students inside and outside of your class.

Next, we move into a very useful oral reporting technique called "the fishbowl." This is a discussion technique you can use in your class. I need four to six volunteers.

(Secure volunteers and continue.)

Let's set up a small inner circle of chairs for these volunteers so that each person in this circle has one, and include an empty chair. Then arrange other chairs in a larger circle outside the smaller one. Other members of the group sit on these as listeners. If one of the listeners wishes to participate in the discussion, make a comment, or ask a question, he or she can use the empty chair—and only then—withdrawing when he or she is finished.

(Set up the situation, then give the inner circle the topic of discussion. Have the topics of discussion—as outlined in the paragraphs below—**typed** on four or five cards for members of the inner circle. As the director, be prepared to "model"—set the example—how to intervene. For example, you may intervene by filling the empty chair.)

The topics for discussion are as follows: (1) What is real and what is unreal on TV? Name as many different things as you can which are real and unreal. Do this before going to question 2. (2) How do you decide which is real or unreal? What about cartoons? quiz shows? commercials? soap operas? sports events? the news? election coverage? (name others.)

You have a total of **10 MINUTES** for this exercise.

15

FIG. 8.4. Instructions for conducting sessions in MARC's CVS program. From Griffith (1980) *Program Guidebook for Planners and Administrators: Growing with Television—A Study of Biblical Values and the Television Experience.* (Copyright © 1980 by Media Action Research Center, Inc. Reprinted by permission.)

suggestions for training teachers how to use *Growing with Television* in their classrooms. The very detailed, minute-by-minute procedures emphasize personalized activities. They relate personal experience of TV and attitudes about it to Biblical values.

Each *Leader's Guide* carefully outlines the purpose and scope of that level's text and supporting audiovisual materials. The two lower levels include: a small long-play disk with soundtrack for one filmstrip, and music for selected activities; filmstrips of equipment used in a TV studio and of "reverse dialogues" between persons on the screen; two posters of Jesus depicting a simple lifestyle. The expectation for all levels is that television set(s) at home will be used as audiovisual instruments for the lessons.

Student "leaflets" are to be distributed for the lesson periods and to be used for "homework" and reading/discussion at home. Each folded, four-page leaflet includes brief explanation of the lesson, photos of technical equipment for TV production, fill-in blanks, and commentary for parents to read to help them discuss the lesson with their children.

Leaders are reminded to stress students' learning through experience, by their verbalizing and doing activities. For the first two elementary levels, "activity centers" are to be set up in the classroom or meeting place: in both levels are an art center (to construct montages and posters), a record and tape center (for playing songs), a filmslip center (to view filmstrips), a drama center (to act out playlets, as for TV), and a TV center (for viewing in class). They are joined in younger elementary by a puppet center (for children to express themselves through puppets), and in older elementary by an "exploring values center" (for writing and comparing lists). For the three upper levels, leaders are urged to encourage students to think about their own values, to respect the contributions of every person, to be positive, and to be flexible in using variety and creativity in applying the organized lessons.

Sessions begin with the activity centers for 25 minutes, then group time for discussion and interaction for 20 minutes, and then assigning homework with the handout sheets.

The text alludes to general findings in behavioral studies about the impact of media on viewers. It puts in brief, understandable form some major concerns about relationships between TV viewing and attitudes and behavior. The data and statements tend to do justice to findings provided by research literature.

Questions put to children to elicit responses and participation are to be nonjudgmental. The pattern of development includes: (a) values to be explored, (b) Biblical examples and scripture passages, and (c) reflections and activities regarding television.

Values considered range widely: excluding others, career and sex stereotypes, friendship (vs. TV's passive isolation), value of self and of neighbor, and problem solving. Representative of the balanced approach to assessing one's own values in relation to television experiences is the discussion (Price, 1980b) about the "sense of authority" television has for viewers of its programs, personalities, and advertising:

It is healthy for young children to begin to discover the reality of advertising. It is good for them to know that they can and should question the
authority of television, that they can trust themselves to research, find
out, ask questions, and make their own decisions. (p. 29)

Again, on the subject of diversity among people and the threat of
exclusion unless one conforms, both the younger and older elementary
texts comment:

Because TV often excludes people, it can encourage children to do the
same. However, if TV is used carefully, with a careful selection of programs that show a wide variety of persons in many activities, television
programs can encourage children to be more open and inclusive. A good
follow-up discussion about the positives and negatives of a program can
help children learn about inclusion and exclusion. (p. 31)

The final, 12th session for the older elementary level (Price, 1980a, p.
27) encourages active letter writing (again, with both positive and
negative comments) to networks and stations as a means of overcom-
ing the feeling of powerlessness while influencing executives' thinking.

This openness to potential values of television is made very explicit
in a paragraph in the *Leader's Guides* for junior high (Sheie, 1980, p.
10) and for senior high (Martens, 1980, p. 9) but is omitted from the
*Guide* (West, 1980) for the adult level:

Few of us are aware enough of the good programming available. Using
*TV Guide,* review a full week's programming and mark all the programs
that seem likely to provide a valuable, positive experience. You'll probably find there's more than you have time to watch. (p. 11)

But all three *Guides* (pp. 10, 10, 11 respectively) include this admoni-
tion to leaders:

It is very important for the group to understand from the beginning that
the series is not anti-TV. Whenever an opportunity arises, mention
positive points about TV.

While following the same topics and similar structure for meetings
and booklet text as well as hand-out sheets, the *Leader's Guide* booklets for the junior high, senior high, and adult levels predictably incorporate progressively more sophisticated concepts, data, and activities.
Group discussions involve reflective analysis of storylines and character development in TV programs viewed.

For example, in treating lifestyles and consumerism (Unit 2, Session 4, p. 15 in each), all three texts note that, whereas advertising and unequal distribution of wealth and world hunger are massive issues, *"the basic problem is really the consumer in each of us."* Participants are to consider what different ways they have discovered to use TV, "awareness of opportunities or concern"; they are to develop specific guidelines for their own use of TV "in creative, intentional, thoughtful ways" (pp. 16, 16, 14 respectively).

The final session for all three groups centers on traditional critical viewing skills by reflecting on how programs and program schedules are constructed, the factors involved in being a TV critic, tactics for planning personal viewing during each week along with reflection and discussion about programs, and communicating those judgments to broadcasters.

Only brief attention is given to production of programs, including special effects (to demystify TV).

The sets of leaflets vary among the three upper levels, not so much in their content as in their form. While covering similar material in the same sequence, the junior high sheets emphasize large black-and-white photographs of scenes from popular television programs. Senior high sheets offer some photographs but many cartoon-like drawings; they also provide more detailed analysis—offering data and commentary about the topics, including a range of quotations from media critics and researchers. And leaflets for adults add yet more sophisticated quotations and data from which to draw their inferences and conclusions. Similarly, orientation toward hands-on activities with younger students gradually gives way to increased discussion and reflection at later levels. Rather than the summaries and even conclusions provided in material for non-adults, more citations and quoted material are provided for adults to analyze.

The balanced tone is sustained throughout the printed materials. Two final examples from the adult worksheets indicate MARC's awareness of complexity regarding television as a major transmitter of popular culture:

It's not that there is too much sex on television. There is simply too much emphasis on the shallow aspects of sex, and not enough portrayal of sex as an act that offers the opportunity of showing love in one of the most profound and expressive ways. Does this absence of genuine, warm sexual relationships on television represent a similar absence in our society? Or is television helping develop this absence by portraying sex as a product to be used to sell goods, gain power, and garner laughter? Or both? In a medium dominated by situation comedies and thirty-second commercials the complexity of our sexual nature is rarely depicted. Conversely, in real life, the complex nature of our sexual life is one of the things that is always with us.

*        *        *

If the sexual relationships, values, and attitudes on television do not agree with those you believe in, there are ways to change the picture. We are responsible for the programs we choose to watch; we do, after all, have the ability to select and to turn off the set. The networks are responsible for the programs offered to the sponsors. Since advertising revenue provides commercial television's operating funds, the sponsors must be held accountable for the type of programs they attach their names to. Therefore, several avenues of action are open to us. We can turn off the set, change channels, or actively try to influence the decisions made by the networks and sponsors. But no one can do it for us.[11]

But other than writing letters of constructive criticism to stations, MARC and its *Growing With Television* writers do not suggest boycotts or other strategies for gaining attention and social leverage. A final positive recommendation to leaders for adults (West, 1980) in their final session is:

The group should consider ways to take advantage of the many good programs on TV, especially the television 'specials' that often deal with social, cultural, educational and religious issues in an entertaining and yet more redeeming manner than do many of the series shows.
The groups should also give some attention to how almost any TV program (excellent, mediocre, or bad) can be used in an on-going process of values clarification. (p. 30)

Throughout all sessions, *Growing with Television* emphasizes relating personal experiences in life with television to values reflected in the Bible, especially in stories taken from the life of Jesus. It seeks to integrate reflections on day-to-day TV experience with scriptural ideals and dicta, as a means of value-formation. As part of that process, participants grow in their understanding of television and become more discriminating in their use of the medium.

## U.S. CATHOLIC CONFERENCE ("THE MEDIA MIRROR")

On the heels of the work of MARC's Protestant coalition in the early 1980s came the United States Catholic Conference (USCC) with its "The Media Mirror: A Study Guide on Christian Values and Television." Developed by the Conference's Departments of Communication and of Education (and funded by the annual Catholic Communication Campaign), it was first published in 1982. It was revised slightly and distributed under the same title in 1984 and thereafter by the National Catholic Educational Association. The pilot phase by USCC was tested in ten dioceses around the country, involving 14,000 students.[12]

*Purposes.* The stated purposes are positive and integrate reflection about Christian values:

- Develop an understanding of the role and influence of TV;
- Foster constructive use of TV and related media;
- Cultivate a better understanding of Christian values as portrayed in popular culture;
- Develop viewers who will utilize choices in TV programming;
- Educate viewers to upgrade the quality of TV programming;
- Develop a national media education program reflecting Christian values.[13]

The third paragraph in the *Teacher's Guide* (Schropp, 1982) emphasizes that "this is not an anti-television course. Television is a technological tool than can be used for good, as well as the not-so-good" (p. 3). And again: "The goal of the critical viewing skills curriculum is to stimulate students to think about TV and to analyze, not to condemn TV or even particular programs" (p. 5).

*Procedures.* The material is intended as a full semester unit that can be used in courses in religion, English, communications, language arts, or social studies, as well as in parish catechetical programs. It consists of a *Teacher's Guide,* and three booklets for elementary Grades 4–6, junior high Grades 7–8, and high school. The 24-page books (32 pages in revised version) are each divided into 10 sessions (nine in the revision, by combining two about external and internal conflict).

The Catholic agency's realistic caution (pessimism?) differs from MARC's expectations regarding familial discussions about TV: "Encourage students to discuss TV with their parents, but do not expect it. Students watch TV alone or with their peers more often than with their parents" (p. 5). This caveat in the omnibus *Teacher's Guide* refers to all students within the scope of the program, from the fourth grade through high school.

*Curriculum: Content.* The syllabus is similar to MARC's T-A-T and *Growing with Television,* especially in linking TV study with direct reflection on scriptural sources and Christian values and behavior. But this Catholic project puts more stress on the structure and components of television as a medium of business and art. Topics for each level are: factual data about television, reality and fantasy, commercials, how a program is developed, conflict (both external action and inner conflict), heroes and models for behavior, relationships among people, problems/solutions in TV vs. real life, and an agenda for further discriminating action.

The *Teacher's Guide,* unlike the prolix *Leader's Guide* of the Protestant agency, is extremely succinct. It devotes only five pages to capsulized information about the 10 (or 9) student sessions. It lists several objectives for each session and then offers a few brief paragraphs about each topic. Four pages outline a detailed schedule for "in-service training" of teachers before they present "The Media Mirror" in their classes. Another five pages of small print list hundreds of cross-references to scripture passages and religious literature related to each session's TV topic; this is for those who incorporate the lessons into parish catechetical programs. The final five pages provide an annotated bibliography of books for teachers, parents, and students; a list of organizations involved with critical viewing projects; and descriptions of 30 audiovisual items to complement the lessons, including films, videotapes, filmstrips, recordings, and slides. The guide mentions two videotapes made by USCC for this project: "The Media Mirror" about the entire CVS program, and "Heroes, Models, Groups" portraying students and teachers using Lesson VII; each is 15 minutes long and sells for the price of duplication ($35 each).

USCC's material for teachers offers tightly condensed factual data for each lesson. And, although it does briefly relate each topic to specifically Christian values from scripture and the life of Christ, the vast majority of objectives pertain directly to understanding, comparing, and evaluating the constructs of television programs and media structures. Rather than directly harnessing students' TV experience as an instrument for growing directly in Christian reflection and values—as do MARC's projects, especially *Growing with Television*—this USCC project emphasizes enlightening students about the nature of the medium, its form, purposes, and some of its effects. This primary focus is linked with Christian background that serves as a source of criteria for judging oneself and society more than the medium. In the 10 lesson plans, 42 "objectives" are enumerated; 23 of them pertain directly to TV as such, 12 draw implications for personal attitudes and behavior, and only 7 comment on explicitly Christian themes and sources related to the topic. For example, "IV. Anatomy of a Program" (Schropp, 1982) lists only three objectives:

1. To understand what it takes to create and produce a television program (people, ideas, resources, talent, skills, time, etc.).
2. To begin to identify shows for their artistic and technical merit.
3. To appreciate the value and results of cooperation and teamwork. (p. 11)

Similarly, "V. Conflict in Action" offers six objectives of the lesson:

1. To recognize what conflict is and to define it.
2. To describe the role of conflict in a television story.
3. To identify the various types of conflict (give examples).
4. To recognize the relationship between conflict and violence.
5. To recognize the problems created for young viewers by excessive violence in television programming.
6. To appreciate how Jesus used conflict in his teaching, but also his strong position against violence. (p. 12)

Student workbooks carry out this theme of studying the medium for its own sake, and secondarily as a context in which to explore Christian values. Again, those values are standards against which to judge oneself and society, and popular culture in general—not just television. In the elementary level workbook, references to specifically Christian points are almost nominal—included as one of several possible examples of the point being made about media. At times, the workbook uses television more as a resource from which students are asked to draw examples to demonstrate the topic of the session. Most analysis is through nondirective questions and also by occasional checklists or fill-in-the-blanks worklist.

The junior high booklet also emphasizes factual information about television and audiences, plus some modest commentary about implications of those data. Not until the end of lesson III are there any references, even brief, to Christianity; and both of them cite scripture references with a few questions appended, such as "How do [the passages] relate to television commercials and materialism?" Further religious allusions are rare. The text is concerned with students' learning about television and their response to it. It offers factual commentary and open-ended questions for discussion, plus occasional checklists and fill-in tables. This booklet is punctuated with photographs of TV scenes and stars (rather than the cartoonish line drawings found in the elementary book).

The high school text (Hawker & Plude, 1982) follows emphases and patterns of the previous material. It offers a few more allusions to Christ and Christian perspective, but does not elaborate. The text apparently assumes students' prior knowledge, or depends on the teach-

er's guidance of discussion. Indicative of the restrained, even telegraphic (and perhaps ineffectual?) references to generalized Christian
values in the context of positive television study is in the text's final
paragraph. It concludes the final session's presentation (followed by
seven discussion questions and seven optional activities):

> As you grow, your interests and tastes should mature as well. Don't limit
> your viewing to entertainment shows. Take advantage of cultural pro-
> grams, documentaries and docu-dramas. Employ some of your valuable
> time viewing programs that enrich you as a person and enable you to
> become better informed about timely issues and concerns within society.
> In every instance recognize the importance of approaching the medium
> as an intelligent and responsible follower of Jesus. Be an active viewer
> who evaluates critically the attitudes, values and behavior presented on
> the programs that you watch. If you are to respect your dignity and
> cultivate your potential you cannot do less. (p. 18)

*Assessment.* The always optimistic and positive commentary includes
somewhat exhortative explanations without specific details to expand
on (although most sessions begin with descriptions of selected scenes
from TV programs as a springboard into the topics). The open-ended
questions for discussion do lead students into ramifications of the topic. And allusions to explicit Christian points are just that: allusions
without detail.

The USCC's media study projects do not bring the sense of urgency
for systemic change in broadcasting called for by the Protestant
churches' MARC nor the National PTA. Those organizations approach
the stance of media critics and educators in Britain and South America: Priorities and the very structure of society must be changed if
mass media are to truly serve that society according to human values
as well as divine ones. Complete media education involves activist
reforms reaching far beyond typical critical viewing skills curricula.

## NOTES

1. Participants in the 1979–1980 poll lived in 38 states and in Canada; but
one-third of all evaluations came from Louisiana. Most participants were students (54.9% were age 14–18, 10.7% were younger than 14, and college students were included in the 10.3% whose age was 19 to 34).

2. Organization president Grace Baisinger was reported (*Variety,* 1978, p.
80) as projecting its potential influence at the time to the PTA's 6.5 million
members in 31,000 chapters.

3. A factor in selecting this theme and treatment for a CVS curriculum was funding by the Edna McConnell Clark Foundation of New York. The foundation's concern was to support understanding of family life, particularly to help children in nontraditional settings (single-parent, adoptive, foster, or extended families) to realize such situations are not abnormal, despite TV's portrayal of the "standard family" lacking those characteristics as an implied role model. In 1982 the PTA entrusted curricular materials to Phi Delta Kappa's Center for Dissemination of Innovative Programs (Bloomington, IN) to oversee typesetting, packaging, and distribution. The Center produced a three-ring custom binder for the two sets of curriculum materials. For further details, see note 4.

4. Information was provided by Neville L. Robertson, director of Phi Delta Kappa's Center for the Dissemination of Innovative Programs [in education], Bloomington, Indiana, by telephone on February 12, 1987 (responding to specific questions about the status of the project, put in a letter to that organization dated January 2, 1987). In personal correspondence dated February 17, 1987, Mr. Robertson offered further data. In 6 fiscal years, almost 90% of CVS booklet sales were in the first 2 years: $6,698 in 1981–1982 and $3,426 in 1982–1983; figures for following years were $893, −$151 (loss from returned books?), $264, and $227. Their records about items sold went back only to 1983. From 1983 to early 1987, they distributed 72 Teachers Manuals K–5, and 45 for Grades 9–12; plus 21 Student Activity Books K–2, 17 for Grades 3–5, and 22 for grades 9–12. No material was produced for Grades 6–8.

5. Ben Logan (Logan & Moody, 1979) noted this distinctive quality: "Since Television Awareness Training uses a values approach in looking at television, it provides a good back-up and expansion of the U.S. Office of Education (HEW) television curriculum which takes a critical viewing approach" (p. 5).

6. Phrases used in responses to questionnaires returned in surveys of 1981 and 1985.

7. Key personnel in the T-A-T program were affiliated with specifically Christian, organized churches that cooperated in planning and conducting workshops around the country: American Lutheran Church, Christian Church (Disciples of Christ), Reformed Church in America, United Church of Christ, Church of the Brethren, Presbyterian Church in the United States, Protestant Episcopal Church, and United Methodist Church, plus the World Association for Christian Communication (WACC) in London, and T-A-T Canada in Toronto. Cited by Logan & Moody (1979, pp. 271–272).

8. In an otherwise very favorable, supportive evaluation, one reviewer (Robbins, 1980) noted: "Scattered throughout the book are worksheets, logs and various other kinds of 'homework' for the diligent television awareness trainee. Some of these I found confusing and unworkable, others struck me as condescending. . . . The book has its share of (to me) unreadable reports of carefully controlled research experiments all leading to the obvious. But there is so much more that is in fact thought provoking, challenging and informative" (pp. 20–21).

9. But in the junior high and adult editions (pp. 4 and 6 respectively) the listing is more specifically both negative and positive: "3. Achieve freedom

from the tyranny of the content values and the presence of TV. 4. Develop critical viewing skills, including an emphasis on seeking out the good TV programs."

10. Prices in the mid-1980s, were $34.95 for a complete "Starter Kit" with a complete set of material for all five age levels, which sold separately: $1.95/each set of 12 student leaflets (one set for each of five levels); $8.95 for leader's guides for younger and for older elementary and for junior high; $2.95 for leader's guide for senior high and adult levels; $2.50 for program guide books. These materials developed by MARC were published by a consortium of six publishers coordinated by the 10-religious-denomination Cooperative Publishers Association.

11. Media Action Research Center (1980a), Session 8 of worksheet leaflets for Adults, pp. 2–3.

12. Dioceses that participated in the pilot program for 1982 were: Boston, Dubuque, Newark, Oakland, Orlando, Paterson, Portland (Oregon), Providence, St. Paul-Minneapolis, and St. Petersburg-Tampa (Schropp, 1982, p. 4). Copies of booklets were available from the Publication Sales Office of the National Catholic Educational Association in Washington, DC: $4.00 for the Teacher's Guide, $3.00 for each of the three student booklets ($1.50 each for orders of 10 or more).

13. National Catholic Educational Association (ca. 1983, p. 3); a similar listing with expanded phrasing is in Schropp (1982, p. 3).

# 9

## Private Companies, U.S., U.K.

Yet another source of critical viewing skills projects and materials are private companies not associated with government, formal education, or national organizations. They include manufacturers and distributors of teaching materials that emphasize audiovisual aids, and national broadcasting corporations that mounted various projects augmenting classroom instruction. USCC's *The Media Mirror* described in its resource manual 30 audiovisual products produced by 16 companies; multiple listings included seven products by Pyramid Films, four each by Churchill Films and The Learning Seed Company, and three products by Mass Media Ministries.

### THE LEARNING SEED COMPANY

A prolific supplier of sophisticated kits for media study is The Learning Seed Company (Palatine, Illinois). Among its products are:

1. *MEDIAKIT: Exploring the Values of Mass Culture*
   Two filmstrips with narration on audio cassette, 35 copies of "The Values of Media Culture" discussion/activity guide, teaching guide ($59).
2. *ADBOX: Advertising as Literature, Education and Persuasion*
   Three filmstrips, four audiocassettes, spirit master and guide ($56).

  3. *AD ANALYSIS*
     36-frame filmstrip and teaching guide ($42).
  4. *NEWSKIT: A Consumer's Guide to News*
     Three filmstrips, two audiocassettes, 35 4-page mini-news-
     papers, and two spirit masters (53).
  5. *SEXISM in Language and Media*
     Two filmstrips, one with audiocassette, 35 activity posters, and
     two spirit masters ($40).
  6. *TELEVISION VIOLENCE*
     63-frame, color filmstrip with audiocassette, two spirit master
     worksheets, and a teaching guide ($24).
  7. *TELEVISION & VALUES: An Exploration of the Values, Mes-
     sages, & Impact of Television*
     75-frame filmstrip with 14-minute narration on audiocassette,
     24 project cards, a spirit master "student monitoring form," 128-
     page *TV Action Workbook,* 220-page TV *Sponsors Directory,* ma-
     terials for classroom simulation "TV on Trial," and a teaching
     guide (originally $43, 1981–1982 edition $58).[1]

*Television and Values.*  The last-named kit (Schrank, 1976) is reviewed here because it most closely resembles CVS projects in its scope
and objectives (see Fig. 9.1). The original version, from 1976 until the
1981 edition was introduced, was used in more than 3,500 classrooms.
The material was organized for "at least one or two weeks of solid
study of television" or selective use of items "for a day or a week" at a
time (p. 3).

*Purposes.*  Differing markedly from CVS curricula by religious organizations (MARC and USCC), the negatively critical stance of the key
filmstrip is acknowledged at the outset as:

> not a balanced or unbiased attempt to evaluate the effect of television on
> human values. Rather, it points out areas that critics and students of
> commercial television have found troublesome. . . . The filmstrip deals
> very superficially with each of the problem areas, thus inviting further
> thought and study. . . . [S]ince the filmstrip concentrates on the negative
> aspects of TV it is likely to stimulate an exchange of viewpoints after a
> showing. (p. 4).

The filmstrip surveys problems arising from TV's pervasiveness,
time consumption, engendering passivity, influence on behavior, violence, role models, instant solutions, ads extolling drugs and poor nu-
tritional eating habits, and consumption of alcoholic beverages. Discussion questions do offer opportunity for reflection and for modifying
the balance of the filmstrip. For example, after noting one assertion in

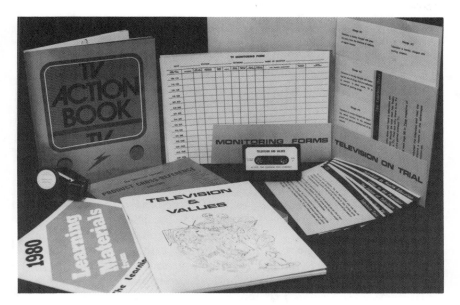

FIG. 9.1. Assignment book, filmstrip, audiocassette, worksheets, project materials, product/advertiser directory and booklets in *Television and Values* kit by Schrank (1974/1976/1978).

the filmstrip, the text asks: "Is this really true or could it be an exaggeration?" At another point, the text inquires:

> What effect has *Sesame Street* had on your household? Remember that the filmstrip does not say anything about the ability of the program to teach the alphabet. Instead, it claims that *Sesame Street* teaches the habit of regular watching. Is this valid? (p. 4)

Although the filmstrip opens with alarmist concepts and wording, the narration qualifies many of the negative assertions including those drawn from research findings. The unhurried, relaxed male voice allows viewers/listeners to assimilate the data and stated implications and—in subsequent discussion—perhaps to sort out the pros and cons of some topics touched on. The teaching guide outlines "A TV Philosophy" that is pessimistic about the pervasive, almost narcotizing impact of television on people's daily living. It marshals negatively critical quotations and data to support condemnation of people's misuse of the enticing, exploiting medium. But care is taken not to make definitive claims:

> We don't know with any degree of scientific certainty if TV shares the blame for a decline in writing and reading skills or the increase in the divorce rate. But there have been some carefully conducted studies that

provide clues. Although unmeasurable, the most pervasive effect of television is that it is an invention which causes the majority of citizens to
spend a huge portion of their lives as passive spectators instead of as
participants in an active process. (p. 15)

The material analyzes many detailed examples of alleged, potential,
and real shortcomings and dangers of television. But it alludes to very
few positive values of the medium. The seven-page essay expands on
themes and specific data briefly treated in the filmstrip, providing
teachers with background for leading discussion—including using the
project cards.

*Support Materials.*   Those 24 stiff 4×6-inch pastel-colored project
cards are for individual and group assignments. They prompt students
to gather further information and to think seriously about TV's social
effects. Each presents an exercise or mini-project to be reported back to
the class. Some require monitoring TV programs, others involve interviewing peers, or creating a hypothetical scenario about a TV issue, or
writing letters to research companies for data, or gathering data from
suggested library resources. Most of them are fact-finding activities,
to gather data substantiating (or not) assertions made in the filmstrip;
the directions on each tend to be non-judgmental to allow students to
learn and judge for themselves.

The "TV Monitor Form" is a 8½×11-inch grid, on which each student is to log programs viewed in 15-minute increments, plus acts of
violence (including kinds, male/female victim or attacker, etc.), guns
and alcohol shown, and product brands advertised. This is to focus
students' attention on those specifics while viewing at home, and to
serve as a basis for discussion back in the classroom, confirming or
qualifying the filmstrip's assertions. Its intent is to prompt students to
watch TV more actively, with critical attention, than they normally do.

"Television on Trial" is a simulation exercise to get students to
check books and periodicals for information as they explore TV's social
effects, especially on personal values. It calls for students to role-play
as judge, jury members, prosecution and defense teams, and witnesses.
It provides details of trial procedure and instructions for each role,
printed on stiff 2¼×4-inch cards in the kit. In effect, it offers a setting
for informed debate about five issues, whereby "television is hereby
charged with . . .":

Stealing years from the lifetimes of millions of regular viewers
inciting violence
fostering the sale of drugs that are ineffective or harmful; in other words,
TV is accused of pushing drugs

turning Americans into spectators instead of participants

teaching values harmful to the personal growth and spiritual development of its viewers.

The kit includes two related publications by other companies. The *TV Action Book* (Schrank, 1974/1978) serves as a reference for teachers and as a resource for students. *The Television Sponsors (Product Cross-Reference) Directory* (Boe, 1979) is a tool for student assignments such as the project cards and writing letters.

The elegantly laid out and printed 128-page *TV Action Book* is precisely what its title states: a manual for consumer activism, using federal regulations as a guide to broadcasters' legal obligations and the rights of members of the public. (But those federal regulations have been much modified since the work was published in the late 1970s.) Technical data about legal forms and procedures are accompanied by lucid, accurate explanations of regulatory and economic points. The book includes study sheets, perforated for easy removal, that provide many neat forms and grids for logging programming, listing news and advertising, and chronicling station ownership. Chapter 5, "Television as a Shaper of Values," most closely parallels the other material in the kit. As do other chapters, it offers reprints of major articles from newspapers and magazines or excerpts from books and public reports. The views about broadcasting vary from conservative to liberal, most emphasizing negative media criticism. Major portions of the publication are intended for consumer activists more than for students in the typical classroom.

The *Television Sponsors Directory* consists of 120 sheets, mimeographed single-spaced on both sides. The 240 pages offer tightly printed listings of more than 9,000 name-brand products, cross-referenced with the corporations and manufacturing divisions that manufacture the products. Company addresses and names of corporate executives are listed. The last 15 pages supply names and addresses of national and state consumer offices, members of Congress from each state (current with the semi-annual printing of each edition), federal and state governmental officials and agencies, and national networks.

## TELEVISION LEARNING, LTD.

Many companies produce isolated materials related to the subject of this report. One has the convoluted corporate title of In Touch With . . . Children/Television/Learning, Ltd. [*sic*], a division of Television Learning, Ltd. in Momona, Wisconsin. It packaged a one-year teaching plan with a 30-minute color videotape and a hardcover text,

*Centering Television* by Rosemary M. Lehman. Unlike many other CVS projects, it deals exclusively with aesthetic and cultural aspects of the medium. It uses television to teach growth in perception and in creative and critical thinking. These skills include seeing, listening, relating, discussing, deciding, and creating. They are emphasized by noting specific elements while viewing TV: "light, color, forms, sound, time-space motion, composition-frame, orchestration-environment, management-execution, and narrative-idea."[2] The arts are the source of comparisons; they are considered as expressing and interpreting behavior and experience. The material was used in California, Oregon, Florida, Louisiana, Minnesota, Illinois, Wisconsin, and in Canada.

## PRIME TIME SCHOOL TELEVISION[3]

Since 1970 this nonprofit national organization developed study guides for significant commercial and public broadcasts. Written by a staff of former educators, the guides included program synopses, background information, discussion questions, optional activities, sources for further study, and charts and graphs. The guides were intended to help teachers assign TV programs for viewing and subsequent class discussion. The guides were distributed as monthly inserts in *Media and Methods* magazine and in the National Education Association's journal *Today's Education,* and also by mail to members of national educational organizations in English and Social Studies.

Prime Time School Television also received funds from the Ford Foundation to prepare units of study on television related to law enforcement and to economics. The American Broadcasting Company contributed funds for elaborately printed booklets of a dozen pages with photographs on the occasion of special programs such as the miniseries "Roots" (200,000 copies) and about themes such as news-gathering, editing, and presentation, in *Making the News.* The CBS Television Network also cooperated with Prime Time School Television. In 1981 it helped develop a 16-page resource publication about the many aspects of TV as an adjunct to the classroom, including its multiple role as language, art form, and information source—involving all types of programs. Organized by subject area to show how TV can be used in the classroom and at home to enrich learning and enhance creativity, the booklet was directed to teachers of primary and intermediate grades. Copies were distributed to over 700,000 educators and librarians. The pages were also printed as a supplement to the National Education Association's journal *Today's Education,* which was estimated to reach over one million teachers, librarians, and parents.

Other materials were financed in part by major corporate and public sources such as Mobil, Exxon, Gulf Oil, McDonald's, the Corporation for Public Broadcasting, and the private Harris and Bush foundations. Evidence for Prime Time School Television's impact was one PBS series for which the organization initially prepared 2,000 copies of its guide; but it received requests for 262,000 copies from day care centers, nursery schools, PTA groups, and schools.[4]

## BROADCASTING COMPANIES

For various motives, companies engaged in professional broadcasting have cooperated with educators in preparing printed and videotaped material designed to sensitize young people to the medium, particularly through scripts and advance information about upcoming television programs. Although not curricular programs in themselves, these intermittent projects were integrated into formal educational settings. Significant efforts in the United States and the United Kingdom are described here.

*Television Information Office/Teachers Guide to Television.* TIO was a service of the National Association of Broadcasters—commercial radio and television companies in the United States.* Since 1967 it cooperated in publishing semi-annual *Teachers Guide to Television.* Each issue offered study guides to a dozen major television programs scheduled by the networks. They included questions for classroom discussion before and after viewing at home; they listed suggested readings compiled by a committee of the American Library Association, plus film references provided by the Association for Education Communications and Technology. The booklets also included essays by educators, broadcasters, and people in government about current issues relating to the medium and its educational potential. The handsomely laid out and printed booklet contained as many as 32 pages, with many photographs of programs reviewed.

*Parent Participation TV Workshops/NBC.* Although Teachers Guide to Television (TGT) as an entity was separate from TIO, it depended on broadcasters' cooperation. In 1976 the National Broadcasting Com-

---

*Three decades after it was created by the NAB, in 1989 the Television Information Office was disbanded. Its activities and resources were relocated among related groups such as the Museum of Broadcasting (New York City) and the Broadcast Pioneers Library (Washington, D.C.).

pany began underwriting costs for TGT's Parent Participation TV Workshops. They promoted dialogue between parents and children through shared viewing experiences—predictably, of TV programs broadcast by the NBC network. Participants gathered to view programs dramatizing sensitive topics (such as freedom/responsibility, sexual relations, abortion, drugs, desegregation); a moderator supported by a study guide helped family members discuss each other's attitudes and feelings prompted by the program. Discussion guides to selected NBC programs were supplemented by articles, preview tapes, books, records, scripts, and papers by educators. Workshops were intended to facilitate communication between parents and children, and to help youngsters choose values and make decisions. Thus they were not truly CVS activities, except insofar as they promoted reflective viewing of television along with critical and creative thinking. But project leaders claimed that "sharing the television experience with their children makes it easier for a family to develop good television habits in their children" such as how much time they spend with TV, what programs they select, and how they respond to what they view.[5]

By 1979 departments of education in Georgia, Michigan, Minnesota, and Pennsylvania adopted the project state-wide; Nassau County in New York, 25 school systems in major cities, and hundreds of other communities, schools, and churches introduced workshops. By 1980 a total of 21 states participated in the workshop project. Local television stations affiliated with NBC cooperated in the activity.

## NATIONAL TELEVISION NETWORKS AND MAJOR BROADCAST GROUPS

*Capital Cities Communications.*   Owner of a large group of radio and television stations,* Capital Cities Communications was among the first broadcast companies to harness TV scripts to school reading programs. It grew out of pioneer work by Dr. Michael McAndrew in the Philadelphia school system. In 1979 Dr. McAndrew introduced into the classroom videotaped TV programs and mimeographed copies of scripts as the "text" used by students to learn or enhance reading skills. In 1976 Dr. McAndrew had received assistance from ABC for scripts for a two-part dramatization of Joseph P. Lash's book *Eleanor and Franklin*. The program's advertising sponsor, IBM (International

---

*In 1985 Capital Cities Communications purchased the four-times larger ABC, merging into Capital Cities/American Broadcasting Companies, Inc.

Business Machines), offered financial support, and the Philadelphia *Inquirer* published the script in a special supplement to the 550,000 copies of its daily newspaper. Gunther (1976, p. 6) estimated that 3,500 other school systems were experimenting with or considering the concept. In the spring of 1977, CBS tested such a project with one of its network programs. During the 1978–1979 school year, school districts in 13 cities joined in a year-long project with Capital Cities, which hired Dr. McAndrew to direct the $250,000 project. Teacher's guides and scripts from the three commercial networks, some bilingual, for each of 10 monthly programs were sent out 2 weeks in advance of broadcasts; 60,000 students in Grades 4–12 participated.[6] Studies conducted by Pennsylvania State University estimated that students engaged in the initial year-long TV reading program, compared with those not involved, scored 20% higher on tests of reading comprehension, vocabulary, and writing and listening skills (Margulies, 1980, p. 43). Because all activities were based on reading the scripts, actual viewing of the programs was not essential. But the National Council for Children and Television (1979) recommended that "if the reader chooses to view the program, further understanding of the medium and of the functions of its behind-the-scene contributors (directors, editors, etc.) will be dramatically demonstrated" (p. 32). To that extent, at least, this and similar programs designed to motivate and enhance reading skills also contributed to critical viewing skills.

*CBS Inc.* CBS (formerly Columbia Broadcasting System) began collaborating in the late 1970s with educational organizations to link television programs with projects promoting literacy (i.e., basic reading skills and motivation to explore literature). In 1977 it introduced a "Television Reading Program" in association with its affiliated stations. The stations in turn worked with local newspapers and corporations to help print and distribute materials.[7] Six to eight special dramas and episodes of prime-time series were selected annually. Complete scripts of those CBS programs were reprinted locally and distributed to teachers and school children, using television as a motivating tool for reading. The scripts contained all dialogue as well as camera and stage directions. They were accompanied by explanations of TV technology and terminology, acquainting young readers with how programs are produced and with some creative elements in TV. The 16- to 24-page tabloid newsprint copies included a final page with six suggestions for parents, recommending they discuss the program and script with their children by asking questions to encourage reflection and creative thinking (sample questions were suggested). Students were to read the script before viewing the scheduled program at home, and perhaps again afterward—even aloud in classrooms, with roles assigned. In some instances, children read the scripts as they viewed the program. Occasionally, bilingual scripts were distributed to Hispanic children. The first was an episode of "M*A*S*H," for which more than 2 million scripts printed in English and Spanish were distributed to elementary and secondary schools in the country. Within 6 years over 23 million students had used the scripts. By late 1986 more than 32 million scripts had been distributed by CBS affiliated stations in more than 110 cities.[8] By 1989 more than 36 million scripts for 53 programs had been distributed to students in all 50 states.[9]

Detailed teacher's guides (spiral-bound, each 40 to 60 pages) helped them initiate classroom discussion and direct students to additional reading, writing, and creative activities related to the scripts. One portion dealt with script format and technical production terms; it suggested classroom activities to help understand TV process by simulating studio production. Another section on "comprehension" analyzed the theme, plot and characters of each story. Less directly related to CVS topics were vocabulary and discussion of personal, ethical, and social values. The "Critical Evaluation" section included questions about specific production characteristics such as music, sound effects, camera angles, video editing, scene sequences and editing revisions. Several pages of worksheets were added to facilitate classroom handling of characters and themes, plus evaluation forms for teacher and students. Professional educators developed the guides as a resource to be adapted freely by teachers to fit local circumstances.

*Testing.* In 1979 CBS conducted detailed studies with 97 schools in 11 metropolitan areas and reported how 262 teachers, 921 students (Grades 7–12), and 95 parents evaluated their experiences with the reading program.[10] Most participants were enthusiastic and claimed the children's interest in reading had risen. So had the expression of ideas and critical thinking in discussions and post-program activities, according to 86% of the teachers. Nine of 10 teachers used the guides; 83% rated them as "excellent" or "very good." Regarding specific CVS concerns, many students said they better understood program content and character motivation by reading the script before a broadcast. Of parents who responded, 85% said the reading program stimulated discussion about the program and characters and helped children understand program content, while it also encouraged them to watch TV with their children. Students were most positive about the experience when they "acted out" scripts or read them aloud in class, when they used broadcast instructions provided, when they compared the script with the broadcast, and when they had studied television terms in the script. Among children, 98% wanted to continue the project; 96% of parents who viewed with their child wanted him or her to work with another script. But less than a third of all parents seemed to agree that the reading program benefited children in specific critical viewing skills. Among the 95 responding parents, only 29 stated it "upgrades child's TV taste," 21 said their child "understands content better," 20 felt it "promotes thinking," and 18 agreed that it "provides understanding of TV production."[11] The study dealt with reactions to one program project in January 1979; the results were positive enough to prompt the network and the wide range of cooperating agencies in the country to continue and expand the program, as already described.

CBS mounted another literacy project in 1979 in collaboration with the Library of Congress, called "Read More About It." At the outset, the Library of Congress annually selected from 10 to 25 CBS "special" programs from outlines and summaries of future programs submitted by the network. At the end of each broadcast a featured performer from the cast spoke to the audience for 30 seconds, urging them to visit local libraries and bookstores to explore several books related to the program's content. Those titles, and a single-page list of other books reflecting a variety of perspectives on the topic, were chosen by bibliographers and reference librarians at The Library of Congress. The complete lists were published in advance of broadcasts in The Library of Congress' "Information Bulletin" and in the American Booksellers Association's "Newswire"; the American Library Association also distributed lists to schools and libraries. And CBS sent lists for each program to its affiliated stations and to print media. By 1988 over 175 programs, plus almost as many rebroadcasts of them, had been part of the project (CBS/Broadcast Group, 1987, p. 1). During each season into the 1990s, some 40 CBS programs are chosen by The Library of Congress for the "Read More About It" messages.[12]

**NBC.** In addition to its funding of the Parent Participation TV Workshops, the National Broadcasting Company (NBC), through local affiliated stations, distributed to teachers and parents its "Viewer's Guides" about selected network programs, to help young people better enjoy and understand the programs. At the end of each monthly program for young viewers, *Special Treat*, brief announcements were made by actors featured in the drama who recommended reading the book on which the program was based as well as other books by that author. The short announcements advocated "When you turn off your set, turn on a book."

NBC also produced study guides for many prime-time special broadcasts, to help teachers and parents assist younger viewers to better understand and enjoy the programs. The first was produced in 1978; 12 or more were prepared in succeeding years. The four-page guides included photographs of scenes from the drama and documentary programs. Only a small part pertained to technical and artistic elements of the programs themselves (visual camera work, sets, characters, settings). Emphasized were the themes and topics, relating them to viewers' lives, and to their reactions and judgments about those topics; they included suggestions for discussion and for further activities and reading. Shorter guides were prepared for the "Project Peacock" programs for younger viewers. The network staff collaborated with outside companies that researched and produced educational materials, including Cultural Information Service (CIStems, Inc.) and Art Worlds, Inc., independent nonprofit educational agencies. More than 100,000 guides were regularly distributed through TV stations affiliated with NBC; direct mailings went to 50,000–500,000 people and groups selected according to each program's subject and theme (e.g., reading, education, religion, theater, retirement). In some instances, "learning packages" with synopses and articles of background information as well as bibliographies and classroom activities were distributed as inserts to daily newspapers in 11 cities. A major instance was in 1980 when material for the mini-series "Shogun" was published in the *Chicago Tribune,* with 100,000 additional copies sent to high schools in that city, and an estimated (Television Information Office, 1980–1981, p. 6) total readership of 15 million in the United States. Additional funding was provided by the Illinois Humanities Council, the National Endowment for the Humanities, and the Illinois State Board of Education.

*ABC.* The American Broadcasting Company (ABC) collaborated with the American Library Association in supplying over 4,000 school libraries with monthly information packages about its *Afternoon Specials* and *Weekend Specials* that were based on books and directed to children. Packages included schedules, posters, program synopses, biographies of authors, and bibliographies of related works. The theme was "Watch the Program; Read the Book."

ABC also funded Drs. Jerome and Dorothy Singer at Yale with a $108,000 grant to develop their major CVS project (described in chapter 7). ABC Wide World of Learning, Inc. distributed seven, 12-minute videotaped segments called "Getting the Most Out of TV," with teachers' guides, as "the first comprehensive program for developing critical television viewing skills in children."[13] (An activity book and a teacher's manual were available through Goodyear Publishing.) The videotape complemented printed materials, based on experimental studies by the Professors Singer. The videos were professionally produced, including music. They used television to explain TV. Taped material was well organized; explanations were clear; good sharp titles of key words were displayed on the screen as they come up in the program. The tapes explained: Technical aspects of TV broadcasting; scheduling and the people who make programs; basic editing procedures and special effects "magic"; characterizations depicted in programming, including stereotyping; action and violence (including make-believe techniques) and moralizing about how to resolve problems properly; TV news, including selective editing, interviewing and documentaries; and commercial advertising (agencies, consumers, persuasive appeals) and public service announcements. Videotapes were targeted to children aged 8 to 10.[14]

*WQED.* The noncommercial public broadcast station in Pittsburgh, WQED mounted an instructional TV series called "Learning with Television" in 1979. Originally funded for 6 months by a modest grant of $5,000 from the Pennsylvania Department of Education and the Pennsylvania Broadcast Council, the project was overseen by an administrator and supported by three staff persons and a teacher/ "trainer."

A pilot workshop in CVS training was developed for June 30 through July 3, 1980. It was based on previous projects, including Television-Awareness-Training, Parent Participation TV Workshops, and the four funded by the U.S. Office of Education. The workshop's purpose was to train teachers (K–12) and other adults—as individual viewers and as parents—"to sharpen their own viewing and television literacy competencies . . . [in order to] be able to teach their children, students, or peers to be more aware of the TV message, to analyze the message, to evaluate the message and to express the evaluation" (Shapiro, 1980, p. 2). Topics included those found in other projects: personal use of TV; the industry's structure, economics, and regulation; commercial advertising techniques; elements of drama (plot-theme-characters-setting); production techniques; news and documentaries; program types and their critical review; TV messages (stereotypes) and consumer organizations. The workshop included activities (role-playing and producing portable video production), hand-out materials, readings, audiovisual materials (videotapes, audiocassettes, 16mm film, slides, filmstrips), and a visit to WQED television production studios.

*Testing.* Formal pre-/posttests indicated significantly more favorable opinion of TV used in instruction, after discovering creative ways to employ the TV programs children viewed at home. The 27 participants evaluated the workshop as good to excellent in all categories (objective, organization, ideas and activities, scope, printed and audio-visual materials). Subsequent workshops based on this model were planned for various regions in the state.

## INDEPENDENT BROADCASTING AUTHORITY AND THE INDEPENDENT TELEVISION COMPANIES (UNITED KINGDOM)

In the United Kingdom, six series of 21 programs were presented in 1980–1981 by non-BBC stations. They were approved by the Educational Advisory Council of the Independent Broadcasting Authority and by educational advisory bodies of the Independent Television Companies. Teachers' notes were compiled into a printed book of 152 pages, with accompanying photographs. It presented essays by experts on each program topic, lists of further reading and of teaching resources, information about specific content of the programs, and several pages of possible activities for students. While "critical study of mass media" was a factor in all programs and their study, it was the primary focus of several programs.

A group of four programs comprised "Viewpoint 2." They examined recurrent patterns in how media represented social aspects of contemporary Britain—media's "image" of youth, Black people, industrial relations, and welfare. They included songs, film clips, interviews, dramatizations, and animation. Booklets (e.g., Bethell, 1980) for students were to accompany study of each program; they were heavily laden with photographs and graphic layouts, and posed open-ended questions for reflection and thoughtful discussion. (Booklets were available from local ITV companies.)

*Purposes.* The purpose was to question mass media's view of the society that students live in, by introducing students briefly to how media work and then to observe examples of how media treated topics in print and broadcasting. Professor Stuart Hall's lengthy essay on "Viewpoint 2" (Griffiths, 1980, pp. 24–45) succinctly described major structures and forces at work in the creation of television news and public affairs coverage. He emphasized the selection process inherent in filming and editing reality. It involved identifying problems and patterns as well, attributing value to them and establishing an agenda of social significance. This necessarily occasioned dilemmas of "balance" or fairness and accuracy in depicting ongoing social, cultural, and political events. His essay and the following pages in the teacher's guide probed in detail the media process of selecting and presenting.

"Working" was a series of five television dramas intended for use in English courses, especially where teachers examined television and TV genres as part of media studies curricula. Two dramas exemplified the popular television forms of situation comedy and episodic serials. Scripts of all five plays were published as a book with the same title *Working*. Mottershead's essay (1980, pp. 58–73) explained television as a commercial system as well as technical production of television drama. He offered an articulate review of the role of TV drama in culture, and of understanding TV drama as symbolic representing society within the constraints of scheduling, format, and conventions of sound and image to produce meaning. The seven pages of "Working Activities" offered detail points for observing and discussing types of TV drama, plot and character, settings and effects and music, and the use of cameras and sound in staging the plays.

A unit on "One World Documentaries" included three entitled "Jonathan Dimbleby in South America" and a fourth in which that same documentarian described how he creates his films about world topics, commenting on journalistic problems involved. The essay in this section of the book consisted of notes from a recorded interview with him (1980, pp. 106–119) about seven Third World countries and also about disasters in general, including his views about responsibility, balance, frustration, and education.

\*       \*       \*

Those varied efforts by private companies sought to engage classroom teachers and their students into becoming active, informed, perceptive, and judging viewers of television drama and news. Many projects were developed and promoted by major broadcasting companies in collaboration with educators and research specialists to ensure validity of televised programs and of printed and audiovisual support materials for institutional use.

The next chapter explores selected major CVS-related projects around the world.

## NOTES

1. Prices are quoted from promotional materials and bibliographies of the early 1980s. Although the prices are subject to change, they indicate the range of relative expense of various kits.

2. Promotional pamphlet by Television Learning Ltd., quoting Lehmann's text. Purchase of book and tape, $225; rental, $45.

3. The author is indebted to others' reviews of activities described in this section of the chapter, when primary sources were not readily available. Regrettably, Prime Time School Television's Chicago address changed at least three times in the 1980s, and inquiries mailed to them were repeatedly returned by the postal service. For good summaries, see "Television for Learning: A Catalog of Reading Programs and Teachers' Guides" in National Council for Children and Television (1979, Fall).

4. Reported in *Variety,* May 14, 1980, p. 105.

5. Data cited in promotional folder by Teachers Guides to Television (ca. 1982), which quoted Dr. Thomas K. Minter, Deputy Commissioner, U.S. Office of Education (identified as "Assistant Secretary, Elementary and Secondary Education"): "Television literacy has the potential for developing other literacies. Specifically, critical and active viewing of television has the potential for stimulating reading. . . . I believe that critical and informed viewing of television programs within a family setting can help strengthen the bridges between home, school, and family which must be the support for equal educational opportunity for all children."

6. Data reported by Television Information Office (1980), LeGrand-Brodsky (1979), and "Helping Johnny Read," *Broadcasting,* January 16, 1978.

7. Data from CBS news releases, October 26 and December 27, 1978. For example, CBS-affiliated station WJBK-TV in Detroit collaborated with the *Detroit Free Press* to print and distribute 100,000 scripts on a program in 1978; 700,000 more copies were printed in that newspaper's Sunday supplement, with reprinting funded by Manufacturers National Corporation (whose headquarters were in that city). Students in 40 cities participated in two other programs in December, 1978; 1.5 million scripts were distributed directly to classrooms by local CBS affiliate stations, and another 2.8 million copies were reproduced as supplements in newspapers in Baltimore, Cleveland, Dayton, Detroit, Houston, Los Angeles, Milwaukee, and St. Petersburg. Numbers of students ranged from 75 in Phoenix to 40,000 in New York and 500,000 in Los Angeles.

8. Data from Television Information Office (1984); CBS news releases, May 20, August 19, and October 31, 1986. More than 1 million scripts were distributed for each of several programs, "A Christmas Carol" (broadcast December 17, 1984), "Alice in Wonderland" (December 9 and 10, 1985), and "Dream West" (April 13, 14, and 15, 1986).

9. Press announcement from CBS/Broadcast Group, CBS Educational & Community services, January 31, 1989, p. 2.

10. The spiral-bound report had 53 pages of text and another 41 pages of tables. Data were analyzed by age, grade, gender, minority status, geographic location, and other categories. See Child Research Service, Inc. (Hyatt-Esserman Research Associates) & CBS Office of Social Research (Economics and Research Division, CBS Inc.), 1979. See also a summary of major findings (25 pp. with promotional photographs), published by CBS Television Network (1982).

11. Data reported in Table 34 of Child Research Service, Inc. & CBS Office of Social Research (1979, n.p.).

12. Cited by Television Information Office (1980, pp. 2–3); also in a 10-page

promotional announcement about the project, by CBS, September 8, 1986, pp. 1–2.

13. Promotional folder by ABC Wide World of Learning, Inc.

14. Prices in the early 1980s for the complete series (84 minutes) were: $1,197 on 16mm film, $850 on videotape cassettes. Individual segments, and "modules" of three or four segments were also available.

# 10

## *Institution-Related CVS Programs in Non-U.S. Countries*

A major factor in introducing and sustaining systematic programs in media education, including television, is acceptance and positive support by institutional authority as well as by peers in the teaching profession. Anderson emphasized that point as critical to the success of any media study program.

Eddie Dick, Media Education Officer for the Scottish Film Council, struggled with gathering data about media education around the world by his questionnaire survey reported in 1987. He acknowledged "the quantity and quality of information received varied widely" from country to country, so no hard comparisons were truly valid. He also noted (1987a):

> Another constraint is that it is not usually possible to write of national provision within any one country. Even in those countries where national curricula exist, education is often administered locally and, in the interstices between pedagogy and administration, the possibility of useful generalisation is lost. On a more formal level, too, countries made up of federal states almost invariably administer education on a state basis. It is not, for example, possible to write of *Australian* media education; rather Western Australia, Victoria, New South Wales and so on have to be written of quite separately. (p. 1)

Some observers (Pungente, 1985, p. 27) consider Australia a leader in these efforts, because their education authorities as well as teachers and parents "understand" media education, they experimented in the field, and associations and meetings as well as media curricula and texts have been widespread for 20 years. In addition to the two Australian projects recounted in chapter 6, the Education Department in New South Wales reflects serious support by the state. In 1981 it asserted that media courses were as appropriate as teaching reading, writing, and mathematics. And a Media Studies Centre in South Australia assists the 80% of secondary schools offering such courses. It offers workshops and conferences and operates a library of media materials. The Centre also provides consultants to primary and secondary schools, making available 40 persons trained to bring information about content and methodology of media courses to administrators and parents as well as to in-service staff.

Elsewhere in the world, CVS efforts in institutional contexts are often carried on without system-wide administrative involvement. Typically, individuals initiated media study on their own—usually within more traditional educational subjects—and slowly expanded their activities. In other instances, a governmental office (ministry of education, culture, etc.) offered optional kinds of media studies to be overlaid on existing curricula.

Several examples from the United Kingdom, continental Europe, and South America exemplify television study courses offered in the environment of formal education, with institutional authority sometimes closely involved and in other instances only partly or distantly involved.

Described here are salient details of organized projects that participated in the 1981/1985 questionnaire surveys and/or submitted sample curricular materials then or in 1988–1989. Further data are added from several recent analytical surveys of media projects world-wide.*

## UNITED KINGDOM

In England and Wales during the last two decades various courses and some formal examinations involved "media education" in the broad sense, including aspects of film, broadcasting, and sound recordings along with more traditional print media. Sustained and structured

---

*The author is indebted to Paul Kenney, S.J. at the Centre for the Study of Communication and Culture, London, for gathering materials and questionnaire responses from CVS-related representatives in this section. More recent data were provided by descriptive worldwide surveys by John Pungente (Canada), Eddie Dick (Scotland), and Valeria Fuenzalida (Chile)—all cited earlier and specifically referenced later in this chapter.

activity was not widespread until the late 1980s, partly because media study was only gradually accepted as appropriate for academic study. In 1987 Eddie Dick summarized the state of media education at the primary level:

> Within the *United Kingdom* things are potentially on the verge of happening. On a formal level there is no provision for primary media education. However, in *Wales* primary projects were established in 18 schools in September, 1987. In *England* many individual projects are scattered throughout the 100 or so education authorities. . . . In *Scotland* curriculum guidelines are, at the time of writing, due to be published in autumn 1987 and a small number of pilot schemes in primary (and secondary) schools are beginning. In all 3 countries there is a sense that the substantial developments apparent in secondary and tertiary are, at long last, percolating into primary. (1987a, p. 9)

But at the secondary level in Britain (England, Wales, and Scotland), Dick noted "major advances" in media education in the 1980s. They included media education opportunities for students aged 16 and above, offered by all five English Examining Boards (including General Certificate of Secondary Education courses) as well as Scotland's "Highers" (examinations) and National Certificate catalogue.*

By 1989, Canadian media analyst John Pungente (1989, Winter) concluded from first-hand observation that "media education is perhaps more developed in Britain than elsewhere in Europe" (p. 3). He cited a 1988 survey reporting some form of media education taught in more than a third of all schools in England and Wales; in Scotland 200 schools and colleges taught modules of National Certificate Media Studies to students 16 and older. Scottish government approval and administrative support in schools strongly encouraged development of media curricula, with plans to train teachers. The British Film Institute (BFI) Education listed almost 40 persons in England, Wales, and Scotland who helped implement media education by providing resources to U.K. teachers. In Britain at the end of the decade, a new national curriculum specified media education to be part of English studies in schools.[†]

---

*It should be noted that for several decades colleges in the United States have offered not only scattered courses on media criticism, including television, but also complete "major" emphases of study for undergraduate and graduate degrees in electronic as well as print and cinematic media, often directed toward professional careers. Many courses develop aesthetic and social awareness and critical judgment of mass media and their product. Somewhat similar academic programs of study have been introduced in the United Kingdom and elsewhere. (See later at note 5.)

†Ireland offered promise when the Curriculum and Examinations Board, established by the Irish government in January 1984, noted in its first publication that media education might be integrated into a new curriculum plan.

## WALES

### Powys, Wales

An early, well-developed project in Wales included one primary and two secondary schools in Powys county (respectively involving 26, 33, and 31 pupils). It was jointly funded over a 14-month period (April 1979 to June 1980) by the Schools Council of Great Britain through its Welsh Committee and by the Powys Education Committee.

*Purposes and Procedures.* The project rejected the "inoculation" approach of preparing young people to defend themselves against media blandishments and excesses. It also eschewed semiotics and analysis of hidden messages and meanings. Instead, Elster (1980) explained, it sought "to return the focus of teaching to the medium itself" under title of "Visual Literacy," emphasizing *how* the medium works in order to "objectify" it for students (p. 3). Students accomplish this by sequenced steps: (a) keeping log books about their personal viewing; (b) discussing programs they were familiar with, including viewing videotapes of recent broadcasts, to learn visual/aural "grammar"; (c) producing amateur programs with basic videotape equipment (emphasizing thematic concepts and fantasy); (d) applying capabilities developed in previous steps by advanced discussion about news and current affairs broadcasts and about methods of persuasion in TV advertising; (e) demonstrating through discussion and written work their grasp of language and concepts taught in previous steps.

The Powys project emphasized as central the mounting of TV productions, so students could experience alternatives possible in producing programs. It also provided critical discussion "in which the children themselves have a stake, namely their own creative work." Using students' productions as well as videotapes of their favorite broadcast programs, teachers involved them in discussing a broad range of CVS topics in addition to those noted earlier, such as program genres, economic basis for program decisions, news as information or opinion or interpretation, and the function and effects of editing. Confirming the orientation toward "hands-on" production as a key to developing critical awareness in students, the project director (Elster, 1980) concluded "we see little profit in a purely abstract approach to our subject. But this does not mean that no education can take place in the absence of a teacher with practical, creative experience in the medium" (p. 16). He noted that many teachers already have some audiovisual experience; and professional broadcasters might be brought in to clarify more technical aspects of programming. Their visits would help demystify the medium, as program production itself was intended to do.

Clwyd, Wales*

During the 1980s the Clwyd Media Studies Unit (or in Welsh: Uned
Astudio Cyfryngau Clwyd) of the Centre for Educational Technology
trained secondary school teachers in media education. More than 90%
of secondary schools in the county of Clwyd provided some form of
media education. It was integrated with English studies, as optional or
core courses in the General Certificate for Secondary Education
(GCSE) curricula for Years 4 and 6, as modules in Technical and Vocational Education Initiative (TVEI) schooling and also toward the Certificate for Pre-Vocational Education (CPVE), and as part of Welsh
examinations in English literature for the "advanced" level. Those
varied forms of media education reached approximately one out of four
senior students (Dick, 1987a, p. 18).

The Unit extended that effort to primary-level teachers in a pilot
program conducted in 1985–1986 and expanded in following years.
The Unit prepared media teaching materials such as 10 booklets on
"Making Sense of the Media" and sets of photographic slides to accompany printed tracts about media in general, television, radio, the press,
popular music, and cinema. It published a 35-page booklet (McIver,
n.d., ca. 1987) outlining the project's basic structure and content. The
Unit also published in 1988 a detailed 48-page report (Twitchin, 1988)
of a year-long evaluation of the project. The handsome typeset book
provides details about procedures and assessments rarely available for
CVS-related projects.

*Purposes and Procedures.* By "media education" the Unit meant
study of images, institutions, and audiences:

> *Learning to read the media.* What sense do we make of different media
> products?
>
> *What are the media?* How and by whom are media outputs produced, and
> how are meanings constructed?
>
> *Consumption of the media.* How do we use media products? What effects do
> they have on us? (p. 5)

Those broad categories were derived from their study program for
secondary media education which follows, as outlined in the Polytechnic of Wales Handbook for the Graduate Diploma in Teaching
Media Studies.

---

*Although questionnaire data (1981, 1985) were not available for this project, later
reports and primary materials used in the project as well as secondary sources provided
adequate information to attempt appraising it according to CVS criteria (part III).

*Secondary Level.*[1] "Block One—The World of Images" studies images and words through textual analysis and semiotics, including signs, codes, and forms of juxtaposing images in sight and sound. Unit 1 explores codes and conventions of photographic and other media images, including those about gender. Unit 2 looks at the way media depict domestic and foreign groups. Unit 3 studies how media are used by people of different backgrounds and values, and how media represent subsets of people representing "textual and social meanings"— specifically analyzing scientists and law enforcers.

"Block Two—The Industry of Images" looks at sociological and historical aspects of media industries and institutions which are factors in shaping media content. Unit 4 covers production practices and creative roles of "the people who 'make sense' professionally [and] also have their own ideas, values and limits" so that mass media are "not only the product of individual professionals but of corporate professionalism as well" (p. 27). Unit 5 analyzes the commercial context of media as industries—ownership, control, and marketing—focusing on the sound recording industry and how personalities serve as commodities. Unit 6 looks at media as institutions: Their historical development, including internal policies, and relationships with government and public.

"Block Three—Images of Audience" looks to quantitative research (ratings) and how media "construct identities for us to make sense of both the programmes and ourselves" (p. 27). It also studies how and why audiences use media in their lives. Unit 7 reviews media's effects and influence on audiences, plus audience's uses and gratifications from media, and considers recent research into how different people form different meanings from the same media messages. Unit 8 analyzes soap operas and serials to observe how "institution assumptions and textual strategies serve to 'position' us in relation to the messages we look at or read" (p. 28), including developing images of various social constructs (family, the nation, housewives, etc.) which audiences incorporate into their own context and daily routines. Unit 9 studies media amid popular culture and as a "consciousness industry," including theories of mass society, ideology and hegemony. This unit concludes by grappling with issues in teaching media studies: pedagogy and developing syllabi and practical exercises not relying on highly technical equipment.

*Primary Level.* Up to the mid-1980s, although secondary-level education proved effective with teacher in-service training linked with school projects, only "pioneering individuals" taught media in primary grades. Meanwhile conferences and national reports (1983, 1985) supported teaching media literacy to young children.[2] So the Clwyd Media Studies Unit adapted to a 1-year pilot project for primary teachers its 12-month part-time program for secondary level offered in collaboration with Polytechnic of Wales Graduate Diploma in Teaching Media Studies.

Five teachers selected by "headteachers" from as many primary schools met on 24 days of released time throughout the academic year, beginning in September 1985. Experienced in the classroom, participants adapted the secondary-level body of knowledge and procedures to teaching younger children. They appraised course content, pedagogy, and logistics of introducing media material into already crowded school schedules. Beyond studying mass communication theories, they also learned skills in producing video and audio materials. Concurrently they applied their media learning to regular classes during the term (for example, they conducted surveys in their classrooms and assigned media diaries to students, discussed children's favorite programs, newspapers, and comics). Television constituted a major portion, directly and indirectly, of media study material; radio, film, recordings, newspapers, and advertising were also treated.

One third (nine sessions) of the experimental training project engaged teachers in discussing media's "importance as a definer of social reality and cultural experience" (McIver, 1987, p. 11). They debated whether they ought teach children "to discriminate between 'good' and 'bad' media products." They considered using "children's engagement with pleasure as a positive learning outcome." They explored "'effects arguments' and studied examples of moral panics." Despite different foci for media topics, the five teachers acknowledged that "every medium has its own language or set of codes and conventions that are understood and interpreted by different people in different ways" (p. 12).

After the second group of nine sessions, plus a special 5-day seminar at Easter, several participants compiled their aims in teaching media (p. 21). "Concepts" included representations of gender/race/age/class, bias, stereotyping, power, construction of media texts, bringing meanings to texts, production processes, image analysis, narrative, and notions of audience. "Attitudes" included open mindedness, ability to question, cooperation, respect for differences in social groups, and pleasure. "Skills" included production skills for various media: group work, analytical skills, media literacy, scripting and storyboarding, and language development.

The final component of the program (another nine sessions) helped teachers better understand media institutions and industries. Concepts included power and control, financing, and professional practices in producing radio, television, and newspapers. Exercises in preparing simulated news presentations gave a sense of constraints in selecting content, editorial control, production and marketing. They explored exercises to acquaint children with technical skills, production techniques, program conventions (e.g., game/quiz shows), TV scheduling, and media audiences.

Five teachers participated in the initial year's project; by the end of the following year (1986–1987), teachers in 16 schools had taken the media training course.

*Assessing Results.* How effective was this pilot project? The Clwyd City Council commissioned The National Foundation for Educational Research in England and Wales to conduct an evaluation in 1987–1988. Beyond assessing results, that review (Twitchin, 1988) chronicles how the course was developed, to serve as a paradigm for others. The study adverts to administrative factors by seeking "to provide Primary teachers and heads with an example of the processes involved in the introduction of a curriculum innovation," including "the parts played by a wide range of institutions and individuals" (p. 3).[3]

At the outset, evaluators noted the CVS project's "*informed* support of the Director of Education" and "a strong commitment by the Local Education Authority," including financial support (p. 10). They allude to the fact that "media education does not appear on the list of national priorities" established by central government (p. 11). Because teacher-participants required released time from school duties on days when media training sessions were held, it was important to market the project by soliciting cooperation from headmasters (principals, "headteachers") sympathetic to curriculum innovation and to media study. Those supervisors nominated their own staff teachers as participants. They also constituted a steering panel during the pilot year for progress reports and comments. When interviewed during the evaluation, some supervisors recommended their participation at earlier stages of planning. They also regretted that steering panels were not continued after the pilot year; such participation by heads, some judged, would ensure their support in implementing media education. In fact, in the second year of the project, two of the five participants were heads of schools; in the third year there were two heads and three deputy heads among eight participants.

After 2 years of training primary-level teachers for media education, the Clwyd Unit reduced the year-long project from 24 to 10 hours, reassessing the structure of the course. They divorced training programs from the formally certified "Diploma" syllabus, replacing it with accreditation leading to a Certificate in the Advanced Study of

Education (CASE). The CASE study program reduced training to 4 units in primary media education:

- Media Education Arguments, claims and moral panics.
- How can we find out: School focussed research.
- Reading Images: A TV Literacy?
- Media Audiences: Who do they think you are? (p. 18).

One concern was the need to obtain academic (scholarly or bureaucratic?) validation for local media training programs so primary-level teachers could progress toward advanced certificates and degrees in their profession.

The evaluation team lauded the project for preparing well crafted printed and audiovisual materials. They stressed that:

> media education lays great emphasis on oral and practical work, but when the credibility of a curriculum innovation is being established, it would seem that print remains the medium that allows the newcomer to gain most purchase on the area. (p. 21)

Evaluators summarized why teachers had volunteered to take the pilot course and two subsequent years of training. Potential career advancement was only secondary to the following major factors:

> The teacher had seen or heard about the classroom work of earlier course members and was impressed with the approach. The teacher had tried media education in a limited way already, and wanted to expand that area of their work. The course was seen as complementing existing skills in a range of media. The teacher was convinced of the need for children to engage more systematically with non-print media. (p. 23)

Responding to the evaluators' questionnaire administered in 16 Clwyd county schools, most teachers judged teaching mass media to primary students as "a good idea" (65%) or "very important" (21%), although 14% rated it "relatively unimportant"; none agreed with the optional choice "that teaching primary pupils about mass media is not the job of the school" (p. 24). Among all teachers, 12% taught regularly about mass media, 51% occasionally, 5% more than once each term, and 30% never taught about mass media. Roughly half of them (48%) taught about media in other curriculum topic areas: language, history, current affairs, mathematics, environmental studies, advertising, communication, art, health education, and sport (p. 24).

A major difficulty was disruption or discontinuity in classrooms as substitutes replaced teachers absent for each of the 24 training days (or 10 days in subsequent years). But teachers found that regimen well suited to swiftly trying out media ideas in classrooms and reporting back to colleagues from week to week to compare results. They preferred that scheduling rather than a block of weeks of intensive, unbroken training, with no opportunity for applying to regular classes. When queried about most apt scheduling, 34% preferred a series of half-day sessions during school, 11% opted for a series of half-days apart from school, 25% supported the series of full-day sessions during school (as conducted in the project), 28% preferred a series of full-day sessions out of school (p. 27).

Teacher-participants found some theory unrelated to classroom application, but useful for personal knowledge and for purposes of diploma certification. They wanted (and had received) flexibility in ideas presented, structure of sessions, and practical exercises. Some were skeptical of or resisted tutors' handling of CVS approaches at times. Many wanted very concrete, pragmatic activities and exercise sheets to apply directly in their classrooms. Tutors "tried not to fall into that trap, because [they] knew they would simply use it as a worksheet, and not incorporate discussion around" the material (p. 31). Some participants were uneasy with allowing students to assume much decision making traditionally left to the teacher.

Evaluators recommended the following strategies:

1. Offer positive reinforcement, by providing sample exercises and materials apt for immediate classroom use and for sharing with colleagues.
2. Hold sessions with teachers of both primary and secondary levels, to share experiences and to demonstrate the need for progressive levels of media education.
3. Provide support by CVS tutors on-site at participants' own schools—helping implement this new curriculum but without intruding—and maintaining contact and support after the program was completed.
4. Use local audiovisual resources to supplement school resources.
5. To extend curriculum innovation, establish a two-person team (the CVS-trained person and a teacher colleague) to "co-teach" at each local school.
6. Early during the CVS classroom course, mount small-scale, localized research projects so pupils can learn by doing and by discovery rather than by lecture.
7. Develop media curriculum outlines attuned to local needs and structures, to interest supervisors in expanding media education locally.

Evaluators of the Clwyd Media Studies Unit's three experimental years of CVS teacher training concluded with recommendations for initiating, implementing, and institutionalizing media education in schools. They advised balancing need for stability with pressure for change. One criterion (by headmasters) was for media education to "enrich current practice—it should be capable of being integrated" (p. 38). Most teachers and heads agreed that media education ought not be offered as a discrete subject but melded into the primary, traditional curriculum of subjects.

Evaluators recommended carefully structured proposals when introducing media education to schools with positive endorsement by school heads, so as to gain priority in local curriculum planning. And media work going on elsewhere should be checked out by visits and interviews, then reported to supplement the local media advocate's perspective, enthusiasm, and skills. Responsibility for implementing media curricula should be shared among colleagues in a school. Further, headmasters and superintendents of schools should be kept advised of progress in introducing media education, as should parents of children in classrooms exposed to CVS activities. Understanding and support by each of these groups makes possible enduring curriculum innovation. Finally, to strengthen continuity of media study programs in schools, policy statements ought be drawn up to guide others, including successors.

*Assessment.* Clwyd county Media Studies Unit's quantitative scope (number of participants directly involved in CVS training) was limited. But its sophisticated use of traditional and contemporary theoretical perspectives coupled with pragmatic activities make it a useful model for others. At many points it incorporates findings and guidelines of current research (including "accommodation theory" as delineated by Anderson and Meyer). The Clwyd project's institutional setting, with overlays of administrative structures and accountability, prompted attention to a central factor in introducing and expanding critical viewing studies in schools: the importance of awareness, endorsement, and positive support by education officials.

The *Primetime* evaluation document lucidly outlines reasonable, pragmatic considerations for developing media education in primary grades, based on the 3-year Clwyd case study. Many recommendations apply similarly to secondary and even higher education—especially state-structured systems—where hierarchical processes of decision making affect potential success of media study programs. The project and its formal evaluation emphasizes the need to work astutely within existing administrative frameworks, not only to innovate CVS studies but to ensure long-term results.

## ENGLAND

### Mayfield School (Southwest London)

*Purposes.* A broad statement of purpose and philosophy in media studies courses was articulated in 1977 (and reprinted in 1980) by James Donald, of British Film Institute Education, a department of BFI's Information Division.[4] He also proposed "practice" and practical "use" as a key criterion of the value of media study courses. He urged this to liberate people from hidden control through media by government and other entrenched institutions. To this he added visual literacy and decoding of "meaning" from images, as well as learning about mass media structures and processes, including program development. These features were represented in a Media Studies syllabus introduced at Mayfield school for girls in Southwest London in September 1977, which he included as a seven-page appendix.

*Syllabus.* The 2-year course at Mayfield was designed (a) to involve students in substantial issues by practical work with multiple media—television, film, radio, advertising, and the press, and (b) to deepen understanding of mass communication's cultural significance (Donald, 1977/1980, p. 9). Course content included visual literacy (understanding images, partly by producing posters and photos); technical competence in several media (scripting, storyboards, interview techniques, tape editing, designing and lay-out of magazines, printing); information about industrial organization of mass media; and cultural effects of mass communication (impact on ideas, attitudes and beliefs, and questions of public participation and of "balance" such as in news). Grades were distributed 55% to written assignments and applied projects such as audiovisual tape montage and story outline or script; 25% to a major audiovisual presentation on social issues by teams of students; and 20% to written examination on material covered.

A useful two-page grid (Donald, 1977/1980, pp. 4–12) outlines five topic areas:

1. Introduction to the language of image and sound.
2. Communication: something to say.
3. Documentaries & news: how it is—or is it?
4. Television fiction: telling the tale.
5. Mass Communication or popular culture?

Each of the topics is described in terms of nine items: aims, media for study, products, skills and activities, concepts, issues, films "&c" [sic], visits (field trips), and simulations (role-playing, as in radio or news-paper operations). In the category "media for study," the first broad-cast medium cited is radio (under the second topic of "communication . . . "); television appears in the final three topics. Videotape re-cording is introduced at the outset in "skills & activities" under Topic 1; and in "products" there appear "taped interviews" under Topic 1 and "video interviews" under Topic 2. (This suggests less than perfect or-ganizing of the curriculum grid.) A two-page bibliography of sophisti-cated readings is intended for teachers; it lists an average of five titles of books or journal articles for each area: ideology, the media, educa-tion, and media studies.

*        *        *

As noted earlier, examination boards and courses of study at univer-sities in the United Kingdom, as in the United States, reflect broad efforts to introduce formal media study, including criteria for assess-ing content and media structures and processes as well as social ef-fects. Complete degree programs are available, often emphasizing hu-manistic, aesthetic aspects or else focused on vocational or profession-al studies oriented toward careers in media industries. For example, the University of Liverpool developed a master's degree in "Media Education" for primary and secondary teachers; taken part time, the course work is completed in approximately 2 years.[5]

## NON-SCHOLASTIC ORGANIZATIONS

In the United Kingdom, curricula for various school levels have been devised by organizations not themselves parts of local school systems. During the decade of the 1980s, regional arts councils in England and councils for education and media in Scotland developed detailed plans for studying mass media. They also helped train teachers how to teach media education. Activities of major organizations are described later.

### Southern Arts Association (Winchester, Hampshire)

British arts councils received governmental funding to experiment with media studies and training. Less formally organized than schools, and without traditional academic constraints, they emphasize creative skills and "hands-on" aspects of media study. The Southern Arts Asso-ciation in Winchester, Hampshire, collaborated with the British Film

Institute, Channel Four Television, Thamesdown Community Arts, and "Swindon Viewpoint." Together they support a resource center called Media Arts Lab. The Association primarily promotes practical use of mass media, specifically preparing programs for the community cable system. It also provides television, film, and audio materials for courses in theoretical and practical aspects of media.

*Media Arts Lab.* The Media Arts Lab offers video and film workshops in south-central England to promote:

> Awareness of the social, cultural, ideological and technical determinants of (primarily) film and television products. Recognition of the influences exerted over an audience/viewer by the programme-makers' choices (of subject, style, editing, relation of sound to image, etc.). . . . To equip the community to produce work of an informed high standard and to study work produced elsewhere. To help schools and colleges to develop film and media study and practice as part of their curriculums.[6]

At the outset, six persons administered and taught workshops, assisted by volunteers and guest speakers; 5 years later one administrator was joined by three teacher/"trainers." In 1981–1982 the Regional Arts Association provided £45,000 to which was added £30,000 locally; in succeeding years the combined funding amounted to £30,000 annually. In mid-1981 some 450 persons affiliated with 12 organizations had participated; by mid-1985 participants were estimated at about 100 per year, with a total of 1,500 involved during the half decade since its inception. Participants ranged from upper elementary grades, through secondary school and college, to adults.

Materials included readings, scripts, study sheets, and media samples (audiovisuals, including TV programs). No workbooks or examinations were employed. Formal courses met weekly for 2 to 3 hours through 8 to 12 weeks. Courses emphasized evaluating media content and preparing alternate programming, not activist letter-writing or contacting media organizations. Courses treated creative aspects of program production, information about media structures and processes, plus TV's effects on attitude and behavior. But they did not include forms of assessing TV's role in individuals' lives (such as logging time spent watching TV and patterns of viewing, reasons for watching, or the medium's impact on reading and other cognitive skills).

Little formal evaluation or results were available; findings were not compiled. Several years earlier the Centre for Mass Communication Research at the University of Leicester had prepared a 49-page typeset report (Cross & Husband, 1975) on the Swindon community television experiment begun in 1973. The Media Arts Lab sought to prepare local working-class residents for opportunities to use the local cable system's "access program."

*Resource Consultant.*   By 1989 a County Advisory Teacher for Media Education served as resource person for in-service training and classroom courses, including nine different workshop courses, for teachers at 600 primary and 500 secondary schools in Hampshire county.[7] Beginning in September 1989, she assisted primary schools in implementing three areas of the United Kingdom's recently introduced national curriculum, with its "Media Education" component as part of teaching English (which included more than the language).

## SCOTLAND

### Scottish Film Council

The Scottish Film Council is a division of the Scottish Council for Educational Technology. The Council ran "weekend schools," funded college courses, published documents, awarded grants to students and educational groups, and presented exhibitions in Regional Film Theatres to foster educational development.[8]

*Curriculum Proposals.*   The Scottish Film Council prepared a 14-page report (1979) on curriculum proposals for media education in Scotland. Although this was a "discussion document" for future planning, it details specific courses for various levels of school.* This (as the Powys Report cited earlier) offers a complete outline of curricular policy for teaching media, including CVS material. It offers a succinct, understandable, and cogent analysis of trends in media study that developed over the past half-century: study of effects, content analysis, "uses and gratifications"; popular culture, anthropology and linguistics as bases for study of media; genre, codes, structuralism and semiology; and sociology, "ideology," and even psychoanalytic perspectives.

*Purposes.*   Media study includes several mass media forms; television, cinema, press and radio—plus some aspects of magazines, comics, and

---

*A decade later (1988) formal Media Education Curriculum Guidelines were finally completed and distributed, as cited later.

paperback fiction. The Film Council's report advises that at least two media ought be studied to understand the "underlying unity of structure and function" among them.

> It is therefore a central concern of these proposals to present media education as a means of helping children and adults towards greater understanding of their own experience of the media by studying media messages or other products in the context of the various industries, institutions and professions involved in their productions; the economic, political and constitutional background to the development of these bodies; and the broader social and cultural setting in which media production and its reception by a variety of audiences, operates. (p. 2)

*Curricula.* The report offers five brief curricula outlines for primary, early secondary, later secondary, "further education and community education," and teacher education. The report recommends that primary-level media education contribute to cognitive development generally, plus teach awareness of mass media and differences among media. It emphasizes practical knowledge of how media work, partly through production activities that lead to discussion. It proposes media study in these early years as an extension of language arts, visual arts, environmental studies, math, and music. The report stresses the importance of involving parents in their children's media work.

For secondary level, the report recommends initial short modular courses within subject areas of English and art and modern studies, but urges that eventually media study becomes a separate subject area. Foci in the curriculum for "early secondary" include ability to articulate personal responses to media experiences, awareness of different functions of media, and the way they present aspects of society. In addition to acquiring vocabulary of media concepts and terms, pupils should begin to understand "the relationship between an individual creator or author within a medium and the institutional nature of that medium." They should systematically examine specific media products—individual shows, program types, and thematic patterns. And they should study directors' and producers' functions and how their viewpoints affect the creative process and product.

The "later secondary" curriculum offers more specialization and depth in understanding media industries' production, distribution, and exhibition. It analyzes specific programs "considered both as the creation of an individual director or artist and as the end-result of an industrial/commercial process." Students are to learn various analytic approaches to media products, partly by studying representative films and programs from different genres.

Only at the level of "further education and community education" does the report explicitly note informational presentations in television and the press, including how media help to create as well as reflect our sense of contemporary reality. (Although that might be implied at earlier stages, artistic and cultural aspects dominate there rather than the sociopolitical.) Here the report stresses pragmatic implications of media for daily living, and potential roles consumers can play through "alternative" media opportunities, including trying to focus public attention on issues. Communication skills, including practical work with video and super-8mm film, are linked to possible vocational as well as personal use in civic and community life. The report also defers to this advanced level (regrettably) attention to "the media as resources for living in life-long education, community development and cultural enrichment."

Finally, the report addresses "teacher education" when it comments on the centrality of media to everyone's experience, noting that the Scottish education system looks to enhanced use of media in classrooms by teachers well-versed in how mass media interact with audiences. As various levels of education gradually incorporate formal media studies, teachers with media expertise will be in demand. Curricula for training teachers, according to the report, should include: (a) studying origins and development of media studies (including content analysis, cultural studies, and semiology); (b) applying those theories and methods to analysis of specific media products; (c) learning about structures and operation of major media institutions and their relationship to government; and (d) acquiring practical skills in at least one medium.

The report acknowledges the limited resources in most schools, but reminds that at least basic hardware is available as well as many "software" media products. It recommends drawing up compilations of available materials, including curricula and complete packages or modules of CVS materials. It urges coordinating media study and materials to avoid duplication, to prevent lacunae, and to support efficiency. Finally, it recommends assessing media study programs according to their stated purposes and objectives.[9]

## MAJOR PROJECTS FOR MEDIA
## RESEARCH AND DEVELOPMENT

In Scotland, two major projects were begun in 1983 to observe, gather data, and evaluate the best ways to develop formal media education. The Media Education Development Project was directed by Eddie Dick,

Media Education Officer of the Scottish Film Council. The Media Education Research Project was conducted by David Butts at the University of Stirling. The first project's ambition to survey the state of media teaching at all levels in Scotland, to identify priorities and methodologies, and to make available audiovisual and print resources—including curricula, syllabi, modular packages, and so forth—to teachers embarking on teaching media. It focuses on pragmatic service to classroom teachers, based on sound conceptual footing. The second research project surveys the media studies scene specifically in Scottish secondary schools and summarized major issues. Both resulted in published books of 49 pages and 177 pages respectively. Although neither is a television-specific "critical viewing skills" curriculum as such, they both reflect the advanced stage of media education in Scotland and so are reviewed here.

*Media Education Development Project.* The genius of this effort was to coalesce data about activities at many levels and kinds of institutions throughout Scotland and the United Kingdom, while involving teachers in identifying patterns of media pedagogy within various conceptual frameworks in order to develop model syllabi for classroom use. One outcome was publication of four major teaching packages, with 1,300 sets sold within a year. Another publication was the 32-page booklet *Teaching Media Studies,* of which 2,000 were distributed in Scotland within a year. The report concluded by recommending establishment of national policy and mechanisms to determine responsibility for media education within the three levels of schooling, to prepare curriculum guidelines and teaching materials suited to each of those levels, to establish programs of study for developing teaching staffs, and to develop some media education outside formal curricula. It further recommended that the Scottish Film Council serve as coordinator and central developer of a national policy, and that it be provided with adequate resources and personnel to do so.

*Purposes and Philosophy.* Eddie Dick (1987b), director of the project, distinguished media education from media studies by how they differ not in issues of pedagogy but rather of administration. That is, media education refers to "permeation" or integration of such study within other traditional disciplines, whereas media studies consist of discrete courses devoted to that topic. The published report describes the scope of media studies as including most kinds of mass communication, including television, radio, print, film, advertising, and the popular music industry. It asserts that media education:

- places an important emphasis on a fruitful blend of analytical and practical work to achieve a balance of understanding and skill, both critical and creative;
- examines how the media construct images of the world and how to analyse these images;
- studies how the media themselves are organised and how their natures affect the images or representations they construct;
- examines the important relationship between socio-cultural contexts of the media and their representations. (p. 4)

Although disclaiming any intent to train technicians or, on the other hand, to create abstracted academic critics, the report proposes the objective of students learning "critical awareness" by "doing" production and analyzing professional structures and products. In a nutshell: "The media are best understood as *sets of processes* (e.g., technical, professional, aesthetic, ideological, economic, political) whose purposes include the social generation of meanings" (p. 5).

The report rejects considering mass media either as reflecting "mirrors" or as "windows" presenting reality. Instead, media are "complex and influential constructs" that are "sets of signifying systems." What they represent in their "texts" derive partly from their "institutional functions and practices" and partly from the sociocultural context of ideology—taken not as "the adherence to a particular political philosophy but as the means by which social consciousness is generated" (p. 6).

The project was engaged in five areas developing curricula, teacher training, preparing teaching materials, disseminating information, and administrative issues ("bureaucratic-political") of collaborating with official authorities, institutions, and teachers' organizations in order to advance media education throughout Scotland.

*Curricula.* Pilot curricula were developed emphasizing induction from practical experiences with various media. Project personnel observed and appraised activities. Keynotes were learning by "doing" (inductive) and flexibility in applying modules to children in classrooms. *Teacher training* experiments drafted courses for "Certificate" (developing personal knowledge and skills with applications to teaching) and for "Diploma" (broader concerns). The certificate curriculum includes four 30-hour modules: media theory and analysis (texts); media institutions (industrial, social influences); media production skills (basic techniques in various media); and course design and methodology. The Degree curriculum adds another five modules to the existing four: Medium-specific study (detailed case study of processes and products of one medium); thematic study (case study across multiple media); advanced media production skills (in a single medium); advanced course design and methodology (pedagogy, assessment); and applied media production skills (production of a teaching package involving several media). The curriculum was designed primarily for inservice training of teachers already in the classroom.

*Teaching materials* included films, storyboards, audiotapes, slides, photographs, and print materials gathered into packages to be applied to projects with different media. Projects pertained to television melodrama, a videotaped football game, an advertising campaign, a newspaper, and video excerpts from motion pictures.

*Database.* The project became a repository for data about media studies, providing a database about Scottish schools, supplying lecturers, and participating in conferences on the subject in the United Kingdom. It also published *Teaching Media Studies* (cited later).

Finally the Media Education Development Project collaborated with media-related groups throughout the land, especially the Association for Media Education in Scotland—an organization of teachers—and its *Media Education Journal*. It also participated in meetings of higher education and the General Teaching Council as well as other groups. To this end, it concludes its report by recommending national and regional policies toward developing coherent, progressive education in all media, both within traditional curricula and as specific courses and programs of study.

*Teaching Media Studies* was originally published in 1983 by Kevin Cowle and Eddie Dick for the Scottish Film Council. It was revised in 1985 and again in 1986, perhaps justifying the claim that it was one result of the developmental project outlined previously (which had only begun in 1983). Subtitled "An Introduction to Methods and Resources," this 32-page booklet provides a brisk run-down of key questions about teaching media. The authors urged teachers to begin with media artifacts and to work outward to broader questions and general issues; or teachers can stress language of sight and sound images in print, film, radio, television media. They offered options for introducing media study into the curriculum, by collaborating departments or subjects (English, art, etc.), by a single department responsible for media training, or by a comprehensive course developed by several departments. They urged teachers "to capitalise on pupil/student confidence in this area; they are well acquainted with media output and they are not in awe of it" (Cowle & Dick, 1986, p. 7) and will quickly enter into discussing and debating media questions.

The authors suggested 20 students as maximum for effective media courses. Studies can be adapted to limitations of local class schedules and time-frames, with from 4 to 6 weeks of intermittent sessions up to modules that each fill 40 hours. Students' work can be assessed by testing knowledge and understanding, measuring analytical skills, and evaluating creative ability. Students' activities to be assessed include case studies, practical simulation, essays, group projects, and productions. In addition to the teacher's appraisal, assessment of a student's achievement can come from that student and from peer groups.

The booklet lists minimum equipment and budget needed for teaching media in a school (pp. 10–11), suggesting "curriculum development" as the category against which charges are made. It also lists individuals and agencies in Scotland that offer advice and support for introducing media studies: Media Education Development Project (funded by the Scottish Education Department and managed by the Scottish Film Council), the Scottish Film Council, and the Association for Media Education in Scotland. It adds the names and institutions of nine regional associations for media studies, 18 "L.E.A. Advisers," and media staff at five colleges (pp. 12–17). The booklet briefly describes media courses available to teachers at the British Film Institute, the Scottish Film Council, the Open University, the University of Edinburgh, the Edinburgh Film Guild, and the Workers' Educational Association. The authors compiled four pages of 54 book titles about various mass media (five of them specifically about TV), plus seven media and trade journals. The final eight pages list analytical descriptions of available teaching materials, of which five video/film/slide packages relate directly to television.

*Media Education Research Project.*   The project began in 1983 and 3 years later resulted in David Butts' report *Media Education in Scottish Secondary Schools: A Research Study 1983–1986.* Until then the "Outline Proposals . . . " of 1979—described at the outset of this section— had been "the most comprehensive description to date of the field of study involved" (Butts, 1986, p. 1). As with many national reports in other parts of the world, the 1979 "Outline" theorizes, stating principles and needs as well as some projections without being based on observed experience. But the 1986 report, after helpfully sketching how media education developed in Scotland, provides one of the most thorough analyses of what was actually going on in classrooms throughout a country. Instead of a broad survey, it selects representative sites for detailed, multi-factored analysis. The report is lucid and readable, filled with concrete, personalized, first-hand descriptive information. These 177 pages report the study first proposed by Stirling University's Department of Education and codirected by Professor A.

T. Morrison of that department and by Mr. D. MacLeod of the Department of Film and Media. (Author-researcher D. C. Butts also chaired the Scottish Council for Educational Technology's Media Education Coordinating Committee.)

*Purposes and Procedures.*   The project observed media education in 10 secondary schools as case studies, including full courses and units of media studies "designed to promote a critical awareness of the ways in which the mass media operate within contemporary society, as production processes and as institutions" (p. 1). The second phase applied those findings to six schools for further evaluation.* It gathered data from schools, teachers, and students to identify theoretical and pedagogic issues in teaching media and to provide data for other teachers and curriculum planners. The project was structured to explore these questions:

1. Concepts
   - On what concept of media studies are the courses based?
   - Is there evidence of 'characteristic' concepts, associated with subject, disciplines, pupil ability levels, teacher experience, etc?
   - What patterns of internal coherence can be discerned within course elements?
2. Curriculum
   - How are media studies being related to existing curriculum structures?
   - What indications are there for models of future developments?
3. Classroom Practice
   - What are the pointers to further investigation/developmental work concerning
     - teaching skills and methods?
     - course design?
     - pupil reactions to different approaches?
     - needs for pre and in-service training?
   - What are the main management and resource problems? (p. 10)

Included were questions relating to cognitive development of students, such as "At what age should [media education] begin? What approaches are appropriate to different age levels? How can coherence across the age range be achieved?" (p. 21).

Many kinds of media instruction were found in the schools. But only

---

*But the concluding chapter states the researcher worked with 20 schools, and carried out extended observation in 15 (p. 159).

after one-third of the report appears the first reference to a school case study with specifically television study—albeit intermingled with film, radio and press (pp. 61 ff.). One complete module on television is reported on pages 84–91. Further information about courses with TV are on pages 97–98 and 101–102. Appendices "Bi" (eight pages) and part of "C" (three pages) offer some television intermingled with other media; Appendix "Bii" [sic] (five pages) is a teaching syllabus wholly devoted to production elements of TV, whereas another part of "C" (three pages) covers those aspects plus a broader range of theory and issues in television institutions, appreciation, and criticism. Clearly, print and other audio-visual media dominate the cases studied. But most include treatment of concepts and values involved in all the mass media, including television, even if not explicitly.

Interviews with a number of secondary teachers, administrators, and college media instructors provide personalized observations about curricular theories and the status of media study in Scottish schools.

*Findings.*   The concluding 16-page chapter 9 offers "Issues for Research and Development" of media education. But modifications of the project's original research design "render it impossible to draw conclusions from empirical work or to make precise recommendations" (p. 159). Instead, the author identified central issues to be resolved only by further investigation. Evolving media studies in Scottish classrooms saw shifting personnel and curricula even during the period researched, with media instructors and researcher "increasingly out of touch" with one another. This was caused partly by restrictions on teachers' in-service training and partly by declining activity of the teachers' own organization, Association for Media Education in Scotland (AMES). Somewhat predictable are the tentative findings of this necessarily limited study, drawing as it does on direct experience of just over a dozen schools.

*Curricula and Outcomes.*   Whereas 13 courses offered a curriculum balancing analysis and pragmatics, another seven stressed practical workshop activity. "Characteristic concepts" in media courses related to the subject discipline in which media were taught and/or to individual teachers' interests and abilities—many of them prior or instinctive ones, and a few with specific training in media education. "Patterns of internal coherence"—fusing words, images, sounds, factors of ownership and control, and production processes—were most effective with specialist teachers of media studies, less successful among interdisciplinary teams offering media study, and least successful where courses were multidisciplinary. Further, students (especially younger ones) did not offer evidence of drawing connections between practical exercises and broader implications for critiquing professional media or for assessing their personal media experiences. As for how media studies related to existing curricular structures, 10 schools taught media courses as part of an established subject, 3 taught them within a multidisciplinary structure, 4 taught them with an interdisciplinary team, and 1 taught them as independent options by "specialist" teachers (p. 163).

*Problems.*   Both inter- and multidisciplinary approaches encountered problems of coherence and organization. Researchers commented on administrative difficulties in placing courses within an established subject, where other parts of the syllabus had to be dropped or truncated to accommodate media material. Difficulties would also arise when creating independent courses that required either releasing teachers from other curricular commitments, or else adding the media courses to their regular academic duties. But:

> In practice, in the schools observed, media studies courses have for the most part been accommodated without any such modifications and there is no sign that media education has been allowed to challenge the existing structure. . . . None of the schools observed had worked out a "whole school" policy for media education. (pp. 162–163)

*Recommendations.*   The report repeats recommendations of a regional study in 1986, calling for adequate in-service teacher training—including released time—and resources to serve schools in each jurisdiction. Findings among those interviewed for this report also support the earlier study's (Stephen, 1986) insistence:

> In secondary schools there is a clear necessity for a coordinator with responsibility for integration and development of media education within the institution and for the coordination of syllabuses and resources cooperatively with other schools/colleges which may be feeders or members of a partnership group. (p. 164)

As to classroom practice, course design and teaching skills and methods required greater attention to students' various stages of cognitive development, better managing of practical exercises, and more skill in inductive approaches and nondirective open discussion—including guiding students to analytical understanding of the significance of pragmatic activities.

*Issues as Challenges.*  Finally, Butts' report acknowledges the under-lying dilemma of formal institutional education: The established cur-riculum resists media education because it presents a challenge to the traditional structure of secondary education. The report cites a formal commentary (Axford, 1983): "how can new ways of looking at the world be accommodated within a curriculum defined within histor-ically determined categories . . . ?" (p. 173). And again, Butts quotes a respondent to the project survey: "a curriculum which would give prop-er cognizance to media education would be very different from the present subject-based curriculum" (p. 173). Media and the study of media cut across sociology, political science, commerce, law, literature, aesthetics, arts (drama, music, etc.), economics, and other identifiable "subject-areas" about human endeavor. Butts concluded from case ob-servation and discussion that, ideally, media study in secondary educa-tion:

> would find its 'natural home' within a broad but unified field of study which aimed at developing pupils' understanding of the society in which they lived and at identifying the forces that shape and animate our patterns of social interaction. The pedagogical problem, of course, would be to hold the elements of such a broad field of study together. But this integrative task might be a function which media education could under-take, since it reaches out one way towards communications and another way towards sociology. (p. 173)

Although strategically (politically or bureaucratically), at least in Scotland, separate subject status would strengthen media education, the more likely prospect is either "a precarious existence as an inter-disciplinary venture; or a safe home within an established subject or subjects" (p. 173).

*National Certificate Curricula.*  In the late 1980s, the National Cer-tificate catalogue for "16-plus" provided 14 "module descriptors" that included some media study.* Three modules pertain to television, two to radio, one to advertising, and one is an introduction to media stud-ies; seven other modules concern print, photography, film, popular

---

*For example, the Scottish Vocational Education Council's module for "Media Stud-ies: Popular Literature"—recommending concurrent study of modules in film, televi-sion, or radio—looks to the "popular literature industry." Proposing to "develop a critical awareness of some of the forms of popular literature in the context of the industry which produces them," it stresses aesthetics of texts in the context of production, distribution, and consumption. The module outlines expected outcomes of learning, teaching ap-proaches, and procedures for assessing students' achievement. Clearly the medium here was print. See Eddie Dick (1987a), Appendix 7 (n.p.).

music and popular literature. By 1985 over 100 institutions (74 primary and secondary schools, 27 colleges) and by 1987 more than 170 secondary schools taught media-related courses by combining various modules. So-called short courses, each totaling 40 hours, were similar to those of Western Australia (discussed earlier). Their six levels typically involved an introduction and then study of media language (words, images, sound), narratives (fact/fiction, genres, authorship), representation (stars, advertising, youth culture), Scottish context (images, industries, broadcasting, print), and media issues (case study, and productions in school and in the community).[10]

*Curriculum Guidelines and Policies.* In February 1988 the Scottish Film Council distributed *Media Education Curriculum Guidelines* to all primary and secondary schools in Scotland, encouraging local teachers and administrators to support such studies.[11] Subsequently, the Council worked with education authorities in Edinburgh, Glasgow, and Stirling to develop "pilot schemes" in four primary and four secondary schools. Linked with the Scottish Council for Research in Education, it obtained funds to investigate those "schemes" of organizing and administering curricular changes amid overall school policies.* Titled "Media Education in Scotland: A Study of Curriculum School Policy and Management," that study was conducted through 1989 and was to be reported in 1990. It sought to identify concepts of media education found in school policies, and how policies influenced curriculum content and development. It also analyzed management issues in introducing media education, as well as effects on teachers and students. It planned to draw guidelines for further development of media education and related school policies.

## FRANCE AND THE NETHERLANDS

Two other (non-U.S.) institution-related CVS programs that returned questionnaires and sent some printed material were in France and The Netherlands. The first was directed exclusively to television, the second to various mass media. They are only partly representative of the continent because many European countries have a tradition of media education.[12]

---

*The investigation was scheduled for October 1988 to December 1989, so results were not available for this present report.

France

*Formation Du Jeune Téléspectateur Actif.* In France, film studies have been long in vogue, usually through film societies (ciné-clubs) associated with schools and youth organizations. In the early 1970s the Ministry of National Education brought to schools under its jurisdiction "Introduction to Communication and the Media" (ICOM/ICAV) to develop responsibility and creativity in students' use of media. Prior to 1982 it was taught outside the regular class schedule and since then within it. But to better interrelate learning of mass-mediated information with formal school learning, the French government mounted the experimental Formation Du Jeune Téléspectateur Actif (Forming the Active Young Television Viewer) in many cities in 1979 to July of 1982. The five ministers of Culture and Communication, of Education, of Youth, of Sport and Leisure, and of Agriculture requested the Fond d'Intervention Culturelle (Fund for Cultural Intervention) to establish such a program. It was introduced in 11 of 90 French academic sectors—"school *departements*"—and was the only national television study program in France. Unlike many projects in the United Kingdom and on the continent, it was oriented exclusively to television. It included children in earliest grades through secondary school and also in homes. It also involved some 500 teachers, 200 nonacademic instructors (e.g., in sports or music), and 200 parents of students. Designers of the plan intended 800 adults to receive television training programs over 10-day periods, who in turn could relay CVS principles to some 24,000 young people (Gagnier, 1980, p. 7).

Although not a formal curriculum, the project relied on readings, parent and teacher guides, and audiovisual support materials for its lectures, discussions and workshops. A dozen videocassette tapes were prepared for the program. An elaborate grid was drawn up, outlining the project's concurrent and successive stages of activity (pp. 36–39). This helped coordinate parents' involvement with more formal instruction.

One specific objective was to help young people understand how broadcasts are created through production and editing, including the possibilities and limitations of electronic "tools." They were to become aware of television as a means of artistic expression formed by and reflecting individual persons, with distinctive genres and styles, employing patterns of images. They also were to understand how television is a social phenomenon on both sides of the interacting communication process—producing and distributing programs and also receiving them. Participants learned something about broader cultural, sociological, and anthropological aspects of mass communication.

They also specifically studied broadcast news, public affairs, and advertising.

The project did not include "consumerism" aspects of writing letters to media decision makers, contacting media organizations, or joining organizations seeking to influence media content.

The French government's participating agencies closely coordinated the entire project. They carefully selected sites for introducing and then expanding the project, coupled with continuing appraisals by participants and observers. Unlike many governmental-supported CVS endeavors in other countries, which were merely funded by the state, this was orchestrated and overseen from its inception by the respective agencies. But by the late 1980s the program was no longer offered.

Meanwhile, during the latter half of the decade, teachers of French and history received training for teaching introductory media courses that by 1990 were offered in Grades 9 to 11 in 300 schools (Pungente, 1990, p. 4). Film and video production was introduced in 1984 as part of a course in art production; by decade's end it was offered in 100 schools.

## Amsterdam

*Stichting Audiovisuele Vorming.* Less ambitious and less complex was the project mounted in Amsterdam by Stichting Audiovisuele Vorming: Project Film Television Reality. Despite its title, the project included print as well as film and electronic media. Although a "national institute" originated the project for 1978–1980, it had no specific funding.[13] Directed to secondary school students, it provided material for teaching young persons how producers of mass media content use the "language" of images and sound to transmit messages selected and edited "for their own purposes . . . motives and criteria." By learning how creators select means and effects, students might thus become more aware of their own response toward media.

The project offered eight 2-hour lessons. Materials included a student workbook, a teacher's manual, and audiovisual items. Supporting audiovisual material were 35mm slides, a feature film, two documentary films, extract of a radio news broadcast, and portions of television news programs and magazines—some to be provided by the teacher. The 47-page workbook for students, *Werkelijkheid? Krant-Radio-Film-Televisie* (Reality? Newspaper-Radio-Film-Television) offers background information, exercises, and photographic examples for the several media, including many excellent reproductions of newspaper pages and film and television scenes. Topics include history of communication in human society vis-à-vis economic, cultural, and political conditions; role of mass media in contemporary living; and especially the selecting and editing process in producing major media, which results in varied representations of reality.

The workbook emphasizes students' experiencing actual media products, then analyzing their components and form of presentation. The printed text suggests avenues of discussion to aid students' observation and assessment, to learn how "reality" presented in media is a conceived one, depending on the creator's aim and intended audience. The project's exclusive theme is understanding how media content is crafted. It does not include most categories found in other CVS projects: time spent with TV, personal viewing patterns, impact of TV on cognitive growth, media organizational and economic structure and relation to government, people's use of media ("uses and gratifications"), advertising, or consumer roles.

*          *          *

A number of similar CVS projects in formal education that were related to institutions but not necessarily formal curricular programs responded to our questionnaire surveys and/or provided material about their activities. They can be briefly acknowledged at this point, while noting that countless others have been mounted in many countries, in association with or informally in the context of educational institutions.

> Jerry Booth, Hull College of Higher Education, Humberside, United Kingdom: Volunteer Centre's Media Project (community groups produce programs and "social action" public service announcements—results of media training)
>
> Helga Keller, School of Education, Tel-Aviv University, Israel (middle-school Grades 5–10; weekly 2-hour sessions to teach "media literacy")
>
> Myron J. Pereira, Xavier Institute of Communications, Bombay, India: Mediaworld (12 sessions about print, film, and broadcasting for high school students—to foster creative imagination about media and to develop a critical attitude toward their values).

Other media literacy projects developed around the world during the decade of the 1980s. Researchers and project directors sent materials in 1988 and 1989 in time for this report's final revision. Despite not being represented in the questionnaire surveys of 1981/1985 (nor in Part III's quantitative tabulations)—indeed, some of them were not even under way early in that decade—their descriptive data help augment the world-wide perspective of media literacy and critical viewing skills education.

## CANADA

Instead of national standards, each Canadian province developed its own curriculum guidelines. Of Canada's 10 provinces and two territories, only Alberta, Manitoba, Quebec, and Ontario had officially enacted some aspects of media education. At the primary level media studies were usually part of language arts and depend on individual teachers' interests. At secondary level, media education was also offered as an elective within journalism or other specific media or general communications; courses cover one or two terms. In Quebec, the full course covered 2 years, or was offered as a half course over several years, or else during the final 3 years was integrated into language arts.

### Ontario.*

Among Canadian provinces Ontario has been the most active in media training. The province mandated integrating media literacy study into English courses for all students in Grades 7 to 13. Its Association for Media Literacy—with 1,100 members in 1989—held teacher-training schools in summer and fall. For 1990 the Association prepared a North American Media Education Conference featuring many theorists and practitioners cited in this report. At post-secondary level, Toronto University's summer sessions in education offered three levels that in three consecutive summers earn a Specialist Certificate in Media Literacy. Ontario's Ministry of Education finally released in 1989 a 232-page handsomely typeset book that had been written in 1986.

*Media Literacy Resource Guide: Intermediate and Senior Divisions, 1989.*[14] The Ministry of Education sent copies of the book with a covering memorandum to directors of education, English coordinators and consultants, principals of secondary schools, principals of elementary schools with Grades 7 and 8, and teachers of media education in Grades 7 to 13, throughout Ontario. The memo noted that "The ideas

---

*Although questionnaire data (1981, 1985) were not available for this project, later reports and primary materials used in the project as well as secondary sources provided adequate information to attempt appraising CVS criteria (Part III).

and activities contained in this document are not specifically assigned to any grade. They are predicated on the conviction that teachers can teach the key concepts of media literacy in some form to all students at any level."[15] These sentences are verbatim in the preface (p. 3).

The resource guide assumes little sophisticated technical equipment available in schools and allows teachers with even "only a minimum knowledge of media literacy" to apply the analytical, practical, and creative material. The book offers necessarily succinct analyses of major factors in media creation, reception, interpretation and impact, because it treats a wide range of media: television (45 pp.), film (24 pp.), radio (16 pp.), popular music including rock video (18 pp.), photography (8 pp.), print (23 pp.), and cross-media themes (50 pp.). As British CVS expert Len Masterman noted while strongly endorsing the book, it sacrifices depth for breadth, not delving into the complexities of media and society. But he praised it as "packed with teaching ideas and underpinned by a clear conceptual structure" (Pungente, 1989, p. 2).

*Purposes and Procedures.*  The comprehensive book (Ministry of Education, 1989) pulls together current themes in critical analysis, including texts and codes, deconstruction, semiotics, negotiating meaning by reading media "texts," and inductive and heuristic discovery rather than a priori lecturing about concepts. The Introduction cautions teachers not to stress negative aspects of media "under the guise of developing a 'discriminating response'" nor to impose elitist values on students. Rather, teachers are to serve as facilitators and "co-learners" in order to help students achieve "critical autonomy." The objective is for young people to become well-informed consumers of media, with neither "a quite unwarranted faith in the integrity of media images and representations" nor "undifferentiated scepticism in which the media are viewed as insidious" (p. 6):

> Media literacy, then, is concerned with the process of understanding and using the mass media. It is also concerned with helping students develop an informed and critical understanding of the nature of the mass media, the techniques used by them, and the impact of these techniques. More specifically, it is education that aims to increase students' understanding and enjoyment of how the media work, how they produce meaning, how they are organized, and how they construct reality. Media literacy also aims to provide students with the ability to create media products. (pp. 6–7)

The introduction's recommendation and tips under "Key Concepts" (pp. 8–10) and "Teaching Strategies and Models" (pp. 11–13) distill most major criteria outlined in part I of this book. It promotes various strategies for teaching CVS. One is the inquiry model of teaching, to help students explore issues through open-ended questions and to seek data for developing informed judgments. Another is critical or dialogical thinking to illuminate multiple points of view and interpretation. Other forms incorporate values education, and integration with other subjects or as part of interdisciplinary teaching.

Attempting to develop cross-media literacy, the book suggests thematic credit courses: pop culture, the world of images, Canadian identity, the information society, television production, and specific media or a genre within a medium. Finally, the introduction suggests practical ways to integrate media study into the curriculum, via courses in English, social sciences, natural sciences, visual arts, music, mathematics, and physical education.

*Support Materials.* The first major portion of the book is about television. Six lucid pages about TV's history, economics, and social impact are followed by two pages of tips for using the medium in the classroom and harnessing home viewing. The next 37 pages present four substantive teaching units: how TV constructs reality, decoding, program types, and "commercial implications" of the medium—including selling ideas as well as products. Each unit consists of suggestions for activities, exercises, and applications of media experiences for classroom discussion and analysis. The units offer various leading questions; provide excerpts from provocative quotations by critics, media creators, and others; and they offer references to related reading and other source materials.

The last chapter, "Cross-Media Studies," looks at how media are closely related and interdependent in news as well as entertainment and advertising. Subjects offered are: advertising, sexuality, violence, Canadian identity and media ownership, and news reporting by various media. A few pages of background data and concepts introduce each section, followed by many pages of open-ended questions for discussion plus practical activities and student projects. Factual data and brief quotations as well as references to further sources generally reflect a range of interpretation, permitting teachers and pupils to develop their own judgments. The book concludes with lists of other resources, names and addresses of major media organizations, and a bibliography.

Masterman nicely crystallized this publication's contribution to media teachers, as offering "integration of accessible theory with a thoroughly workable and down-to-earth classroom practice" (Pungente, 1989, p. 2). That it does, although a large portion does not relate directly to teaching specifically television critical viewing skills.

## LATIN AMERICA

Reports, articles, and other documents about media education in South and Central America reflect a thrust different from most projects in English-speaking countries. Instead of concentrating on broad cultural and aesthetic values and on consumers' "images" and understanding of their own world and of themselves, Latin American projects tend to be less personally narcissistic. They look beyond to the very structures and processes of volatile and often repressive society around them. Developing Latin countries as well as more advanced ones share concern about transcultural imperialism (Anglo-American program forms and content, images and values) but especially about repressive authoritarian and economic control of the people and their destiny. Motives and content of CVS projects reflect pressing needs of people widely divided between the very rich and the destitute. Mass media, especially television, are seen as a key to shifting oppressive structures and almost as a tool of nonviolent revolution. The terms and tone of marxist reaction to dominating socioeconomic forces inspire as well as inform typical critical viewing skills endeavors in Latin nations.

Introducing his report on critical TV viewing projects in four Latin American countries, Valerio Fuenzalida (1987) noted that half of all Latin America television consists of imported programs (vs. the one third average for non-U.S. countries worldwide).[16] Programs are mostly entertainment, depicting consumerism societies and promoting products of multinational corporations. He cited a 1979 document issued from Puebla, Mexico, by the Catholic Church, which chastised political and economic powers seeking to maintain the status quo by ideological and political manipulation. Fuenzalida (1987) paraphrased the document's Section 1094 criticizing that status quo "which is thereby being propagated: the LA [Latin American] masses are submerged in poverty, marginalization, injustice and violation of human rights" (p. 6). He recounted that document's list of other social evils caused by repressive policies reinforced by mass media, including manipulation of local and national news by those in power. His summary of Latin American countries' rationale for CVS education quoted the Church document's support for "teaching the receiving public to exercise a more critical attitude towards the impact of the ideological, cultural and advertising messages with which we are continually bombarded, in order to counter the negative effects of manipulation" (p. 8).

To that end, Fuenzalida surveyed five projects in four countries.* He

---

*Most data in this section, including important sources in Spanish-language publications, are drawn from Fuenzalida's detailed report; this author is indebted to him for much of this material. Eddie Dick's survey also provided complementary information as well as analysis of Latin American projects (along with other countries).

selected them as representative of three social spheres: family, social groups, and school. Further, these specific projects had the widest scope in Latin America, with the broadest institutional base, including duration and continuity: and they have influenced other institutions in those countries. Projects reported are:

- FAMILY
  Costa Rica: Latin American Communications Pedagogy Institute
  Uruguay: Plan DENI [*desde niños*—"from childhood"]
- SOCIAL GROUPS
  Brazil: Brazilian Social Communications Union
  Chile: Centre of Cultural and Artistic Enquiry & Expression
- SCHOOL
  Chile: Robert Bellarmino Educational Foundation

All five projects were associated directly or indirectly with the Catholic Church, but they did not limit participating teachers or children to members of that church. The Costa Rican Institute and Chilean Centre were legally organized nonprofit organizations. In Uruguay, Plan DENI was a division of the Catholic Cinema Office, whereas the Chilean Foundation was operated by Jesuit priests and conducted CVS study programs in private and church-related schools. The Brazilian Union consisted of Christians across several faiths who were engaged in media activity. (Also reviewed later is CVS-related activity by Univérsidad de Playa Ancha de la Educacion, in Chile—reported from sources other than Fuenzalida.)

## Costa Rica

*The Latin American Communications Pedagogy Institute (ILPEC).* ILPEC offered an educational program created to counter the impact of television on the family, especially children and their homework studies. The program, conducted by ILPEC's Department of Communications and New Technologies Pedagogy, considered the problem rooted not in TV and its programs but rather in "family relationships to which its presence gave rise. This conclusion was later confirmed" (Zamora, 1986, p. 11).

*Purposes.* The project's objective was to improve family relationships affected by television. It looks to the medium itself and the affected environment, not so much to the message(s). Developers judged that healthy family relationships depended neither on the amount of time spent viewing TV nor even on the quality or "moral suitability" of programs, but rather on the extent to which TV prompts "new and creative dialogue within the family." The project sought to educate the public how to harness television to promote meaningful family discussion. ILPEC's project was more positive and optimistic than those of other Latin American countries. It discounted the dominating function of the medium, instead placing responsibility on the family for properly using potentially enriching TV material. And by stimulating viewers' creativity, it lessened their "being reduced to mere objects of outside forces" while growing in selectivity and critical reception of media content.

*Procedures.*   The program's pedagogy was founded on the approach of "Total Language" (*Le Langage Total*), emphasizing semiotic over semantic aspects of mass communication media, "since it is through semiology that defensive instruments against massification and domestication can be developed" (Zamora, 1986, p. 13). ILPEC presented two days of 9-hour workshops for parents and their children. The first of three phases explores family relationships, first *ideally* with and without television and then *actually* as they experience one another in their homes along with TV viewing. Discussion and some practical exercises follow. The second phase moves from domestic situations just analyzed to viewing and discussing samples of television programs. Although discussion is unstructured, the procedure used is recommended for the home: first view the program, then (after rerunning the program if possible) discuss it, and finally identify the program's meaning and values. While parents practice the procedure during the workshop, children write scripts and videotape-record them—as an exercise in familiarization with and demystification of media. Then all view the videos, again following the aforementioned procedure for discussing TV. The third phase seeks various ways to make the methodology work in participants' homes by planning the family's week of activities. Back home, for several months, family members take part in activities that reinforce and strengthen the three-step procedure learned in the workshop.

*Assessment.*   Limited data for the present report are drawn from a secondary source, with no information about whether printed materials accompany the television programs viewed in the workshops. ILPEC claims "a very appreciable increase has occurred in new interfamily relationships producing a healthy influence at the community level" (Zamora, 1986, pp. 15–16). The number of workshops grew in Costa Rica; and they occasioned experiments introducing television to improve school curricula. From available data, the project appears somewhat idealistic and ambitious in terms of goals despite short-term and fairly unsophisticated methods.

## Uruguay

*Plan DENI.* This project was part of a seven-nation film/television education program mounted since 1960 by the Latin American Secretariat of the Office Catholique International du Cinéma.* The media study Plan DENI (*desde niños*—"from childhood") was developed in 1968 by Luis Campos Martinez in Quito, Equador. It originally emphasized training primary school teachers, through annual courses of 7 to 10 days and subsequent monthly meetings. Although procedure differed widely among countries—Bolivia, Brazil, Colombia, Dominican Republic, Paraguay, Peru, and Uruguay—Plan DENI is usually conducted in primary schools either integrated into formal courses or else as an extracurricular activity.

But Uruguay's Catholic Cinema Office until 1983 engaged in teaching critical film viewing and creativity in colleges and cinema clubs. The next year the Office developed a course emphasizing television, for groups of parents.

*Purposes.* Objectives were to make parents aware of TV's impact on behavior and personal development, to help them understand and analyze the medium's content and forms ("language") and to promote changed attitudes about television and its role within the family. Half the course is devoted to cultural and social aspects of the medium, including conceptual instruments for analyzing mass communication media. They include semiotics as the background to studying elements of technical aspects of media images, plus such concepts as signifier and signified, denotation and connotation, and functions of language, as well as implications for course subjects listed later.

*Procedures.* The group listens to recorded presentations introducing each of 10 topics; then they read brief booklets on the topics, after which they gather for group discussion with a coordinator. Next they engage in exercises in ways to view TV reflectively and critically. Finally the coordinator evaluates the session.

---

*Background data on non-Uruguay countries were provided by Centre for the Study of Communication and Culture, "Research Trends in Religious Communication," *Communication Research Trends*, 3:2 (1982), p. 11.

*Printed Materials.*   Complementing the recorded talks are 10 booklets (8 to 16 pages each) on the topics: TV as a problem, audiovisual social communication, film language (two of the booklets), concepts for semiological analysis, advertising, information and news, entertainment and comedy, TV drama, and the TV serial.

*Assessment.*   This approach is more conceptual than others in the Latin American group. It depends on semiotic and linguistic analysis and reflects approaches taken by the French school's "total language" and UNDA-UNESCO's "Educommunication" (see last section of this chapter). At the same time it offers progressive development through printed and audio-visual support materials, guided by experienced coordinators, for parents to apply in their home environment.

## BRAZIL

### Brazilian Social Communications Union (UCBC)

The Brazilian Social Communications Union promoted activities among social groups, concerned with "liberating" the poor in Latin America. That stance evolved out of work in the early 1970s with critical reading/viewing courses, based on "Television Awareness Training" of the Media Action Research Center (New York). UCBC progressed from what Fuenzalida (1987, p. 33) termed "a moralistic and denunciative stance" (concerned with media excesses of violence, sex, and depicting stereotypes) to active involvement vis-à-vis television on behalf of liberating the poor under-class in Latin America. Until 1982 UCBC concentrated on teachers along with church and social leaders; subsequently it shifted direction to poor groups in rural areas and on the outskirts of cities.

*Purposes and Procedures.*   UCBC drew on contemporary liberation theology as a foundation for its activity of popular education and "liberation communication." Its meetings and seminars—including 20-hour courses—presented topics on liberation theology, liberation communications, and communication theology. That conceptual approach put at the center of the communication process the land's broad social classes and popular organizations. It analyzed how the affluent dominate TV and society through ideological messages perpetuating interests of the "ruling class" hegemony. It also explored how to harness mass media for creating social awareness and organization among disadvantaged people. UCBC examined the media system as an industry of mass culture:

> [T]he objective was to denounce manipulation by mass communications and alert those responsible for communications of the dangers of control and manipulation of information; in other words, the social, political and cultural system existing in Brazil and in the world as a whole.[17]

UCBC moved beyond sharing theoretical knowledge with participants—merely objectively analyzing codes and language and content as well as production systems and ideological interests. It studied subjective "reading" of media texts to discern the gap between values and needs of the common people contrasted with those of the dominant class. Through participants' inductive study of concrete instances, the project intended to bring each social group to: (a) shared awareness of how they were involved in the process, (b) *as* a group analyze mass media messages, and (c) reinforce their group awareness through commitment to changing the mass communication process by developing alternate media outlets such as leaflets, community newspapers and theater, and video.

*Evaluation* of results was under development at the end of the 1980s. To be assessed were methods and procedures of "critical reading" training and how they benefited social groups, mutual commitment of groups and how they communicated among themselves, and also how personnel were assigned to assist groups subsequent to training periods.

## CHILE

### Centre of Cultural and Artistic Enquiry and Expression (CENECA)

Directed to social groups, the Centro de Indagacion y Expresion Cultural y Artistica since 1981 promoted education for "active reception" of television. It trained leaders to apply concepts of active viewing promulgated through workbooks. Those concepts explored how various audiences relate to different television "texts." CENECA directed its program to specific groups: students in secondary schools, in extracurricular activities; young persons through informal education; women in poor urban areas; and rural people generally. Chilean television is not operated by private commercial interests but by the state military government and universities; still, it is strongly influenced by advertising. According to Fuenzalida (1987, pp. 37–38), the Centre looks to the country's return to a democratic regime as opportunity for restoring the medium's original social orientation. This offers promise of "democratizing" television, in the sense of liberating TV and the general populace's interaction with it.

*Purpose and Procedures.*[18]   The Centre's goal was to help selected social groups develop their own meanings from TV content, and to strengthen the groups' cultural perceptions so they could actively demand programs matching their needs. The workshops trained different groups in methods of teaching—analyzing television as an industry and as language—and about how institutional contexts affect implementing media teaching. CENECA shifted focus from traditional "passive critical viewing" with its decodifying and dymystifying, to positive "active reception" aimed at transforming the television experience. This referred to viewers' judging TV content and making active demands on it. It also referred to their influencing television's social organization to integrate indigenous culture—interests and needs of various levels of social groups. The viewers' judging, of course, involves active construction of meaning from the medium's messages. And with CENECA, judgment about the value and ideological (class) content of TV along with its cultural significance is to be reached through group discussion. The group's evaluation and meaning, or "semanticization," may well not reflect the meaning intended by producers or broadcasters or even semanticists.

The Centre's approach emphasizes simulation games; through discussion and judgments participants "discover" forms of TV messages and conceptualize principles. Printed materials support those group activities, while providing basic theory.

*Support Materials.*   CENECA's books and manuals for group study and application include: for intermediate and high schools, *TV Education Module* (1983, second edition 1984); for urban youngsters, *TV and Active Reception* (1985); for parents and teachers, *TV—Parents—Children* (1985); and for women's groups in cities, *TV—Women* (1986). A workbook guide was planned for peasants in rural areas. The range of publications reflect CENECA's view that a single, universal form of TV education is inappropriate because various sociocultural groupings relate differently to interpreting and finding meaning in TV content— what Fuenzalida (1987, p. 28) phrased "varying semantization relationships with TV messages." In 1986 CENECA published Paula Edwards' key book *De la Educación para la TV a la Recepción Activa,* describing the projects and regional trends.


## Robert Bellarmino Educational Foundation

Similar to Brazil's UCBC, the Foundation worked with social groups, mindful of the desire to "liberate" the poor in Latin America. Its Social Communications Department in 1985 published *Programa de Educación para la Televisión,* a 108-page book outlining a curriculum for classroom teachers to use progressively through the 12 primary and secondary years. Programmed activities were mostly in private and Church-related schools, focusing less on individual teachers than on the schools in order to establish continuity of institutional support for CVS studies. The Bellarmino Centre (or, variously, Foundation) since 1985 stressed teacher-training workshops; in that year alone almost 400 teachers participated.

*Purpose and Procedures.*   The curriculum is cautious about TV's role as an

> instrument which might potentially be used to extend and democratize culture. However, experience has shown us that media frequently becomes [sic] an instrument of alienation when, for instance, used for ideological manipulation or to boost consumerism or encourage irresponsible escapism.[19]

The goal is to develop a context in schools that supports children's progressive development of critical skills in how they view television. "Progressive" refers both to successive levels of content and to respective stages of cognitional development. Objectives include growing awareness of TV's communication processes, understanding indirect and implicit messages, analyzing content and form, and creating alternative communication. This curriculum provides for learning through group activity and exercises rather than through lecture and "direct transfer of information." This promotes inductive discovery of how communication works and affects society.

*Curriculum Content.*   The curriculum promotes a learning *process* developed right up through primary and secondary grades. Relative to different ages of students, it develops objectives according to four major themes (summarized by Fuenzalida, p. 20):

| THEMES | OBJECTIVES |
|---|---|
| 1. Communications | —Identify and evaluate communication processes in which one participates |
| 2. TV and living | —Identify TV's role in one's life and social milieu |
| 3. What TV offers | —Analyze content and form of most popular TV programs |
| 4. Expressing creativity | —Experiment with creating alternative uses for mass communication processes |

*Assessment.*  The formalized curriculum provides a guide for systematically developing media education in classrooms on a regular and long-term basis. But the fairly brief book is directed to all 12 years of schooling. So teachers must be innovative, creating effective applications of the limited printed material at different grade levels, while addressing the "evolutionary psycho-pedagogy in the child and adolescent" (p. 36). Fuenzalida noted potential shortcomings with this approach. There is the problem of rigidity with a preset curriculum, which used over 12 years might also become repetitious. That challenge must be met with each teacher's originality and with children's spontaneity. Further, in Latin America school attendance is typically low (less so in private schools) and large numbers of older children drop out of school, especially in rural areas where 40% of the population resides. Fuenzalida (1987, pp. 41–42) concluded that such limitations favor "active reception" projects centered in the home and in social groups, as described later.

*       *       *

*Assessment* of the five Latin American programs surveyed by Fuenzalida is provided in his own summation, in addition to commentary already cited. "Television education" projects developed through the past 2 decades among various target groups: families, schools, and social groups. Most projects were influenced by Paulo Freire's educational philosophy and methodology. Their scope in studying TV ranges from trying to improve family life and relationships within the home, through conceptual (semantic and semiotic) understanding of media messages and processes, to active involvement in influencing mass media programming and preparing media materials. The broadest goal is to affect sociocultural transformation on behalf of repressed populations by challenging and changing the status quo of media dominated by affluent, corporate, governmental, and/or foreign interests.

Fuenzalida judged that the very diversity of Latin American CVS-related projects engendered a growing body of theory and practical experience, coupled with continuity as they evolve. He cautioned against short-term projects that offered no lasting impact. Continuity within and between Latin American projects and also appraisal of their results were needed to assist continual revising of CVS training. He observed that projects had to be better based in theory, drawing from developments in both education and communication. He found little research on Latin viewer's reception processes. Training methods needed more careful planning along with better preparing coordinators. Also lacking were evaluations of project processes and materials, and also post-training observation of group results. Fuenzalida (1987) called for more positive, active use of television not only at home and in school but in social and civic life. This includes "cultural productivity and creativity, and with the capability to make demands on TV and to gain access to programming" (p. 44). Those goals relate to the UNESCO declaration in 1982, crafted in part by Len Masterman of the United Kingdom, which calls for both critical awareness and greater competence among users, not only conceptually and analytically but in practical applications: "Ideally, such programs should include the analysis of media products, the use of media as means of creative expression and effective use of and participation in available media channels."[20]

# CHILE

## Univérsidad de Playa Ancha de Ciencias de la Educacion

As a prerequisite to classroom CVS studies, educators and researchers in Chile since 1982 mounted pilot projects and systematic follow-up courses precisely for teachers—either as part of their preparatory degree work in education, or as in-service workshops. Miguel Reyes Torres, director of Centro de Investigacion de Medios para la Educacion at Playa Ancha University of Sciences of Education (Valparaiso, Chile) judged that only through trained specialist teachers could critical viewing skills be introduced effectively on a long-term basis to the nation's schools. Further, from experience, project directors retreated from pressing for separate courses of media study in the curriculum, looking instead to integrate media study with traditional academic subjects. Despite the prospect of reaching fewer students, this strategy proved more accessible while also providing holistic involvement of media programs with school subjects related to media content and people's daily lives.

In teacher-training institutes, workshops and courses, this Chilean university's media center presented conceptual foundations drawn from various theoretical perspectives, practical exercises with applications to classrooms and to family viewing contexts, and evaluations of methodologies and materials. They moved beyond studying "defensive" and passive reaction toward TV programming to more positive, dynamic interpretation of media messages, becoming active participants in the social communication process.

In 1984 the University collaborated with the Municipal Corporation for the Social Development of Valparaiso and the Vicariate of Education of the Episcopate of Valparaiso on a course for teachers from 10 institutions who presented their methods for teaching CVS. Other projects engaged small numbers of participants at various schools in the region. In 1984–1985 the University created a series of "modules" and teaching units about demystifying TV, commercial TV publicity, and family reception of television. It also published four booklets on those subjects, each from 31 to 52 pages long. Various conferences were held during the decade to explore concepts and methodologies for helping teachers prepare for teaching media in classrooms. In 1988 the first teachers completed a curricular plan of three academic terms, covering two subjects each term: (Term 1) Media and Education (educator's role with new technologies), and Media Literacy; (Term 2) Media Impact on Children and Teenagers, and Media Education Methods; (Term 3) Curricular Design Dealing with Media, and Educating with Media Workshop.[21] The Center's director (Torres, 1986) asserted that mandatory media training in all teacher-education curricula was necessary for expanding CVS studies in schools and thereby having impact on individual viewers, families, social organizations, and ultimately the media themselves. Beyond that, in-school training must be accompanied by family applications of critical viewing skills in the home. This calls for media training sessions for parents, and mutual support of teachers and parents in creating a context for children to develop skills in understanding media.

## WORLDWIDE: UNDA/UNESCO

A major collaborative effort to apply Minkkinen's theories expounded in *A General Curricular Model for Mass Media Education* was organized by UNDA—Association Catholique Internationale pour la Radio et la Télévision—under contract with UNESCO. The Belgium-based Catholic organization reported in 1980 an experimental 10-lesson media course applied in four countries in Africa, two each in Asia, and Europe, and in one country each in Central America and Oceania. Locations for this experimental media study program were:

| | | |
|---|---|---|
| AFRICA | Libreville, Gabon | 236 students |
| | Beau Bassin, Ile Maurice | 64 students |
| | Niamey, Nigeria | 120 students |
| | Kigali, Rwanda | "1 group" |
| LATIN AMERICA | Cuernavaca, Mexico | 49 adults |
| ASIA | Wonju, Korea | 36 students |
| | Tiruchirapalli, India | 12 students + 24 adults |
| EUROPE | Trent, Italy | 179 adults |
| | Florania, Malta | 21 adults |
| OCEANIA | Wellington, New Zealand | 60 students |
| | (project still under way at time of UNDA Report) | |

At least 6 of the 10 projects were specifically under auspices of local Roman Catholic church agencies. Despite limited data to report, this worldwide effort to introduce a single program of media study deserves some attention here.

*Purposes and Procedures.* Although content and general procedures were often similar, effectiveness differed from region to region. UNDA organizers of the project considered "media" as similar to language in general, possessing structure and techniques just as traditional language; radio, cinema, television, and the press were looked on as specific forms of that language. They are found in various media.[22] The effort to study and teach media was called *éducommunication* (a neologism coined in Munich in 1977). Objectives of *éducommunication*, although expanded to several mass media in addition to television, were similar to other CVS programs:

> *Rendre conscient l'usager des médias, de leur impact sur la vie sociale, culturelle et politique. C'est-à-dire, expliquer comment fonctionnent les médias, exposer leurs objectifs, leurs contraintes et leurs limitations, décrire comment ils exercent leurs effets, pour le meilleur et pour le pire.*[23]

Thus an important purpose in studying media was to ascertain their social and political as well as cultural impact (but see the following, regarding the text). This had important implications in developing countries where the experimental program was carried on.

Lessons emphasized "hands-on" skills so participants could learn by practical application rather than by abstract theorizing. The projects stressed the role of citizens not only as media consumers but also as potential producers. Where actual media facilities were unavailable, lessons offered examples of simulations (e.g., drawing complete story-boards with scripts, to learn how program elements are planned and edited). The project was limited by time as well as local resources. It was contracted in August 1979 with UNESCO; planning until the new year was followed by implementation from January to August 1980, with a report drawn up in November, 1980.

*Curriculum and Content.* Applications of the project varied widely. Some were integrated into courses, others were offered outside of class, and still others were offered once or twice a week or every other week—sometimes in the evening. Ages ranged from classes of 12-year-olds, to mid- and late-teenagers, to advanced students in their mid-20s. Young adults were in their mid-20s to mid-30s.

The 10 lessons revolved around engaging students in looking at newspapers, viewing films and TV, and then eliciting by questions what they noted in those experiences of specific media products— leading them to further reflection and analysis of their perceptions and reactions. Lessons successively treated the following topics:

1. *The different media:* Factual information and practical exercises involving newspapers, radio, and TV.
2. *Information:* Activities for comparing coverage and viewpoints of various media.
3. *Sound:* The role of sound and music, by experimenting with audio recorders, films, and videotapes.
4. *Tape recording:* Interviewing, editing (including scripting).
5. *"Reading the Picture":* Visual elements in film, TV, photography; camera shots, angles.
6. *Advertising:* Print and broadcast appeals to buy luxuries and necessities; values reflected.
7. *"Writing through the picture":* Production of an audiovisual montage of photo-slides and recorded sound, plus critique.
8. *Film analysis:* Questions for discussing an 11-minute animated cartoon (with no narration) about nuclear war.
9. *Comparison between a book and a film:* Questions for discussing the screen adaptation of a short story or novel.
10. *Produce a newspaper:* Simulation of the process of creating a

newspaper for school or neighborhood—its purpose, finance, circulation problems, news gathering/writing/editing, layout, illustrations, printing and selling.

The 25 pages offer a concrete, applied set of basic exercises to familiarize students with elements of media. The lessons are uncomplicated, provide little background explanation (no statistical or factual data or readings), and rely on students' heuristic explorations engendered by the media activities and question-periods. Unlike Latin American projects described in the preceding section, the jejune text only briefly alludes to socioeconomic-political implications.

*Assessment.* Three short questionnaires for presenters and for students were appended to the lessons, to evaluate the project. Those questionnaire responses from sites in nine countries (the 10th, New Zealand, had not completed the project) provided the basis for UNDA's report to UNESCO.

Directors reported that they and most of the participants judged this initial effort at organized media study useful and effective, within the limitations noted here. Some judged parts of lessons as too simple and obvious, whereas other parts were complicated and depended on resources often not available. For example, specific audiovisual items recommended in the lessons were in French or English, which could not be used at sites in India and Korea, among others. Some respondents claimed lesson guidelines were too skeletal; they suggested complete book or study plans with details for applying variations to different contexts. One project director assessed the lessons as deficient in television study and exercises, with too much time devoted to film, which was deemed less intrusive in today's society. A general problem in these scattered sites was unavailability of some specific audiovisual support material (16mm film) cited in the lesson plans. Another was the lack of time to complete all the activities, especially in detail (some recommended more sessions and more time in which to present the media lessons). Extrinsic complications included multiple hurricanes in one country, and civil riots followed by restrictions on public meetings in another country. Low literacy by village people prevented understanding of some materials; their limited prior exposure to media hindered active crafting of simulated media productions.

On the other hand, project directors noted that applied lessons in this experimental project were far more appropriate than Minkkinen's more theoretical and detailed curriculum outline. Reactions to Minkkinen's analysis included: too intellectual and abstract a model without concrete examples, too general and inapplicable equally to children and adults and persons with ranges of intelligence and experience, the division of material is more philosophically than pedagogically sound, training in applied technical areas (e.g., preparing newspaper articles and TV programs) is wholly absent, the materials in each chapter make uneven demands (some need only a lesson or two, others need months to cover); and the model should be revised to address first children and then adults in developed countries, and secondly children and then adults in developing countries—with specific programs of study and concrete suggestions for exercises and audiovisual support material.[24]

From this initial experiment, UNDA's report urged further international organizing—through various publications and organizations—to help spread the two-pronged development *"d'information et d'approche pratique"* in media study.

                              *         *         *

As noted earlier, many of the CVS training programs reported in this chapter were not included in the 1981/1985 questionnaire surveys, so they were not part of the comparative analysis tabulated in Part III. But they were included here to supplement data gathered for previous chapters, to represent recent developments in media literacy and CVS studies around the world.

                              *         *         *

## SUMMARY OF PART II

The seven chapters of Part II reviewed structured programs of critical television viewing skills. Chapter 4 surveyed major projects (by questionnaires in 1981 and 1985 and by correspondence), summarizing their general characteristics and patterns. Chapters 5 and 6 then analyzed goals, content, structure, format, printed and audio-visual materials, and effects (where available) of experimental projects funded by the U.S. government and also systematic formal instruction in school districts. Chapters 7, 8, and 9 analyzed those elements in projects by individual persons, by national nongovernmental organizations, and by private nonprofit and commercial corporations including broadcast companies. Chapter 10 reviewed institution-related programs in formal and informal education in countries outside the United States.

Part III of this report identifies criteria (from Part I) for evaluating CVS projects, then inventories their presence or absence in major programs selected from Part II.

## NOTES

1. The following analysis is drawn from the report by McIver (1987, pp. 26–28).

2. The H.M.I. Report, *Popular Television and School Children,* was published in spring of 1983; national conferences on primary media education were held at Leicester and Nottingham in 1983 and at Bradford in July of 1985, which produced a *Primary Sector Report.* Cited by McIver (1987, p. 9).

3. The study involved questionnaires for *all* teachers in the 16 schools, not only those who took the media course; and it conducted structured interviews with all teachers and heads of schools involved, plus course tutors, education officials, and staff from validating agencies. Further citations listed later are noted by page references within the text.

4. The British Film Institute joined with the Department of Education and Science to create a Working Party on Media Education. They strove to promote "informal research" on teaching and learning media studies at the primary level, and to promote "good practice" in teaching media education. See Dick (1987a, p. 57).

5. For example, West Glamorgan Institute of Higher Education (Wales) includes study of film and television as part of the Modern English Studies in a 3-year honors BA degree; similarly, the University of Birmingham (England) offers Communications and Cultural Studies—including TV production and analysis of media issues—as part of a degree in the Faculty of Arts. The University of Stirling (Scotland) has long offered degree programs in mass media studies, similar to undergraduate "majors" in many U.S. universities. For detailed descriptions of representative undergraduate and postgraduate courses and degree programs in broadcasting and cinema (theoretical studies rather than production courses) available in the United Kingdom, see Orton (1987). A companion booklet about courses in technical production of programs was prepared by BFI Education (n.d., ca. 1987). Another BFI descriptive survey with critical analyses of examination syllabi for film, TV, and media studies in England, Wales, and Scotland is Hayward and Blanchard (1987).

6. Questionnaire response, David Altshul, Film Officer, Southern Arts Association, Winchester, Hampshire, U.K.

7. Data derived from Pungente (1989, pp. 3–4).

8. Kevin Cowle, Film Officer, The Scottish Film Council, in correspondence dated May 18, 1981, responding to Paul C. Kenney of the London Centre for the Study of Communication and Culture. He added a 14-page report in response to the questionnaire survey.

9. In the mid-1980s the first issue of a specialized journal chronicled the growth and sustained governmental support for media curricula and teacher-training: *Journal of the Association for Media Education in Scotland,* Number 1 (1984).

10. See McMahon and Quin (1988, p. 3), whose data were derived from *Media Education Curriculum Guidelines* (Glasgow: Scottish Film Council, with Scottish Curriculum Development Service & Association for Media Education in Scotland, 1988).

11. Data in this paragraph are drawn from John Pungente's (1985) account, pp. 9–11.

12. Again, John Pungente's (1985) worldwide regional review provides a glimpse of these patterns, as does Eddie Dick's (1987a) global survey.

13. Questionnaire response from Stickting Audiovisuele Vorming, via Paul Kenney, S.J., research associate, Centre for the Study of Communication and Culture, London.

14. Published by the Ministry of Education—Chris Ward, Minister, and Bernard J. Shapiro, Deputy Minister (Ontario, Queen's Printer for Ontario, 1989). No authorship is cited. The collaborative work lists as project co-directors Jerry George (Ministry of Education) and Pierre Lalonde (Ontario Teacher's Federation), 13 members of the "writing team," 9 members of an advisory committee, and 30 "validators" from local and regional boards of education.

15. Memorandum from Sheila Roy, Ontario Ministry of Education, undated, p. 1. A copy of the memo was sent to this researcher by Jerry George (Centre for Secondary and Adult Education, Ministry of Education) with a complimentary copy of the publication; the undated memo was received on August 29, 1989.

16. Fuenzalida (1987, p. 5) cited 1983 data reported by Varis (1984a, pp. 10–16).

17. Gomes (1986), quoted by Fuenzalida (1987, p. 24).

18. This information is drawn from reports by Dick (1987a, p. 54) and Fuenzalida (1987, p. 34).

19. Fundación Educación Roberto Bellarmino (1985), quoted by Fuenzalida (1987, p. 36).

20. Quoted by Dick (1987a), Appendix 1 (n.p.), and by Masterman (1985b, p. 341).

21. See Torres and Méndez (1989, in press); p. 6 of manuscript published by Educational Media International, December 1989.

22. Cf. Dessaucy (1980, p. 3). All information about experimental projects related to the Minkkinen model was obtained from this 168-page compendium and its 48 pages of three appendices.

23. Quoted by Dessaucy (1980, pp. 9–10). Cf. chapter 4, endnote 5, for translation.

24. See Dessaucy (1979), pp. 1–4 following p. 168, Appendix (number 1).

# III

# EVALUATION OF CVS PROJECTS AND RECOMMENDATIONS FOR FUTURE PLANNERS AND IMPLEMENTERS

Part I presented conceptual foundations and the contemporary context of critical viewing skills projects. From them were drawn principles and criteria for assessing CVS programs described in Part II. In Part III, chapter 11 employs quantitative listings to measure those projects against the criteria, profiling their relative emphases and strengths. (Some readers may prefer to skim or skip entirely this quantitative analysis of data, directing their attention instead to the interpretive analysis in the following chapter.) Chapter 12 offers a qualitative review of projects, noting patterns among CVS projects which can guide curriculum designers to resource materials appropriate to their contexts. Chapter 13 presents a final summary and some recommendations to those planning and implementing television media studies.

# 11

## Quantitative Profile of CVS Projects

Major projects are inventoried here according to criteria drawn up in Part I, in an attempt to sketch patterns of emphases and strengths in quantitative terms. Of the original 32 projects that provided primary data and also participated in the questionnaire survey (1981, 1985), the 23 directly related to CVS are listed in following tables. Another four non-U.S. projects were added (out of 11 described in chapter 10) for which material became available in 1987–1989, despite no previous questionnaire data. Projects were excluded from tabulations when their scope was tangential to critical viewing skills or else representative material was too limited to permit reasonable estimates of how they embodied specific criteria.

The summary of criteria offers guidelines drawn from theorists and experienced practitioners, reflected in the literature (Part I). Although not strictly prescriptive, the list of criteria does suggest ideal characteristics for CVS programs. Not all characteristics would be expected to appear in all programs because of the variety of contexts. Robert White, after previewing the criteria and analyses in Part III, observed that this report properly does not intend "to give the definitive evaluation of these programs. [It does] rate them according to the criteria, but [is] more interested in what we can learn from the *experience,* [including] the seeming limitations (always seen as limitations in which people tried to do the best under the circumstances or with certain premises)."[1] He added that local and national contexts might even demand different combinations of such guidelines: "Thus, the criteria pose questions implying that there are *different* valid responses to these questions or major dimensions that should be present in some way."

Criteria developed in chapters 1 and 2 are again listed here. Subsequent tables refer to them by their two sets of prefixed letters (A–T, a–j).

*Breadth*

A.  A project should study the broad social context and impact of television as well as intrinsic aesthetics of the medium.

B.  It should include social, political, aesthetic, and ethical perspectives, including "administrative" analysis (functional, utilitarian, experimental, behavioral—atomistic) and "critical" analysis (judgmental, value-oriented, sociopolitical, cultural, interpretative—holistic).

*Scope*

C.  A media literacy curriculum has greater value to the extent that it is (a) adaptable to a wider range of educational emphases, orientations

D.  (b) well organized and sustained over time, by numbers of people and institutions, in more than one place or region.

*Individuality and Values*

E.  It must respect the individuality of the person, including their distinctive upbringing by family, so they are not merely indoctrinated with others' opinions and conclusions.

F.  Values presented should not be narrowly instructional nor exclusively moralistic in a single tradition. But the project ought not be valueless; it should relate to the broad humanistic heritage and and Judeo-Christian ethic.

G.  It should not limit itself to one form of critical assessment; even the criteria should be questioned and analyzed.

H.  Contexts of norms addressed are to be clearly identified, noting various levels of such categories (e.g., economic, legal, ethical, aesthetic, social, technical—normative statements as criteria).

I.  Programs should acquaint participants with constitutive parts of media, including the larger communication process (not labeling the entire television phenomenon as "good" or "bad"): Sensitize viewers to their role in the bi-polar communication process of mutual responsibility of sender/receiver.

*Validity and Reliability; Accuracy*

J.  Project should present factual data based on valid sources and research, eschewing merely conventional assumptions (commonly accepted but misinformed assertions).

K.  They must acknowledge (at least implicitly) research findings and incorporate those conclusions and implications into the content and manner of presenting CVS projects (Those studies are touchstones for determining validity of assumptions, assertions, and directives for training programs).

L. Ideally, projects should be tested and evaluated for results with subjects through time.

*Cognition: Developmental*

M. Projects should properly address stages of students' growth in thinking ability—preoperational (up to 7 years), operational (7–10+)—as well as social cognitional experience and moral development.

N. They should observe, appraise, and train children as children in their responses to specific TV exposure, in accord with children's true state of personal experiencing and cognition (not as "little adults").

*Cognition: Reasoning Skills*

O. Projects should train participants in the process of selective discrimination, analytical observation, and reasoned assessment based on factual data judged according to meaningful criteria.

P. The process should begin with analysis and end with synthesis, merging learned factual data with receivers' experience of TV and own value-system; it should stress inductive (heuristic, a posteriori) exploration from which principles are drawn out, along with the deductive (a priori) process.

*Pragmatics of Media Education*

Q. Projects should include "a systematic approach to a set of objectives supported by instructional routine and devices"—usually involving a curriculum publicly available.

R. Major areas in projects might include:
- media effects on audiences (impact mediation)
- uses and gratifications (goal attainment; interaction with media)
- cultural understanding (symbol-systems reflecting society)
- visual literacy (media techniques, grammar, syntax).

S. Projects should reflect the diversity of the total TV medium: information, persuasion, education, entertainment: quality programming as well as popular kitsch content. But selective perception, in context of uses and gratifications, emphasizes the role of the receiver/viewer rather than the content itself; interactionist approach is more revealing about TV's effects than logical positivist (content analysis).

T. The project should provide detailed audiovisual/print materials supporting the conceptual development in the program.

The following supplemental list adds specific characteristics for significance and feasibility as well as validity of CVS programs:

a.  Project appropriate for intended audience/age-groups?
b.  Ingredients of the project, including procedures and techniques: Realistic, adequate to stated goals and purposes?
c.  Principles stated, assumptions, assertions, conclusions, recommendations-to-action consonant with scientific (behavioral, educational) data?
d.  Accuracy of data, level of scholarship (range of sources, methodologies).
e.  Consistency in development of program: Does the logic of the "argument" break down; internal inconsistencies in practices, applications?
f.  Balanced perspective regarding media: Neither defensively supportive nor cynically negative?
g.  Adequacy of funding for program attempted; sources of funding a factor influencing objectives of program?
h.  Environment of the project (laboratory, field—classroom, home): Factors affecting the integrity or effectiveness of the project, its goals and procedures?
i.  Level of exposition (writing, audiovisual presentation): Clear, explicit? Apt for intended audience(s)? exhortatory, proselytizing?
j.  Extent of resources provided to explain, advance, promote the program: Number, quality, relevance, availability of workbooks, study sheets, teachers' guides, audiovisual materials, and so forth.

Measured against these criteria are projects surveyed in Part II, to identify distinctive patterns found in CVS programs individually and in selected groupings. Table 11.1 inventories projects according to the criteria: 23 projects of the original 32 in Table 4.1 (chapter 4, pp. 130–131) plus four more projects of the 11 added in 1988–1989 (marked by #).* Projects are numbered in Table 11.1 corresponding to their positions in Table 11.2.

Criteria are identified in Table 11.2 according to their alpha listings

---

*Details of all 43 projects were described in Part II; but here some projects are grouped under collective headings in Table 11.1, such as "National Television Networks" which includes three corporations. The new list excludes those for which scant primary material was available (such as East Syracuse, NY) or whose purposes and activities were tangential to formal CVS programs (NAFBRAT, American Council for Better Broadcasting, and all projects in category "E. Private Companies, U.S., U.K." except The Learning Seed Company).

TABLE 11.1
Selected Major CVS Projects Inventoried by Criteria

---

*A. Projects Funded by U.S. Government*

---

1. Southwest Educational Development Laboratory (Grades K–5)
2. WNET/Thirteen, New York City (Grades 6–8)
3. Far West Laboratory for Educational Research and Development (Grades 9–12)
4. Boston University (Post-secondary and Adults)

*B. School Districts (Systematic, Formal Instruction)*

---

5. Idaho Falls School District No. 91 (Grades 3–6)
6. Eugene (Oregon) Public School District 91 (Grades 4–8, 9–12)
7. New York City Board of Education (Grades K–9)
8. Catholic Education Office (Sydney, N.S.W.) (Grades K–6, 7–12)
#a. Ministry of Education (Western Australia) (Grades 1–7, 8–12)

*C. Projects by Individuals: Collaborative and Individual*

---

9. Aimee Dorr et al. (Harvard/Univ. of Southern California)
10. Dorrothy and Jerome Singer (Yale/ABC)
11. Rosemary Lee Potter et al. (Pinella County Schools, Florida)

*D. National Organizations (Non-Governmental), U.S.*

---

12. Congress of Parents and Teachers (National PTA)
13. Media Action Research Center: Television Awareness Training
14.  "       "       "       "    : Growing with Television
15. U.S. Catholic Conference: The Media Mirror

*E. Private Companies, U.S., U.K.*

---

16. The Learning Seed Company

*F. Institution-Related CVS Programmes: Non-U.S. Countries*

---

17. Powys (County) Education Committee (Wales)
#b. Clwyd (County) Media Studies Unit (Wales)
18. Mayfield School (Southwest London)
19. Southern Arts Association (Winchester, Hampshire)
20. Scottish Film Council (Scotland)
#c. Media Education Development Project (Scotland)
21. Formation Du Jeun Téléspectateur Actif (France)
22. Stichting Audiovisuele Vorming (Amsterdam)
#d. Ontario: Media Literacy Resource Guide (Canada)
23. UNDA/UNESCO (Worldwide)

---

on the preceding three pages: A–T and a–j. Each of the 30 criteria is noted as either present, partly absent, or wholly absent, in each major CVS project. Identification of each criterion's presence/absence in the projects is coded:

5 = all elements clearly, directly evident
4 = implicitly present, but not stated

## TABLE 11.2
### Presence of Criteria in Selected Major CVS Projects

*Two Sets of 30 Criteria (Alpha-Numerics: cf. pp. 276–279)*

| PROJECT | BRDT | | SCOP | | INDIV/VALUES | | | | | VAL/REL | | | COGd | | COGr | | PRAG EDUC | | | | CONCRETE SPECIFICS | | | | | | | | | | TOTAL |
|---|---|---|---|---|---|---|---|---|---|---|---|---|---|---|---|---|---|---|---|---|---|---|---|---|---|---|---|---|---|---|---|
| | A | B | C | D | E | F | G | H | I | J | K | L | M | N | O | P | Q | R | S | T | a | b | c | d | e | f | g | h | i | j | |
| *A. USOE* | | | | | | | | | | | | | | | | | | | | | | | | | | | | | | | |
| 1 SEDL | 0 | 5 | 5 | 1 | 5+ | 4 | 3 | 3 | 5+ | 3 | 4 | 3 | 4 | 5 | 3 | 5 | 3 | 0 | 5 | 3 | 5 | 3 | 5 | 3 | 1 | 5 | 5 | 5 | 5 | 4 | 110 |
| 2 WNET | 3 | 3 | 4 | 3 | 5 | 5 | 2 | 5 | 5 | 5 | 4 | 3 | 5 | 5 | 5 | 4 | 3 | 4 | 5 | 5 | 5 | 5 | 5 | 4 | 3 | 5 | 5+ | 5 | 4 | 5+ | 127 |
| 3 FarWest | 4 | 5 | 5 | 1 | 5 | 5 | 2 | 5 | 5 | 5 | 5 | 4 | 4 | 3 | 5+ | 5 | 5 | 5 | 4 | 5+ | 5 | 5 | 5 | 5 | 4 | 5 | 5 | 5 | 3 | 5+ | 134 |
| 4 BostnUn | 5 | 5 | 4 | 1 | 5 | 5 | 5 | 5 | 5 | 5 | 5 | 3 | 5 | X | 5 | 5 | 5 | 5 | 4 | 5+ | 5 | 5 | 5 | 5 | 4 | 5 | 5 | 4 | 5 | 5 | 135 |
| *B. SCHLDstr* | | | | | | | | | | | | | | | | | | | | | | | | | | | | | | | |
| 5 IdaFalls | 5 | 5 | 4 | 5 | 5+ | 5 | 2 | 5 | 5 | 5 | 5 | 5+ | 5 | 5 | 5 | 5+ | 5+ | 4 | 5+ | 5 | 5 | 5 | 5 | 5 | 4 | 4 | 4 | 5 | 5 | 5 | 146 |
| 6 Eugene | 3 | 5 | 3 | 5 | 4 | 2 | 2 | 4 | 5 | 5 | 4 | ? | 4 | ? | 5 | 5 | ? | 4 | 5 | 5 | 4 | 4 | 4 | 4 | ? | 5 | ? | ? | 4 | 5 | 127 |
| 7 N.Y.C. | 3 | 3 | 0 | 0 | 2 | 3 | 3 | 3 | 5 | 3 | 3 | 0 | 5 | ? | 5 | 5 | ? | 4 | 0 | 4 | ? | 3 | 3 | 3 | ? | 2 | ? | ? | 2 | 1 | 64* |
| 8 Sydney | 5 | 5 | 5 | 5 | 3 | 5 | 5 | 4 | 5 | 5+ | 5+ | 3 | 5 | 2 | 5 | 3 | 5 | 5 | 5+ | 5 | 5 | 5 | 5 | 5 | 5 | 5 | 5 | 5 | 4 | 5 | 139 |
| #a W.Aust. | 5 | 5 | 5 | 4 | 5 | 5 | 5 | 4 | 5 | 4 | 4 | 1 | 4 | 3 | 5 | 5 | 4 | 4 | 4 | 4 | 5 | 4 | 4 | 4 | 4 | 5 | 3 | 4 | 4 | 4 | 127 |
| *C. Indivs.* | | | | | | | | | | | | | | | | | | | | | | | | | | | | | | | |
| 9 Dorr | 5 | 5 | 1 | 1 | ? | ? | ? | 5 | 5 | 5 | 4 | 5 | 5 | 4 | 4 | 5 | 3 | 3 | 3 | 3 | 5 | 5 | 5 | 5 | 5 | 5 | ? | 5 | ? | 3 | 107* |
| 10 Singers | 5 | 5 | 5 | 4 | 5 | 5 | 3 | 5 | 5 | 5 | 5+ | 5+ | 5 | 5 | 5 | 5 | 5 | 5 | 5 | 5 | 5 | 5 | 5+ | 5+ | 5 | 5 | 5 | 5 | 5 | 5+ | 146 |
| 11 Potter | 3 | 3 | 5 | 3 | 5 | 3 | 3 | 3 | 5 | 5 | 5 | 0 | 5 | 5 | 4 | 5 | 3 | 4 | 5 | 5+ | 4 | 4 | 5 | 4 | 5 | 5 | 3 | 5 | 5+ | 5+ | 127 |

| Section / Project | Ratings (left → right) | Partial Total |
|---|---|---|
| **D. Orgn's.** | | |
| 12 PTA | 2 3 1 3 5 5 1 3 5 5 1 4 3 5 1 1 5 5 0 ? ? 5 3 ? | 79* |
| 13 MARC TAT | 5 5 5 5 3 3 5 5 5 5+ 1 5+ 5 5 4 3 5 4 4 5 5 5 5 3 | 126 |
| 14 " GWT | 3 3 5 5 3 3 5 5 5 5 5 4 5 5 4 4 5 5 4 5 5 5 5 4 | 133 |
| 15 USCC | 5 5 5 5 3 3 5 5 5 5 4 4 5 5 3 3 5 4 4 5 4 5 5 4 | 126 |
| **E. Pvt.Co.** | | |
| 16 LrnSeed | 3 3 4 1 3 5 4 5 3 4 2 4 4 5+ 3 5 4 3 X 3 5 3 5 5+ | 101 |
| **F. Instit.*** | | |
| 17 Powys | 0 0 0 0 3 5 3 5 5 5 1 2 3 1 5 5 1 1 1 2 5 3 3 | 62* |
| #b Clwyd | 5 4 3 4 5 3 4 5 5 4 5 4 4 4 4 5 4 4 2 3 3 3 4 1 | 120 |
| 18 Mayfld | 5 3 ? 1 3 5 4 3 1 1 3 4 3 1 5 5 2 ? ? ? 3 3 ? 1 | 64* |
| 19 SoArts | 5 5 1 5 ? 5 ? 2 ? 1 ? 4 4 2 5 5 5 5 1 5 3 3 ? 0 | 65* |
| 20 ScotFlm | 5 5 5 4 5 5 5 3 5 2 5 4 4 0 5 5 3 3 3 3 4 3 2 3 | 108* |
| #c MEDevP | 4 4 3 3 4 5 4 4 4 0 5 4 5 3 4 4 2 3 4 4 2 4 ? 3 | 103* |
| 21 FDJTAct | 5 5 5 5 5 4 1 1 3 0 5 4 4 5 4 4 3 2 3 4 5 5 5 5 | 84* |
| 22 SAVormg | 0 0 1 5 5 5 3 ? 1 0 1 2 0 ? 5 ? 3 2 ? ? ? ? ? ? | 43* |
| #d Ontario | 4 4 5 2 4 5 4 5 5 1 4 4 4 3 3 5 5 5 5 5 2 2 5 4 | 119 |
| 23 UNESCO | 3 5 1 3 3 5 4 ? 3 3 5 2 ? 1 1 1 1 0 ? 5 3 0 1 | 56* |

5 = all elements clearly, directly evident
4 = implicitly present, but not stated
3 = considerably evident, but lacking elements
2 = some elements present
1 = a bit present, sometimes ambiguous (from data)
0 = definitely absent (although could be appropriate)
X = not applicable to this project
? = inadequate primary data to determine

*Indicates partial totals: project profiles based on incomplete data (cf. ? indicators).
#a–d: projects not surveyed by questionnaires (1981, 1985): data received 1987–1989.

3 = considerably evident, but lacking elements
2 = some elements present
1 = a bit present, sometimes ambiguous (from data)
0 = definitely absent (although could be appropriate)
X = not applicable to this project
? = inadequate primary data to determine

This necessarily subjective assessment was based on primary materials exhaustively detailed in Part II and on secondary data, including published sources cited in the endnotes and references.

It is important to stress once again that some criteria were not universally appropriate because projects had differing purposes and target audiences. Thus "low marks" do not necessarily reflect negative value judgments. Any attempt at comparative evaluation among the projects is bound to be inadequate because their cultural, economic, and political contexts varied widely. And projects often had differing purposes, structures, and funding. Furthermore, data gathered over several years during the course of this study were uneven.* Especially lacking were consistent, comparable materials from non-U.S. sources whose projects were represented often by limited printed materials and by interviews and/or questionnaires administered by a third party and relayed to this researcher. Further, data submitted from overseas during 1987–1989 did not provide some information derived from earlier questionnaire surveys (in 1981 and 1985).

Yet, impressions of projects drawn from almost 300 pages of analysis (involving subjective interpretation) in Part II are broadly supported in this effort to put into some kind of quantified order admittedly different kinds of data. This crude exercise does suggest relative strengths or emphases although not necessarily effectiveness of projects in demonstrating various CVS criteria. It even makes possible, albeit only partly valid, a rank-ordering (Table 11.3) according to the extent they reflect criteria—keeping in mind previous qualifiers and disclaimers.

Projects in Idaho Falls (collaborating with Anderson and Ploghoft) and by the Singers at Yale University enjoyed the scholarly expertise of pioneers in applied CVS research. They stood out above others in meeting desirable criteria, each totaling 146 estimated "points." The second cluster of four projects (ranging from 139 to 133 "points") in-

---

*Similarly, Eddie Dick lamented the variance in responses to his world survey, including nonresponses and kinds of information not easily categorized (cited earlier at the beginning of ch. 10).

TABLE 11.3
Ranking of CVS Projects by Dominance of Implemented Criteria

| | | *Number of Instances for Appraisal "Points" Estimates* | | | | | |
|---|---|---|---|---|---|---|---|
| # | Project | "5+" | "5" | "4" | All Others | X/?* | Total |
| 5 | Idaho Falls | 5 | 21 | 4 | 0 | | 146 |
| 10 | Singers | 5 | 22 | 2 | 3 | | 146 |
| 8 | Sydney | 3 | 21 | 2 | 11 | | 139 |
| 4 | Boston Univ. | 1 | 22 | 4 | 4 | (1) | 135 |
| 3 | Far West | 3 | 18 | 5 | 9 | | 134 |
| 14 | MARC: GWT | 0 | 19 | 5 | 18 | | 133 |
| 11 | Potter | 2 | 16 | 4 | 21 | | 127 |
| 2 | WNET | 2 | 14 | 6 | 23 | | 127 |
| 6 | Eugene, Ore. | 0 | 15 | 11 | 8 | (1) | 127 |
| #a | W.Australia | 0 | 12 | 15 | 7 | | 127 |
| 13 | MARC: T-A-T | 2 | 17 | 5 | 11 | | 126 |
| 15 | USCC | 0 | 13 | 10 | 21 | | 125 |
| #b | Clwyd | 0 | 8 | 15 | 20 | | 120 |
| #d | Ontario | 0 | 12 | 11 | 15 | | 119 |
| 1 | SEDL | 2 | 11 | 4 | 29 | | 110 |
| 20 | Scot Film | 0 | 15 | 2 | 25 | (2) | 108* |
| 9 | Dorr | 0 | 17 | 2 | 14 | (5) | 107* |
| #c | MEDevP | 0 | 6 | 15 | 13 | (3) | 103* |
| 16 | Lrng Seed | 2 | 6 | 8 | 29 | (1) | 101 |
| 21 | FDJTAct | 0 | 12 | 2 | 16 | (7) | 84* |
| 12 | Nat'l PTA | 0 | 7 | 1 | 40 | (3) | 79* |
| 19 | So Arts | 0 | 9 | 1 | 16 | (9) | 65* |
| 7 | New York City | 0 | 4 | 2 | 36 | (6) | 64* |
| 18 | Mayfield | 0 | 5 | 2 | 31 | (8) | 64* |
| 17 | Powys | 0 | 7 | 0 | 27 | (2) | 62* |
| 23 | UNESCO/UNDA | 0 | 5 | 0 | 31 | (5) | 56* |
| 22 | SAVormg | 0 | 5 | 0 | 18 | (6) | 43* |

*Lack of data for some projects precluded determining extent to which all criteria were manifested. Each "?" entry for a criterion lessened by 5 "points" the possible total of 150 (based on 30 criteria, each with up to 5 points where "clearly, directly evident" in the project).

cluded two religious-oriented programs (Sydney and MARC/"Growing with Television") and two USOE-funded projects (Boston University and Far West). A third group (127–125 "points") consisted of one individual (Potter), one USOE project (WNET), one collaboration with researchers (Eugene, Oregon), a non-U.S. regional school district (Western Australia), and two religious-oriented organizations (MARC/"Television Awareness Training" and U.S. Catholic Conference "The Media Mirror"). Excluding those projects for which data were limited and totals thus misleading, a final cluster of four projects (120 to 110 "points," plus one with 101) included two non-U.S. projects (Clwyd

County in Wales and Ontario province in Canada), followed distantly by a USOE-funded project (Southwest Educational Development Laboratory), with a private U.S. company (The Learning Seed) totaling fewest points by far.

Among those CVS media education programs whose totals were incomplete (marked by asterisks in Table 11.3) because of limited data available for this review, two national projects in Scotland and one individual researcher in the United States stood out from the others (Scottish Film Council, Aimee Dorr, and Media Education Development Project—with totals ranging from 108 to 101). The remaining eight projects, of which six were non-U.S., grouped somewhat closely except for the French activity (Formation Du Jeun Téléspectateur Actif, 84) and the National Parent-Teacher Association (79) at the high end, whereas The Netherlands (Stichting Audiovisuele Vormin/ Amsterdam, 43) was at the low end of the "point" rankings.

What does all this tell us? Primarily, that no one type of project source accounts for strongest or for least strong programs (at least as measured here). At best, one can identify among those most consistently meeting criteria two USOE projects and two school districts along with a research team and one religious-oriented organization. But almost as many in each of those categories are found mid-way and even toward the lower end of the rankings in Table 11.3.

The practical implication is that one ought to seek out projects that not only in source and context (school district, organization, church-related group, etc.) but also in purpose (Part II, plus chapter 12) and emphases or strengths (Table 11.2) best reflect one's own context, purpose, and points of desired emphasis. No one or other project is best for all. Many manifest desirable characteristics, yet may lack some aspect or procedure important for others mounting critical viewing skills. To repeat the caveat: Projects not fully represented by data that could be definitively appraised have artificially "low ranking." Persons interested in adopting—and adapting—specific CVS activities ought look not to gross totals, but rather to discrete points listed after specific criteria they consider particularly significant for local implementation (Table 11.2).

Patterns can be discerned among various criteria by studying data in Table 11.2. Those totals are synthesized according to categories of criteria in Table 11.4.

Of the 30 CVS criteria listed, those represented most strongly and widely in projects (with notations of $5+$, 5, or 4) were in categories of "Cognition: Reasoning Skills." They totaled 129 for "P" (inductive) and 123 for "O" (analysis and judgment). The highest possible total was 135, with a maximum of 5 points for each of 27 projects reported.

TABLE 11.4
CVS Criteria: Patterns of Incidence in Major Projects*

| Category | Number of "5+/5" | "4" | Sum of Points for All Others | "X/?" | Total Points |
|---|---|---|---|---|---|
| BREADTH | | | | | |
| A. Social & Aesthetics | 13 | 3 | 23 | | 100 |
| B. Atomistic/Holistic | 15 | 3 | 21 | | 108 |
| SCOPE | | | | | |
| C. Wide orientation | 12 | 4 | 14 | | 90 |
| D. Organized time/space | 6 | 4 | 25 | | 71 |
| INDIVIDUALITY & VALUES | | | | | |
| E. Individual's values | 12 | 3 | 17 | (6) | 89 |
| F. Not narrow/valueless | 14 | 2 | 11 | (5) | 89 |
| G. Multiple criteria | 5 | 2 | 28 | (7) | 61 |
| H. Levels of norms clear | 11 | 5 | 27 | | 102 |
| I. Sender/receiver roles | 19 | 4 | 7 | (1) | 118 |
| VALIDITY/RELIABILITY & ACCURACY | | | | | |
| J. Factual, valid sources | 12 | 4 | 20 | (2) | 96 |
| K. Founded on research | 9 | 10 | 7 | (2) | 92 |
| L. Tested results | 4 | 3 | 20 | (1) | 52 |
| COGNITION: DEVELOPMENTAL | | | | | |
| M. Child's growth levels | 13 | 6 | 10 | | 99 |
| N. As youths, not adults | 6 | 5 | 28 | (5) | 78 |
| COGNITION: REASONING SKILLS | | | | | |
| O. Analysis, judgment | 19 | 4 | 12 | | 123 |
| P. Inductive/Deductive | 23 | 2 | 6 | | 129 |
| PRAGMATICS OF MEDIA EDUCATION | | | | | |
| Q. Systematic, curriculum | 12 | 3 | 22 | (1) | 94 |
| R. Efcts/U&G/Cult/VisLit | 7 | 16 | 6 | | 105 |
| S. TV Divrsty/Interactn | 13 | 7 | 15 | (1) | 108 |
| T. Print/A-V materials | 12 | 4 | 16 | (1) | 93 |
| SPECIFIC CONCRETE CRITERIA | | | | | |
| a. Apt for participants | 24 | 1 | 1 | (1) | 125 |
| b. Apt for goals | 13 | 5 | 21 | (1) | 106 |
| c. Consonant w. science | 13 | 4 | 22 | | 103 |
| d. Scholarship accurate | 8 | 8 | 17 | (2) | 89 |
| e. Consistent | 6 | 9 | 14 | (5) | 80 |
| f. Balanced +/− re media | 18 | 3 | 10 | (2) | 112 |
| g. Adequacy of funding | 10 | 1 | 24 | (6) | 78 |
| h. Environment integrity | 15 | 3 | 20 | (1) | 107 |
| i. Clear, apt exposition | 8 | 6 | 16 | (6) | 80 |
| j. Support resources | 12 | 6 | 13 | (1) | 97 |

*For descriptions of alpha-listed topics see the first pages of Part III (pp. 276–279).

Category "a" (project's aptness for intended participants) rated 125 for all CVS programs. Most projects also met criterion "I" (teaching totality of communication process that included receivers' role as well as senders'), totaling 118 points. But in the same group of criteria, "G" (using multiple forms of critical assessment, even questioning those criteria themselves) ranked second lowest, with 61 points. Lowest ranked of all characteristics found in projects was "L" (testing and evaluating results with subjects through time), with only 52 points— 11 projects evidencing none, plus five others mostly pretesting subjects and/or materials but not posttesting for valid effects of their media study programs.

Among other criteria widely found in these projects were "i" (level of written and audiovisual exposition apt for intended audiences) with 118 points; and "f" (balanced perspective of media) with 112 points. "B" (breadth, including sociopolitical and aesthetic and ethical perspectives, both atomistic and holistic) and "S" (medium's diversity included, with interactive/transactional use stressed over content/effects) each rated 108 points. Almost equal to those were "h" (project environment: factors affecting effectiveness, goals, and procedures) totaling 107 points; "b" (procedures and techniques realistic, adequate to stated goals) with 106 points; and "R" (incorporating media effects, uses and gratifications, cultural understanding, and visual literacy), 105 points. Nearly as high with 103 points was criterion "c" (principles and conclusions consonant with behavioral and educational data), and "H" (varied norms and context identified for levels of criteria) with 102 points.

Most other criteria were manifested in a number of projects with varying levels of completeness, but not at all in some of them. The range of evaluations of how CVS criteria were manifested in the 27 projects skewed towards the high end (within a "high" of 5/5+ and a "low" of 0) when overall totals were considered, even when projects lacking complete data (marked by *) were included. The mean was 95.8 (compared with highest possible mean of 135); the median lay between 96 and 97. Thirteen criteria described in preceding paragraphs ranked at the high end—rating respectively 129, 125, 123, 118, 112, 108 (2), 107, 106, 105, 103, 102, 100. Five ranked at the low end—totaling 52, 61, 71, 78 (2). The other 12 criteria fell in the 80s and 90s.

As for sets of grouped criteria, the means were:

104.    Breadth (A, B)

 80.5   Scope (C, D)

 91.8   Individuality & Values (E, F, G, H, I)

 80.    Validity/Reliability & Accuracy (J, K, L)

88.5   Cognition-Developmental (M, N)
126.   Cognition-Reasoning Skills (O, P)
100.   Pragmatics of Media Education (Q, R, S, T)
97.7   10 Specific Concrete Criteria (a–j)

As noted earlier, projects most consistently manifested characteristics of cognition-reasoning skills (O, P), with a mean of 126 out of possible 135. Clustered somewhat distantly behind were: projects' breadth of sociopolitical context and media aesthetics (A,B), with a mean of 104; pragmatics of media education where the four categories (Q–T) averaged 100; and the 10 specific concrete criteria (a–j) with 97.7. Least intensively present in the 27 projects were: validity and reliability of research bases and accuracy of data and especially testing and evaluating of project materials and results (J–L), averaging 80; and care to address stages of cognitional development in students (M–N), with a mean of 80.5.

It was apparent that most projects incorporated high levels of training in analytical observation and reasoned assessment based on factual data (generally) judged according to meaningful criteria. And they clearly stressed heuristic, inductive exploration over deductive, a priori training based on transmitting principles through lectures and reading texts and published commentaries. Most projects had participants bring their own values (and their families') along with those of their peers, in collaborative discovery, to bear on a synthesis of what they had observed and reflected on in their media experiences.

\*    .    \*    \*

These raw, quantitative data are fleshed out in the following chapter, which reviews main characteristics of CVS projects in light of the 30 criteria. That summary of their respective emphases, strengths, and highlights as well as shortcomings can help potential users determine which are most appropriate and feasible for them to consider adapting for local use.

## NOTES

1. Robert A. White, executive director, Centre for the Study of Communication and Culture in London, subsequently editor of Sage's Communication and Human Values series, Rome; in extended critique with personal correspondence to author, November 9, 1988.

# 12

## *Qualitative Review: Distinctive Characteristics of CVS Projects*

After synthesizing broad patterns of emphasis recurring among television media education projects worldwide, this chapter reviews distinctive characteristics of each project, and then categorizes them among various theoretical and research approaches.*

### GENERAL PATTERNS

Predictably, critical viewing skills curricula for lower primary grades are relatively simplified, leaning heavily on "hands-on" activities and on observing TV and responding to questions put by teachers and parents.† Even at upper grade levels, including secondary school, most projects in the United States do not directly include sophisticated aspects of media in society, such as complex social and political considerations recommended by Minkkinen (UNESCO) or Masterman (United Kingdom) or Freire (Latin America). They emphasize personal experi-

---

*Projects include the original 32, of which 23 were tabulated in the preceding chapter, plus the later 11 non-U.S. projects, of which four were analyzed in that chapter.

†This chapter employs the present tense, for purposes of readers searching CVS projects for clues and guidelines to be applied to their own circumstances. Principles and procedures endure, as do support materials, beyond periods of time reported for both terminated and continuing activities.

ence of the TV medium and subjective evaluation based on values common to American families and schoolrooms. These include some basic aesthetic/artistic considerations, the role of persuasive commercials in young people's lives, and inchoate value-formation reflecting exposure to entertainment, information, and advertising in American mass media. Projects directed to very young people emphasize the more immediate and obvious aspects of broadcast media. Although they do advert briefly to the industry's economic and legal structures (networks, stations, agencies, government), they stress images presented in characters, plots, dialogue, and through production techniques of television. This reflects their effort to match the TV project with youths' level of cognitional development.

CVS projects for primary grades tend to reflect research findings about the less-than-absolute impact of television in lives. Most consider the medium as offering useful experiences when used in moderation, with forethought, and with some reflective evaluation afterwards. They look on TV as a potential ally in the home for shared experiences by the family, especially when workshops, meetings, workbooks, and exercises were attended to by both children and parents. They stress interactionist aspects (child to TV, child among peers, and child within family context when viewing) rather than logical positivist (content analysis, with effects largely determined by the medium as stimulus-source).

Almost all projects for youngsters emphasize heuristic, a posteriori approaches to studying television. Direct TV viewing experience is coupled with exploration, usually by responding to nondirective questions. The basis for discussion is children's own perceptions, not abstract principles enunciated and applied to the medium as if for adults experienced in reflective reasoning.

Some projects negatively assess television and its impact. In the United States three of the four nongovernmental national organizations are themselves activist oriented, which their projects reflect. The National Parent-Teachers Association's project voices somewhat alarmist cautions about omnipresent TV's corrosive influence; it emphasizes therapeutic inoculation or intervention to protect youngsters exposed to the medium. The Media Action Research Center (MARC) is more balanced in its appraisal but its two projects (Growing with TV and Television Awareness Training) train viewers to protect themselves against the value system portrayed in entertainment programs and also to take active effort to influence TV decision makers.

Among non-U.S. countries, the Sydney project (parochial school system) carefully notes ambiguities of research findings and positively endorses media per se. At the same time it seeks to guide viewers toward appraising social values and even religious implications of media fare, and also towards active involvement in communicating their judgments to media leaders. CVS projects in some Latin American countries and Britain have been mounted in reaction to class-oriented, foreign-influenced (if not dominated) media systems.

Non-U.S. projects generally emphasize aesthetic and cultural understanding of the medium. In some instances—especially in Britain where Masterman's views have particular impact—they concentrate on amateur television production to learn "from within" in a concrete, skills-oriented experience how the medium functions and produces content for the TV screen. British and Latin American projects also stress social, economic, and political aspects of the medium, its messages, and its impact on society. They train citizens to participate in local media, to influence media planners and programmers and even media structures themselves. Some non-U.S. projects look to develop alternate media forms to counter established TV media systems.

Projects intended for schools are usually integrated into already existing courses rather than as separate subjects, to facilitate introducing CVS into schools' established curricula. Projects typically succeed in providing for systematic instruction by preparing curriculum outlines and sequences of materials for classroom use and at home. Various projects evidence a wide range of applied creativity, especially those supported by USOE funding. To workbooks and teachers' guides are added flash cards, hand-out sheets, transparency masters, game boards, videotapes, "cue cards" with modules of instruction for teachers, and (for later grades) filmstrips and audio recordings. They represent heavy investment of pragmatic skills in developing tools for students and teachers alike. In most instances, support materials are provided as a resource to be used selectively by teachers on-site, who are expected to adapt them for their respective charges.

Many American projects, both institutional and private, prepared extensive and highly organized printed materials supplemented in many instances by sophisticated audiovisual materials. Some corporations joined with scholar-educators in producing elaborate kits of filmstrips, sound-recordings, printed cards, and master-sheets for reproducing copies of data and exercises. Those planning to introduce critical viewing skills in their own educational context would find most of the projects' materials readily adaptable to local circumstances. But occasionally some material seems inconsistent or uneven in content and expression. (For example, lucid and specific explanations progress slowly and methodically, then suddenly insert complicated concepts, including technical terminology not truly relevant to youngsters' understanding of the medium.)

Non-U.S. materials tend to be more conceptual and less prolix, offering principles and guidelines for application by teachers without heavily structured lesson-plans and proliferation of sample hand-out materials. Projects in those countries stress training teachers—in workshops and with syllabus guidelines that include conceptual analysis along with theoretical readings and practical exercises for their students.

## PROJECTS FUNDED BY U.S. GOVERNMENT

### Southwest Educational Development Laboratory

Among projects heavily funded by the U.S. government, the Southwest Educational Development Laboratory's materials for teachers offer limited organization but high flexibility, to integrate TV study into related academic subjects in lower primary grades. They emphasize children's current use of TV, especially in the normal family context of viewing at home, as the matrix for questions and guided discussion about their experiences with the medium.

This project provides a single workbook guide for teachers that contains considerable explanatory material as well as hefty appendices with readings and extended booklists of sources. Although some explanatory material is simplistic or assumes too much and provides only limited supporting data, many references are made to "studies" and "research findings" as the basis for identifying problem areas and efforts to resolve them. Interpreting and applying this material is left to individual parents and teachers. The focus in adults' workshops—and applied to working with children—is on consciousness-raising techniques to stimulate interaction among the participants. SEDL's approach is always positive about the medium, and techniques are realistic and practical. Materials are presented succinctly. The five brief brochures ("Television: A Family Focus") and the teacher "Cue Cards" offer specific concrete activities geared to precise grade ranges. Academic skills are correlated with TV viewing skills in each exercise. For each set of material to be used in training general audiences, adults, parents, teachers, and youth leaders, SEDL clearly defines objectives, CVS skills intended, research basis, and rationale by staff. The "cue cards," boardgames, and other supporting materials (described in Part II) are used when teaching CVS to children. Focus is on aesthetic aspects and some social implications, but not on more judgmental areas.

That differs somewhat from the Sydney approach as well as from

MARC, and especially from several projects in the United Kingdom and in developing countries (Latin American and UNESCO projects), which stress social and even religious values.

## WNET/Thirteen

For upper primary grades, WNET/Thirteen's "Work-A-Text" offers perhaps the *single* most organized and usable material for teaching critical viewing skills. This is because the composite teacher's guide reproduces in half-size on every page the corresponding page from the student workbook. With this single book, a teacher has literally in hand the contextual data, explanatory guidelines, suggestions for initiating and guiding discussion, and the reproduced information and worksheets from the students' books. This publication is eminently functional for presenting a CVS program. Its shortcomings include lack of information about economic bases and their potential impact on programming, and putting off to the very end more analytical and valuational considerations of the total medium. And, as with most USOE projects, this one emphasizes harnessing students' current viewing behavior and experiences rather than prompting them to explore other kinds of programming than they regularly watch. This does avoid imposing implied judgments or values, much less proselytizing. But it assumes the status quo of mass media as an insurmountable or even acceptable given, without exploring larger social or ethical/moral questions. (Granted that these are still preteenagers, but non-U.S. media curricula regularly look to those larger issues in ways adapted to young people.)

## Far West Laboratory for Educational Research and Development and Boston University

Similarly cautious or even reticent about socially and morally significant avenues of discussion about television are the federally funded projects for secondary level and college/adults by, respectively, the Far West Laboratory for Educational Research and Development (with WGBH Educational Foundation) and by Boston University's School of Public Communication. They both prepared, with ample governmental funds of some $400,000 each, elaborately printed texts supplemented by highly detailed worksheets. Each set of materials provides instructors with considerable background information, factual data, guidelines for questions and discussion, and suggestions for activities and projects. They are highly organized and complete. The Far West Lab offers the most immediately usable sets of published materials among projects studied. Boston University's printed texts and workbooks are also instantly applicable in classrooms by instructors. Both projects present many simulations, role-playing, and other participatory activities to engage students in raising consciousness (not necessarily conscience) about television in their lives.

Among the four federally-funded projects, Boston's texts for advanced students and adults most related to social, economic, and even ethical implications of television in society. These issue-oriented topics are presented objectively and neutrally, to prompt students to reflect about them apart from a priori judgments. But if there is an implied stance in the materials, it is one of cautious acceptance and even optimism rather than hostility to the medium and its effects. Regrettably, its published revised text deleted the extensive excerpts from readings that in the original draft had provided helpful background information and interpretations and even somewhat value-oriented analyses of media.

An important consideration in the first two (SEDL and WNET) was the expectation that CVS materials developed by them would be integrated into existing courses, often used as instruments for supporting other traditional skills such as reading and the humanities generally. They did not foresee much possibility for CVS as an independent coherent part of the formal curriculum. Anderson and Ploghoft's experimental projects in several school districts led them to support critical television viewing as an integral part of the language arts and social studies curriculum.

The latter two (Far West and Boston University) respectively emphasized workshops for administrators and sessions for adults—parents and teachers—as effective means to introduce CVS into educational structures. Boston judged that long-lasting effects on children and even on media producers would come only through adult participation in the entire process. This reflects some of Don Agostino's and James Anderson's cautions at the 1979 conference in Philadelphia: The structural/administrative and political/economic realities—of school systems and of mass media—to a large extent will much determine whether, how, and with what effectiveness critical viewing skills are introduced into schools and gradually have impact on the mainstream of television experience. Similarly, Eddie Dick of Scotland in the late 1980s referred to the "bureaucratic/political" aspects of introducing long-term media studies into educational institutions.

All four CVS projects stress harnessing viewers' current habitual viewing patterns, with little attention to reaching out to new TV experiences by watching other kinds of programs. Although there is sound pedagogical purpose in helping students reflectively analyze their present media diet (which already interests them), it limits their perspective and inhibits growing to new levels of perception from first-hand experience. Edgar Dale's dictum about mass media appreciation one third of a century ago is relevant, without necessarily implying elitism: "Good taste comes from tasting good things."

## SCHOOL DISTRICTS

### Idaho Falls; Eugene, Oregon; East Syracuse, New York

In this report, CVS projects developed for comprehensive school jurisdictions include three school districts that collaborated with scholar-researchers Anderson and Ploghoft. The programs predictably encompass the philosophy, goals, and procedures of those collaborating pioneers. They emphasize nondirective, inductive experience by school children, centering on their interaction with the TV medium in their own homes. The family context was critical to the success of the projects.

Perhaps the best organized for systematic application progressively through four lower grades was *Idaho Falls School District #91*. The teachers' guides alone provide most support material needed, including pages able to serve as masters for reproducing all hand-out items. A strength of the Idaho Falls project is that all material, including mastersheets for photocopying or making overhead transparencies, are systematically provided in each of the large teachers guides, so no other materials (except the optional video- and audiotapes) are needed to present the CVS project locally. However, the guides provide only brief background information for teachers, with little or no supporting evidence or discussion, as noted earlier. Without more introductory data—in the form of workshops or substantive orientation sessions— the project's integrity relies heavily on the competence and prior research of the academic consultants who assisted in developing it. Those implementing the project must have confidence in its consultants and creators. Unless they obtain a copy of Anderson and Ploghoft's books, teachers will have limited information to guide them when presenting CVS activity. (Of course, those consultants have published widely, making available much conceptual and factual material for those seeking it.)

Idaho Falls served as paradigm for the two other projects. All three seek to integrate media skills activities into preexisting traditional curricular subject areas, partly for administrative feasibility. They are strong in relating media literacy modules within courses and between courses and different years of schooling.

## New York City Board of Education

The school system in New York City had prepared only a prototype curriculum with modest, even meager, resource materials suggested in the succinct proposal. Although generally even-handed, source material tended to be negative about the medium's role and impact in society.

## Catholic Education Office, Sydney

The extensive and well-established curriculum in the Catholic schools of Sydney, Australia, is well developed. The Catholic Education Office in Sydney takes an active, positive stance vis-à-vis media. That administrative support throughout the system is a distinctive mark of the project (and it reflects similar effective endorsement of a Media Studies Centre by the secular Education Department in New South Wales). It looks to media education to help train youths to become active, discriminating users of broadcast, film, and print media through attempting to support those media's favorable characteristics while avoiding "less good" aspects. Media education from Grades 1 to 12 depends on parents and teachers as crucial to any effective, integrated use of media in home or school. The Sydney project presents a balanced rationale for such study, explicitly based on extensive sound research published in recent decades. The even-handed analysis notes modest, ambiguous causal relation between television and effects on viewers. But it does not overlook the medium's influence and impact on attitudes and behavior; it assumes by common sense that media—in concert with other social agents of family, school, peers, and church—have some effect on viewers, especially young people. The project prepared printed booklets and audiovisual items for teachers and parents. Those materials provide purposes and structured guidelines, as well as a plethora of specific questions and concrete activities suggested for children.

Media education is shown to relate to many traditional academic disciplines, partly because a separate course in media study would be difficult to squeeze into present curricula. Although their questionnaire response (1981) indicated exclusively "deductive" teaching in the Sydney parochial school curriculum, that is more the case only with background information provided to teachers and parents. The material and recommended procedures for teaching children is heavily or almost solely inductive—through asking questions, guiding discussion, prompting reflection, and assigning tasks for first-hand experience and individual perceptions. Religious characteristics are seldom introduced; they are broadly Christian except when referring to major Roman Catholic documents about media as sources of guidance. The value system implied is similar to most other media study programs, reflecting concern for individuality, interpersonal and social sensitivity, and awareness of and involvement in social processes.

## Western Australia, Ministry of Education

Different educational systems in various Australian states each developed media education syllabi, reflecting differing philosophies, purposes, and emphases. Western Australia's key objective is to foster literacy in the broadest sense. Media studies are generally dominated by television, especially at senior level. They encompass culture, languages, economic factors in mass media, and audiences' drawing meaning from media messages via codes, conventions and social implications of media. This program promotes active viewers. It eschews mere inoculation in favor of cultural, critical analysis. It analyzes values, including issues and topics related to media images of Australia.

The media education program promotes exercises but cautions against skills as ends in themselves. It requires only limited audiovisual facilities for media studies, thus differing from some projects in the United Kingdom such as Masterman's, grounding CVS studies in applied media production.

Western Australia integrates media studies into existing courses, but at upper levels introduces some separate media courses. Curricular structures for media study are closely similar to Scotland's, after which they patterned themselves.

The Ministry prepared teachers' guides with listings of media resource materials, including tips for classroom activities. Limited in detail, support material urges flexibility by on-site teachers who are to apply as appropriate to students and circumstances. The project stresses students' creative, critical thinking regarding media, with some guidance but not directed or limited by teachers. It proposes many controverted topics for classroom analysis. To be effective this plan requires creative teachers adept at open discussion. The curriculum covers topics of cultural images, social controls, and media structures; but it does not promote activist responses to mass media.

# PROJECTS BY INDIVIDUALS: COLLABORATIVE AND INDIVIDUAL

Independent of institutionally structured forms of CVS programs are individual persons (often associated with education) and private companies. The individuals pioneered experimental and research foundation for their work; the companies professionally manufactured and marketed support materials for teaching critical viewing skills.

In the United States, Aimee Dorr and Dorothy and Jerome Singer conducted formal laboratory and field research in the process of developing CVS activities. Rosemary Potter drew on others' research, using first-hand teaching experience to apply media literacy skills in her own elementary classroom. Both the Singers and Potter subsequently produced manuals and workbooks for teaching media study.

*Aimee Dorr* and her associates confirmed effective results of teaching media literacy to youngsters and adults; but their limited research did not predict impact on subjects' future use of TV. The scope of her earlier work (in this report's limited review*) includes only entertainment programming; and sessions with youthful subject were conducted a total of 6 hours.

The *Singers* fused concern about potential media impact on youth with their first-hand field research and developed a balanced approach to guiding children's use of television. They reflect social concern in their introductory analysis of media's influence in contemporary society. Their research findings and subsequent CVS curriculum look to parental habits of television viewing and their role in the domestic use of TV as the best predictors of how youngsters use and respond to the medium. Limited experimental applications of their curriculum demonstrated that children could be taught elements of critical viewing, including recognition of program types and fantasy as well as commercials. These can be taught within traditional disciplines, strengthening their skills in reading and writing as well as in elementary critical thinking. Their "values" are similar to those of other curricular proponents: socio-cultural and aesthetic integrity of cognitive experience, to avoid the distortions and blandishments of television. But moral implications are not explicitly explored, although alluded to.

They employed an arsenal of available research to establish their well funded projects with youngsters. Their field study, under normal television viewing conditions, underscored the trans- or interactional

---

*Dr. Dorr, as well as the Drs. Singers, continued to conduct related research throughout the 1980s; reports of their project design and findings can be consulted in major journals.

context of that viewing experience as central to children's use and understanding of TV. The eight lessons (totaling about 6 hours) over 4 weeks relate to viewing and discussion at home, mediated by parents. The Singers' two books provide research premises, rationale, and complete exercises with directions for carrying out similar media study programs. They include almost all essential elements for critical viewing skills listed among the 30 criteria in chapter 11. Their materials are complete, clear, balanced, and offer guidelines and concrete material to conduct media sessions for children up to age 10.

*Rosemary Potter,* drawing on her individualized classroom experiences with media study, wrote syndicated articles about her activities, and collaborated with others to produce elaborate audio-visual kits for national distribution. Her several books and multimedia kits are variously intended for work with primary and secondary school children. Her early premise was that TV, despite having little merit, is widely popular and can serve as an enticing tool for teaching traditional skills of reading and critical thinking. Gradually that negative approach grew into more positive study of television's form and content, its social implications, and ways to respond effectively (selective viewing, communicating with media executives).

Her many and well worked out materials in the kits offer flexibility for wide-ranging adaptation by teachers and parents; they are not rigidly ordered. In her later materials, including professionally produced filmstrips, soundtracks, flashcards, hand-out sheets, and teacher's guides, data about the broadcasting industry are complete and accurate. But at times the material is overly technical in detail, especially if the goal is merely to support reading and other skills rather than comprehension of the medium itself. The material indirectly refers to larger social issues involving TV and society, but that is not its focus. Published materials in the kits acknowledge the status quo of TV as a given, looking more to the viewer's positive reactive role in using it wisely—while continuing to exploit TV as a handy and effective means for developing other non-media skills. Guidelines for teachers stress the need to let children observe and respond for themselves, using their comments about personal TV experience as the basis for class discussion; teachers are cautioned not to be judgmental but rather to "be a learner." Teachers with interest and initiative will find these handsomely boxed materials a cornucopia of options for introducing TV critical viewing skills into their classrooms.

## NATIONAL ORGANIZATIONS (NONGOVERNMENTAL)

A number of scattered organizations throughout the decades pioneered monitoring media content and alerting audiences to listen/view selectively. They also promoted forwarding criticism to leaders in media and government through correspondence and participation in activist groups. Generally the organizations served as self-appointed "watch-dogs," often assessing media programming and distributing evaluation lists in newsletters to members. Clearly these groups are "value oriented," emphasizing critical analysis of programs, and directed to personal action (in avoiding programs and in contacting media organizations). Although initially concerned with TV's depiction of crime and violence, they later added elements related to sex.

The *National Association for Better Radio and Television* stands out as the prime representative of such activities. It was highly critical of some media content and was vocal, sometimes strident, in its efforts.

The *American Council for Better Broadcasts* avoided that adversarial role, instead promoting programs of higher quality. It enlisted people across the country to submit their personal judgments about media fare, then published results of that poll—identifying only the positive choices from its pluralistic constituency. It sought not media reform but rather audiences' recognition of personally acceptable programs already available, encouraging them to tune in those broadcasts. The organization urged that the *process* of critical viewing—not predetermined structures or conclusions—be introduced into classrooms. That process was to depend not on teachers inculcating lists or criteria but rather on interchange among students and teachers to tap varying tastes and judgments among entire groups who together developed guidelines and assessments of media. Most ACBB activities were communicated in a bi-monthly newsletter to members. The organization produced no formal support materials for media study.

The *National Congress of Parents and Teachers (National PTA)*, to the kinds of activities described earlier, added national "hearings" about negative impact of media. It published selective "findings" from those multiple sessions. It later moved from critical attack to training enlightened users of media by mounting a CVS program. The purpose was inoculation—to limit negative effects of TV on viewers. The PTA developed curricula for elementary and high school levels, which were not fully completed and distributed. They sought to remain neutral about television. Study guides, worksheets, and some videotaped material were to acquaint students with most of the usual elements in critical viewing: production, industry structure, content and form of programs, characterizations, and advertising. A "pilot" experimental workbook about special effects, intended for early grades, offered exercises about techniques; but it was not subsequently distributed. A second curriculum on the theme of "family awareness" prepares lessons for lower primary grades, with lengthy teacher's manuals and exercise sheets. It has children compare their own families with those depicted by TV. One sixth of the lessons include brief information about how television operates. This curriculum does not explore the nature of the medium or the many larger issues of TV in society.

The next two groups are associated with specifically religious organizations, one a mainline Protestant coalition and the other Roman Catholic. Religious values alluded to are broad Christian ones rather than sectarian. Although both were value-oriented, a specifically religious perspective was central only to MARC's "Growing with Television" project.

*Media Action Research Center (MARC)* produced two major curricula that were carefully developed and widely used. MARC marshalled its national constituency to present workshops to teachers and parents so they could relay principles of media analysis to young people. Teachers desiring better understanding of factors in media structure, content, research, impact on society, and interaction with viewers might find illuminating as well as motivating the extensive compilation of reprints in *Television-Awareness-Training* (or T-A-T). That organization's approach is assertive and exhortatory as well as valuative, with a priori principles involving value-systems. MARC's strong behavioral orientation—committed to changing selves and affecting broadcast structures—reflects something of the European/Latin American posture opposed to "the monolithic system" of competitive (read "capitalistic") free enterprise.

T-A-T relies heavily on its 280-page *Viewer's Guide* of analysis, readings, and exercises. The book treats most CVS topics, often in a questioning and even critical way. Some social and personal topics such as sex and TV are presented in great detail, extremely frankly but sensitively. The lengthy reprints represent a range of views, the majority of them negative about television's role and impact. Nevertheless, T-A-T prompts individuals to arrive at their own assessment after reviewing the materials and reflecting about their own exposure to the medium. This MARC project urges viewers to make individual evaluations by drawing on their respective beliefs and value-systems. The lengthy readings and some of the lesson material lean, however, more to deductive exercise from stated principles and comments. The book's lessons and readings are not structured for systematic use in formal educational settings. They are meant to be integrated as appropriate in various contexts, primarily in the home and also in classrooms and church meetings. A feature of the material is repeated suggestions about how viewers can take an active stance not only in revising their own media habits but also in communicating their criticism to broadcasters and governmental agencies either personally or through consumer organizations. Concluding essays stress Christianity as the source of criteria for evaluating television programming and its impact.

That theme is taken up in a direct way in the second MARC project, *Growing with Television: A Study of Biblical Values and the Television Experience.* It is intended for use in churches, schools, and organizations. This sophisticated, well organized set of printed and audio-visual materials is directed to five levels covering most ages. Although the sequence of topics is similar for all levels, the supporting information (such as excerpts from readings, and technical information about media structures) is progressively more detailed and complex at the latter three levels. It orchestrates a wide range of very specific classroom procedures and activities—all optional, to be applied as appropriate—in the series of lesson plans and supporting materials. Home viewing is an integral part of the process that includes group discussion. This MARC project stresses criteria for Christian living based on belief drawn from scripture, and systematically compares Biblical values to what television portrays. The project harnesses TV as a vehicle for assessing values in individuals' lives—Biblical versus secular (mediated by TV). But it acknowledges television's positive contributions as well as negative effects. Its perspective and judgments are based on research literature. The project promotes students' learning through personal experience, including verbalizing their reactions and personal assessments. To this end, it urges viewers to communicate their favorable and critical comments to broadcasters; but it does not suggest boycotts or other strategies for influencing media. The essence of *Growing with Television* is personal values-clarification, using television as a counter-source to the Bible; it does not focus on the medium's intrinsic aesthetics and cultural elements for their own sake.

The *U.S. Catholic Conference* looks more directly to television as such, with less specific religious orientation, despite the title of its "The Media Mirror: A Study Guide on Christian Values and Television." Like MARC's project, it is neither anti- nor pro-television. But it differs in exploring the nature of the medium and its programming. It reflects the range of common media literacy topics. A slim (even skeletal) teacher's guide and three levels of exercise workbooks (middle and late primary, and secondary school) are structured for a full semester unit integrated into traditional classroom subjects. This teacher's guide offers little of the precise and helpful detail for classroom use that MARC's "Growing with Television" provides; but it does list hundreds of cross-references to scripture passages, and religious literature related to TV topics in the ten sessions. Most questions for analysis are open-ended, nondirective. This Catholic project reflects little of the sense of urgency for systematic change in broadcasting found in

CVS programs by the Protestant churches' MARC and by the National PTA.

## PRIVATE COMPANIES: UNITED STATES, UNITED KINGDOM

Privately owned corporations collaborated with individuals or teams of scholar-teachers to prepare elaborate kits or detailed books for teaching critical viewing skills. Effective marketing—including promotion and distribution—ensured wide use of these sophisticated teaching aids that often include professional audiovisual components. *The Learning Seed Company* produced several products related to media—including one closely following CVS lines, "Television & Values: An Exploration of the Values, Messages, & Impact of Television." It was designed for one or two intensive weeks of TV study, or else selective use "for a day or a week" at a time. More even than PTA or MARC, it strikes out at perceived weaknesses and excesses of television. It acknowledged that it presents "not a balanced or unbiased attempt to evaluate the effect on human values" but rather serves as a devil's advocate to stimulate young viewers' perceptions, data gathering, and evaluation. Supporting material quoted from the literature tends to be negative and pessimistic about people's misuse of the enticing, exploitative medium. But the text does acknowledge the tentative nature of research findings about media effects. A highly professional film-strip with audiocassette soundtrack accompany printed cards of fact-finding exercises and for role-playing in a mock court trial of the medium. Two massive books by other publishers complete the kit. A directory of sponsoring advertisers offers specific information for relaying criticism to financial supporters of programs. The *TV Action Book* is a 128-page manual for consumer activism, offering detailed guidance for enlisting federal agencies in the pursuit of better programming. It includes excerpts from mostly negative commentaries about TV; only one chapter closely parallels typical CVS topics.

Many other companies produce isolated materials related to critical viewing skills. Their work is usually highly professional and forwards the purposes of CVS—helping viewers understand the medium better and use it selectively with reflective analysis. Often these materials are used widely by schools to augment classroom instruction. But they are not complete, coherent programs in themselves nor integrated into formal education or systematic instruction within national organizations.

For example, *Television Learning, Ltd.* packaged a one-year teaching plan about TV aesthetics. It offers a 30-minute videotape and a text, *Centering Television,* which have been used in seven of the United States and in Canada.

National broadcast networks cooperated with the nonprofit organization *Prime Time School Television* in periodically distributing to schools up to hundreds of thousands of handsome guides featuring lengthy analyses of major TV programs. They also cooperate with educators in preparing printed and videotaped material designed to sensitize young people to the medium, particularly through advance information and scripts for scheduled programs—linked to widespread projects to enhance youngsters' reading experience. Multi-station owner *Capital Cities Communications* pioneered literacy-oriented script distribution. Workshops sometimes accompanied the printed materials, as with *Teachers Guide to Television* and its *Parent Participation TV Workshops* supported by NBC. They expanded to include 21 statewide projects and hundreds of individual communities and school systems. Each U.S. commercial network—the *American Broadcasting Company, CBS* (formerly Columbia Broadcasting System), and the *National Broadcasting Company*—fund occasional viewer guides distributed nationally to schools prior to their respective programs, often as part of school literacy programs. ABC also underwrote seven 12-minute videotapes used in conjunction with the Singers' media skills research projects and their resulting teacher's manual.

All such activities seek to sensitize viewers to their media experience: to view programs selectively, to reflect about what they see and hear—including aesthetic and systemic aspects of mass media as art and industry—and to assess that experience. The industry-supported projects regularly advocate youngsters viewing with their parents who can prompt children to more careful perception and critical thinking about what they view. Subsequent testing documented considerable success in many aspects of some projects.

Noncommercial station *WQED* in Pittsburgh offered a workshop for teachers and adults, promoting understanding and skills similar to other CVS projects on which it was based. It included many kinds of support materials, both printed and audio-visual.

In the United Kingdom, *Independent Broadcasting Authority* and the *Independent Television Companies* collaborated with educational advisors in preparing six series of 21 programs along with a 152-page teacher's book. Attractive booklets for students provide supplementary material, partly on critical study of all mass media—emphasizing how media (mis-)portray portions of society. Open-ended questions elicit students' thoughtful reactions to their own media experience. Readings offer data and commentary about how media operate and affect society. Various themes study social interaction and mass mediation of perceptions and values.

## INSTITUTION-RELATED CVS PROGRAMS (NON-UNITED STATES)

Many projects in the United Kingdom and continental Europe have been mounted by individuals or by government-related offices but often without fully integrated, long-term support by educational institutions. Critical viewing skills projects in Latin America countries have been offered, often by church-related organizations.

### United Kingdom

The short-term project by an instructor in *Powys* county, Wales, was funded by the Schools Council of Great Britain and the Powys Education Committee. It emphasized producing amateur TV programs to learn how the medium works, to objectify and demystify it and as a basis for discussing program form and content. Labeled a "visual literacy" program, it avoided the common CVS elements of "inoculating" students from potentially harmful aspects of TV. It rejected analyzing images and hidden meanings of purported sociopolitico-economic significance (differing from the approach by Masterman and others in Britain).

*Clwyd* county's Media Studies Unit provides a thoughtful application of broadly scoped media study, with a strong component of television. The range of topic areas well represents major aspects of media study and various "theoretical" perspectives. It builds explicitly on extensive research findings and literature as well as others' experiences. The project was somewhat limited in number of teacher-participants and the extent to which it was implemented throughout the county.

Developers of the media program collaborated with an institution of higher education as they systematically planned and organized secondary and then primary school media studies curricula. The project's strength came from working closely with major administrators at local schools. By gaining their effective support, the project was able to recruit teachers and get their schedules modified, including released time for media training. It also succeeded in introducing media education into the curriculum. Their experience led them to prefer integrating media studies into other courses, rather than to try to develop individual media courses to be inserted into the curriculum, with teachers set apart for such.

The project emphasized teacher training periods as important to provide competent as well as enthusiastic instruction. But they avoided preparing detailed materials such as handout sheets, transparencies, and examination questions, lest teachers simply use them instead of creating their own materials directly suited to their own students and class levels. Still, the project did generate a moderate amount of support materials within a limited budget.

Another distinctive feature was a thorough outside analysis of the project's principles, procedures, pedagogy, and materials. That review describes many pragmatic "oughts" and "shoulds" in light of the several-year pilot experience—providing tips and concrete caveats to others.

An instructor at *Mayfield School* in southwest London designed a somewhat more comprehensive curriculum that involved common CVS elements. His 2-year curriculum offered practical application of production skills to creating programs as central to media study, to liberate people from hidden control through media. It also included study of media structures as well as images and cultural impact of programming.

The *Southern Arts Association in Winchester,* Hampshire, through its Media Arts Lab resource center stressed hands-on production skills for the practical purpose of preparing programs for the community cable system. Sustained funding through a half decade helped large numbers of all ages to learn in formal courses about producing alternative program content and about evaluating media content, including media structures and social effects. They directed no effort to contacting or influencing media leaders. Nor did they use workbooks or examinations.

Far more advanced and organized than these three projects was the *Scottish Film Council's* many forms of media study for most grade levels. Their planned curriculum embraced all major elements of CVS study. Theirs most resembles the broadly developed plans of major U.S. projects. As in other U.K. projects, emphasis is on practical production of media product. One shortcoming is relegating to adult education the study of media information (news and its relation to reality) and how media serve as resources for education and cultural enrichment throughout life. Although acknowledging as temporarily expedient the fusion of media study with existing school subjects, it looks to eventually establishing independent media study courses. Despite not being fully implemented, this proposal forcibly charted a path for comprehensive media study in formal education in Scotland.

The *Media Education Development Project* had a pragmatic organizational purpose: to develop curricula, train teachers, prepare teaching materials, disseminate information, and address administrative (bureaucratic-political) issues.

While emphasizing the inductive approach, it equally proposes technical skills as well as abstract theory. Learning by "doing" is based on viewing TV/media. It focuses on media as processes amid social, cultural, and economic contexts. It offers practical advice, pragmatic tips and recommendations for effectively conducting media study classes. Class sessions are intended to be integrated into other disciplines, but discrete courses are also possible.

The *Media Education Research Project* is not itself a CVS project but rather an exhaustive, specific analysis of the status of media studies in Scotland. It offers concrete instances, surveying not broadly but in depth selected case studies in schools. Yet the author disclaims the possibility of conclusions or even recommendations partly because of the study design and partly due to the continually shifting scene of media education.

The report reflects limited attention to TV medium, more to the several other mass media. It explores in great detail important aspects to be assessed when planning and evaluating media education programs. Very straightforward, with little rhetoric or promotional attitude, it searches for data and observable results (reportable by interviewees among faculty and administrators) demonstrating whether media education is effective. Teachers and media planners would find this a dispassionate, detailed review of major aspects of teaching media studies.

Among its candid, practical observations it finds a need for more central organization of media studies in each school, and the need for more administrative support and leadership. Also lacking were coordination among and between schools and other institutions. It observes that the traditional established curriculum resists "intrusion" of media study even when integrated into other courses, but especially when introduced as separate courses. The report notes that more attention must be given to students' cognitive stages. Teachers require more skill in inductive approaches, and in guiding students to analytical understanding of principles behind applied exercises.

### France and the Netherlands

Whereas various forms of media education in Europe for many decades explored aesthetic-cultural characteristics of media, especially film, only two CVS-related projects are analyzed in this book—based on availability of returned survey data.

The French government mounted *Formation Du Jeune Télespectateur Actif* in many cities to interrelate media study with formal education. This national project involves children throughout the 12 years of schooling and also in their homes. There were 1,000 adult participants who were to relay to 24,000 students the result of their 10-day media study programs. Although highly structured administratively, this does not have a formal curriculum; rather, it provides readings, guides, and audiovisual support materials for the workshop sessions. It sought to coordinate parents' involvement with formal instruction. Goals include most of the major ones for CVS except for "activist" forms of contacting media leaders or joining organizations to influence media content.

In Amsterdam, *Stichting Audiovisuele Vorming*'s less complex project for secondary school students was similar to that in Powys, Wales. It stressed technical production of amateur programs as the means to learn how media work, and partly as the object of analysis as a micromodel of professional media and their depicting of reality. Artistic aspects of media's form and content constitute most of this effort. It eschews most other elements common to CVS study (personal use of TV, economic structures and relations to government, impact on cognitive growth, advertising, or consumer roles). Thus its impact is narrow.

## Canada: Ontario

The Ministry of Education distributed the comprehensive, practical workbook *Media Literacy Resource Guide* to most levels of teaching in the province. It covers a wide range of mass, popular media. Its breadth and pragmatic, lucid exercises and explanations are based on essential and recent research and theoretical investigation reported in the literature. It lacks only depth in treating each of the many media-related topics. It is balanced in its perspective, and flexible—accommodating various levels and stages of cognitive growth, to be applied by teachers on the local scene. And it stresses the need for objective, balanced analysis of media—neither cynically negative nor naively accepting. Although not elaborating conceptual foundations, it implies them and provides bibliographical references for other source materials. Two distinctive strengths are incorporating at all points traditional and contemporary key theoretical materials and concepts in education and media literacy studies, while also providing clear, practical, exercises for students' individualized heuristic investigation of media. A weakness is that it relies on individual teachers' interest and instinctive ability to interpret and apply the manual's material, without the advantage of any special study or teacher training.

## LATIN AMERICA

Five projects in four countries were developed among social groupings: families, schools, and special social groups. They seek to improve family relationships within the home, understanding of media messages, and active involvement in producing media materials. Usually their long-term goal is not only to affect but also to transform mass media systems to respond to the needs of society's poor and disenfranchised. The diversity of contexts in different countries and the breadth of application (through 12 years of schools, or to urban and rural poor plus young people, etc.) make it difficult to focus the projects. Little systematic study of short- or long-term effects of media education had been conducted by the end of the 1980s. But observers cited the need for better planning and coordination, and for more training of teachers.

The *Latin American Communication Pedagogy Institute* (ILPEC) in Costa Rica focuses on children in the family setting, emphasizing not so much television appreciation but TV as a catalyst for interrelationships and communication among family members. The project is concerned not with time spent viewing nor even content, but rather with TV as a vehicle for promoting family discussion. It emphasizes family members' responsibility to use the medium positively. It stresses semiotics—signs and images—over semantic meanings to protect viewers from anonymous "massification" and from being manipulated by media. The pedagogy involves viewing programs, re-viewing them if possible, and then discussing them. Parents are trained apart from children whose activities are directed more to media skills. The project's expectations seem optimistic despite short-term, fairly unsophisticated methodology.

*Plan DENI* is carried out in seven Latin American countries. It involves study of film and TV "language" coupled with making films and related· audio-visual products. Originally directed to primary schools, Plan DENI in Uruguay has presented a media course for parents since 1983. The course is split between sociocultural theoretical aspects of TV, plus semiotics as background to analyze concrete TV presentations. Recordings and booklets provide the basis for discussion guided by coordinators.

*Brazilian Social Communications Union* (UCBC) is concerned with liberating the poor and oppressed by working among social groupings. In the 1970s, it originally employed North American "Television Awareness Training" materials. Later it moved away from the analytical, critical approach to more active involvement in media. Initially directed to teachers and leaders in church and society, after 1982 it shifted its activity to poor rural groups. Meetings and seminars explore "liberation communication" theory, looking on television as a system fostering mass culture, manipulating under-classes for the benefit of media industries—often dominated by foreign interests. From that counter-culture analysis, it seeks to develop alternate media products affecting the process of mass mediation in the country.

The *Centre of Cultural and Artistic Enquiry and Expression* in Chile since 1981 has trained leaders and produced a series of workbooks to encourage active reception of television. It concentrates on several kinds of groups: students, young persons, urban women, and rural residents. Those groups are taught to understand TV's cultural biases, then to demand media programs more suited to their real needs. Perceptions about TV's content and hidden motives are to be sharpened by group discussion and simulation games.

The *Robert Bellarmino Educational Foundation* works with social groups in Chile, to ameliorate the status of the poor. It complements its media study book for primary and secondary schools (1985) with teacher-training workshops. Although cautiously acknowledging media's potentially positive role in society, it seeks to help viewers learn media's manipulations. It offers structured study analyzing TV's content and role in society, plus hands-on production of media materials. Its broad curriculum depends on creative implementation by individual teachers at various school levels. And it emphasizes an evolving process of group exercises rather than lectures and a priori principles.

The *Univérsidad de Playa Ancha de Ciencias de la Educacion* in Chile looks to trained teachers specializing in media studies for long-term effectiveness. It has developed projects and courses to train teachers—toward academic degrees in education and as in-service workshops. They emphasize integrating media study into traditional academic subjects rather than introducing new courses dedicated to media education. Training includes conceptual foundations from a range of theoretical perspectives, plus applied exercises and also evaluation of methods and materials. They include active media involvement among their CVS goals. Conferences, booklets, workshops, as well as curricula and modules of instruction all contribute to helping teachers bring critical viewing skills to classrooms. They promote out-of-school support for media studies, urging that parents also be exposed to media education.

## Worldwide: UNDA-UNESCO

This loosely confederated effort to apply Minkkinen's theoretical curriculum of media study was organized by UNDA (international Catho-

lic association for broadcasting) in very limited experimental projects
in 10 mostly developing countries of the so-called Third World. The
succinct (even telegraphic) text attempts to touch on major CVS topics,
including viewers' role as citizens and potential producers as well as
consumers of media (treated briefly). Despite the lack of technical
equipment at many sites, the projects include practical media skills,
often through stimulation exercises.

Many extrinsic circumstances as well as internal problems limited
some projects' success. They were directed to wide age-ranges among
participants in the various countries, and were variously parts of formal courses or extracurricular or community exercises. Subsequent
critiques commented as much on the strengths and weaknesses of
Minkkinen's conceptual model as on those of the text and projects.

*To Sum Up.*    Many of the projects described in this international non-
U.S. section suffered from limited data or support and source materials, from narrow focus or partial coverage of the broad range of
important CVS topics. But they did evince orchestrated efforts in some
cases, especially in Scotland and Canada and in the geographically
scattered activities undertaken by UNDA/UNESCO.

*       *       *

By way of synthesis, Table 12.1 outlines salient features of media
literacy projects related to critical viewing skills which are reviewed in
this book. Those wishing to identify projects conducted at specific *sites*
similar to their own, can note which ones were intended for school
classrooms, or to be applied in homes, or else conducted by organizations or by church groups, or in workshops. Various CVS projects' *targeted users* are listed as: children (preschoolers), students in primary
and/or secondary grades or college, adults (as individuals), parents,
and teachers. The final column in the table recapitulates premises and
featured emphases in the CVS programs.

Although most projects are developed for use in schools, many of the
materials prepared for teachers can be adapted by parents for use in
the home. The intended age of participants in each school project is
indicated by the range of grades listed. In many instances, materials
have been prepared for workshops with teachers and adults who are
parents, who in turn present CVS principles and activities to their
students and children. That two-step process results occasionally in
only seeming discrepancies between "sites" and "targeted users."

Equally important to those exploring potential media literacy projects are varying *premises and featured emphases*. Those characteristics

TABLE 12.1
Major CVS Projects: Sites, Targeted Users, Premises

| A. Projects Funded by U.S. Government | Site | Targeted Users | Premises & Featured Emphasis |
|---|---|---|---|
| 1. Southwest Educ'l. Dev. Lab. (Grades K–5) | SHO | Sp P | Mediation/protectionist (Material directed primary to P, T) |
| 2. WNET/Thirteen, N.Y. (Grades 6–8) | SH W | Sp A T | Critical thinking/skills, artistic (Material directed to T, Leaders) |
| 3. Far West Lab (Grades 9–12) | S W | S s PT | Critical thinking, related cognate areas |
| 4. Boston Univ. (Post-secondary & adults) | O W | S u PT | Understanding media structure/processes; accept status quo + note social impact |
| **B. School Districts** | | | |
| 5. Idaho Falls (Grades 3–6) | SH | S s PT | Analytical, imteractionist (in home), recognize implied values in media |
| 6. Eugene, Oregon (Grades 4–12) | S | Sps T | Integrated into other courses |
| 6a East Syracuse, N.Y. (Grades 6–12) | S | Sps T | Integrated into other courses |
| 7. N.Y. City Board of Education (Grades K–9) | S | Sp T | Media structure/processes; protectionist |
| 8. Cath. Educ. Office, Sydney (Grades K–12) | SH C | Sps APT | Moralistic values, social influence, some activism |
| #a. Ministry of Education, W. Australia | S | Sps | Broad literacy, socioeconomic contexts of media; *vs.* inoculation |
| **C. Projects by Individuals** | | | |
| 9. A. Dorr, Harvard/USC (Primary/secondary) | S C | Sps A | Demythologize; modify TV's effects; reduce TV's availability to children |
| 10. D. & J.Singer, Yale/ABC (Grades K–6) | SH C | Sp P | Transactional, interventionist; books on parents' role in child's TV viewing |
| 11. R.L. Potter, Pinella C'y, Flo. (Grades 1–12) | S | Sps T | Diversionary: TV as tool for learning other disciplines; kits, books, A–V |
| **D. National Organizations (Non-Gov.), U.S.** | | | |
| 12. Congress of Parents/Teachers: Nat'l PTA | S | Sp T | Initially adversary to TV; later TV as aid to analyzing family relationships |
| 13. MARC: Television Awareness Training | W | PT | Moralistic, personal value-oriented; deductive, some call to social action |

(*continued*)

TABLE 12.1 (*Continued*)

*D. National Organizations (Non-Gov.), U.S.*

| | | | | | | |
|---|---|---|---|---|---|---|
| 14. MARC: Growing with Television | C | | Sps | A | T | Bible-related analysis; protectionist, but positive perspective re TV |
| 15. U.S. Catholic Conference: The Media Mirror | S | | Sps | | T | Social-cultural analysis; "realistic caution" but TV medium as business & art |

*E. Private Companies, U.S., U.K.*

| | | | | | | |
|---|---|---|---|---|---|---|
| 16. The Learning Seed Co. | S | | Sps | | | Protectionist; negative re TV in society, promotes reactionary consumer activism |
| 16a Prime Time School Television | S | | Sps | | T | Cultural, aesthetic appreciation of TV |
| 16b TIO: Teacher's Guide to Television | S | | | | T | Cultural, aesthetic appreciation of TV |
| 16c Parent Participation Workshops/NBC | H | W | | | P | Mediation, transactional; parents role with child's TV viewing |
| 16d Capital Cities Communication | S | | Sps | | | Learn to read with TV scripts & viewing |
| 16e CBS Inc. | S | | Sps | | | |
| 16f NBC | SH | | | | PT | Learn to read with TV scripts & viewing + program appreciation (aesthetics) |
| 16g ABC | S O | | Sps | | | |
| 16h WQED, Pittsburgh | | W | | A | T | |
| 16i IBA/ITV (U.K.) | S | | | | T | Analyze programs, social context |

*Institution-Related Programs (Non-U.S.)*

| | | | | | | |
|---|---|---|---|---|---|---|
| 17. Powys Educ'n. Comm. | S | | Sps | | | Pragmatic: produce programs |
| #b Clwyd Media Studies Unit | S | | Spsu | | T | Certified teacher training |
| 18. Mayfield School | S | | S s | | | Applied media projects |
| 19. Southern Arts Assoc. | | W | SpsuA | | | Creative skills, cable TV |
| 20. Scottish Film Council | S | | Sps | A | | Progressive media curricula |
| #c Media Educ'n Dev. Proj. | S | | | | T | Media resources, curricula |
| 21. Form. Du Jeun Télésp. Actif | SH | W | Sps | | PT | Statewide; social, aesthetic TV |
| 22. Stichting Audiovis. Vorming | S | | S s | | | How media content made + social |
| #d Media Lit. Resource Guide | S | | Sps | | T | Media theory, classroom practice |
| #e Latin Amer. Comm's. Ped. Inst. | H | W | | | P | TV to promote family interaction |
| #f Plan DENI—Cath. Cin. Office | S O | | Sp | | PT | Conceptual TV analysis for home |
| #g Braz. Social Comm's. Union | | O W | | A | | Social activist, alternate media |
| #h Centre Cult./Art. Enq./Expres. | S | W | Sps | A | | Youth, rural groups; simulations |

(*continued*)

TABLE 12.1 (*Continued*)

*Institution-Related Programs (Non-U.S.)*

| #i Rob. Bellarmino Educ'l. Fndtn. | S | W | Sps | T | TV ideology, teacher training |
|---|---|---|---|---|---|
| #j Playa Ancha Ciencias d. Educ. | | W | | T | Teacher ed.: conceptual, applied |
| 23. UNDA/UNESCO (World-wide) | S | CW | Sps A | | Sociopolitical/cultural + skills |

| Code | Site: | S School | Targeted Users: | C Children | A Adults |
|---|---|---|---|---|---|
| | | H Home | | S Students: | P Parents |
| | | O Organization | | p primary grades | T Teachers |
| | | C Church | | s secondary grades | |
| | | W Workshop | | u college/university | |

were detailed exhaustively in Part II and sketched earlier in this chapter. They are reviewed here to note patterns of assumptions and perspectives among these representative television literacy projects.

## Theoretical and Research Approaches

Adapting a schema by Keval Kumar (1985, pp. 1–9) and analyses by Halloran and Jones (1984) provides a typology for classifying CVS projects. They reflect two broad sectors that can be identified as humanities and social sciences. Under either area (or sometimes, both) fall most categories of media literacy programs.*

The area of *humanities* encompasses theoretical perspectives focusing on the individual person. These include cultural aspects such as aesthetics and ethics: (a) moral approaches—protectionist and interventionist, (b) discriminating, critical viewing—personal mediation and even inoculative at times, (c) images and consciousness—including symbols, codes, myths (recall Gerbner, Newcomb), and (d) pragmatic or utilitarian, even "diversionary"—using media as a tool for learning other kinds of skills such as reading.

The area of *social science* focuses, first, on micro-social considerations of the individual and personal associations. Included are elements of: (e) developmental psychology (Piaget's biology of genetic influences, plus cultural environmental factors) and (f) social psychology including domestic contexts of family, parents, siblings, and peers plus one's living context that partly determines media impact and affects interpreting meaning and significance of media.

---

*Descriptions of listed categories are expanded in the following pages. Tabulations are analyzed in Table 12.2.

TABLE 12.2
Major Theoretical Approaches Among CVS Projects

*A. Projects Funded by U.S. Government*

| | | | |
|---|---|---|---|
| 1. | B c | e F | h | Southwest Educational Development Laboratory |
| 2. | B C | e | h | WNET/Thirteen, New York |
| 3. | B c | E | H | Far West Laboratory, Educ'l. Research/Development |
| 4. | B c | | G h | Boston University |

*B. School Districts*

| | | | |
|---|---|---|
| 5. | b C | E F | Idaho Falls School District No. 91 |
| 6. | b C | E F | Eugene (Oregon) Public School District |
| 7. | A b | G | New York City Board of Education |
| 8. | A  c | F H | Catholic Education Office, Sydney (Australia) |
| #a. | B c | G | Ministry of Education (Western Australia) |

*C. Projects by Individuals*

| | | | |
|---|---|---|
| 9. | B C | E | Aimee Dorr et al. (Harvard, USC) |
| 10. | A B | E F | Dorothy & Jerome Singer (Yale/ABC) |
| 11. | B  D | G h | Rosemary Lee Potter et al. (Pinella County, Flo.) |

*D. National Organizations (Non-Gov.), U.S.*

| | | | |
|---|---|---|
| 12. | A B | d | F | Congress of Parents & Teachers (National PTA) |
| 13. | A B | d | F G h I J | Media Action Research Cntr: TV-Awareness-Training |
| 14. | A B | D | H i | Media Action Research Cntr; Growing w. Television |
| 15. | a B c D | G | US Catholic Conference: The Media Mirror |

*E. Private Companies, U.S., U.K.*

| | | | |
|---|---|---|
| 16. | A B | g h I j | The Learning Seed Company |
| 16a | b C D | | Prime Time School Television |
| 16b | B C D | | TIO: Teacher's Guide to Television |
| 16c | b  D | f | Parent Participation Workshop/NBC |
| 16d | b  D | | Capital Cities Communication |
| 16e | b  D | | CBS Inc. |
| 16f | b  D | | National Broadcasting Company |
| 16g | B  D | | American Broadcasting Company |
| 16h | B | F G h | WQED, Pittsburgh |
| 16i | B C | G h | Independent Broadcasting Authority/ITV (U.K.) |

*Institution-Related Programs (Non-U.S.)*

| | | | |
|---|---|---|
| 17. | B | g H i | Powys (County) Education Committee (Wales) |
| #b. | B C | f G H I | Clwyd (County) Media Studies Unit (Wales) |
| 18. | C | g h  J | Mayfield School (Southwest London) |
| 19. | B C | g H I j | Southern Arts Association (Winchester, Hampshire) |
| 20. | B C d e f g h | Scottish Film Council |

(continued)

TABLE 12.2 *(Continued)*

| | | | |
|---|---|---|---|
| #c. | B C | g h | Media Education Development Project (Scotland) |
| 21. | B C | f G | Formation Du Jeun Téléspectateur Actif (France) |
| 22. | b C d | g | Stichting Audiovisuele Vorming (Amsterdam) |
| #d. | B C | g | Ontario: Media Literacy Resource Guide (Canada) |
| #e. | A CD F | | Latin American Comm'n. Pedagogy Inst. (Costa Rica) |
| #f. | A b C e | | Plan DENI—Catholic Cinema Office (Uruguay) |
| #g. | a c GHIJ | | Brazilian Social Communications Union (Brazil) |
| #h. | B c g H J | | Centre Cultural/Artistic Enquiry/Expres'n. (Chile) |
| #i. | a B EF IJ | | Robert Bellarmino Educational Foundation (Chile) |
| #j. | B c f | | Univ. Playa Ancha, Ciencias dela Educacion (Chile) |
| 23. | a b c HI | | UNDA/UNESCO (Worldwide) |

| CODE | HUMANITIES | SOCIAL SCIENCES | |
|---|---|---|---|
| | *Cultural* | *Psychological/Social Psychology* | *Sociology/Economics/ Political Science* |
| | A Moral, protectionist<br>B Critical viewer, self-mediation<br>C Images, symbols, codes, myths<br>D Utilitarian, pragmatic | E Developmental, cognitive<br>F Social psych: home, peers | G Socioeconomic context<br>H Political economy, groups<br>I Community media<br>J Liberation communication |

Code letters: CAPITALS = primary emphasis; lower case = secondary emphasis or "partly"

Secondly, social science involves macro-social characteristics—institutional, systemic aspects of economics, political science, and sociology: (g) socioeconomic contexts, (h) "political economy" (Masterman), plus (i) community media (Britain) and (j) "liberation communication" (Latin American countries).

Table 12.2 lists CVS-related projects according to these 10 areas. Clearly, some categories necessarily overlap. And many media literacy projects incorporate multiple categories. This chapter concludes by commenting on patterns of these categories among the critical viewing projects.

Differing approaches to research and theory are closely associated if not identified with several of the categories. Emphasis on media *effects* underlies much of category (a) "moral, preventionist"; study of *uses and gratifications* is related to category (b) "critical viewer, self-mediation" and also with (f) "social psychology: home, peers"; *semiotics* is linked with (c) "images, symbols, codes, myths"; and *critical analysis of social structures* is associated with all four categories (g), (h), (i), and (j) relating to socioeconomic and political implications of mass media.[1] Anderson and others, as discussed in Part I, would be quick to point out that "effects" of mass media really involve complex interactions between media producers' programs and individuals in heterogeneous mass audiences.[2] Viewers' cognitive development (category "e") as well as interactive contexts (category "f") play important roles in the process. Thus one can look to the relationship between media and viewers as involving media effects but manifested in *traditional* uses and gratifications approaches (in both Humanities/cultural [category "b"] and Social Sciences/psychological [category "f"]), as well as in *interpretive* approaches (mostly category "c," but partly "b"), and also in what Anderson terms *social action* models (category "f", involving one's daily routines of living)—not to be confused with social activism of the four categories under "sociology/economics, political science."

Tabulations in Table 12.2 predictably reflect widespread emphasis on "B—Critical Viewer" and "C—Images, symbols, codes, myths" (38 and 27 instances, respectively).* Midway in frequency with 20 instances each were "G—Socioeconomic context" and "H—Political economy, groups." "D—Utilitarian, pragmatic" was found in 15 projects; "F—Social Psychology: home, peers" in 14; and "A—Moral, protectionist" in 13 of them. Least often part of projects reviewed were "E—Developmental, cognitive" (in 10) and, not unexpectedly least, "I—Community media" (in 9), and "J—Liberation communication" (in 7 projects).

The most comprehensive projects, merely in terms of offering the widest range among the 10 categories, were Media Action Research Center's "Television-Awareness-Training" and the Scottish Film Council. They included aspects of eight and seven categories, respectively. Most projects were distinguished more by their "primary" stress on one or two categories, with two or three other "secondary" areas of attention. Least substantive for critical viewing skills were projects supported by five of the private companies in the United States. Typically, they used television programming and scripts as instruments for addressing other goals such as learning to read ("D—Utilitarian, pragmatic"), with lesser or even distant attention to growth in critical viewing skills ("b—Critical viewer, self-mediation"), and no other categories manifested.

Those wishing to identify CVS projects that emphasize characteristics relevant to their own situations may be aided by the following elaboration of each of the 10 categories—referenced to projects reviewed.

---

*Assessments of project content and purposes were derived from data presented in Part II and summarized earlier in this chapter. Identifying the characteristics of projects by coded categories involved some degree of interpreting those data.

## HUMANITIES: CULTURAL—INCLUDING AESTHETICS, ETHICS

*Moral, Protectionist.* This approach considers mass media as harmful to culture and social values. It is concerned with inoculating viewers against media's damaging influence. It tends to be elitist, critical of mass culture. Parental intervention is a means to protect viewers against media's bad effects. This is found in writings and projects in the United Kingdom and West Germany as well as in the United States.* Projects with this approach include the New York City Board of Education, the Catholic Education Office in Sydney, work by the Doctors Singer, the National PTA, the Media Action Research Center, the Learning Seed Company, and two Latin American projects— ILPEC in Costa Rica and Plan DENI in Uruguay.

*Critical Viewer, Self-mediation.* Found in most projects, this involves learning skills to manage one's media use and hence media's influence. It is a form of personal interventionist mediation of television's impact. It includes learning discrimination and selectivity. This relates to uses and gratifications or purposefulness of viewers. It is found in projects in the United States, Canada, and Australia, as well as in Britain and parts of Latin America.

*Images, Symbols, Codes, Myths.* This involves aesthetics and "demystifying" programming and its hidden ideologies of media creators. Again, the great majority of projects include this, especially those funded by the U.S. government and school districts in the United States and Australia. England, Wales, and Scotland as well as France stress this, but Latin American countries tend not to do so.

*Utilitarian, Pragmatic.* This uses television as a tool for teaching other skills and disciplines, partly as an attractive adjunct for youngsters' attention and partly as a device to aid exercises in reading, studying subjects treated in programs, and the like. But the purpose is not to understand and grow in selective appreciation of the medium itself. The four national organizations with "moral, protectionist" zeal also include some purposes extrinsic to media experience, such as using TV to study the Bible or to serve as a catalyst for family interaction. The private companies generally center on this approach in their projects; most of them are television broadcasting corporations sup-

---

*These profiles and some examples of countries are partly derived from Kumar's review (1985).

porting reading programs while promoting mass audiences (perhaps more than viewers' comprehension and appreciation).

## SOCIAL SCIENCES

### Psychological/Social Psychology

*Developmental, Cognitive.* Emphasized are various stages of cognitive growth, drawing on Piaget's developmental psychology, plus cultural environment of young persons. This is found in CVS projects either conducted by researchers (Anderson-Ploghoft, Dorr, the Singers) or assisted by research consultants (USOE-funded), and also by ones involving scholars familiar with research findings (Scottish Film Council, Plan DENI in Uruguay, and Robert Bellarmino Educational Foundation in Chile).

*Social Psychology: Home, Peers.* This approach takes into account family context of parents, siblings, and peers where viewing takes place. This domestic environment influences media's impact because it affects viewers' interpretation and meaning derived from shared media experiences. This may involve parental mediation, evoking aspects of "moral, protectionist" intervention. The Anderson projects (Idaho Falls and Eugene) stress this interactionist milieu, as do the Singers and MARC's Television-Awareness-Training. Others including this in their projects are Southwest Educational Development Laboratory, WQED-Pittsburgh, ILPEC in Costa Rica, and Robert Bellarmino Educational Foundation in Chile. It is a less prominent feature in Parent Participation Workshops/NBC, Clwyd Media Studies Unit in Wales, the Scottish Film Council, Formation Du Jeune Téléspectateur Actif in France, and Univérsidad Playa Ancha in Chile.

### Sociology/Economics/Political Science

*Socioeconomic Context.* This concerns competitive economic factors in media, where profit is the driving motivation behind creative processes and techniques. Thus "media competence" is important to enable one to deconstruct programming "texts" to understand their rationale. Which leads to "wary appreciation" of media. This perspective appears scattered among various projects in the United States; it is commonly found in most media literacy programs in the United Kingdom, Europe, and Latin America.

*Political Economy, Groups.* This reflects a perspective of mass media as part of the total process involving politics and financial systems, and includes ideologies—social, cultural, political interests—of media producers. It considers television as a "consciousness industry" shaping audience's views. A tactic for learning first-hand how this comes about is to engage in group discussions and simulations, and preparing media materials, to learn how they are shaped by the creators. All USOE-funded projects have some such elements, as do the Sydney and MARC projects as well as Potter, Learning Seed Company, and WQED. Partly influenced by Masterman, activities in the United Kingdom all reflect this as one of their primary or secondary thrusts. Two Latin American projects (Brazilian Social Communications Union and Center in Chile) plus the UNDA/UNESCO experiment also stress this approach.

*Community Media.* Widely found outside the United States (including Italy, Finland, India), this perspective is alert to mass media as an instrument of "big business" in the capitalist tradition—which must be resisted by viewer-consumer reaction. This can include developing alternate "amateur" media forms to counter the dominant influence of mega-media. In addition to projects in the United Kingdom and Latin America, a few U.S. activities reflect this approach: MARC's two projects and The Learning Seed Company's materials.

*Liberation Communication.* This is a logical extension of the previous category. Its concern is not only consumerism and materialism, but capitalist dominance of a country's media and lower economic classes—especially by foreign mega-corporations. Reaction reflects Paulo Freire's strategy of self-expression and participation in forms of media. This includes group discussion and simulation and also producing media products—even seeking to establish alternate mass media systems to counter dominating forces. Traces of this approach are in MARC's Television Awareness Training and in The Learning Seed Company's material; it appears with some prominence in CVS projects in Britain, Brazil, and Chile.

\*     \*     \*

This qualitative analysis concludes the detailed review of representative critical viewing skills projects in the United States and other selected countries. It provides the background and basis for making recommendations in chapter 13 about television literacy programs, particularly for curriculum designers and those planning and implementing projects.

## NOTES

1. This four-fold division of major patterns of media research and theory was proposed by Bennet (1976).

2. A succinct analysis is provided by Anderson and Avery (1988).

# 13

## Retrospect and Prospects: Toward CVS Media Education in the 1990s

This chapter reviews the ebb and flow of systematic educational programs of media literacy and television critical viewing skills. It sketches recommendations to designers, administrators, and implementers, drawn from the previous 12 chapters.

### EVOLVING CYCLES OF CVS

The ground swell of exploration and experimentation in the 1970s grew into a proliferation of CVS projects by the early 1980s in the United States. But as initial intrigue and enthusiasm gave way to pragmatic, sustained application in schools and adult organizations, funding sources shifted to other priorities—leaving in limbo many short-lived projects such as four massive ones underwritten by the U.S. Office of Education. Clearly 1978 to 1982 were watershed years for organized, widespread developing of formal programs in critical viewing skills in the United States. But by the mid-1980s many projects were quiescent. Perhaps most regrettable is that published materials, often quite sophisticated and carefully developed, were not even available a few short years after some projects were terminated. The whirlwind of data gathering, analysis, philosophical justification, and production of printed and audiovisual materials often resulted in extremely short-term, hard-to-locate reports and support materials. This was true with some school districts, the National PTA, and especially projects heavily funded by governmental agencies intended as "seed" experiments to serve as paradigms for others in the field of education.

During the 1980s the CVS baton was passed, as it were, from the United States to Britain, Australia, and a number of developing countries. To adapt Riesman's (1950) classic terms, emphasis moved away from *inner-directed* viewers' aesthetic understanding of media to *outer-directed* active response to socioeconomic and political implications of mass media. A number of those non-U.S. projects—such as some in Scotland and in far-flung experimental sites by UNDA/UNESCO—have also become quiescent. Yet in many lands, aggressive individuals as well as institutions continue to explore and apply variations of media literacy to television, while espousing various purposes and procedures. In the meantime, interest has revived in the United States among foundations and organizations, paralleling growing international efforts to promote "critical viewing skills" under various forms of media literacy education.

*Contemporary Developments.* In 1987 Strategies for Media Literacy was founded in San Francisco, California, to distribute research findings and to promote media literacy. In 1989 publishers of the journal *Media & Values* expanded into a Center for Media and Values to serve as a clearing house of information about media influence and media literacy programs. At the end of that same year, media educators in France established *L'Association Europeenne pour l'Education aux Media Audiovisuels,* to promote integrating media studies into general schooling.

On May 10–12, 1990, Ontario (Canada) Province's Association for Media Literacy—1,100 members in 1989—presented at the University of Guelph a North American media conference on "The New Literacy: Media Education in the 1990s." Featuring major theorists and practitioners cited in this report, it attracted 420 participants from five countries (plus another 100 applicants for whom space was not available). A similar assembly for media teachers and professionals, "New Directions in Media Education," was organized for July 2–6, 1990, in Toulouse, France, by the British Film Institute, UNESCO, and the Centre de Liaison de l'Enseignement et des Moyens d'Information (CLEMI—created in 1983 by the French Ministry of National Education).

*Patterns.* During the early years, broadcast media study and criticism often presented a moralistic stance. This was especially true with organizations promoting "public interest" perspectives and agenda.

Those groups of concerned citizens, sometimes entire memberships of churches, sought to remove alleged objectionable program content first from radio and then from television. Educators and researchers gradually entered the field of media analysis with more objective and dispassionate views and purposes. Media criticism became increasingly pluralistic, nondirective, and nonvalue-laden. But the next wave of media concern grew out of desperate social and economic contexts, with strong valuative judgments directed against mass media empires. Instead of religious perspectives distressed about language and behavior (particularly depicting sexual and violent activity), or the later cultural-aesthetic analysis, more recent media criticism fostered audience responsiveness, responsibility, and reaction to media structures in order to liberate the common people from class domination. Although patterns overlapped through the decades, they successively emphasized religion and rightness ("inoculation" approach), then sensitive discriminating responsiveness ("critical viewer"), and more recently anti-media resistance and rebellion—even consumer revolution in extreme instances ("community media"). These three patterns respectively reflect UNESCO's 1984 *Media Education* document reviewing inoculation, critical viewer, and community media approaches.[1]

## FUNCTION OF THIS BOOK

This compilation intends to do more than chronicle the rise and passing and resurgence of a dynamic era linking formal education with developing selective, discriminating, responsive viewers of television. It can also serve as a repository of major samples of notable CVS programs, providing not only a guide to various kinds of projects but also substantial extracts from them—statements of varying purposes, descriptions of methodology, and extended portions of their content. Perhaps this review can provide a menu of possible agenda for the next wave of educators who realize anew the significant link between television viewing and social, aesthetic, economic reality as well as specific learning skills.

## THE KEY: COMPREHENSIVE COLLABORATION IN EDUCATIONAL STRUCTURES

*Administrative Support.*   A major caution and recommendation is reiterated by James Anderson, Don Agostino, and a number of researchers, innovators, and evaluators in Britain and Latin America. Administrators in school systems and individual schools must endorse and support critical viewing programs if they are to take on a life of their own, not wholly dependent on the inspiration, perspiration, and serendipity (or good fortune, translated "luck") of isolated teachers.

To succeed, a curricular program of critical viewing skills must be developed through collaboration among teachers, administrators, and specialists and also with parents, who together must build it into the systematic educational process. That means progressively developing studies geared to the participants' successive levels of cognitive development, based on educational as well as behavioral research findings. It also means studies continuing and integrated into successive grade levels through the school years. Otherwise it will be nonsubstantive and peripheral to the process of students' becoming educated in the fullest sense.

*Training Teachers.* Projects around the world have underscored the need to train teachers for media education. Competence in effectively integrating media studies and in applying specific media procedures and materials in classrooms cannot be assumed. Administrators must permit teachers to enroll in comprehensive workshops to study media phenomena and the resources of literature and support materials; they must have planned time to learn with colleagues effective, sophisticated ways to teach critical viewing skills. They must be given the opportunity to become adept at integrating media literacy into traditional curricular subjects. Experience has demonstrated repeatedly in various parts of the world, in varied contexts, how ineffective are facile, poorly informed and untrained efforts at media education. Instructors also need appropriately reduced teaching loads and released time during the regular school term in order to prepare complex media-related materials (especially when first embarking on teaching CVS studies).

*Holistic, Integrated CVS Curriculum.* For sustained impact among students and on families, and ultimately on the media themselves, media literacy training must be incorporated into systematic curricula as a substantive area of study. It must not be a mere appendage or an attractive instrument by which to teach other subjects and skills. Worldwide experience to date suggests that separate media courses as separate subjects can be introduced only with difficulty, but that CVS modules can be integrated efficiently within existing courses and curricula. Although not ideal, this option is at least feasible; it meets with least resistance for scheduling and competent staffing.

*Parents and the Home.* A key component to effective, longlasting television media education is involving parents and families in the process. Many projects, especially in Latin American countries, focus primarily on the home viewing environment and interaction among family members as the "lived" context of how mass media are in fact consumed. Many projects direct their efforts primarily or even exclusively to parents, mounting workshops by which media skills can be relayed by parents to their children. Printed materials for most projects can be used by parents, just as by teachers, with their own children—always adapting it to match youngsters' individual stages of cognitive development.

## ROLE OF RESEARCH, EVALUATION

Important for the whole field of critical viewing skills is sophisticated, valid research about the effectiveness of various kinds of projects. In order to measure outcomes, to evaluate effectiveness of media literacy projects, curriculum designers must identify at the outset their goals and objectives: the behavioral skills, cognitive abilities, and attitudes regarding the television medium. When it is difficult to measure "target outcomes" in education because they consist of long-term goals in a person's growth and media use, Flagg (1990, p. 230) cited the need for traditional methods of assessing on-going and preliminary results: by task analyses, learning hierarchies, behavioral/motor skill taxonomies, and interim cognitive and affective outcomes. Ideally, surveillance and testing coupled with evaluation ought come at stages during the course of a project so that its conduct can be corrected while "in process" in light of those findings.

The Singers, Anderson-Ploghoft, and Dorr conducted some of the more detailed testing for results. David Butts oversaw exhaustive analysis of media education in Scottish secondary schools. Other projects pretested initial curricular materials, and sometimes tested while conducting media projects. But it is usually difficult to assess the real value of most projects by determining how effectively they achieved what they set out to do. That is why long-term sustained programs with systematic curricula offer better prospects for verifying over time their level of success.

Flagg (1990) stressed the need for continued interaction among administrators, planners and curriculum designers, and those who implement educational programs.

> The goal of formative evaluation is to inform the decision-making process during the design, production, and implementation stages of an educational program with the purpose of improving the program. . . .

How can one increase the likelihood that formative evaluation results actually will be used by decision makers? . . . Creating a working dialogue and trusting relationship between formative researchers and decision makers is critical to the eventual utilization of results. . . . Besides producing results that are timely and relevant to the needs of developers, evaluators must be able to communicate the results in an understandable, nonthreatening, and brief manner. . . . Making recommendations requires that evaluators have knowledge of the constraints on the project—thus, stressing again the necessity of a good relationship with the developers. (pp. 241–242)

## MODE OF EDUCATIONAL INQUIRY

The mere transmission of information will not promote critical viewing skills. Individualized discovery must be allowed so that children and other CVS participants can learn for themselves by viewing and reflecting and judging about their television experience—often in discussion with peers. Nondirective questions can stimulate personal involvement in the process, while not abdicating a context that draws on values of the children and their families, churches, and peers. The inductive, exploratory approach was used almost universally by media projects reviewed here.

*Content of CVS Education.* Individual teachers and administrators must determine what content and format best suits their local circumstances. That is why this book has been so prolix in excerpting major portions of project texts, and exhaustively described details of procedures and materials. This book focuses on specifically television viewing skills, but many media studies courses embrace a wide range of mass and non-mass media—cinema, radio, newspapers and magazines, photography. Beyond determining major purposes such as inoculative, critical viewing, and community media, designers of curricula and teachers of syllabi must consider the proper balance of theoretical (critical appreciation) and practical (creative program crafting) activity. (Recall that many programs, especially in Britain, look to creative efforts using equipment to produce amateur programs as a sine qua non of developing in children true critical awareness and understanding of media.) They must select from paradigmatic projects the extent to which they want to study mass media as "texts" to be read and deconstructed and demystified or demythologized, as semiotic phenomona (with connotation, representation, and ideology), and as industries (including issues of ownership and control). Further, they must determine whether they can develop independent media study courses or else must fuse such study into areas of social studies or humanities or even science-related courses if technology is emphasized.

As stated earlier, curriculum designers and administrators, as well as practitioners who implement CVS in the classroom, must determine at the outset what kinds of media education best match their needs and circumstances. By reviewing projects reported here they can consider various premises and theoretical approaches possible, such as critical social analysis or (following Keval Kumar's categories) political economy, environmental, psychological, cultural, or liberation perspectives.

*Cultural and Social Values.* A dilemma arises about guiding, without channeling, young people to come to understand the multiple roles of the mass medium of TV in society, and the extent to which it is implicated in setting agenda and affecting—even forming—values for the contemporary world. Although aesthetics of the medium itself (that is, visual literacy) is paramount, the larger social and economic and political aspects of the medium must be explored. Whether that leads to consumer activism depends on the participants as much as on the teacher, if the proper mix of open-ended discovery and unbiased evaluation takes place.

*Aesthetics and Social Impact.* Critical viewing skills training should not be limited to "visual literacy"—studying the medium's aesthetic creativity and semiotics.* Beyond that, the intent should be to improve "the way our culture interacts with the medium" (in David A. England's phrase). That is, individual viewers, viewers as members of families, and viewers as citizens grow in their understanding of the medium, in their critical judgment about its content and processes, and in their reaction to it by modifying their own media behavior and by entering actively into the sender-receiver process by communicating with and attempting to influence the media.

Thus, viewers should not only enhance their appreciation of media product, but also grow in realization of "mediation" in society which is a function of the traditions, ideals, myths, and established forces (business, government, socioeconomic ideology itself) driving that society and its values. This underscores the need for inductive CVS programs, allowing independent critical thinking.

---

*When beginning this study (too many years ago), the author of this report held for such a limited perspective. But, especially in reviewing non-U.S. projects of the 1980s, he broadened his view to include socially reactive roles as proper to comprehensive, responsible media literacy programs.

## RESPONSIBILITY AND VALUES

This relates at another level to the whole concept of a critical conscience among the citizenry, not mesmerized by a medium that can distort reality and social priorities, but rather discerning and demanding of that medium and, through it, challenging the very structure of society. This suggests Freire's thesis that, in the broader sense of communication, all people are to participate in building their national culture. Or, as Minkinnen put it: "An important issue in the field of ethics is whether one takes a stand in respect of the kinds of interests, and whose interests, the outputs of the media and those who provide them should serve."

Critical viewing skills projects in the United States rarely touch on these broader themes, unlike some programs in the United Kingdom and in developing countries, especially in Latin America. But the United States projects do recommend conveying criticism to media leaders.

*The U.S. Media Scene: Role of Responsive Viewers.* CVS projects in the United States often urge viewers to communicate to media their critical judgments about programs. Is that realistic, or doomed to be ineffectual? Generally, broadcasters engaged in capitalistic, free enterprise are in business to reach large audiences attractive to advertisers. Criticism reflects disaffection by some of that mass audience. Therefore media executives are not simply indifferent to negative comments. At the same time, viewers' criticism is typically rare and often not well stated; it is deemed not necessarily representative of even a large minority of those masses. To the extent that great numbers of people grow in critical viewing skills and exercise participatory or "democratizing" communication, the media will be made increasingly aware of negative reactions by the audiences they are trying to woo.

And yet, if CVS programs are to be truly successful, they will not indoctrinate but rather stimulate individualized assessments that will be pluralistic. They will foster personalized critical thinking. So not all viewers—even when trained in media literacy—will react the same way to given programs or media policies. It would seem that only a massive spontaneous outpouring of similarly critical comments would affect media decisions—as well as concerted action orchestrated by a large group with like interests. But the latter kind of effort contradicts the nondirective approach of preferred media training programs, which rely on values brought to the exercise by participants from their own spheres (families, churches, friends), rather than instilled by a group leader or teacher.

In the United States, the broadcasting industry is regulated by the federal government which licenses individual stations and indirectly affects national networks. Until the mid-1980s, that status provided opportunity for individuals and groups to get the attention of media leaders, sometimes even results. Networks were especially sensitive to public criticism, partly on behalf of their affiliated stations, partly out of enlightened self-interest (not to antagonize investors, major advertisers, or opinion-leaders in the national community including government), and partly out of a somewhat lofty perspective of the larger issues of media and society. But with the Federal Communications Commission's shift to a "degregulatory" agency, coupled with permissiveness of alternate television sources such as pay TV and cable and satellite services, standards and sensitivity of the traditional network/station medium have deteriorated.

Audience reaction no longer has the at least moderate impact of previous decades. Similarly, the "creative community"—of writers, producers, directors, actors, and others who are not themselves broadcasters but craft the entertainment programs—was in the past often vocal about restrictions on creativity and about shortcomings of the commercialized industry. But they now have more options for creating and selling their programs, and they also realize the lesser role assumed by government in overseeing media content; so they are less critical of the commercial industry that gives them work. The broadcast system in America has become at the same time more pluralistic and less susceptible to "pressure" from audiences and critics. But that kind of interrelation is subject to the swings of evolving social priorities; the pendulum shows signs of reversing its course in the early 1990s. At the very least, a viewer who does not even attempt to communicate with media decision-makers abdicates a potential role as effective participant in the media process.

Finally, mass media claim to give the public what it wants. In this sense, media decision makers are not leaders so much as followers, trying to discern the interests and tastes of potential mass audiences so that programs can be scheduled to respond to their preferences. Survey ratings measure how much of the public "wants" given programs or at least tunes in to the limited choices provided. Comments submitted by members of that audience can offer qualitative data about "wants" and "likes." And occasionally an enlightened broadcaster operates on the principle enunciated by former NBC executive Franklin Dunham: "Give the public what it wants most of the time, and a little of what it would want if it only knew about it." Thoughtful, articulate, constructively critical letters from the public audience can reassure and support such conscientious broadcasters.

# THE BIG PICTURE: MEDIA IN NATIONAL/INTERNATIONAL SOCIETY

Beyond that, this anthology of data, interpretations, and recommendations can end on a note similar to that sounded by media critics and educators in Britain and South America: Priorities and the very structure of society must be changed if mass media are truly to serve that society according to human values, including religious ones. Complete media education involves activist reforms reaching far beyond typical critical viewing skills curricula.

Even as this book reached final manuscript form for the publisher, major shifts in media structures occurred weekly. Across the face of an approaching European Economic Community of countries to be interrelated by common currency and interchanged mass media descended television signals from orbiting satellites of transnational consortia. Meanwhile mass media news organizations and private hand-held camcorders documented rapidly evolving events as Eastern European bloc nations struggled for independence from the Soviet sphere. Governments around the globe—even in the Soviet Union—liberalized media coverage and access; many nations degregulated media systems, permitting commercial-supported entertainment-oriented programming to compete with traditionally state-operated media monopolies. The United States and Japan rushed headlong with partners and against competitors in Europe to high definition, wide-screen, stereo-sound television transmission by optical fiber and by direct broadcast satellites simultaneously to dwellings across entire hemispheres. The world picture—how media depict the world's people, its governments, its cultures, its customs—was modified daily.

So how ought educators of various countries and various regions and various school systems and various classrooms most effectively use what paradigm of media education, specifically critical viewing skills?

In the final analysis there *is* no final analysis.

Whether media studies ought be mandated in all primary and secondary schools, whether such should be separate courses or integrated into traditional ones, how teacher training programs can be most efficiently mounted and competent teachers selected for released time inservice media training, how media institutes and workshops should be offered to parents and citizens generally, how media resource centers can be established—these and other important questions must be addressed and responded to by respective teachers, administrators, and curriculum designers in concert with colleagues and supported by continuing research findings.

As Scottish expert Eddie Dick (1987a) concluded his own world survey of media education:

> This, perhaps, should be the place where a sequence of conclusions is offered. However, on the basis of the evidence available, such a closure to this document would verge on the foolish and prove less than useful. Let the descriptions speak for themselves. (p. 69)

Similarly, David Butts (1986) concluded his extensive formal research study of Scottish media education by acknowledging that the continually changing status of CVS projects coupled with modifications necessary for his case studies "render it impossible to draw conclusions from empirical work or to make precise recommendations" (p. 159).

*A Pragmatic Invitation.*   Perhaps the most apposite concluding remark is the cliché: Don't re-invent the wheel. Much useful material for fostering critical viewing skills has already been explored and put into organized printed and audiovisual materials, often in full-blown curricular teaching plans. Massive funding accompanied some of that work. The heritage includes widespread experimentation as well as formal research. Classroom teachers, theoretical scholars, as well as pragmatic broadcasters and corporate businessmen have collaborated over time on the many kinds of projects described in this review. Their work should not be overlooked, but rather tapped.

The hope is that this book can help subsequent explorers and practitioners of critical viewing skills review the kinds of results already achieved so they can build on that foundation, even utilizing some of the extensive materials already in the field.

## NOTES

1. Cf. Butts (1986, p. 7), citing summary by Professor Halloran, director of the Centre for Mass Communications, University of Leicester.

# Appendix A:
# Initial Three-Page Questionnaire, 1981 Survey

"CRITICAL VIEWING SKILLS" PROJECTS

MAJOR GOALS, CONTEXTS, PARTICIPANTS, TECHNIQUES

*In questions with checklists, please check appropriate categories that reflect your activity and then briefly describe major details. Add any further comments on the back of the sheets.*

1. Please state succinctly (a brief paragraph of several sentences) what you mean to include in "critical viewing skills" or "media literacy" or [your phrase] _____.

2. PURPOSE OR "MOTIVATION" OR ORGANIZING SOURCE: State very briefly why this project got started: *Check major motive(s), then describe.*
   [  ] Education                       [  ] Ethical/Moral
   [  ] Public relations                [  ] Research
   [  ] Religious (Church-related)      [  ] Other:_____

3. What are specific GOALS of this activity—what is to be achieved with participants in the program?
   [  ] Educational                     [  ] Ethical/Moral
   [  ] Cultural/Aesthetic              [  ] Media reform
   [  ] Other:_____

4. When did your activity/project begin?_____, 19___
   Is there a terminal date to your project? [   ] No
                                             [   ] Yes:_____,     19___

5. Who originated this project? (E.g., local individual, local organization or
   school, school system, national office, etc.)

6. How many people are involved in administering the project?
   _____ Administrators              _____ Teachers/"Trainers"
   _____ Staff: clerical, research   _____ Other:

7. Is this project funded?   [   ] No        [   ] Yes
   If so, by what source?_____
   For what amount? $_____Over what period of time?_____

8. How many participants ("trainees") are in the project?
   *(Answer whichever categories best reflect the scope of your activity)*
   _____ Persons       _____# classes      _____# churches
   _____ Families      _____# schools      _____# organizations
                                                   (chapters/units)

9. At what levels is their participation?
   SCHOOL      *(Circle*              CHURCH  ORGANIZATION  HOME
      *range of grades)*     Children. . . [   ] . . . . . . . . [   ] . . . . . . . . [   ]
   [   ] Pre-school         Teenagers. . [   ] . . . . . . . . [   ] . . . . . . . . [   ]
   [   ] Elementary: K 1    Adults. . . . [   ] . . . . . . . . [   ] . . . . . . . . [   ]
      2 3 4 5 6 7 8
   [   ] H.S.: 9 10 11 12
   [   ] College
   [   ] Postgraduate/
      extension (adult)

10. What approach do you emphasize?
    [   ] Deductive (theories, philosophy, applying principles)
    [   ] Inductive (experiential, explorative, "heuristic," processing data)

11. What techniques are used?
    [   ] Lecture        [   ] Workshop                    [   ] Readings
    [   ] Discussion     [   ] Curriculum (formal courses)  [   ] Other:

12. What materials are used?
    [   ] Readings     [   ] Tests, quizzes       [   ] Study sheets
    [   ] Scripts      [   ] TV programs          [   ] Teachers/Parents'
                           (viewing)                  Guides
    [   ] Workbooks    [   ] "Voting" checklists (for monitoring)
    [   ] Audio-visuals: slides/filmstrips, records, audio/video-tapes, etc.
    [   ] Other:

13. Approximate number of hours/week for participants in program:___hours
Participants ("trainees") meet how often? FREQUENCY:_____
LENGTH OF TIME:_____

14. If a school-related project, this activity is:
[  ] Integral part of curriculum:  (  ) required;  (  ) elective
[  ] Extracurricular activity apart from formal schoolwork

15. Media emphasized:
[  ] Television     [  ] Film/Motion Pictures     [  ] Print: Newspapers,
[  ] Radio          [  ] Records                          magazines
                                                  [  ] Other:

16. Involvement with television media:
"Active":  [  ] writing letters                    [  ] Prepare media
           [  ] contacting media organizations          material
                                                         (programs)
                                                   [  ] Other:
"Passive": [  ] selective viewing  [  ] evaluations, appraisal of media
                                        content

17. Topic areas for television activity:
[  ] Time spent with TV
[  ] Program viewing patterns
[  ] Impact of TV on reading, speaking, other cognitive skills
[  ] TV's form and format: schedules, techniques of camera, sound; plot,
                character, dialogue
[  ] TV's structure and processes: advertising supported, government reg-
                ulated,  industry/art  of  stations/net-
                works/producer-suppliers
[  ] How people use TV: uses & gratifications (needs, desires, preferences,
                choices in context of other media/leisure acti-
                vities)
[  ] What TV does to people: effects of viewing on attitudes, behavior
[  ] Kinds of TV: (  ) entertainment; (  ) news, public affairs
[  ] Advertising: commercials (appeals, "values," weaknesses)
[  ] Consumer roles: (  )writing; (  )joining organizations to affect media
                decision-makers; (  )other:
[  ] Other:

18. Sources for establishing norms, standards, for categorizing and evaluating
media content and practices:
[  ] Originators/leaders of project     [  ] Published books, articles
[  ] Professional educators             [  ] National office of
[  ] Professional media persons              organization
[  ] Research reports                    [  ] Other:

19. Briefly note kinds of testing/measuring to evaluate materials, methodology, effects of this media project activity.

20. Have you compiled your findings: results and measured/reported effects of this project? [   ] Yes *(Please append to this questionnaire, if possible)*
    [   ] No

21. Do you have (documented) reactions, appraisals by leaders, participants (including children, parents, teachers)? [   ] Yes *(Please append, if possible)*
    [   ] No

*Thank you for your patience in responding to this inquiry. Please return the questionnaire and any supplementary material that you wish to:*

> *JAMES A. BROWN, Ph.D.*
> *School of Journalism*
> *University of Southern California*
> *Los Angeles, California 90007*

# Appendix B:
# Follow-Up One-Page
# Questionnaire, 1985 Survey

"CRITICAL VIEWING SKILLS" PROJECT

QUESTIONNAIRE UPDATE, 1985

ORGANIZATION/PROJECT: ----------------------------------------------------------------

*(Numbers refer to items in previous questionnaire, returned by you in 1980)*

4. Has your projected terminated (since 1979–1980)?
   [   ] Yes: 19_____
   [   ] No. Is there a terminal date? [   ] No
                                             [   ] Yes: 19_____

6. Either presently, or back towards the end of an already terminated project, the number of people involved in administering the project included how many:
   _____administrators             _____teachers/"trainers"
   _____staff: clerical, research     _____other:

7. Has this project been funded since 1979–1980?
   [   ] No
   [   ] Yes. Source of funding:_____
                  Amount:_____Over what period of time?_____

8. How many participants ("trainees") have been in the project?
   *(Because various projects coincide with school years, or conduct short-term self-contained workshops, etc., please respond in whatever categories best reflect your activities)*

|               | Current No. | Avg. per year | APPROX. TOTAL TO DATE* |
|---------------|-------------|---------------|------------------------|
| Persons       | _____ | _____   | _____            |
| Families      | _____ | _____   | _____            |
| Classrooms    | _____ | _____   | _____            |
| Schools       | _____ | _____   | _____            |
| Churches      | _____ | _____   | _____            |
| Other organizations | _____ | _____   | _____      |

*(or to date of termination)

19. Briefly note kinds of testing/measuring to evaluate materials, methodology, effects of this media project. *(Continue on other side of sheet)*

20. Have you compiled your findings: results and reported effects of this project?
    [  ] No
    [  ] Yes. (If possible, please append to this questionnaire; or else note what kinds of evaluative material and how it may be obtained: titles, cost)

21. Do you have documented reactions or appraisals by leaders, participants (including children, parents, teachers, administrators)?
    [  ] No
    [  ] Yes. (Please append if possible; or note how we may obtain them)

PLEASE ADD ANY OTHER INFORMATION OR COMMENTS THAT MAY HELP US BETTER UNDERSTAND AND ACCURATELY REPRESENT YOUR ACTIVITY.    *Many thanks for your cooperation!*

# Appendix C:
# Sources of Information and
# of Printed and Audiovisual
# Materials for CVS Projects

## A. PROJECTS FUNDED BY U.S. GOVERNMENT

(United States Department of Education, Washington, DC 20202)

SOUTHWEST EDUCATIONAL DEVELOPMENT LABORATORY
  Division of Learning and Media Research
  211 East 7th
  Austin, Texas 78701
    Project Director: Dr. Charles Corder-Bolz

WNET/THIRTEEN (New York City)
  356 West 58th Street
  New York, N.Y. 10019 (212)560-2000
    Manager, School Services: Debbi Waserman Bilowit
    **Printed materials available through:**
    Globe Book Company, 888 Seventh Ave., New York, N.Y. 10106
    (Same address: Cambridge—the Basic Skills Company [a N.Y.
    Times Company])

*FAR WEST LABORATORY FOR EDUCATIONAL RESEARCH AND DEVELOPMENT
  1855 Folsom Street
  San Francisco, California 94103  (415)565-3000
    Project Director: Dr. Donna Lloyd-Kolkin
    Subsequent contact: Debra Lieberman (415)565-3002

*WGBH EDUCATIONAL FOUNDATION [*jointly with above]
  Office of Radio & Television for Learning
  125 Western Avenue
  Boston, Massachusetts 02134
    Project Director: Douglas Smith
  **Major materials available through:**
    Science and Behavior Books, Inc., P.O. Box 11456, Palo Alto, CA
    94306

BOSTON UNIVERSITY
  School of Public Communication
  6450 Commonwealth Avenue
  Boston, Massachusetts 02215  (617)353-3364
    Project Director: Dr. Donis Dondis [deceased]
  **Materials distributed by:**
    Dendron Press, P.O. Box 24, Kenmore Station, Boston, MA 02215

*B. SCHOOL DISTRICTS (SYSTEMATIC, FORMAL INSTRUCTION)*

IDAHO FALLS SCHOOL DISTRICT NO. 91
  690 John Adams Parkway
  Idaho Falls, Idaho 83401  (208)522-0063
    Project Director: Elizabeth Moll
    Director, Federal Programs: Craig Ashton

EUGENE (OREGON) PUBLIC SCHOOL DISTRICT 91
  School District 4J
  Eugene Public Schools
  Eugene, Oregon
    Curriculum Specialist: Melva Ellingson

EAST SYRACUSE, NEW YORK
  East Syracuse-Minona Central Schools
  Syracuse, New York
    Contact: Suzanne Schaff
    Administrator, Broadband Telecommunications: Rosemary M.
    Lehman

**NEW YORK CITY BOARD OF EDUCATION**
Office of Media & Telecommunications
City of New York
New York, New York (718)935-4400
Contact: Noel White, Carole Haber

**CATHOLIC EDUCATION OFFICE, SYDNEY, NEW SOUTH WALES, AUSTRALIA**
P.O. Box 145
Broadway, New South Wales, 2007, Australia
Executive Director of Schools: Kelvin Canavan
**Materials published/distributed by:**
Longman Cheshire Pty Limited, 346 St. Kilda Road; Melbourne 3004, Australia
Catholic Audiovisual Centre, 50 Abbotsford Road; Homebush, N.S.W. 2140, Australia
(02)760-459 [80 35mm slides & audiocassette]

**MINISTRY OF EDUCATION, WESTERN AUSTRALIA**
Media Studies
151 Royal Street
East Perth, Western Australia 6000 (09)420-4111 / 4731 / 5005
Senior Curriculum Officer: Barrie McMahon
**Audiovisual materials (films, videos, slides) distributed by:**
Audio-Visual Education Branch, [same address]

*C. PROJECTS BY INDIVIDUALS—COLLABORATIVE AND INDIVIDUAL*

**AIMEE DORR** *et al.* (Harvard/Univ. of Southern California)
Graduate School of Education
University of California at Los Angeles
Los Angeles, California

**DOROTHY AND JEROME SINGER** (Yale/ABC)
Family Television Research & Consultation Center
Department of Psychology
Yale University
405 Temple Street
New Haven, Connecticut 06511 (203)436-0356 / 432-4286
Co-directors: Dr. Jerome Singer, Dr. Dorothy Singer
Project Director: Dr. Diana M. Zuckerman

**Materials published by:**
*Getting the Most Out of TV:* Goodyear Publishing Co., Inc., Santa Monica, California 90401

Film/Videotape series based on above: MTI Teleprograms, Inc., 3710 Commercial Ave., Northbrook, Ill. 60062

*Teaching Television: How to Use TV to Your Child's Advantage:* The Dial Press, 1 Dag Hammarskjold Plaza, New York 10017

ROSEMARY POTTER *et al.* (Pinella County Schools, Florida)
Harbor Middle School
Clearwater, Florida
Contact: Dr. Rosemary Lee Potter
**Materials published by:**
Educational Activities, Inc., P.O. Box 392, Freeport, New York 11520

Charles E. Merrill, Publishers; 1300 Alum Creek Drive; Columbus, Ohio 43216

Educational Services, Inc., P.O. Box 2319, Stevensville, Michigan 49127

Churchill Films, 662 North Robertson Blvd., Los Angeles, California 90069

## D.  NATIONAL  ORGANIZATIONS  (NON-GOVERNMENTAL): UNITED STATES

NATIONAL ASSOCIATION FOR BETTER RADIO AND TELEVISION / . . . FOR BETTER BROADCASTING
P.O. Box 43640
Los Angeles, California 90043

AMERICAN COUNCIL FOR BETTER BROADCASTS / NATIONAL TELEMEDIA COUNCIL
120 E. Wilson St.
Madison, Wisconsin 53703 (608)257-7712
Contact: Dr. Leslie Spence

NATIONAL CONGRESS OF PARENTS AND TEACHERS (NATIONAL PTA)
700 N. Rush St.
Chicago, Illinois 60611-2571 (800)323-5177; (800)942-4266 (Ill. residents)
Project Coordinator: Marion R. Young
William M. Young & Associates, 911 S. Oak Park Ave., Oak Park, Illinois, 60304

**Printed materials distributed by:**
Phi Delta Kappa, Center for Dissemination of Innovative Programs, Eight Street & Union Avenue, Box 789, Bloomington, Indiana 47402 (812)339-1156
Director, PDK Center: Neville L. Robertson

MEDIA ACTION RESEARCH CENTER (MARC)
475 Riverside Drive - Room 1370
New York, New York 10027 (212)865-6690 / 663-8900
Director: Dr. William F. Fore
(a)"Television Awareness Training" ("T-A-T")
Project Director: Shirley Whipple-Struchen
(b) "Growing with Television"
**Material published variously by:**
Abingdon (Nashville, Tennessee), John Knox Press (Atlanta), Warner Press, Inc. (Anderson, Indiana), Judson Press (Valley Forge, Pa.), the Brethren Press (Elgin, Ill.), for Cooperative Publication Association, Box 179, St. Louis, Missouri 63166 & The Seabury Press, 815 Second Ave., New York, N.Y. 10017

U.S. CATHOLIC CONFERENCE ("THE MEDIA MIRROR")
Department of Communication
1011 First Avenue, Suite 1300
New York, New York 10022 (212)644-1894
Project Director: Henry Herx
**Materials published by:**
U.S. Catholic Conference, 1312 Massachusetts Ave. N.W., Washington, D.C. 20005
National Catholic Educational Assoc., 1077 30th St., N.W. - Suite 100; Washington, D.C. 20007 (202)293-5954

*E. PRIVATE COMPANIES: UNITED STATES, UNITED KINGDOM*

THE LEARNING SEED COMPANY
145 Brentwood Drive          21250 Andover
Palatine, Illinois 60067     Kildeer, Illinois 60047
Contact: Jeffrey Schrank
**Materials published by:**
McDougal, Littell & Co., Box 1667, Evanston, Illinois 60204
Everglades Publishing Co., P.O. Drawer Q, Everglades, Florida 33929

PRIME-TIME SCHOOL TELEVISION
[See below: "Media and Methods")

## TELEVISION INFORMATION OFFICE/TEACHERS GUIDES TO TELEVISION
745 Fifth Avenue
New York, New York 10022 [Office closed 1989]
  Contact: National Association of Broadcasters
          1771 N Street, N.W.
          Washington, D.C. 20036 (202)429-5350

## TEACHER'S GUIDES TO TELEVISION
Teacher's Guides Company
699 Madison Avenue
P.O. Box 564 - Lennox Hill Station
New York, New York 10021 (212)688-0033
  President: Edward Stanley

## PARENT PARTICIPATION WORKSHOPS/NBC
699 Madison Avenue
New York, New York 10021
  [+ See above: "Teacher's Guides. . . "; see below: "NBC"]

## CAPITAL CITIES COMMUNICATIONS
Capital Cities Television Reading Program
4100 City Line Avenue
Philadelphia, Pennsylvania 19131
  Director: Dr. Michael McAndrew

## NATIONAL TELEVISION NETWORKS (U.S.)

ABC - Capital Cities/American Broadcasting Company, Inc.
  ABC Educational Projects
  77 West 66th Street
  New York, New York 10023-6298 (212)456-7777
      ABC Community Relations: Pamela N. Warford
CBS Inc. (formerly Columbia Broadcasting System, Inc.)
  CBS Television Reading Program
  CBS Educational and Community Services
  51 West 521 St.
  New York, New York 10019 (212)975-8743
      Director: Joanne Brokaw-Livesey
NBC - National Broadcasting Company, Inc.
  NBC Educational Projects
  30 Rockefeller Plaza - Room 1806
  New York, New York 10020 (212)664-5443
      Director, Children's Informational Services: Dr. Ellen Rodman

INDEPENDENT BROADCASTING AUTHORITY & INDEPEN-
DENT TELEVISION COMPANIES (ENGLAND)
Thames Television Limited
149 Tottenham Court Road
London W1P 9LL, England (01)388-5199
Education Officer: Peter Griffiths
**Materials distributed by:**
Hutchinson Educational publishers (copies of scripts)
Film Forum, 56 Brewer Street, London W1 (01)437-6487 (6
documentaries)

## F. INSTITUTION-RELATED CVS PROGRAMS IN FORMAL EDUCATION

POWYS (WALES)
Powys County Council: Schools Council, Powys Education
Committee
Brecknok Area Office
Watton Mount, Brecon, Powys, LD3 7BE Tel.: (0874)4411
Contact: M. Eslter
Director of Education: Robert W. Bevan

CLWYD (WALES)
County Civic Centre
Media Studies Unit, Theatr Clwyd
Mold, Clwyd CH7 1YA, Wales Tel.: (0352)55105
Director of Education: Keith Evans

SOUTHERN ARTS ASSOCIATION, WINCHESTER, HAMPSHIRE
(ENGLAND)
19 Southgate St. - Law Courts
Winchester 9EB, Hampshire S023, England
Film Officer: David Altshul
Media Arts Lab
Town Hall Sudios, Regent Circus
Swindon SN1 1QF Tel.: (0793)26161
Director: Martin Parry

SCOTTISH FILM COUNCIL (SCOTLAND)
Scottish Council for Educational Technology
Dowanhill
74 Victoria Crescent Road
Glasgow G12 9JN, Scotland
Head of Education and Training: Kevil Cowle
Media Education Officer: Eddie Dick

FORMATION DU JEUNE TÉLESPECTATEUR ACTIF (FRANCE)
CNDP/Centre National de Document Pedagogique
29 Rue d'Ulm
75005 Paris, France
    Contact: Olivier Gagnier

STICHTING AUDIOVISUELE VORMING, AMSTERDAM (NETHER-
LANDS)
Oude Zijds Voorburgwal 129
1012 EP Amsterdam

MEDIA LITERACY GUIDE, ONTARIO (CANADA)
Ministry of Education
Mowat Block, Queen's Park
900 Bay Street
Toronto, Ontario M7A 1L2  (416)965-2666
    Contact: Jerry George
    Director, Centre for Secondary & Adult Education: Sheila Roy

LATIN AMERICAN COMMUNICATIONS PEDAGOGY INSTITUTE
(COSTA RICA)
ILPEC
Apartado 210
Heredia, Costa Rica Tel.: 37.27.19

DENI PLAN—CATHOLIC CINEMA OFFICE (URUGUAY)
Oficina Católica de Cine
Cerrito 475
Montevideo, Uruguay Tel.: 91.19.05

ROBERT BELLARMINO EDUCATIONAL FOUNDATION (CHILE)
Fundación Educación Roberto Bellarmino
Almirante Barroso 24
Casilla 10445
Santiago, Chile Tel.: 60.68.442

CENTRE OF CULTURAL & ARTISTIC ENQUIRY & EXPRESSION
(CHILE)
CENECA
Santa Beatriz 106
Providencia
Santiago, Chile Tel.: 43.772
    Contac: Valerio Fuenzalida

UNIVERSIDAD DE PLAYA ANCHA DE CIENCIAS DE LA EDUCA-
CION (CHILE)
Facultad de Ciencias de la Educacion
Centro de Investigacion de Medios Para la Educacion
Avda. Playa Ancha 850
Casilla 34-V Valparaiso, Chile Tel.: 25.45.04
Director, Centro: Miguel Reyes Torres

BRAZILIAN SOCIAL COMMUNICATIONS UNION (BRAZIL)
UCBC
Praça da Sé, 21, 6 andar - Sala 612
Edificio Sao Marcos
01.001 Sao Paulo SP Brazil Tel.: 37.76.10

UNDA/UNESCO — Worldwide: various countries
UNDA/Association Catholique Internationale pour la Radio et la
Télévision
Rue de l'Orme 12
1040 Brussels, Belgium Tel.: 734.63.61
Contact: Jacques Dessaucy

UNESCO/United Nations Educational, Scientific and Cultural
Organization
7, Place de Fontenoy
75700 Paris, France
Contact: Herbert Marchl

* *OTHER SOURCES OF CVS-RELATED MATERIALS*
ACTION FOR CHILDREN'S TELEVISION, INC.
46 Austin Street
Newtonville, Massachusetts 02160
Executive Director: Peggy Charren

BRITISH FILM INSTITUTE
BFI Education
81 Dean Street
London W1V 6AA (01)437-4355
Contact: Philip Simpson

CENTRE FOR THE STUDY OF COMMUNICATION & CULTURE
"Communication Research Trends"
221 Goldhurst Terrace
London NW6 3EP, England Tel.: (01)328-2868

JEA BOOKS [Journalism Education Association]
Tomahawk Trail
Shabbona, Illinois 60550

JESUIT COMMUNICATION PROJECT
10 Saint Mary Street, Suite 500
Toronto, Ontario M4Y 9Z9, Canada (416)923-7271
Editor, *Clipboard:* John J. Pungente, S.J.

LE LANGAGE TOTAL
Institut du Langage Total
21, rue de la Paix
42000 Saint-Etienne, France
Contact: Antoine Vallet
Centro Latinoamericano de Lenguaje Total
SEC - SAL - OCIC
Av. 9 Diciembro (Paseo Colón) 378
Lima, Peru
Contact: Francisco Gutiérrez Perez
Paseo Colón 378 - Apartado 44; Lima, Peru

MEDIA & VALUES (magazine + coordinating center)
*Media&Values* [sic]
1962 South Shenandoah
Los Angeles, California 90034
Executive Editor: Elizabeth Thoman, CHM

MEDIA AND METHODS (magazine, prints Prime Time School Television study guides)
401 North Broad Street
Philadelphia, Pennsylvania 19108

NATIONAL COUNCIL FOR CHILDREN AND TELEVISION/
... FOR FAMILIES AND TELEVISION
20 Nassau Street - Suite 215         3801 Barham Blvd. - Suite 300
Princeton, New Jersey 08540         Los Angeles, Calif.
90068 (213)876-5959
President: Tricia McLeod Robin

PBS - PUBLIC BROADCASTING SERVICE
"TV for Learning"
1320 Bradock Place
Alexandria, Virginia 22314-1698 (703)739-0775

+ "Reading Rainbow"
202 Riverside Drive, 9B; New York, New York 10025 (212)666-1800
    Associate Producer: Lynne Brenner Ganek

PRIME TIME SCHOOL TELEVISION
120 South LaSalle St. - Room 810
Chicago, Illinois 60603
    [+ see above, "Media and Methods"]

SCHOLASTIC MAGAZINES
50 West 44th St.
New York, New York 10036

STRATEGIES FOR MEDIA LITERACY (newsletter + coordinating
agency)
347 Dolores Street - Room 306
San Francisco, California 94410 (415)621-2911
    Executive Director & Editor: Kathleen Tyner

TEL-AVIV UNIVERSITY
School of Education
Tel-Aviv University
Ramat Aviv, Israel
    Contact: Helga Keller

UNIVERSITY OF STIRLING
Film & Media Department
University of Stirling
Stirling FK9 4LA, Scotland
    Contacts: Dan MacLeod, David Butts, John Izod
    Department of Education: Eric Drever

WQED: "LWT—Learning with Television"
WQED Educational Services
Metropolitan Pittsburgh Public Broadcasting, Inc.
4802 Fifth Ave.
Pittsburgh, Pennsylvania 15213 (412)622-1398

*      *      *

# References

Altheide, D. L., & Snow, R. P. (1979). *Media logic*. Beverly Hills, CA: Sage.

Alvarado, M., Gutch, R., & Wollen, T. (1987). *Learning the media: An introduction to media teaching*. London: Macmillan.

American Council for Better Broadcasts. (ca. 1960). *Teaching evaluation of drama and informational programs as aired on radio and television*. Madison, WI: Author.

American Council for Better Broadcasts. (1980). *Look-listen opinion poll / 1979–1980*. Madison, WI: Author.

American Council on Better Broadcasts. (1980, March-April). *Better Broadcast News*. Madison, WI: Author.

An interdisciplinary symposium on mass communications research. In S. Bamberger (Ed.). (1975). *Communications research: Reports and studies: No. 1*. Rome: Jescom Research Unit.

Anderson, J. A. (1980). The theoretical lineage of critical viewing criteria. *Journal of Communication, 30*(3), 64–70.

Anderson, J. A. (1981). Receivership skills: An educational response. In M. Ploghoft & J. A. Anderson, *Education for the television age* (pp. 19–27). Athens, OH: Cooperative Center for Social Science Education.

Anderson, J. A. (1983). Television literacy and the critical viewer. In J. Bryant & D. R. Anderson (Eds.), *Children's understanding of television: Research on children's attention and comprehension* (pp. 297–330). New York: Academic Press.

Anderson, J. A., & Avery, R. K. (1988). Review and criticism—the concept of effects: Recognizing our personal judgments. *Journal of Broadcasting and Electronic Media, 32*(3), 359–372.

Anderson, J. A., & Meyer, T. (1988). *Mediated communication: A social action perspective*. Newbury Park, CA: Sage.

Anderson, J. A., & Ploghoft, M. E. (1977, June). *Television receivership skills: The new social literacy*. Paper presented at International Communication Association conference, West Berlin.

Anderson, J. A., & Ploghoft, M. E. (1978). *The way we see it*. Salt Lake City, UT: Media Research Center.

Anderson, J. A., & Ploghoft, M. E. (1980a). *Receivership skills: The television experience*. Paper presented at International Communication Association convention, Acapulco, Mexico.

Anderson, J. A., & Ploghoft, M. E. (1980b). Receivership skills: The television experience. In D. Nimmo (Ed.), *Communication yearbook 4* (pp. 293–307). New Brunswick, NJ: Transaction Books.

Arnheim, R. (1971). *Visual thinking*. Berkeley, CA: University of California Press.

Ashton, N. C. (1981). The way we see it: A program design for instruction of critical viewing skills. In M. Ploghoft & J. A. Anderson (Eds.), *Education for the television age* (pp. 55–63). Athens, OH: Cooperative Center for Social Science Education.

Ashton, C., Moll, E., & Rinaldi, F. (1981). *The way we see it: A project to develop analytical televiewing skills* (Teacher's guides for third, fourth, and fifth grades). Idaho Falls, ID: Idaho Falls School District No. 91.

Axford, M. T. J. (1983, Autumn). Media studies in Scottish schools. *SED Occasional Papers*.

Baime, C. (1980, March-April). Of special interest to teachers: Considerations for developing critical attitudes toward TV and radio. *Better Broadcast News*, p. 8.

Bamberger, S. (Ed.). (1975). *Communications research: Reports and studies: No. 1*. Rome: Jescom Research Unit.

Barnett, E. (Ed.). (1981). *Television literacy: Critical television viewing skills* and *Television literacy: Workbook* and *Television literacy: Instructor's guide* (rev. ed.). Boston: Dendron Press & Boston University School of Public Communication. — Original edition was in four sets of books, copyrighted 1979 and 1980: (a) *Television literacy / Critical television viewing skills / module I* and . . . *Workbook;* (b) *Persuasive programming / module II critical television viewing skills* and . . . *Instructor's guide* [includes workbook pages]; (c) *Entertainment programming / module III / critical television viewing skills* and *Instructor's guide* [includes workbook pages]; (d) *Informational programming / module IV / critical viewing skills* and *Instructor's guide*.

Bennet, S. (1976, Spring). Mass media education: Defining the subject. *Screen Education*, pp. 15–21.

Bethell, A. (1980). *The English programme: Viewpoint 2*. London: Thames Television Limited.

BFI [British Film Institute] Education. (n.d., ca. 1987). *Film & TV training: A guide to film & video courses*. London: British Film Institute.

Bilowit, D. W. (1981). Critical television viewing: A public television station reaches out. In M. Ploghoft & J. A. Anderson (Eds.), *Education for the television age* (pp. 64–70). Athens, OH: Cooperative Center for Social Science Education.

Blake, R. H., & Haroldsen, E. O. (1975). *A taxonomy of concepts in communication*. New York: Hastings House.

Boe, J. O. (1979). *Television sponsors [Product Cross-Reference] directory*. Everglades, FL: Everglades.

Boston University School of Public Communication. (ca. 1980). *Critical television viewing skills* (Pamphlet). Boston, MA: Author.

Boutwell, W. D. (Ed.). (1962). *Using mass media in the schools*. New York: Appleton-Century-Crofts.

British Film Institute. (1979). *Television studies: Four approaches* (Educational advisory document). London: Author.

Bruner, J. (1962). *On knowing: Essays for the left hand*. Cambridge, MA: Harvard University Press.

Bryant, J. B., & Anderson, D. R. (Eds.). (1983). *Children's understanding of television: Research on children's attention and comprehension.* New York: Academic Press.

Butts, D. (1986). *Media education in Scottish secondary schools: A research study / 1983–1986.* Stirling Scotland: University of Stirling.

Canavan, K. B. (1975). *Mass media education.* Sydney: Catholic Information Office.

Canavan, K. B. (1975/1976). *Mass media education: Curriculum guidelines for primary schools / years 1–6.* Broadway, New South Wales: Catholic Education Office.

Canavan, K. B. (1975/1979). *Mass media education: Curriculum guidelines for secondary schools / years 7–12.* Broadway, New South Wales: Catholic Education Office.

Canavan, K. B. (1978). *Life in the media age.* Sydney: Catholic Education Office.

Canavan, K. B. (1978/1979). *Mass media education—why? how?* (Folder accompanying a 23-minute slide/sound package). Homebush, New South Wales: Catholic Audio Visual Centre.

Canavan, K. B. (1980). *The development of mass media education in catholic schools: A personal perspective* (Report). Sydney: Catholic Education Office.

Canavan, K., McGuiness, R., Blaney, B., & Davis, P. (1974/1978). *Mass media activities 3.* Melbourne: Longman Cheshire Pty Ltd.

Canavan, K., McGuiness, R., Blaney, B., & Davis, P. (1975/1978). *Mass media activities 4.* Melbourne: London Cheshire Pty Ltd.

Canavan, K., Slattery, P., Tarrant, W., & Threlfo, C. (1974/1979). *Mass Media activities 1.* Melbourne: Longman Cheshire Pty Ltd.

Canavan, K., Slattery, P., Tarrant, W., & Threlfo, C. (1975). *Mass media activities 2.* Melbourne: Longman Cheshire Pty Ltd.

Carey, J. (1975). A Cultural Approach to Communication. *Communication, 2,* 1–22.

Carey, J. (1988). *Media, myths, and narratives: Television and the press.* Newbury Park, CA: Sage.

CBS/Broadcast Group. (1987, September 29). [Press release by CBS Educational and Communication Services.] New York: CBS Inc.

CBS news releases. (1978, October 26 and December 27; 1986, May 20, August 19, and October 31). New York: CBS Inc.

CBS Television Network. (ca. 1982). *Television and the classroom—a special relationship: The CBS television reading program* (Report). New York: CBS Inc.

Child Research Services, Inc. (Hyatt-Esserman Research Associates) & CBS Office of Social Research. (1979). *A study of the CBS television reading program / May 1979.* New York: Economics and Research Division, CBS Inc.

Colder-Bolz, C. R. (1980a). Critical television viewing skills for elementary schools. *Television and Children, 3*(2), 34–39.

Colder-Bolz, C. R. (1980b). Critical TV viewing-mediation: The role of significant others. *Journal of Communication, 30*(3), 106–118.

*Communication abstracts: An international information service* (quarterly, 1978–....). Beverly Hills, CA: Sage.

Comstock, G., Chafee, S., Katzman, N., McCombs, M., & Roberts, D. (1978). *Television and human behavior.* New York: Columbia University Press.

Conklin, G. C. & McFadden, L. W. (1979). Television: Television and theology. In B. Logan & K. Moody (Eds.), *Television awareness training: The viewer's guide / for family and community* (pp. 153–157). New York: Media Action Research Center.

Cowle, K., & Dick, E. (1986). *Teaching media studies: An introduction to methods and resources* (2nd rev. ed.). Glasgow: Scottish Film Council.

Cross, P., & Husband, C. (1975). *Communication and community: A study of the Swindon community television experiment* (Report). Leicester: University of Leicester, Centre for Mass Communication Research.

Dessaucy, J. (1979, November 30). Rapport a l'UNESCO concernant le programme d'etudes portant sur l'enseignement des mass media. In J. Dessaucy, *Rapport a l'UNESCO: Concernant le programme de récherche et d'experimentation portant sur l'educommunication* (pp. 1–4). Brussels: UNDA/Association Catholique Internationale pour le Radio et la Télévision.

Dessaucy, J. (1980, December). *Rapport a l'UNESCO: Concernant le programme de récherche et d'experimentation portant sur l'educommunication* (Report for UNDA). Brussels: UNDA/Association Catholique Internationale pour le Radio et la Télévision.

Dick, E. (ca. 1987a). *Descriptions and some observations on media education developments in a miscellany of countries throughout the world* (Report No. D/3215). Edinburgh, Scotland: Scottish Film Council.

Dick, E. (ca. 1987b). *Signs of success: Report of the media education development project.* Glasgow: MEDP/Scottish Education Department (?—no indicia for place, agency, or date).

Dietsch, J. A. (writer), Young, M. R., & Maley, B. S. (Eds.). (1982). *Critical viewing skills curriculum / teacher's manual K-2 & 3-5* (includes accompanying texts of K-2 and 3-5 Student Activity Books). Chicago: National Congress of Parents and Teachers (National PTA).

Dimbleby, J. (1980). One world. In P. Griffiths, *The 1980-81 English Programme* (pp. 106–119). London: Thames Television Ltd. (& ITV Companies).

Donald, J. (1977, November; reprinted 1980, October). *Media studies: Possibilities and limitations* (report for BFI Education department). London: British Film Institute Information Division.

Dondis, D. (ca. 1980). *A Guide to critical television viewing skills.* Boston: Boston University, School of Public Communication.

Dondis, D. (1980, Summer). Critical television viewing skills for adults. *Children & Television, 3*(2), 49–52.

Dorr, A. (1979). In the land of the one-eyed monster the two-eyed parent rules. In B. Logan & K. Moody (Eds.), *Television awareness training: The viewer's guide / for family and community* (pp. 217–219). New York: Media Action Research Center.

Dorr, A., Graves, S. B., & Phelps, E. (1980, Summer). Television literacy for young children. *Journal of Communication, 30*(3), 71–83.

Education Department of Western Australia. (1987, March). *"The unit curriculum" media studies (English, languages and communication* (rev. ed.; report). East Perth, Australia: Author, Curriculum Branch.

Education Department of Western Australia. (n.d., ca. 1988). *Media studies year 11 and year 12* (report). East Perth, Australia: Author, Media Studies Curriculum Branch.

Edwards, P. (1986). *De la educación para la TV a la recepción activa.* Santiago, Chile: CENECA/Centre of Cultural and Artistic Inquiry and Expression.

Ellingsen, M. (1981). Television viewer skills project / Eugene, Oregon school district. In M. Ploghoft & J. A. Anderson (Eds.), *Education for the television age* (pp. 88–90). Athens, OH: Cooperative Center for Social Science Education.

Elster, M. (1980). *Schools council/Powys education committee visual literacy project in Powys schools - April 1979/April 1980 / Report* (Report). Powys, Wales: Powys Education Committee.

Ewen, S., & Ewen, E. (1982). *Channels of desire: Mass images and the shaping of American consciousness.* New York: McGraw-Hill.

Faber, R. J., Perloff, R. M., & Hawkins, R. P. (1982, Spring). Antecedents of children's comprehension of television advertising. *Journal of Broadcasting, 26*(2), 575–584.

Fiske, J. (1987). *Television culture.* London/New York: Methuen.

Fiske, J., & Hartley, J. (1978). *Reading television.* London: Methuen.

Flagg, B. N. (1990). *Formative evaluation for educational technologies.* Hillsdale, NJ: Lawrence Erlbaum Associates.

Ford Foundation. (1975). *Television and children: Priorities for research.* Reston, VA: Author.

Fore, W. F. (1979). The role of mass communication in society. In B. Logan & K. Moody (Eds.), *Television awareness training: The viewer's guide / for family and community* (pp. 261–267). New York: Media Action Research Center.

Foster, H. M. (1979). *The new literacy: The language of film and television.* Urbana, IL: National Council of Teachers of English.

Fransecky, R. B., & Ferguson, R. (1973). News ways of seeing: The Milford visual communications project. *Audiovisual Instruction,* April 1973, pp. 44–49; May 1973, pp. 47–49; and June-July 1973, pp. 56–65.

Fuenzalida, V. (ca. 1987). *Education for critical TV viewing: Five experiences in Latin America* (Report). Santiago, Chile: CENECA/Centre of Cultural and Artistic Inquiry and Expression.

Fundación Educación Roberto Bellarmino. (1985). *Programa de educación para la televisión.* Santiago, Chile: GALDUC.

Gagnier, M. O. (1980). *Formation du jeune téléspectateur actif: Un an d'actions—bilan du programme experimental Fond d'Intervention Culturelle, 1979–1980* (Report). Paris: Fond d'Intervention Culturelle.

Gerbner, G. (1981). Education for the age of television. In M. Ploghoft & J. A. Anderson (Eds.), *Education for the television age* (pp. 173–178). Athens, OH: Cooperative Center for Social Science Education.

Gitlin, T. (1983). *Inside prime time.* New York: Pantheon Books.

Gomes, P. G. (1986). Educación para la TV en la opción por los pobres. In *Educación para la comunicación televisiva.* Santiago, Chile: CENECA/Centre of Cultural and Artistic Inquiry and Expression.

Gordon, G. N. (1975). *Communications and media: Constructing a cross-discipline.* New York: Hastings House.

Graves, S. B. (1979, September). *Content attended to in evaluating television's credibility.* Paper presented at meeting of the American Psychological Association, Washington, DC.

Griffith, R. J. (1980). *Growing with television: A study of biblical values and television experience—program guidebook for planners and administrators.* Anderson, IN: Warner Press (for Media Action Research Center).

Griffiths, P. (1980). *The English programme 1980–81.* London: Thames Television Limited (& ITV companies).

Gross, L. (1973). Art as the communication of competence. *Social Science Information, 12,* 115–141.

Gross, L. (1974). Modes of communication and the acquisition of symbolic competence. In D. R. Olsen (Ed.), *Media and symbols: The forms of expression, communication, and education* (73rd Yearbook of the National Society for the Study of Education, pp. 56–80). Chicago: University of Chicago Press.

Grossberg, L. (1979). Interpreting the 'crisis' of culture in communication theory. *Journal of communication, 29*(1), 56–68.

Gunther, M. (1976, September 4). How television helps Johnny read. *TV Guide,* p. 6.

Hall, S. (1980). Viewpoint 2. In P. Griffiths (Ed.), *The English programme 1980–81* (pp. 24–45). London: Thames Television Ltd. (& ITV companies).

Hall, S., Hobson, D., Lowe, A., & Willis, P. (Eds.). (1980). *Culture, media, language.* London: Hutchinson.

Hall, S., & Whannel, P. (1964). *The popular arts.* London: Hutchinson.

Halloran, J. D., & Jones, M. (1984). *Mass media education: Education for communication and mass communication research.* Leicester: UNESCO & International Association for Mass Communication Research.

Harris, W. H., & Levey, J. S. (Eds.). *The new Columbia encyclopedia.* New York: Columbia University Press.

Harrison, B. G. (1977, October). How TV can be good for children. *McCall's.* Cited by New York City Board of Education, *TV and growing up* (Report draft). New York: Board of Education.

Hawker, J., & Plude, F. F. (1982). *TMM [the media mirror] / High school level.* Washington, DC: U.S. Catholic Conference.

Haywood, P., & Blanchard, T. (1987). *Media studies at 16+ with special TVEI supplement: 1987 survey.* London: British Film Institute/BFI Education.

Head, S. W. (1985). *World broadcasting systems: A comparative analysis.* Belmont, CA: Wadsworth.

Head, S. W. (1987). *World broadcasting systems: Update notes, December 1987.* Unpublished manuscript, University of Miami, Florida.

Head, S. W., & Sterling, C. (1990). *Broadcasting in America: A survey of electronic media* (6th ed.). Boston: Houghton Mifflin.

Hefzallah, I. M. (1987). *Critical viewing of television: A book for parents and teachers.* Lanham, MD: University Press of America.

Heintz, A. C., Reuter, M. L., & Conley, E. (1972). *Mass media: A worktext in the processes of modern communication.* Chicago, IL: Loyola University Press.

Heller, M. A. (1982). Semiology: A context for television criticism. *Journal of Broadcasting, 26*(4), 847–854.

Helping Johnny read. (1978, January 16). *Broadcasting,* p. 53.

Himmelstein, H. (1981). *On the small screen: New approaches in television and video criticism.* New York: Praeger.

Hodgkinson, A. W. (1964). *Screen education: Teaching a critical approach to cinema and television.* Paris: UNESCO.

Hoover, S. M. (1979). Television: Strategies for change. In B. Logan & K. Moody (Eds.), *Television awareness training: The viewer's guide / for family and community* (pp. 113–122). New York: Media Action Research Center.

Hoover, S. M. (1988). Television myth and ritual: The role of substantive meaning and spatiality. In J. W. Carey (Ed.), *Media, myths, and narratives: Television and the press* (pp. 161–178). Newbury Park, CA: Sage.

Jones, A. M. (1948, April). Television and the cinema. *Penguin Film Review, 6.*

Journalism Education Association. (1976). *Me and my TV.* Shabbona, IL: JEA Publications.

Kane, H. L. (Ed.). (1980). *Critical television viewing: A language skills Work-a-text—teacher's annotated edition.* New York: Cambridge [now Globe].

Katz, E., Gurevitch, M., & Hass, E. (1973). On the uses of mass media for important things. *American Sociological Review, 38,* 164–181.

Kuhns, W. (1971). *Exploring television: An inquiry/discovery program.* Chicago, IL: Loyola University Press.

Kumar, K. J. (Ed.). (1985). Media education: Growth and controversy [Special issue]. *Communication Research Trends, 6*(4), 1–9.

Lee, C. (1981). "Media imperialism" and the Third World. *Television & Children, 4*(1), 53–67.

LeGrand-Brodsky, K. (1979, October). Television and reading: Industry initiatives. *Journal of Reading, 23*(1), 9–11.

Lelley, M. R. (1983). *A parent's guide to television: Making the most of it.* New York: Wiley.

Lieberman, D. (1980a). *Trainer's manual (volume I) / Critical T.V. viewing workshops for high school teachers, parents and community leaders.* San Francisco: Far West Laboratory.

Lieberman, D. (1980b). *Workshop handouts (volume II) / Critical T.V. viewing workshops for high school teachers, parents and community leaders.* San Francisco: Far West Laboratory.

Lloyd-Kolkin, D. (1981). The critical viewing project for High school students. In M. Ploghoft & J. A. Anderson (Eds.), *Education for the television age* (pp. 91–97). Athens, OH: Cooperative Center for Social Science Foundation.

Lloyd-Kolkin, D., Wheeler, P., & Strand, T. (1980). Developing a curriculum for teenagers. *Journal of Communication, 30*(3), 119–125.

Logan, B., & Moody, K. (Eds.). (1979). *Television awareness training: The viewer's guide / for family and community.* New York: Media Action Research Center.

Maddison, J. (1971). *Radio and television in literacy: A survey of the use of the broadcasting media in combating illiteracy among adults.* Paris: UNESCO.

Mann, T. (1927). *The magic mountain.* (Original work, *Der Zauberberg,* published in 1924).

Margulies, L. (1980, Spring). Reading, 'riting and television. *Emmy Magazine,* p. 43.

Martens, S. M. (1980). *GWT [growing with television]: Leader's guide / senior high.* Anderson, IN: Warner Press.

Masterman, L. (1980). *Teaching about television.* London: Macmillan.

Masterman, L. (1982). Television and the English teacher. In A. Adams (Ed.), *New directions in English teaching* (pp. 43–77). Barcombe, England: The Falmer Press.

Masterman, L. (1983). Media Education in the 1980's. *Journal of Educational Television, 9*(1).

Masterman, L. (1985a). *Television mythologies.* London: Comedia.

Masterman, L. (1985b). *Teaching the media.* London: Comedia.

McAnany, E. G., & Williams, R. (1965). *The filmviewer's handbook.* New York: Paulist Press.

McCain, T. A. (Ed.). (1981). Children Using Television [Special issue]. *Journal of Broadcasting, 25*(4), 327–402.

McIver, L. (ca. 1987). *Primary media education project: 1985–1986.* Mold, Clwyd (Wales): Clwyd Media Studies Unit.

McMahon, B., & Quin, R. (1986, July). *An approach to the teaching of television.* Paper presented to the International Television Studies Conference, [location not cited].

McMahon, B., & Quin, R. (1988, October). *Media studies in schools—Into the next era.* Paper for "Audiovisual Massmedia and Education" special edition of *Tijdschrift voor theaterwetenschap.*

Media Action Research Center/MARC. (1980a). *Growing with television* (five sets of worksheets). New York: Author.

Media Action Research Center/MARC. (1980b). *T-A-T workshop* (printed flyer). New York: Author.

Media Action Research Center/MARC. (1984). *What is MARC?* (folder). New York: Author.

Ministry of Education. (1989). *Media literacy resource guide: Intermediate and senior divisions, 1989.* Ontario: Queen's Printer for Ontario.

Minkkinen, S. (1978). *General curricular model for mass media education.* Paris, UNESCO.

Mottershead, C. (1980). Working. In P. Griffiths, *The 1980-81 English Programme* (pp. 58–73). London: Thames Television Ltd. (& ITV Companies).

Murray, J. P. (1980). *Television & youth: 25 years of research and controversy.* Boys Town, NE: Boys Town Center for the Study of Youth Development.

NAFBRAT. (ca. 1960). *National association for better radio & television.* Los Angeles, CA: Author.

NAFBRAT. (1960, Summer). *NAFBRAT Quarterly.*

National Catholic Educational Association. (ca. 1983). *The media mirror: A study guide on Christian values and television* (pamphlet). Washington, DC: Author & U.S. Catholic Conference.

National Council for Children and Television. (1979, Fall). Television for learning: A catalog of reading programs and teaches' guides. *NCCT Forum, 2*(3), 32–36.

National PTA Television Commission. (1977). *Violence on TV / the effects of television on children and youth: A report on the findings of the public hearings conducted by the National PTA Television Commission 1976–77* (Chicago, IL: National Congress of Parents and Teachers.

National PTA TV Action Center. (1978). *TV program review guide.* Chicago, IL: National Congress of Parents and Teachers.

New York City Board of Education. (1978). *TV and growing up* (Report, typewritten draft). New York: Author.

Newcomb, H. (1980, Summer). Television as popular culture: Toward a critically based curriculum. *Television & Children, 3*(2), 22–27.

Newcomb, H. (1981). Television as popular culture: Toward a critically based curriculum. In M. Ploghoft & J. A. Anderson (Eds.), *Education for the television age* (pp. 9-18). Athens, OH: Cooperative Center for Social Science Education.

Newcomb, H. (1983). *Television: The critical view* (3rd ed.). New York: Oxford University Press.

Newcomb, H. (1986). American television criticism: 1970-1985. *Critical studies in mass communication, 32*(2), 217–228.

Newsome report. (1963). *Half our future.* London: Ministry of Education.

Orton, L. (1987). *Studying film & TV: A list of courses in higher education* (Report). London: BFI/British Film Institute.

Parsley, J. F., Jr. (1980, Summer). In support of teaching critical thinking & critical televiewing in schools. *Television & Children, 3*(2), 28–31.

Parsley, J. F., Jr. (1981). Critical receivership skills: The need for innovation at the local school district level. In M. Ploghoft & J. A. Anderson (Eds.), *Education for the television age* (pp. 132–138). Athens, OH: Cooperative Center for Social Science Education.

Perez, F. G. (1971). *"Total language": A new approach to education* (Monograph). Rome: Multimedia International.

Phelan, J. M. (1980). *Disenchantment: Meaning and morality in the media.* New York: Hastings House.

Piaget, J. (1970). *Structuralism.* New York: Basic Books.

Ploghoft, M. E. (1981). What is basic about critical receiver skills? In M. Ploghoft & J. A. Anderson (Eds.), *Education for the television age* (pp. 125–131). Athens, OH: Cooperative Center for Social Science Education.

Ploghoft, M. E., & Anderson, J. A. (Eds.). (1981). *Education for the television age.* Athens, OH: Cooperative Center for Social Science Education.

Ploghoft, M. E., & Anderson, J. A. (1982). *Teaching critical television viewing skills: An integrated approach.* Springfield, IL: Charles C. Thomas.

Porter, G. S. (1989, April). *Audience-response criticism and studies of popular television.* Paper presented at meeting of Popular Culture Association, St. Louis, MO.

Potter, R. L. (1976). *New season: The positive use of commercial television with children.* Columbus, OH: Charles E. Merrill.

Potter, R. L. (1979, Fall). TV and my classroom: An evolutionary tale. *NCCT Forum, 2*(3), 19–20.

Potter, R. L. (1981). *The positive use of commercial television with children* (Reprint of Potter, 1976). Washington, DC: National Education Association.

Potter, R. L., Faith, C., & Ganek, L. B. (1979). *Channel: Critical reading/TV viewing skills.* Freeport, NY: Educational Activities, Inc.

Potter, R. L., Hanneman, C. E., & Faith, C. (Eds.). (1980, 1981, 1982). *TV readers skills kit.* Freeport, NY: Educational Activities, Inc.

Potter, R. L., Hanneman, C. E., & Faith, C. (1981). Television behind the scene: Teachers guide. In R. L. Potter, C. C. Hanneman, & C. Faith (Eds.), *TV readers skills kit.* Freeport, NY: Educational Activities, Inc.

Price, A. F. (1980a). *GWT [growing with television]: Leader's guide / older elementary.* Anderson, IN: Warner Press.

Price, A. F. (1980b). *GWT [growing with television]: Leader's guide / younger elementary.* Anderson, IN: Warner Press.

Pungente, J. (ca. 1985). *Media education in the global village* (Report on world-wide inspection of media education sites in 1983–84). Toronto: Jesuit Communication Project.

Pungente, J. (1989, Winter). Out and about Britain 89. *Clipboard: A media education newsletter from Canada, 4*(1), 3.

Pungente, J. (1990, Summer). International clippings. *Clipboard: A media education newsletter from Canada, 4*(2), 4.

Rapaczynski, W., Singer, D. G., & Singer, J. L. (1981, March). *Teaching television to kindergarten, first and second grades* (Report). New Haven, CT: Yale University, Family Television Research and Consultation Center.

Rapaczynski, W., Singer, D. G., & Singer, J. L. (1982, Spring). Teaching television: A curriculum for young children. *Journal of Communication, 32*(2), 46–55.

Reed, S. (1950). Teaching film for seven years without a projector. *The Bulletin.* London: SFT.

Riesman, D., Glazer, N., & Denney, R. (1950). *The lonely crowd.* Garden City, NY: Anchor Books.

Robbins, M. P. (1980, Winter/Spring). Television awareness training / the viewer's guide for family and community: A review. *NCCT Forum, 2*(4)/*3*(1), 20 [double issue].

Roberts, E. J. & Holt, S. A. Television and human sexuality: There's more to sexuality than sex. In B. Logan & K. Moody (Eds.), *Television awareness training: The viewer's guide / for family and community* (pp. 81–85). New York: Media Action Research Center.

Rowe, M. (1989, Winter). NTC active since radio days. *Strategies: A Quarterly Publication of Strategies for Media Literacy, 2*(1), 1–2.

Rubinstein, E. A. Television and the young viewer. In B. Logan & K. Moody (Eds.), *Television awareness training: The viewer's guide / for family and community* (pp. 61–70). New York: Media Action Research Center.

Samples, B. (1979, October). New modes of knowing (Part 2): Seeing the forest, not just the trees. *Media & Methods, 16*(2), 78–83.

Schrank, J. (1974/1978). *TV action book.* Evanston, IL: McDougal, Littell.

Schrank, J. (1976). *Guide to: Television and values.* Palatine, IL: The Learning Seed Co.

Schropp, M. L. (Ed.). (1982). *The media mirror: A study guide on Christian values and television / teacher's guide*. Washington, DC: U.S. Catholic Conference.

Schwartz, T. (1981). *Media: the second God*. New York: Random House.

Scottish Curriculum Development Service & Association for Media Education in Scotland. (1988). *Media education curriculum guidelines*. Glasgow: Scottish Film Council.

Scottish Film Council. (1979). *Media education in Scotland: Outline proposals for a curriculum*. Glasgow, Scotland: Author.

Shapiro, M. (1980, November). *Critical television viewing skills: Report to WQED-TV and Pennsylvania Department of Education* (Report).

Sheie, N. (1980). *GWT [Growing with Television]: Leader's Guide / junior high*. Anderson, IN: Warner Press.

Shorr, J. (1978, April/May). Basic skills of TV viewing. *Today's Education*, pp. 72–75.

Singer, D. G., Singer, J. L., & Zuckerman, D. M. (1979/1980). *Final report: Teaching elementary school children how to use television effectively* (Report). New Haven, CT: Yale University Family Television Research and Consultation Center.

Singer, D. G., Singer, J. L., & Zuckerman, D. M. (1981a). *Getting the most out of TV*. Santa Monica, CA: Goodyear Publishing.

Singer, D. G., Singer, J. L., & Zuckerman, D. M. (1981b). *Teaching television: How to use TV to your child's advantage*. New York: Dial Press.

Singer, D. G., Zuckerman, D. M., & Singer, J. L. (1979, September). *Teaching elementary school children critical television viewing skills: An evaluation*. Paper presented at meeting of American Psychological Association, New York.

Singer, D. G., Zuckerman, D. M., & Singer, J. L. (1980, Summer). Critical TV Viewing: Helping Elementary School Children Learn about TV. *Journal of Communication, 30*(3), 84–93.

Singer, D. G., Zuckerman, D. M., & Singer, J. L. (1981). Teaching elementary school children critical television viewing skills: An evaluation. In M. Ploghoft & J. A. Anderson (Eds.), *Education for the television age* (pp. 71–81). Athens, OH: Cooperative Center for Social Science Education.

Singer, J. L. (1977). *Television, imaginative play and cognitive development: Some problems and possibilities*. Paper presented to meeting of American Psychological Association, San Francisco, CA.

Singer, J. L. (1980). The powers and limitations of television: A cognitive-affective analysis. In P. Tannenbaum (Ed.), *The entertainment function of television*. Hillsdale, NJ: Lawrence Erlbaum Associates.

Singer, J. L., & Singer, D. G. (1979). *A parent's kit for television* (Report). New Haven, CT: Yale University Family Television Research and Consultation Center.

Singer, J. L., & Singer, D. G. (1980). Television viewing, family style and aggressive behavior in preschool children. In M. Green (Ed.), *Violence in the family: Psychiatric, sociological and historical implications* (Symposium series). Washington, DC: American Association for the Advancement of Science.

Singer, J. L., Singer, D. G., & Sherrod, L. R. (1979, March). *Prosocial programs in the context of children's total pattern of TV viewing* (Report for Yale University Family Television Research and Consultation Center, funded by National Science Foundation). Paper presented at meeting of the Society for Research in Child Development, San Francisco, CA.

Sirota, D. R. (n.d.) *The development of critical television viewing skills in students: Proceed with caution*. (Rep. No. IR-007-581). New York: New York University, School of the Arts. (ERIC Document Reproduction Service No. ED 175 417).

Snow, R. P. (1983). *Creating media culture*. Beverly Hills, CA: Sage.

Starr, J. A. (Ed.). (1979). *Training manual for teaching critical TV viewing skills.* Austin, TX: Southwest Educational Development Laboratory.

Teachers Guides to Television. (ca. 1982). *Parent participation TV workshop project* (Promotional folder). New York: Author.

Television Information Office. (1980, Fall). *TV sets-in-use* (No. 1). New York: Author.

Television Information Office. (1980–1981, Winter). *TV sets-in-use* (No. 2). New York: Author.

Television Information Office. (1984, Spring/Summer). *TV sets-in-use* (No. 12). New York: Author.

Torres, M. R. (1986). Education of television audiences: Nature and objectives. *Prospects, 16*(3).

Torres, M. R., & Méndez, A. M. (1989, December). *Introducing media education in Latin America: How we train teachers in Chile* (Manuscript published by Educational Media International).

Twitchin, R. (1988). *Primetime: Evaluating INSET in primary media education.* Mold, Clwyd (Wales): Clwyd Media Studies Unit.

Tyner, K., & Lloyd-Kolkin, D. (1990). *Media and you.* San Francisco, CA: Educational Technology Publishers.

United Nations Educational, Scientific, & Cultural Organization. (1977). *Media studies in education.* Paris: UNESCO.

United Nations Educational, Scientific, & Cultural Organization. (1982). *International symposium on education of the public in the use of the mass media: Problems, trends and prospects.* Paris: UNESCO.

United Nations Educational, Scientific, & Cultural Organization. (1984). *Media Education.* Paris: UNESCO.

*Variety* editors. (1978, March 15). PTA starts a 3-year project for teaching TViewing skills to kids. *Variety,* p. 80.

*Variety.* May 14, 1980, p. 105; April 15, 1981, p. 42.

Varis, T. (1974, Winter). Global traffic in television. *Journal of Communication, 24*(1), 102–109.

Varis, T. (1984a). Flujo internacional de programas de televisión. *Chasqui,* No. 9 (Enero-Marszo), 10–16. Quito, Ecuador: CIESPAL.

Varis, T. (1984b, Winter). The international flow of television programs. *Journal of Communication, 34*(1), 143–152.

West, P. J. (1980). *GWT [Growing with Television]: Leader's guide / adults.* Anderson, IN: Warner Press.

White, N. (1980a). *Inside television: A guide to critical viewing.* Palo Alto, CA: Science and Behavior Books.

White, N. (1980b). *Teacher's guide to Inside Television: A guide to critical viewing.* Palo Alto, CA: Science and Behavior Books.

White, R. A. (1975). New directions for mass media communications research. *Communications Research: Reports and Studies,* No. 2. Rome: Jescom Research Unit.

White, R. A., & Kenney, P. (Eds.). (1982). *Communication Research Trends, 3*(2). London: Centre for the Study of Communication and Culture.

Williams, R. (1975). *Television: Technology and cultural form.* New York: Schocken Books.

Wills, H. R. (1959, October). Editorial. *Screen Education.* No. 1.

Wolf, M. A., Abelman, R., & Hexamer, A. (1982). Children's understanding of television: Some methodological considerations and a question-asking model for receivership skills. In M. Burgoon (Ed.), *Communication Yearbook 5* (pp. 405–431). New Brunswick, NJ: Transaction Books.

Worth, S. (1981). *Studying visual communication* (L. Gross, Ed.). Philadelphia, PA: University of Pennsylvania Press.

Wyman, M. F. (Ed.). (1990). *Project look-listen-think-respond/1989–1990.* Madison, WI: National Telemedia Council.

Zamora, M. I. (1986). Interrelaciones familia-TV. In *Educatión para la comunicación televisiva.* Santiago: CENECA/Centre of Cultural and Artistic Inquiry and Expression.

Zuckerman, D. M., Singer, D. G., & Singer, J. L. (n.d., ca. 1982). *Children's television viewing, racial and sex-role attitudes"* (Report funded by American Broadcasting Companies, Inc). New Haven, CT: Yale University, Family Television Research and Consultation Center.

# Author Index

# Subject Index